trade options online

trade
options
online

Second Edition

GEORGE A. FONTANILLS

WILEY

John Wiley & Sons, Inc.

Published by John Wiley & Sons, Inc., Hoboken, New Jersey.
Published simultaneously in Canada.

For general information on our other products and services or for technical support, please contact our Customer Care Department within the United States at (800) 762-2974, outside the United States at (317) 572-3993 or fax (317) 572-4002. Wiley also publishes its books in a variety of electronic formats. Some content that appears in print may not be available in electronic formats. For more information about Wiley products, visit our Web site at www.wiley.com.

Library of Congress Cataloging-in-Publication Data:

Fontanills, George.
   Trade options online / George A. Fontanills. – 2nd ed.
     p. cm.
   ISBN 978-0-470-33602-1 (cloth)
  1. Options (Finance)–Computer network resources.   2. Investments–
Computer network resources.   3. Electronic trading of securities.   I. Title.
   HG6024.A3F663 2009
   025.06′33263228–dc22

                         2008038658

Printed in the United States of America.

10 9 8 7 6 5 4 3 2 1

To my beautiful wife, Charlene, who has added so much to my life and shown me that there is much to enjoy every day. Thanks for opening my eyes and heart. I am so fortunate to have you in my life.

contents

acknowledgments   ix

introduction: online trading in the twenty-first century   1

chapter 1   the options market today   13

chapter 2   online investing 101   31

chapter 3   online trading resources   63

chapter 4   a primer for trading stocks and options   81

chapter 5   basic option trading strategies   109

chapter 6   vertical spreads   135

chapter 7   delta neutral strategies   153

chapter 8   ratio spreads and backspreads   173

chapter 9   sideways strategies   193

chapter 10 the futures market   **219**

chapter 11 online trading from A to Z   **233**

chapter 12 the quest for the ultimate online brokerage   **281**

chapter 13 order processing   **323**

chapter 14 ready, set, engage   **339**

appendix a useful tables, data, and strategy reviews   **349**

appendix b market analysis terminology   **375**

appendix c financial software guide   **393**

appendix d financial web site guide   **399**

appendix e online brokerage directory   **429**

index   **451**

acknowledgments

Napoleon Hill, a motivational speaker, believed that "Man alone has the power to transform his thoughts into physical reality; man alone can dream and make his dreams come true." I have always lived my life by making my dreams come true, and find myself surrounded by talented people who also live by this code.

My main mission is to develop, teach, and trade high profit/low risk trading strategies to people who want to learn how to become successful options traders. I would like to take this opportunity to acknowledge the dedication of all our staff who continually contribute to my success and that of our companies. Our educational company, Optionetics, is totally committed to the welfare of our students by teaching them how to successfully make high profits while managing the risks of trading. Thank you to our wonderful staff who ensure that the students around the world select Optionetics as their first choice for quality financial education. I am grateful to them all and I would like to take this opportunity to mention some of the essential people in my life who inspire and support me. In particular, and in no order of importance, I would like especially to thank the following:

As always, my appreciation and gratitude go to my trading family and friends, who have supported and believed in me for the past 19 years. One of the most rewarding and amazing parts of business is the diversity of people that you meet. My good experiences represent time spent with highly talented individuals who give without expectation of reward or self promotion. Their kind deeds and actions have helped raise my performance to higher levels. Tom Gentile, Richard Cawood, and Tony Clemendor are excellent business associates and I'm lucky to call them friends as well. I also want to extend a special thank you to Frederic Ruffy and Kym Trippsmith for all of the invaluable research, writing, and editing they've done for Optionetics throughout the years.

Good luck and great trading!

George Fontanills
Founder, Optionetics

introduction

online trading in the twenty-first century

assessing today's options market

So much has changed since I wrote the first version of *Trade Options Online* approximately eight years ago. Technology has improved and is vastly superior today to what it was then. In addition, it is easier than ever to open a brokerage account and begin trading options online. Buy and sell instructions are sent with the left-click of a mouse, and most orders are now submitted to the exchanges through electronic networks. The live broker has become a much less important part of the process. The net result is faster and more efficient trading.

Indeed, the landscape has also changed a lot since the technology boom of the late 1990s. The number of brokerage firms that offer online trading has been reduced to a few key players. Some of these firms offer a wide range of services. Others specialize in specific types of investments, like stocks or options. Markets have become much more volatile in this new age of electronic trading as computers are now the primary drivers. Orders can come into a market to buy and sell at a furious rate, causing wild swings in the markets, which makes using options even more critical to any investment plan.

Meanwhile, the options industry continues to see exponential growth. In the year 2007, 2.86 billion contracts traded in the United States alone, which represents a 41.2 percent increase from 2006 (according to the Options Clearing Corporation). It also represents a 470 percent increase from the year 2000—the year after the first version of *Trade Options Online* was released.

The ease of electronic trading, along with a variety of new products—including new indexes and ways to trade volatility—has helped spur the ongoing growth in the options market during the past few years. New products have been created with the individual investor in mind and have become important drivers of innovation in the options market.

At the same time, while the options industry has been growing exponentially, technology and the way people invest continues to evolve. Not only are executions happening at the speed of light, but the Internet is transforming the way people live their lives and interact. Some call it an *information revolution*. However, it's really much more than that. I prefer to think of it more as a communication or cultural revolution.

Message boards, weblogs, virtual reality, and social networking communities continue to change the way people see and use the Internet. According to an April 2007 publication from the research firm Gartner, 80 percent of Internet users will take part in a virtual world by 2011. These worlds give people a so-called second life where they can participate in other societies and live different lives, including jobs, hobbies, and pets.

But the Internet is much more than a tool for disseminating and collecting information. It has become an important part of everyday life. Without it, economies would crash, which would trigger a seismic shake-up in the fabric of today's society.

Suffice it to say, the Internet has changed a lot since the first version of this book and will continue to evolve in very unpredictable and dynamic ways. For investors, the growth is clearly a positive force. The information available is cheaper and better. The playing field is almost level, with off-floor traders (or those who trade for personal accounts and not for firms) now having access to the information that was once available only to investment professionals. In fact, the cost of sophisticated software programs for analyzing the market has come down considerably. The cost of computers has also plummeted and new technology is readily available. In addition, the new software and hardware give traders the ability to analyze thousands of trades in a matter of seconds. Researching a company or a potential trade these days is as simple as a few strokes on the keyboard.

However, while advances in online trading have made the process faster and easier, there is a pitfall. An online trader has to assume complete responsibility for understanding the intricacies of the marketplace and making good trading decisions. The computer can help in many ways; but comprehensive market knowledge and experience are equally important to long-term success. Point-and-click investors cannot invest as though they are playing video games. As the recent collapse on Wall Street demonstrates, there is real money at risk, and the stakes are extremely high.

---

portfolio trackers
a portfolio tracker is an online service provided by a financial web site or an online brokerage that enables an investor to keep track of the daily price movement, breaking news, and investor sentiment of a chosen list of stocks and indexes.

Not all investors depend solely on online tools. Some still rely on telephones and newspapers to find opportunities. They might scan newspapers for clues to profitable trading opportunities and send orders by phone. But these traditions have given way, in large part, to the new world order of megabytes and modems, search engines and online brokerages. Today, online trading is an anomalous entity with a life all its own. Research is done with electronic, rather than print, publications. Orders are sent electronically rather than with spoken words.

These new tools for trading online are powerful and give investors a great deal of independence when making investment decisions. If you are reading this book, you are probably a do-it-yourself investor seeking that independence. It is certainly rewarding to have full control in the decision-making process and be successfully building wealth from the comfort of your PC. However, it also takes time to learn and understand the financial markets, and to develop an arsenal of trading strategies that can build capital and generate income. Education is the key.

> **the *wall street journal***
> with worldwide distribution and an extensive readership, the
> *Wall Street Journal* (*WSJ*) is packed with financial information
> and has the ability to significantly influence the makets. If a
> company gets into the *Wall Street Journal*, it's news!
> (www.wsj.com)
>
> ***investor's business daily***
> founded by William J. O'Neil, the *Investor's Business Daily* (*IBD*)
> was originally developed to add a new dimension of crucial
> information for the investment community. The *IBD* focuses on
> concise investment news information, sophisticated charts,
> tables, and analytical tools while adding valuable information
> that the *Wall Street Journal* may not provide.
> (www.investors.com)

Now, you might also be wondering just how safe online trading
is. There are some horror stories of entire systems shutting down
totally for hours on end, and of online brokerages not being able to
execute orders or handle the volume of calls. This has become the
online trader's nightmare. Your money is locked up, you're stuck on
hold for hours, and you can't access your account.

However, although there are outages, they are rare and of short
duration. The exchanges and brokerage firms are very dependable
and reliable. If there is a problem, it is often on the customer's end.
For that reason, before trading, always check to make sure your
Internet provider is reliable and will not fail you just as you are
about to enter or exit a position.

the amazing versatility of options

What about options? Aren't they risky? There is an adage among
options traders that goes like this: Options don't lose money, people do. There is no question that many investors have lost money—
sometimes large amounts of money—making poor decisions on options. While options can provide a lot of leverage to boost returns,
options have earned a bad reputation among some observers. They
argue that using leverage is no different than betting on horses
or playing roulette. According to the critics, investors should use

other strategies like buying a diversified portfolio of stocks and bonds. To some critics, options and other derivatives are simply too risky.

While options are sometimes associated with speculation or gambling, the story doesn't end there. Options are used as much for hedging risk as they are used for speculation. Some investors, known as *hedgers*, turn to the options market to protect existing stocks or portfolios. A hedge is a position designed to offset the risk of an adverse move in an underlying security. When used as a hedge, options can greatly reduce the risk of buying and holding stocks or bonds. In fact, not using options is actually a big mistake for most traders and investors. They are missing not only the huge potential profits but, more important, the ability to hedge risk like a professional. As far as I'm concerned, it is irresponsible *not* to use options as part of your investment plan.

> **hedger**
> an investor in the financial markets looking for ways to protect an investment. For example, farmers sometimes hedge their crop prices with futures contracts.
>
> **speculator**
> an investor in the market trading aggressively in search of short-term profits.

While speculators use options to make leveraged bets and hedgers use them to protect positions, another group of investors is also active in the options market: the strategists. These savvy investors use options to make profits in different types of market environments, which can vary from aggressive or high risk to conservative and safe. Profits can be made if the market moves higher or lower. Other strategies are used to generate income when the market moves sideways. For the options strategist, the options market represents limitless opportunities. The keys to your success include understanding the fundamentals, consistent financial education, and, above all, perseverance.

Some investors will never trade options and never trade online for fear of losing money. They might doubt the reliability of the Internet or worry about lost orders. These investors are quickly becoming the minority. Instead, most are moving, or already have moved, toward online trading. Many are also beginning to understand the advantages of adding options to their portfolios. One broker we talked to said that less than 1 percent of orders at his firm are executed through a live broker.

Another dilemma, however, is the risk of information overload. With the profusion of financial resource web sites and online brokerages, the initial foray into online trading might seem overwhelming and confusing. Too much information can be crippling. In order to reap the advantages and avoid the growing pains currently afflicting the online trading industry, serious investors need to develop a systematic approach to investing online.

For an options investor, the battle is even more complex. Although options augment the diversity of an investor's portfolio, they also increase the number of choices to be made. Just finding an online brokerage with the right combination of variables could take weeks of investigative research. There are many factors that require review (including commission costs, customer support, option services, timely executions and exits, and the ease of access to accounts especially during high-volume sessions). Many investors simply don't know where to start or whom to trust. Others simply don't have time for this kind of in-depth research.

---

option
a trading instrument that represents the right to buy or sell a specified amount of an underlying stock at a predetermined price within a specified time period. The option purchaser has the right, but not the obligation, to exercise the specifics of the contract. The option seller assumes a legal obligation to fulfill the specifics of the contract if the option is assigned to an option buyer.

spread orders
the simultaneous purchase and sale of at least two different option contracts on the same underlying stock.

The bottom line is, to become adept at trading options online, you have to have a working knowledge of options strategies, enough computer savvy to give you a competitive edge, and an online brokerage that can handle complex options strategies. This book is designed to provide you with the means to develop your skills as an online options trader. The journey into this new world is in your hands. Let's get started.

trading options online

In 1969, the U.S. Department of Defense developed a labyrinth of networked computers to enable the exchange of information to and from anywhere in the world. In its early stages, the Internet was little more than basic text. But in 1989, an interconnected information network called the "World Wide Web" introduced a multimedia format with text, graphics, sound, and video. The Internet has since become a global communications system for commerce, research, entertainment, and investing. It has, for many people, become a part of everyday life, much like the automobile, the telephone, or the television.

Meanwhile, options are also a relatively new instrument. Options were traded over-the-counter (OTC) by a limited number of put/call dealers up until 1973, when the Chicago Board Options Exchange (CBOE) formally established a standardized list of recognized options. In 2007, the exchange traded 944.5 million options contracts. The CBOE is an auction market system that employs floor brokers and market makers to execute customer orders and inspire additional competition in the markets.

Today, a number of other exchanges have entered the scene. The CBOE is the oldest and still accounts for a large percentage of the options traded in the United States. However, it has also developed electronic trading systems and relies less and less on the auction-style market. In addition, four other exchanges now compete with the CBOE in the options market. The American Stock Exchange (AMEX), the Philadelphia Stock Exchange (PHLX), the NASDAQ, and the New York Stock Exchange (NYSE, formerly known as the Pacific Stock Exchange, or PCX) also list options.

Two of the newer U.S. exchanges are focused on options trading: the Boston Options Exchange (BOX) and the International Securities Exchange (ISE). The BOX made its debut in February 2004, and the ISE became the first new U.S.-based exchange in a quarter century when it opened in May 2000. In addition, the BOX and the ISE are both all-electronic options market. Unlike the CBOE or the AMEX, there is no trading floor; there is only screen-based, or electronic, trading. Both exchanges, especially the ISE, have been growing steadily and their success reflects the growing investor interest in both electronic trading and the options market.

More recently, the NASDAQ Stock Market launched its own options market and became the seventh exchange to list puts and calls. The all-electronic exchange received Securities and Exchange Commission (SEC) approval on March 12, 2008, and started trading options shortly thereafter. Like the six other exchanges, the NASDAQ Options Market offers trading in equity, exchange-traded funds (ETFs), and index options.

As professional traders, we could not trade options without the use of electronic investing technologies. Millions of investors and traders seem to agree. Prestigious full-service brokers have lost ground to online brokerages that offer 24-hour access and cheaper commissions. Although you still need a broker who is reliable and easily accessible, your scope of interest needs to go beyond the person at the other end of the phone line.

You are forging a new relationship, and your ability to prosper depends primarily on how well you can use the tools the Internet offers. This places new demands on you as a trader, increasing by tenfold the scope of details you have to keep track of. You are no longer dependent on the whims of your broker. You are self-reliant, and this self-sufficiency requires you to balance independence with increased responsibilities (i.e., your ability to respond). Increased autonomy is one of the main attractions that makes trading options online continue to grow at such a phenomenal rate.

online pros and cons

Online trading offers options traders an assortment of advantages over traditional full-service and discount brokerages. One important advantage is that online brokerages have severely reduced their commission costs from the lofty levels set by traditional brokers. Some have even tried to offer *free* online trading, but that model has been difficult to implement.

Instead, brokers today get paid a commission fee each time an order is placed or exited. The amount of this commission depends on what kind of service the broker provides. Each transaction is called a *round turn* and costs as little as a few bucks at an online brokerage and over $100 at a full-service brokerage. Ultimately, the commission schedule depends on the type of brokerage firm you're dealing with. Meanwhile, commissions keep dropping while services available to the trader and investor keep expanding.

Three main kinds of brokers dominate the playing field: full-service, discount, and deep-discount brokers.

1. *Full-service brokers* charge higher commissions because they offer more services, like researching markets and making recommendations.
2. *Discount brokers* offer lower commissions because they limit their services to placing orders and facilitating exits.
3. *Deep-discount brokers* offer even lower commission rates as they primarily trade large blocks for big investors.

Online brokerages have broken the mold completely by offering the lowest commission costs ever via easy computer access. Although their services differ, timely executions and good fills are still the most important part of a brokerage's services. Since a small difference in execution can cost you a bundle, we encourage investors to balance low cost with reliable service and good fills—a topic that we take up in more detail throughout this book.

Another major improvement comes in the form of information. Online brokerages offer real-time quotes, charts, news, and analysis as well as the ability to customize this information to fit your portfolio. Today's investors have the means to research stock tips immediately, read up-to-the-minute news almost as it happens, monitor the mood of markets throughout the day, and access option premiums for price fluctuations and volatility. You no longer have to sit on hold waiting for your broker to say, "I'll get back to you on that." The marketplace is alive and you're right there with it.

In the old days, one of the best ways to find a good broker was through the recommendation of other traders. This hasn't changed much. For your convenience, we review and discuss the main players in later chapters of this book. We also have a brokerage review section that is regularly updated on our Optionetics web site (www.optionetics.com).

Computerized trading also offers traders the chance to use powerful software programs. Various analyses can be performed that directly access real-time and/or delayed stock and option quotes. One of the most popular functions is called *screening*. Screening enables traders to choose a specific set of criteria—market outlook, strike spread, maximum risk, and volatility assumptions—in order to search for trades that meet those requirements. In the blink of an eye, you have a list of viable trades that can be further explored for signs of profitability.

> **real-time quotes**
> streaming quotes that are received as the prices change at the exchanges.
>
> **delayed quotes**
> quotes that are displayed up to 20 minutes after the actual price changes at the exchanges.

Finally, although commission fees are not tax deductible, online investors can sometimes deduct computer-related costs. Monthly Internet service provider (ISP) fees, online subscriptions, and computer costs can be listed under "miscellaneous itemized deductions." When it comes to taxes, it's best to seek professional help; but it doesn't hurt to save those receipts!

The disadvantages of online trading are primarily for new investors. Trading options requires a broker who can understand and handle more advanced trading strategies. If you are just starting your trading career, you need a broker who is going to help you, not harm you. If your broker is little more than an order taker, then you are 100 percent responsible for every little detail—a precarious position for a new trader. If you are a novice trader, you need to find a broker who understands options trading and can give you the support you need to become a successful trader. We review the "dynamic dozen" (i.e., 12 qualified firms) in Chapter 12.

getting the most from this book

The text of this book concentrates on two main areas of focus: option strategies and online trading. The first few chapters center on introducing online trading practices into your everyday life as a trader. Since there is an overabundance of financial information available online, the web sites, brokerages, and products selected for review are those that we believe to be most useful to options investors. Each chapter includes personal tips and insights designed to enhance the online experience and act as building blocks for investment success.

Chapter 4 takes you step-by-step through stock and options basics (experienced traders may wish to skip this chapter). Chapters 5 through 9 provide a detailed analysis of various managed-risk option strategies that are designed to take advantage of everyday market opportunities using online resources. In order to enhance your ability to understand each strategy, I have included a hypothetical trade that details how to compute each strategy's maximum risk, maximum profit, breakevens, and exit alternatives. A great deal of effort has been expended to test these strategies and to develop off-floor techniques that enable traders to consistently build up their trading accounts.

By focusing on clear explanations of how to really make money in the markets using options, this book refrains from exposing readers to information that is overly theoretical or technically complicated. In fact, technical analysis has been intentionally avoided. I want to help you integrate these options-based trading techniques into a comprehensive strategic trading plan that fits your own personal profile.

Chapter 10 takes a closer look at the futures market. Then we look at ways to improve the quality of the information used in the decision-making process by "Streamlining Your Approach" in Chapter 11. Chapter 12 offers concrete information regarding online brokerages and their ability to cater to the unique needs of the options trader. Following this in-depth review of available online brokerages, Chapter 13 delves into placing a trade online; although each online brokerage has its own unique design format, we take a walk through the basic online trading process. In Chapter 14, we delve into ways to manage trading risk and end this exploration by taking a look at the big picture.

In addition, several appendixes offer a variety of information geared to helping investors find what they need in order to maintain a competitive online edge. Appendix A contains a summary of key investment strategies; reviews profit, risk, and breakeven calculations; and supplies various tables that provide useful definitions, market acronyms, and other need-to-know material. Appendix B contains a glossary of fundamental and technical analysis methodologies. This handy reference guide is designed to help you define some of the more complex techniques that may be referenced over the Internet as clues to forecasting market price movements. Appendix C contains a short list of options trading software and the Internet sites where they can be reviewed. Appendix D features reviews of more than 200 financial resource sites broken down into the following categories: supersites, news, research, education, technical analysis, options, webzines, high technology, exchanges, advisers, specialty sites, and fun and games. This exhaustive list of resource sites and reviews is the most comprehensive list I've ever run across and I'm proud to be able to share this wealth of knowledge in this book. Finally, Appendix E surveys online brokerages as they compare to one another in services, commissions, and resources.

This book is designed as an instructional guide to help you unleash the unlimited power of your computer and take advantage of what the Internet has to offer you as an options trader. It is also an instructional manual with the lowdown on managed-risk option strategies that allow you to make the most out of today's volatile markets. If you're ready, it's time to join the fresh breed of online investors who are forging a new path with a wealth of resources at their fingertips. It is my deepest hope that this book may inspire you to become as passionate about online trading as I am. It's time to seize hold of your financial destiny—mouse in hand—and venture forth into cyberspace in search of the next great trade.

chapter 1

the options market today

trading options today

The Internet has gone from an abstract concept to a global information network with endless applications in everyday life. By 2007, more than 160 million adults (age 18 or older) in the United States were surfing the Net. Almost 75 percent of U.S. households now have Internet access. Odds are you are connected. In fact, there is a good chance that you bought this book online.

People use the Internet in different ways. The rise of online media is giving television a run for its money. People are no longer satisfied digesting spoon-fed TV news or programs. They want to download their own podcasts, you-tubes, music videos, and movies. People want greater control of the content they digest into their systems. In many cases, they have even become broadcasters of their own media.

In addition, e-commerce is altering the way people spend their hard-earned dollars. As this immense shift in control takes place, the nature of the human adventure evolves and entire new industries are booming. Bookstores are trying harder to lure in customers to compete with Amazon.com, car salesmen often look over empty lots because sales are taking place on autotrader.com, and there are very few lines waiting for bank tellers as online banking has transformed the way people handle their finances.

The success of the Internet has also created a maelstrom in the investment world. Conventional brokers, the traditional intermediaries of an investor's game plan, are losing ground as more than seven million investors move to online brokers instead. Reduced commissions and lightning-fast information access have enabled online trading enterprises to redefine the role of a broker.

With a keystroke, traders can access real-time quotes, annual reports, breaking financial news, technical and fundamental analytical data, and investing tips from a multitude of insightful (and not so insightful) market analysts. In seconds you can find out which stocks are hitting new highs or new lows or review an option's volatility. It has become possible to look over charts and graphs, and then, with the click of a mouse, enter an order to buy or sell that stock or option.

Meanwhile, news sites compete for readers by offering daily market analyses, economic reports, and shrewd investment commentary. Market research firms maximize the investment community's ability to track ever-changing fundamentals and technical indicators. Even exchanges offer a variety of free services geared to educate and inform the Net-surfing masses.

In fact, there is so much information available on the Internet that it can be overwhelming. There's just too much to be able to digest it all. The key is to develop a comprehensive game plan that enables you to systematically trade to win. This involves more than just marking your favorites in your Web browser; you have to learn to filter out all the noise and useless information that won't help you make a dime. This book, especially this chapter and the two that follow, is designed to help you cut through the information clutter by highlighting the most important and useful online sources of options-related information.

the exchanges Options trading volume continues to set records year after year. In 2007, six different U.S. exchanges listed put and call options. According to the Options Clearing Corporation (OCC), a total of 2.9 billion contracts traded hands that year, which represents a 45 percent increase over the roughly 2.0 billion contracts that traded in 2006.

How do traders use options? In a variety of ways. A call option can be used to participate in a move higher in a stock. An investor can buy a put option to bet on a decline in a stock price. For example, an investor who bought put options (which give the right to sell a stock) on Intel on December 31, 2007, would have seen the value of the put option more than triple when the stock fell 18 percent over the next few weeks. During that same time, Citigroup fell 3 percent, and put options on its stock rose 32 percent.

So options can be used to profit from price changes in a stock, whether higher or lower. Puts and calls can also be used to profit from price changes in a variety of other assets, known as *underlying securities*, including gold, oil, bonds, the stock market, and specific sectors. Furthermore, there are a variety of more advanced strategies (covered later in this book) that can generate profits if the underlying asset moves higher, lower, or sideways.

---

underlying asset or underlying security
the security (stock, index, or futures) from which an option (put or call) derives its value.

The versatility of options explains why the options market has become one of the fastest-growing areas of finance today. The seven exchanges that offer options trading—the American Stock Exchange (AMEX), the Chicago Board Options Exchange (CBOE), the International Securities Exchange (ISE), the Boston Options Exchange (BOX), the New York Stock Exchange Arca (NYSE), the NASDAQ, and the Philadelphia Stock Exchange (PHLX)—continue to see steady order flows and strong business. Table 1.1 breaks down the total volume by exchange on a typical trading day in 2008.

In fact, the ISE, which was the first all-electronic options exchange, was acquired by Eurex, a European exchange, in 2007. The year before, the New York Stock Exchange (NYSE) bought out Archipelago and, in the process, acquired the options trading business of the Pacific Stock Exchange, which is now known as NYSE Arca. More recently, the NASDAQ Stock Market launched its own options market and became the seventh exchange to list puts and calls. The all electronic exchange received SEC approval on March 12, 2008, and started trading options shortly thereafter. Like the six others,

table 1.1   percentage of market share by exchange

	Options Contract Totals by Exchange:				
	Equity Total	Equity %	Index/Other Total	Index/ Other %	Exchange Total	Total %
AMEX:	631,058	5.65%	12,373	1.24%	643,431	5.29%
BOX:	576,910	5.17%	1,510	0.15%	578,420	4.76%
CBOE:	3,356,567	30.07%	929,403	93.00%	4,285,970	35.24%
ISE:	3,381,628	30.30%	40,643	4.07%	3,422,271	28.14%
NSDQ:	159,650	1.43%	0	0.00%	159,650	1.31%
NYSE:	1,086,910	9.74%	1,078	0.11%	1,087,988	8.95%
PHLX:	1,969,564	17.64%	14,306	1.43%	1,983,870	16.31%
Total:	11,162,287	100.00%	999,313	100.00%	12,161,600	100.00%

source: the options clearing corp. (9-29-08)

the NASDAQ options market offers trading in equity, ETF, and index options. In addition, the exchanges are becoming more efficient with the help of technology. Options trading has never been easier or more popular among individual investors. It is a strong trend that is showing no signs of slowing.

At the same time, while the exchanges have been growing, they are also competing for investor attention and order flow. Consequently, the exchanges have become important sources of information regarding industry trends. For example, a visit to the CBOE web site provides a plethora of useful options-trading information, much of it free. This includes not only product specifications but also quotes, research, and historical data. The AMEX, NASDAQ, ISE, and PHLX also provide useful information on their respective web sites, listed below and in Table 1.1 for your convenience:

American Stock Exchange, Inc.

86 Trinity Place

New York, New York 10006

(212) 306-1452

www.amex.com

Boston Options Exchange

(866) 768-8845

www.bostonoptions.com

Chicago Board Options Exchange, Inc.
400 LaSalle Street
Chicago, IL 60605
(312) 786-7705
www.cboe.com

International Securities Exchange
60 Broad Street
New York, NY 10004
(212) 943-2400
www.iseoptions.com

NASDAQ Stock Market
One Liberty Plaza
165 Broadway
New York, NY 10006
(212) 401-8700
www.nasdaq.com

NYSE Arca
(Formerly Pacific Stock Exchange)
301 Pine Street
San Francisco, CA 94104
(415) 393-4000
www.nyse.com

Philadelphia Stock Exchange, Inc.
1900 Market Street
Philadelphia, PA 19103
(215) 496-5000
www.phlx.com

reality check for online traders

These days, most option orders are sent electronically to the exchanges. When I first started trading, this kind of technology didn't exist. Customer orders were sent to the brokerage firm by phone and then the order was usually sent from the firm to the exchange through a direct line. Sometimes the order went through several individual brokers before finding its way to the pits of the exchange floor. Electronic trading has changed all that; now customers can often send orders directly to the exchanges where the best prices exist.

Since options are *multiple listed*, the same contract can be listed simultaneously on several different exchanges. For example, the January 30 calls on Intel might be quoted at $3.00 on the ISE and $3.05 on the CBOE. In that case, the customer would want a buy order to go to the ISE. However, that doesn't always happen due to poor execution on the part of the brokerage firm handling the order. For that reason, many active traders prefer to deal with a *direct access* broker, or one that allows customers to direct their orders to specific exchanges.

direct access broker
a brokerage firm that allows customers to direct orders to specific options exchanges.

Obviously, with the help of technology, online trading is changing the nature of investing more than we can even begin to understand. It remains to be seen whether the proliferation of online trading—especially in options—is a dramatic shift in the way investors trade or just a hyped-up way for investors and traders to lose money faster in the markets. I hope it is not the latter, but I must be realistic. After all, the faster someone can trade, the more likely that person is to trade more often.

Moreover, the ease with which investors and traders are able to move in and out of the market may very well be inversely correlated to the amount of research they actually do to find and manage investment opportunities. It is paramount to your success as a trader to fight against this kind of gambler mentality when it comes to online trading disciplines. Don't try to make up for losses by trading more and more aggressively. Instead, if you have a series of losses, stop trading.

It's important to let the power of the Internet work for you. Online trading services increased the speed of the transaction, lowered the cost, and gave traders unimaginable access to information from which knowledgeable investment decisions can be made.

Brokerage firms have never offered more objective information to their customers. It's online and often free to customers. At the same time, the costs of trading are still falling. According to the annual ranking of online brokers by *Barron's* ("Making It Click: Annual Ranking of Best Online Brokers," by Theresa Carey, March 17, 2008), "Overall, our analysis puts the average commission at $6.52 this year, up a bit from $6.35 last year, for a 500-share block. A number of firms, meanwhile, cut their options commissions last year." The days of paying $25 or $50 for an options order execution are over.

However, although the trend of falling commissions is clearly working in our favor as options traders, the psychology of trading hasn't changed much. Just like with most jobs, there are fast days and there are slow days in the financial markets. You never know what might happen next. Perhaps it's the uncertainty that's so exhilarating.

For most professional traders, financial markets are exciting. It's the most exhilarating game. Every morning you wake up early and have no idea what might happen next. The key to long-term success is the ability to make good decisions quickly; this is also the backbone to making consistent profits. Time waits for no one, especially the trader. However, the one attribute all traders must learn is *patience*. Many of the best trades take time to mature. So be patient, especially if you have placed a delta neutral options trade. Sometimes it is better to wait than to keep reacting to the market's every whim. In fact, since many other traders are also reacting to the same news, it is almost impossible to get an edge by trading on news alone.

So while, on the outside, trading consists of buying and selling stocks and stock options, on the inside, market sentiment and trader psychology can rip the novice trader apart. Even experienced traders can get caught up in periods of market euphoria or panic. Instead, try to keep your wits and withstand everything the marketplace has to throw at you—from bidding wars to international market collapses. The first rule: Don't panic. By remaining calm, you harness the clarity to make decisions quickly in order to protect your investments against losses.

So what is the key to remaining calm when the majority of other investors are caught up in the chaos? Risk management. I discuss risk management in the final chapter of the book; in the meantime, it cannot be understated. Always look to protect your capital by using strong risk control techniques. Try to place yourself in a position to profit by choosing trades with limited risk and plenty of time to mature to profitability. And finally, have an exit plan already in place before placing a trade. The lack of a profit and loss plan is like not having a fire escape route—don't get burned!

the land of opportunity

Now that I've probably scared you half to death, let's explore some of the great things about trading options online. For one thing, there is no limit to how successful you can become. There is no bias toward race or ethnicity and no glass ceiling. The playing field is absolutely level. You can start with relatively little capital and, over time, build that capital into considerable wealth.

In addition, the opportunities have never been better for investors, even those with relatively little capital, to get started. Some brokerage firms have no restrictions on the amount of money needed to open an account. An investor can start with as little as $500. In short, trading options doesn't require a large capital investment to get started.

In addition, a wide variety of contracts have recently been created to appeal to the smaller investor. Examples include a variety of exchange-traded funds (ETFs), new futures contracts, and the so-called *mini-indexes*. For example, the Dow Jones Industrial Index ($DJX) is a mini-index equal to 1/100th of the Dow Jones Industrial Average ($INDU). You have probably heard stock market reporters talk about "the Dow" on the evening news, especially when it achieves milestones like the 10,000 level. When the Dow breaches key levels, it is a sign that the stock market is performing well. It is also viewed as a good omen for the economic outlook. However, while the fact of the Dow moving above 10,000 might be newsworthy, options traders can't participate directly as the cost of the options would be sky high. Hence, although the Dow is probably the most widely watched barometer for the stock market, there are no options listed on it.

While the industrial average is not practical to trade, the mini-Dow is equal to 1/100th of the industrial average; when the Dow hit 10,000, the mini-index rose to 100, which is a much more manageable level for an options contract. In short, the advent of many mini-indexes (discussed in more detail in Chapter 2) opens up a world of opportunities for options traders looking for ways to profit from moves in the stock market. There has been a lot of innovation in terms of the financial products available to smaller investors. The development of many mini-indexes is just one example.

getting the right stuff

While the cost of trading has come down over the years, so has the cost of technology. It is cheaper and easier than ever to get hooked up to the World Wide Web. In fact, at this point, most readers probably have access to the Internet at home. If so, the following section on computers may not offer much new information.

However, to the uninitiated, getting hooked up to start trading options probably seems like a daunting prospect. Not only does trading options involve a learning curve, but technology is always changing, and getting the right tools to trade is a task in itself. But regardless of all the potential frustrations, getting online to trade is not that difficult. There are four essential products and services that you need: a working computer, a high-speed connection, an Internet service provider (ISP), and a browser.

computers   While some traders seem to get by okay with personal digital assistants (PDAs) or handheld devices to trade options online, it makes sense to have either a desktop or notebook computer, or both. The technology to trade with PDAs is certainly in place, with many brokerage firms offering a variety of tools for doing so. However, handheld devices don't offer much screen real estate for looking at charts or doing research.

---

laptop computer
a portable personal computer that is small enough to fit in a person's lap. Weighing less than eight pounds, laptop computers usually have a flat screen and LCD display, and are powered by a rechargeable battery. They can be connected to a larger monitor or other peripherals when back at the office.

desktop computer
a stationary computer with a full-size monitor and hard drive.

The next questions: personal computer (PC, meaning IBM or IBM-compatible) versus Apple, and notebook versus desktop? In the past, trading software for Apple computers was practically nonexistent. However, now Apple Computers can run most Windows-based software and the difference isn't that important. It all comes down to individual preference. Either will work fine.

A more important consideration for traders is whether to invest in a notebook or a desktop computer. The cost of desktops has come down considerably in recent years. If you're primarily trading at home, there's really no reason to spend more money on a notebook computer. However, if you travel a lot (like I do), then a notebook is worth the extra money, as having all of your software and research on a portable computer is a very valuable asset. Again, the individual trader must decide: If you're an on-the-go kind of person, then a laptop is probably the ticket.

---

chip
a microelectronic device that can store copious amounts of information. A chip is comprised of miniature transistors on a very thin silicon or sapphire rectangle. The type of chip you use contributes to a computer's speed.

Obviously, technology is rapidly changing, and computers are becoming not only cheaper but also faster and more efficient. I really can't recommend the best computer for you because your needs are unique and computer technology changes at a dizzying pace. However, as a general rule, I recommend buying a computer that gives you the most bang for your buck. In today's market (which will probably have changed by the time this book is actually in print), you can get a very good computer (with 250 gigabytes of hard drive space, 2 gigs of SDRAM, and an Intel Pentium processor) for less than $800.

---

random access memory (RAM)
RAM is the memory available for use while you are working (or playing) on your computer. RAM memory controls just how many software applications you can open simultaneously and stores information before it is saved to a disk or the hard drive. When a computer is turned off, RAM memory shuts off as well, and any material not saved is lost into the great beyond.

meg
short for megabyte, which means one million bytes or information units, each consisting of eight bits apiece.

---

hard drives (storage memory)   A hard drive stores all the information on your computer even when the computer is shut down. While the prices of hard drives continue to fall, their memory capacity has been steadily increasing. Most new computers come with 250-plus gigabytes of storage memory. You're probably wondering just how much room you'll need; the answer depends on how many programs you want to run. Comprehensive trading programs may need as much as 350 megs of hard drive space for real-time or delayed data collection. Normally, with new computers today, hard drive space isn't an issue for trading options online. Again, the general rule is the more megabytes the better.

---

hard drive (HD)
the hard drive is a disk permanently installed inside a computer that acts as a permanent storage area for large amounts of information including programs, files, and graphics. Hard disks are measured by how many megabytes of information they can store.

---

monitors   A good monitor is an essential part of your computer setup. A 17-inch monitor is fairly standard and does the job reasonably well. A 21-inch monitor is the next step up, but at a steeper price. One alternative to buying a 21-inch monitor is to buy a video card (a part that will go inside your computer with one edge of the card showing on the outside) that will allow you to use two monitors on the same computer. The two monitors together give you the same picture that you get on one monitor; it will just be stretched over two screens. If you are a heavy trader, consider two 17-inch monitors or a single 21-inch monitor. Either way, the newer flat-screen monitors thankfully use a smaller footprint.

modems   A modem is a small communication device that connects your computer to the outside cyberworld. Modems basically come in two varieties: internal and external. Almost all of the newer computers come with an internal modem, which costs a little less and attaches to the inside of the computer box with one edge on the outside of the computer.

Speed is one of the most important factors when dealing with Internet connections. Most serious Internet users today are connected through cable, satellite, or DSL. However, dial-up modems, which dial in to the Internet service provider, still exist. While speeds have improved, modems are clearly inferior. If you are serious about trading, a high-speed connection will save you a lot of time and frustration.

In addition, using DSL or cable modems will keep the phone line available to call the brokerage firm when needed. This might occur, for example, if you have a power outage in your home or your ISP goes down. Keep your broker's phone number handy, perhaps attached to your computer monitor on a Post-it note, for those times when you need to phone an order in to a live broker.

DSL
digital subscriber lines use standard telephone wires to carry data at much higher speeds than regular modems, which often require the user to have separate phone lines for outside communication.

WiFi
a wireless networking technology that utilizes radio waves to provide wireless high-speed network and Internet connections.

---

internet service providers   An Internet service provider (ISP) allows you to access the Web through its Internet server. You will want to consider two different types: direct ISPs and indirect ISPs. A direct ISP will hook you directly to the Internet without organizing much material for you to look at. It opens the door and then lets you wander around inside, trying to find what you want. If you know where to find what you want, the direct ISP will get you there fastest. Some U.S. direct ISPs now cover large parts of the country and also provide local access in certain overseas cities. An indirect ISP gives you access to the Internet and provides a large amount of information, search engines, and links to both financial and nonrelated topics. The best-known indirect ISPs are AOL and MSN.

> **internet service provider (ISP)**
> a company that provides a connection between individual
> computer systems and the Internet.

Direct ISPs and indirect ISPs cost about the same for unlimited access. I prefer a direct ISP because they tend to have less advertising, which helps the screens move faster. This isn't as big a problem as in the past, but a consideration nevertheless.

The most important factor is reliability. Don't wait to get online before finding out how often the server fails. If you are trading online, outages can cost you money. Call a few ISPs and ask them a few questions, such as how much mail can be received before your mailbox is full. Is there an extra charge for a personal Web page? Make sure you keep track of how long you had to sit on hold waiting for a live customer service representative. Ask your friends about their experience with the reliability of their ISP and make an informed choice.

internet browsers   If you use a direct ISP, you will need to download an Internet browser. A browser is a software program that hosts your Internet journeys. The most popular and widely used browser is Internet Explorer. While some people swear by it, other browsers, such as Mozilla Firefox, also exist. Again, if you are just starting out, ask friends, family, and fellow traders what browsers they like and why.

> **browser**
> a client program that allows users to read hypertext documents
> on the World Wide Web, and navigate between them. Most
> computers come with Microsoft Internet Explorer, but other
> browsers are also available.

data providers   Serious traders need to subscribe to a data provider for real-time, delayed, or end-of-day price quotes. To determine which service fits your trading style best, you need to identify several factors. Do you want to pursue long- or short-term investments? What specific markets do you want to trade? How much money can you commit to your trading account?

Table 1.2 is designed to help you decide which kind of data reception is best suited to your needs. Bottom line: if you're going to trade and compete with commercial and professional traders, you need to have the same data they do. Although the siren song of real-time data feeds and day trading is very seductive, if you are just starting out, delayed feed is more than enough to help you get your feet wet. It has everything you'll need to learn and practice trading systems as well as find, place, and exit trades.

---

data provider
a source of information that provides you with current price data on stocks, futures, and options, as well as up-to-the-minute news and market analyses. This information can be accessed in a variety of ways including online, cable, FM, satellite, and wireless networks.

Lastly, you need to take a look at price. Trading is a business. If you sign up for real-time data feed, expect to pay (including exchange fees) anywhere from $50 to $500 a month. This monthly expense almost immediately forces you to make trades to generate profits to cover your data cost. Forced trades are seldom profitable. To become a successful trader, you have to learn to walk before running. That's why conservation of capital through controlled expenses is a must. As your experience level increases, you can always increase your data speed.

The good news is that many web sites offer free delayed quotes and charts. Meanwhile, some brokerage firms today offer free real-time streaming quotes. Consequently, paying a lot of money for data today isn't the norm that it once was. If you already have a brokerage account, ask your broker what type of online quotes and charts they offer. It might make sense to shop around for different brokers if their answer doesn't include the words "real time."

table 1.2   types of quotes

Type of Quote	Description	Advantages	Disadvantages
End-of-day	Anything from paper charts to Internet remote quotes and chart retrieval or a dial-up download of end-of-day data directly to your computer for analysis.	1. Cheapest form of data available. Much of it is even free and readily available online. 2. Many part-time traders can use end-of-day data to find opportunities after the market closes and place trades before the market opens the next day. 3. Available free with some software packages, including ProfitSource (www.profitsource.com).	1. If you are an intraday trader, end-of-day data is of little use to you. 2. Impossible to monitor live quotes and verify the quality of execution on your buy and sell orders.
Delayed	Real-time streaming data that is delayed by 15 to 20 minutes.	1. Available through a variety of web sites at no charge. 2. Can be used by many trading software analysis programs to find longer-term investment opportunities. 3. Available free from many brokers.	1. Comes at least 15 minutes after the actual event. If you are trying to trade during the day using delayed data, you will not enjoy as much success as you would with real-time data, because by the time you see a big move in a stock with delayed data, the big move is over.

(Continued)

table 1.2 *(continued)*

Type of Quote	Description	Advantages	Disadvantages
			2. Difficult to monitor live quotes and verify the quality of execution on your buy and sell orders.
Real-time	Tick-by-tick streaming data received from a quote service as the prices at the exchange change.	1. Widely available and easy to install. Online collection data is continuous feed, which will be collected and stored at your PC for review and analysis. 2. Receive real-time quotes directly over the Internet from vendors that resell data in real-time format. 3. Can be used by many trading software analysis programs to find various investment opportunities. 4. Sometimes available free from a broker, sometimes for an additional charge. 5. Gives you the ability to closely monitor the market and verify the quality of execution on buy and sell orders. 6. You can create short-term charts using intraday data.	1. Can be expensive depending on the level of service you need. 2. Not necessary for longer-term buy-and-hold investors or occasional traders.

conclusion

This chapter was designed to provide most of the information you'll need to get up and running. Once you decide what kind of information is necessary to your trading process, you can easily find it on the Internet at either a free site or one that charges a small subscription fee. Do not underestimate the importance of choosing wisely when it comes to your Internet connection. Prices on hardware and software have come down so much that it makes little sense to try to trade without the latest technology.

Once you've made your purchases and hooked everything up, you're ready to go online and take your first steps toward financial independence. But don't jump the gun. There are still a number of decisions to make. You have to choose an online brokerage, pick out trading software, and determine which resource sites (if any) are worth the price of subscription. This process can be quite time-consuming, especially when you're champing at the bit to start trading. Practice patience. Take your time. Don't worry about missing some trend or losing out on the next winning initial public offering (IPO). There's always another great trade on the horizon. Take the time to arm yourself well; it'll pay off down the road.

The road to online investing prosperity is an individual experience. On your journey, you will undoubtedly encounter certain obstacles that block your path. Although no one can really tell you how to navigate around these impediments, you can try to learn as much as possible from your own mistakes. No doubt your journey will encompass both victories and losses. I hope you can use some of what I've learned to avoid making the mistakes I've made.

chapter 2

online investing 101

assessing the trading environment

"A good traveler is not intent upon arrival." The wisdom of these words is as applicable today as it was when the renowned philosopher Rumi spoke them back in the thirteenth century. In every aspect of life, it is the journey itself that is truly important.

In the world of online trading, technology and innovation have dramatically changed the landscape; the path to financial success is now a vastly different process than it was 20 or 30 years ago. Many of the investment principles or fundamentals are the same, but the modus operandi for options traders has changed considerably. It is still an exciting journey and one that never really ends, as the financial markets are always changing. Technology and information, however, have universally conspired to change the way most of us trade today.

Today's trading environment is unlike anything we've ever seen before. Mega computers using high-speed Internet connections led to the development of cutting-edge tools and resources. Thanks to the vast number of online financial information resources, investors have access to instant news as well as lightning-quick online transactions. Traders can either use this information intelligently or become so overwhelmed by the magnitude of information available that they develop analysis paralysis—the inability to make decisions due to information overload.

Since online trading is a balancing act, it's up to you to determine what information is most important to monitor, find out where it can be easily located, and decide how you want to keep track of it. For example, you might want to compile a list of your favorite web sites and bookmark these pages for easy access.

The Internet is literally overflowing with financial investment sites and online brokerages. To lend order to the seemingly infinite nature of available information, it is important to cut through the clutter and filter what is truly important for the investment decision process. One approach is to forge consistent investigative patterns while leaving a little room for spontaneous forays into uncharted territory. Over time, there will be some sources of information that are accessed daily, like your brokerage firm, and others that might be viewed once a week or even once a month.

There are very few shortcuts in this process. Finding the optimum combination of resource sites as well as the best online brokerage for you is a process of evolution. You just have to surf from site to site until you develop a daily ritual that works for you. This process will take its own sweet time but, as Rumi reminds us, it's important to enjoy each part of the journey.

Likewise, to enjoy online trading you have to delight in cultivating your own resources, investigating specific industry sectors, developing a watch list and a portfolio, and keeping track of your positions. In Chapter 3, we explore some of the web site resources that are the most useful and popular among options traders today. First, however, let's examine some of the basics of the stock market and highlight what information or research is truly worthwhile when looking for opportunities for placing options trades online.

analyzing the market

Each day, millions of shares of stock are traded around the globe, from Australia to Asia, the Middle East, Europe, and North America. These stocks change in price due to a myriad of factors. More often than not, the price changes are due to the arrival of new information. For example, a stock price might move higher if the company reports strong profits, or the price may fall if there are important news events related to the industry or the economy. These news events cause investors to buy or sell the shares, which causes a change in the supply and demand dynamic, which moves the price.

---

stock
a stock, also called a share, is a unit of ownership in a company. The value of each share is based upon a wide variety of factors including the total number of outstanding shares, the value of the company, its earnings and debts, what the company produces now and is expected to produce in the future, and the overall demand for the stock.

So at any moment, the mass psychology of the trading public can shift, triggering trend reversals that often defy the odds. Perhaps that's why trying to analyze a stock in order to forecast price movement is so challenging; the number of variables and methodologies seems to be infinite. To take advantage of trading software or financial research sites, the first step is to develop a healthy understanding of fundamental market data, technical indicators, and the effects that news, commentary, and analysts have on market opinion. When asked what separates successful customers from unsuccessful ones, the president of one online brokerage firm tells us:

> Consistently successful customers in the options space have much in common with those who invest in the underlying equity directly. They understand the fundamentals of their strategies and the companies they are investing in and they are diversified both by strategy and security. No lottery playing. Just good fundamental investing.

> —John Hass of OptionsHouse

In short, one of the first goals of new options traders should be to understand the fundamentals that drive both the underlying stock and the options prices. In general, traders analyze stock fundamentals based on expectations of future events. Current events change prices by changing the way investors forecast the future prospects of a company (i.e., profits), the industry, and/or the economy in general.

For that reason, the stock market is said to be a *discounting mechanism*. That is, it discounts or reacts to information before it happens. The present plays a role, but since that information is already known, most investors base their investment decisions on what will happen in the future. Getting an edge often requires peering into the future to anticipate events better than the mass of other investors.

This area of trading can be overwhelming to a novice trader. There seems to be no end to the details that need to be taken into account. To become adept, you have to be willing to persistently reconnoiter the markets on a day-to-day basis. In the beginning, you may feel buried by an avalanche of numbers, statistics, and indicators. Just keep reading and watching how the markets react to such things as earnings estimates, analyst upgrades and downgrades, the release of new products, management changes, and the threat of interest rate adjustments.

As a small investor, you have to carefully select your analysis tools because you are competing with traders who have access to scores of analysts studying a wide array of price variables daily. In order to help you, I have divided the complex realm of market research and price forecasting into three basic fields:

1. Individual stock assessment.
2. Broad market analysis.
3. Psychological market criteria.

The first category—individual stock assessment—can be further broken down into fundamental and technical analysis. Let's take a closer look at these elemental research and analysis fields.

individual stock assessment

For the beginner, picking the right stock is a great starting point. If you can find a stock or market with very bullish or bearish fundamentals, the process of selecting option strategies becomes a lot easier. Eventually, the stock price will move to reflect those fundamentals.

For example, in 2007 Apple Computer (AAPL) shares rose 133.5 percent. Why? Apple had unveiled a series of new electronics that were seeing strong sales, including iPod music players, new notebook computers, and the iPhone. Investors who bought shares in 2006 in anticipation of the launch of the innovative and extremely popular products were well rewarded in 2007. Of course, hindsight is always 20/20, but the point is that a company with strong underlying fundamentals is generally rewarded with an appreciating stock price. The key is to isolate those companies with improving fundamentals from those with deteriorating fundamentals.

bearish
a declining market, especially over a prolonged period of time. A bearish market is often caused by the mass conviction that a weak economy depresses corporate profits.

bullish
a rising stock market, especially over a long period of time—at least six months. A bullish market is often caused by the mass conviction that a strong economy produces increased corporate profits.

In the past, fundamental research was an arduous task. The process involved sifting through mountains of printed information and crunching numbers with a handheld calculator, which is why professional analysts got paid big bucks for giving buy and sell recommendations on individual stocks.

But times have changed. Stock screening programs act as online data research engines, enabling traders to analyze individual stocks with the click of a mouse. Just choose which parameters are important and your computer will instantaneously generate a list of stocks that fit these criteria. A multitude of software programs and online sites offer stock screening functions. Some of the online sites are free and others require a monthly subscription fee for more advanced searches. Examples are discussed in the chapters that follow.

While stock screening yields some very useful information, to effectively use it you must understand the inner workings of specific fundamental parameters. Understanding the value of individual stock indicators is a complex process. Let's take a look at a few of the more important fundamental and technical analysis indicators in order to get a basic sense of how search engines can be programmed. (A comprehensive list of analysis methods can be found in Appendix B.)

fundamental analysis

Fundamental analysis forecasts price movement by focusing on hard company-specific data. Corporations have miles of paper trails that review every contributing factor of a company's strength, including product development and reception, targeted customer identification, consumption, profit outlook, management strength, and supply and demand for products. Economic data includes income statements, past records of earnings, sales records, present assets, annual reports, and new product consumption rates. Fundamental analysts use this data to determine whether a stock's current market price is overvalued or undervalued and to anticipate stock price trends and the future success or failure of the company.

---

fundamental analysis
an approach to trading research that seeks to predict stock price movements using a variety of indisputable basic facts including income statements, past records of earnings, sales, assets, management changes, and products and services.

In its most refined state, fundamental analysis produces two basic theories that affect market perception: If a stock's fundamentals are bullish, the stock's price should rise; if a stock's fundamentals are bearish, the stock's price should fall. Low prices relative to the company's real value increase demand, which in turn drives up the price of the stock. Higher prices reduce the demand for shares, and the ensuing increase in the supply of shares leads to lower prices. This cycle feeds on itself, deftly creating market dynamics.

Traders must also pay attention to the competition among different companies in the same industry sector. For example, there is extreme competition among high-tech corporations where breakthroughs in technology spawn dramatic market movement. Trying to stay on the cutting edge of these markets is a full-time job. Studying the entire industry is vital to being able to forecast a company's success. And that's where the money is!

Most of the information you gain from television or newspapers is fundamental analysis. Perhaps a company's product is selling like hotcakes, or a management change is altering the direction in which a corporation is going. Perhaps a disaster occurred, triggering the selling of a corporation's stock shares. Fundamental analysis ranges from the mundane to data that is so economically complicated it may require a degree in business to understand it. As you progress as a trader, you will learn to gauge which data is important enough to take notice of and what can be filtered out. This process is subjective; hence, there is no right or wrong. Anything that helps you to get a feel for a market is valid. It simply takes time and energy to develop a discerning ear for fundamental information, and practice to know how to apply it correctly.

A plethora of finance-related web sites offer basic fundamental information. In fact, my own web site, Optionetics (www.optionetics. com), provides easy access to stock quotes, charts, and fundamental data. Just type in the stock's symbol on the home page and you'll instantly find a snapshot of a company, which includes stock data and fundamental information (see Figure 2.1).

figure 2.1 AAPL snapshot

AAPL Apple Inc (NASDAQ GS)				
Last **$174.67**	Change: ▲ +$2.3	% Change: +1.33%		As of 12:55 PM ET

Quote/Chart/News	Option Chain	Interactive Chart

Open:	$171.30	Yield:	n/a	Shares Out:	881.62 Million
High:	$174.99	P/E Ratio:	36.01	Market Cap:	$153.99 Billion
Low:	$169.07	EPS:	$4.85	52 Wk High:	$202.96
Bid:	$174.65	Ex Date:	n/a	52 Wk Low:	$111.62
Ask:	$174.68	Dividend:	n/a	Volume:	21.27 Million
Future Earnings Date:		07/21/2008			
EPS Estimate:		$1.07			

News Headlines

10:55:00 AM	6/16/2008	BeaconEquity.com Issues TraderNotes on Market Movers MCII, EFGU, EBAY, SYMW, PWRD, PGOG, AAPL, and BRCM -PR Newswire
6:00:37 AM	6/16/2008	Widevine(R) Connects Cable, Telco and Satellite Services to Apple, Adobe and RealNetworks Players -Market Wire
12:10:46 PM	6/13/2008	*APPLE INC. DOWN 1% AT $171.56 IN PREMARKET TRADING -Xinhua Financial News

source: www.optionetics.com, reprinted with permission.

ticker symbol
each stock and options contract is assigned a symbol that is used
to find quotes and create charts. For example, the symbol for
Apple Computer is AAPL and for Coca Cola it is KO.

A stock's quarterly earnings growth is one of the critical pieces
of information to consider when assessing its profitability. The earnings per share value (EPS) is calculated by dividing the net income
(i.e., the profits) of the company in one quarter by the number of outstanding common shares. A comparison between the current EPS
and that of the same quarter of the previous year can be used to
determine earnings growth from one year to the next. In addition,
analysts project a company's earnings, and the price of the stock
often reflects that projection.

Since profits are an important driver of stock prices, quarterly
profit reports can cause volatility in the stock price. *Volatility* simply
means a larger than average move in the stock price. In addition,
since profit reports are released quarterly, there is often speculation
as to whether a company can live up to its EPS projection at the end
of each quarter. If it reports earnings that fall short of expectations,
the stock may fall. This is known as an *earnings miss*. However, if
earnings are above analyst estimates, it is an *earnings surprise* and
the stock usually moves higher. This speculation about whether a
company will miss or surprise often inspires volatility in the stock—a
key to finding successful options trades.

Price-earnings ratio (P/E) is another important value because it
compares a company's stock price to the earnings per share. Computed by simply dividing a stock's price by the annual earnings, it
tells you how many times the earnings a stock is trading at. The
P/E of individual stocks is then compared to the P/E for all stocks
of a given industrial sector. Be aware that many new and emerging
companies do not have valid P/E ratios because they are operating
at a net loss and still enjoying unparalleled success when it comes
to demand for shares of stock. The sales-to-price-per-share ratio is
a much more accurate benchmark for evaluating emerging-growth
companies.

As a general rule, the faster a company's growth rate, the higher
its P/E ratio. This has given rise to another valuation technique

known as the price-to-earnings growth rate formula, or PEG. The formula is straightforward; it is calculated by dividing the P/E ratio by company's earnings growth rate.

- If a high-growth company has a P/E ratio of 100 and an expected annual earnings growth rate of 50 percent, the PEG ratio is 2.0 (or 100/50).
- If a slow-growth company has a P/E ratio of 5 and an EPS growth rate of 7.5 percent, the company's PEG ratio is 0.67 (5/7.5).

The general rule is the lower the PEG ratio, the better the value. Hence, a stock with a high growth rate and a low P/E ratio is better than a stock with a high price-to-earnings ratio and a low earnings growth rate. In this example, the slow-growth company is better than the fast-growth company because its earnings growth rate is much better relative to its P/E ratio. Table 2.1 summarizes what to look for when looking at PEG ratios. A ratio below 0.5 is a good reason to consider bullish trades on a stock. When the reading is 1.7 or more, look out—the stock could be overvalued.

Earnings, P/E ratios, and earnings growth rate formulas are not the only fundamental factors to consider when looking at individual stocks. Price-to-sales ratios, book values, dividends, and a variety of other hard data can also help traders make sense of whether a stock is under- or overvalued. For those investors interested in a more in-depth look at fundamental analysis, we encourage you to read one of my most comprehensive books (cowritten with Tom Gentile), *The Stock Market Course* (New York: John Wiley & Sons, 2001).

table 2.1 PEG ratio and strategy selection

PEG Ratio	Strategy
Less than 0.50	Aggressively bullish
0.50 to 0.70	Moderately bullish
0.70 to 1.00	Neutral
1.00 to 1.30	Moderately bearish
1.30 to 1.70	Bearish
1.70 or more	Aggressively bearish

technical analysis

While fundamental analysis focuses on a company's earning potential and growth prospects, technical analysis is built on the theory
that market prices display repetitive patterns that can sometimes
be used to forecast future price movement. The keys to this type of
analysis are price behavior, volume, and charts, which are used in
combination to gauge strengths and weaknesses in a stock or in the
market. Technical analysis is best used in combination with a study
of the fundamentals.

A multitude of technical analysis techniques exist, including
Bollinger bands, chi-squares, the Elliott Wave theory, candlestick
charts, Kagi charts, and the maximum entropy method. Most of these
technical methods are very complicated and require computer programs to view. It is definitely worthwhile to become familiar with a
few of these techniques even if it's just to know what the competition is using. However, do not feel compelled to buy every technical
analysis book you can find—it will only lead to analysis paralysis.
We encourage you to use what's available first, and then gravitate to
those indicators that seem to make the most sense and are the most
helpful for the type of trading you do.

For example, when considering individual stocks, we pay close
attention to the 52-week high and low because this indicates where
the current price is in relation to where it's been. Volume is another
important factor as it defines the number of shares that have traded
over a specific period of time (daily, weekly, monthly). Volume is
used to confirm moves higher and lower. A stock that is advancing on
increasing volume is said to have strong technicals. Also, traders look
for volume spikes, or big sudden increases in volume, to signal that
buying or selling interest is picking up. I recommend avoiding stocks
with less than 300,000 shares trading daily. Bottom line: volume is
an extremely important technical indicator in many ways.

Accumulation/distribution (A/D) is a useful indicator of a
stock's strength or weakness. A more advanced technical indicator, it reflects a stock's daily long shares compared to short stock
shares. Daily Graphs (www.dailygraphs.com) provides an accumu-
lation/distribution rating. In general, a stock with an A rating means
there is plenty of demand for the stock (high volume) and the price
will probably continue to rise. A stock with an E rating means that
the supply for a stock is greater than the demand and could trigger a
drop in price. Over the years, I have focused on "A" stocks for buying
and "E" stocks for a bearish approach.

long versus short stock shares
investors buy shares when they expect a company to perform
well over time and the stock price to rise. However, traders also
short sell shares when they expect the company to perform
poorly and the stock to fall. Short stock is actually stock borrowed
from the broker and sold into the market. If the stock falls, the
trader can cover the position by buying the stock back at a
cheaper price and returning it to the brokerage firm.

Since trading is a game of timing, charts were devised to speed
up the process of information gathering. When I first started trading,
charts were only available in print. Later, a few software developers
created very expensive programs to help technical traders plot price
moves. Today, a variety of web sites offer free interactive charting
capabilities that allow users to plot a variety of technical indicators
as well.

In its simplest form, a chart shows the stock's price movement
over time. The vertical axis represents price fluctuation and the horizontal axis denotes time. Additionally, charts can be constructed
to represent specific time perspectives—intraday, daily, weekly, or
monthly. A longer-term (monthly) chart might look very different
from a short-term (five-day) chart.

In general, we look at technical indicators and trends under
three time frames: short-term, intermediate-term, and long-term.
When there are conflicting signals from the charts, we defer to the
longer-term chart because it has the most longevity and power.
Stated differently, there are three main kinds of trends: major, intermediate, and minor.

1. A **major** trend is one that lasts more than six months.
2. An **intermediate** trend lasts from one to six months.
3. A **minor** trend lasts less than a month.

As an options trader, it's optimal to look at markets over the
longer term. Hence, to assess a market's movement, learn how to
use annual charts, and always pay close attention to the most recent
few weeks.

technical analysis
technical analysis uses historical price movement and volume to predict a market's future strength or weakness. Since price is the bottom line, technical analysts look primarily at price movement to determine price patterns. From these patterns, technical analysts try to extrapolate future price movements.

trends
a market that is increasing steadily to the upside or decreasing steadily to the downside is said to be a trending market. Catching the trend is one of the keys to successful trading — "the trend is your friend" is a familiar adage.

There are three basic kinds of charting techniques: bar charts, line charts, and candlestick charts. A bar chart, sometimes called an *open high low close* (OHLC) chart, uses vertical lines, each with two small horizontal bars at 90-degree angles. The vertical line itself represents the stock's price range for a specific period of time (hourly, daily, etc.). The horizontal bar to the left indicates the opening price; the one to the right, the closing price. (In Figure 2.2, notice the volatility around the time of the earnings report—denoted with an E on the chart.)

While OHLC charts plot the day's high, low, open, and closing price, line charts are less complex. They just show a stock's closing price from day to day, week to week, and month to month, like some kind of financial connect-the-dots game. While some traders may use line charts, I find them clearly inferior to OHLC charts as they provide no additional information beyond the closing price of the day.

Candlestick charts are the most elaborate. Like bar charts, they show a stock's daily price range. But they are also color-coded to reveal the relationship between a stock's open and closing price (see Figure 2.3). If a stock closed higher than it opened, the body of the candlestick is light (often green), indicating a bullish market. If the candlestick is dark (often red), then the stock closed lower than it opened, indicating a bearish market. Various other patterns are associated with candlestick charts, but those lie outside the scope of this book. Readers interested in a more detailed description of candlesticks are encouraged to visit StockCharts.com (stockcharts.com/school).

figure 2.2   OHLC chart

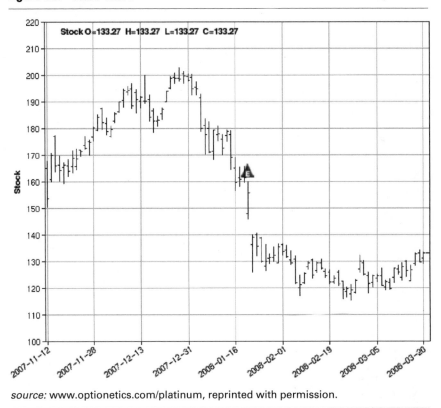

source: www.optionetics.com/platinum, reprinted with permission.

A multitude of web sites offer free stock charting and analysis that can show you a lot more than just the price movement over various time spans. You can easily check out a stock's daily movement for the past year with one keystroke. However, it's one thing to gauge a market's movements by looking at a chart and another to be able to insightfully analyze what you see.

Technical analysts have a broad range of additional analysis tools and patterns that can be used to try to forecast price movement. Price patterns are signposts, not laws, but these signposts help you gauge and understand the mass psychology of the marketplace. A pattern has influence only if people believe it to be true. Therefore, although it is helpful to know the difference between a head and shoulders pattern and a double top and bottom

figure 2.3 japanese candlestick chart

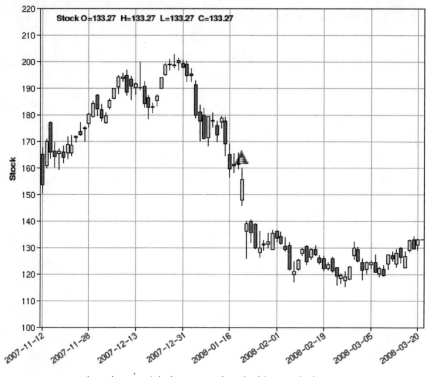

Stock O=133.27 H=133.27 L=133.27 C=133.27

source: www.optionetics.com/platinum, reprinted with permission.

(see Appendix B for pattern definitions), it is not as essential to the process as many technical analysts would have us think. But since many investors look to pattern analysis, it doesn't hurt to know what they're thinking.

For example, support and resistance are basic technical indicators used on stock charts by a number of traders. *Support* is the level at which a stock price stops falling and begins moving higher. This often occurs at round numbers such as $50 or $100 a share. *Resistance* is the opposite. It's a price level where prices find a ceiling and can't move any higher. When a stock breaks through support or resistance, it will often see a flurry of buying (as it breaks through resistance) or selling (as it falls through support). For example, in

Figure 2.4, Apple Computer saw a few days of heavy selling when the stock fell through $170 a share in mid-January 2008.

Volume is another important element of chart pattern analysis that helps traders assess a trend's strength or weakness. Volume bars can usually be found at the bottom of price charts. Each bar corresponds to the number of shares traded—the taller the bar, the heavier the volume. Strong uptrends are usually accompanied by heavy volume. When an uptrend starts to lose momentum, volume decreases. A divergence occurs when price and volume start to move in opposite directions, signaling an end to the trend.

I like to look for dramatic volume increases to catch a trend as it takes off. Figure 2.4 shows an example of a volume bar chart, with the lighter bars representing up days and the darker ones reflecting down days. The taller, darker bars are indicative of increasing selling pressure. For example, after the 133.5 percent rally in Apple shares in 2007, sellers started to surface in early 2008; the dark bars were getting taller, and the stock started a multimonth downtrend.

You can also use indicators to track existing trends. There are two basic kinds of indicators: lagging indicators and oscillators. Lagging indicators are techniques that confirm a trend divergence after it has happened. Oscillators forecast a market as overbought or oversold by assessing when a market has reached a high to the upside or a low to the downside. When a market reaches a peak in either direction, it is ripe for a reversal, and managed-risk strategies can be applied to take advantage of this movement.

---

overbought
a sudden and rapid move higher in the price of a security that has pushed it too far in one direction. Once a stock is overbought, it is likely to see corrective action and move lower.

oversold
a sudden and rapid move lower in the price of a security that has pushed it too far in one direction. Once a stock is oversold, it is likely to see corrective action and move higher.

A moving average (MA)—the analysis of price action over a specified period of time on an average basis—is one of the most popular lagging indicators. A moving average adds together the

figure 2.4   AAPL price chart (top) and volume chart (bottom)

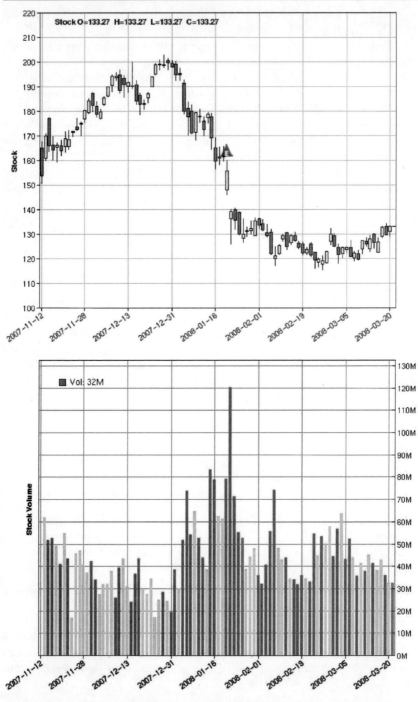

source: www.optionetics.com/platinum, reprinted with permission.

closing prices of a market over a period of time—50 or 200 days is standard—and then divides the sum by the number of days used. Each day a new number is added and the oldest is dropped, creating a slightly different average. You can either look at one moving average line at a time or check out more than one time frame to look for crossovers. For example, you may look at the price of IBM trading right now and how that price compares to the average of the past 50 days and the average price over the past 200 days. When the 50-day average goes below the 200-day average, you sell; conversely, when the 50-day average goes above the 200-day average, you buy. In Figure 2.5, the moving averages are very close to giving a "buy" signal. (Note: "D" = dividends, "E" = earnings.)

figure 2.5   IBM with 20- and 200-day moving averages

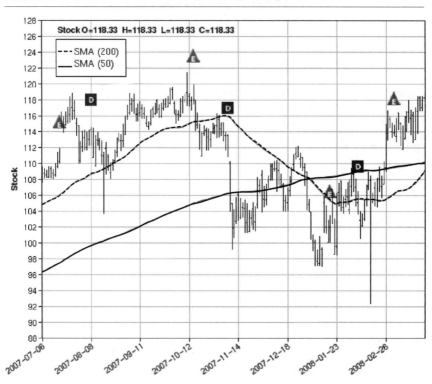

source: www.optionetics.com/platinum, reprinted with permission.

Technicians go to great lengths to fine-tune which time spans and moving averages to use. Moving averages can serve as important indicators of overall trend and often serve as key support and resistance areas. However, although you can play around with different MAs and study a variety of time spans, we focus on the 50-day or 200-day average as a base because they are the most commonly used.

---

lagging indicators
a method of technical analysis that confirms a trend divergence after it has happened (like a moving average) and gives clues to where it is headed, or an economic indicator that lags behind the overall pace of economic activity (like the unemployment rate).

oscillator
a technical indicator used to identify stocks and options with overbought or oversold prices that may trigger a trend reversal.

moving average
a moving average—probably the best known and most versatile technical indicator—is a chart used for judging a market's current trend. The moving average uses a simple mathematical procedure to smooth or eliminate the fluctuations in data and to assist in determining when to buy and sell.

Oscillators are indicators that help traders to predict a market's momentum by focusing on the rate at which a market is moving. Utilizing price and volume statistics, oscillators are used to predict the strength or weakness of a current market, determine overbought or oversold conditions, and locate turning points within the market.

Stochastics are one of the more widely used oscillators. The stochastic indicator is based on the observation that as prices increase, closing prices tend to accumulate ever closer to the highs for the period. Conversely, as prices decrease, closing prices tend to accumulate ever closer to the lows for the period. Trading decisions are made with respect to divergence between the percentage of *D* (one of the two lines generated by the study) and the item's price. When the stochastic indicator moves higher, the trend is bullish. However, when it moves above 80 percent, the stock is overbought and could head lower. Stochastics are available with most options trading software and are generally plotted below the stock chart (see Figure 2.6).

Geologists study volcanoes looking for indications of impending movements that may lead to eruptions. It's the same with momentum investors. They study the markets, watching for pressure to start building, followed by an explosion, and then the calm thereafter. You might catch the first move, place the appropriate strategy, and then get off when the momentum fizzles. A slowdown follows the eruption, often triggering a reversal. If you miss the eruption, you can still make a profitable trade by using a contrarian approach—a practice in which you trade against the majority view (i.e., fading the trend). In general, fast moves up lead to fast moves down, and vice versa.

figure 2.6   stochastics indicator

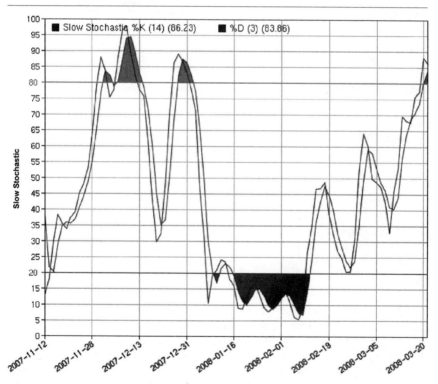

source: www.optionetics.com/platinum, reprinted with permission.

Hence, traders want to trade with the momentum until the stock or market is overbought or oversold on the long-term charts. Then it pays to become more defensive and maybe even take a contrarian approach.

momentum
when a market continues in the same direction for a certain time frame, the market is said to have momentum. A momentum indicator is a technical indicator that utilizes price and volume statistics for predicting the strength or weakness of a current market. Momentum trading exists when a trader invests with (or against) the momentum of the market in hopes of profiting from it.

contrarian approach
a contrarian is said to fade the trend by going against the majority view of the marketplace.

Admittedly, we have only scratched the surface of technical analysis and technical indicators. Fortunately, many online brokerages and web sites provide more detailed descriptions. In addition, a lot of information can also be learned the old-fashioned way—by reading books. Two that come to mind are *Technical Analysis of Stock Trends* by Edwards and Magee (Amacom, 2001), and *Trading for a Living* by Alexander Elder (John Wiley & Sons, 1993).

At the same time, there are many web sites dedicated to providing technical analysis tools and data for the online investor. BigCharts (www.bigcharts.com) and StockCharts.com (www.stockcharts.com) are two of the best. Both are easy to understand. They also offer a wide variety of technical charts and graphs at no cost. Just type in a stock's ticker symbol and click on "Interactive Chart" (at BigCharts) or "SharpChart" (at StockCharts.com). The next screen will provide you with an abundance of charting choices, from moving averages to stochastics. You can also save your favorite charts for easy reference.

broad market analysis

There are three distinct ways for the stock market as a whole to move: up, down, or sideways. If the market moves up, it is a bullish market. If it declines, it is a bearish market. If it stays in the same place, it is a neutral market. Discerning this distinction is the fundamental issue of a broad market indicator.

One of the primary methods of assessing stock market activity is to review the performance of indexes. An index is a group of stocks that make up a portfolio in which performance can be monitored based on one calculation. Broad market indicators use indexes as the basis for several analyses. For example, the Dow Jones Industrial Average (DJIA)—probably the best-known index—is widely quoted as the quintessential economic indicator of market direction. Everyone has heard the Dow mentioned on the evening news as a key indicator of the day's trading performance. The closing prices of the DJIA stocks are averaged to determine if the overall mood of the marketplace was bearish or bullish.

But what is the Dow and how did it get started? In 1884, Charles Dow surveyed the average closing prices of nine railroad stocks and two manufacturing companies that in his opinion represented the general trends in the national economy. He printed the results in his newspaper, a forerunner of today's *Wall Street Journal*. Twelve years later, he created an average of a dozen industrial companies. In 1896, Charles Dow began to publish this list and the overall average every day. Today's Dow Jones Industrial Average reflects the performance of 30 major companies representing a variety of industries including finance, technology, health care, energy, and consumer products. It is no longer just a barometer for "industrial" companies, but for the U.S. stock market and the economy as a whole. That's why you'll hear about how the Dow traded every weeknight on the local or national news station.

In today's highly unpredictable markets, there are several other indexes that track market movement in an attempt to forecast stock performance and direction. The New York Composite Index represents all stocks traded on the NYSE. Likewise, the AMEX Market Value Index and the NASDAQ Composite Index monitor all of the stocks traded at their respective exchanges.

There are, in fact, too many indexes to name. However, a few stand out as important to options traders. For example, the S&P 100 ($OEX) is one of the more popular indexes for options traders because it was the first index to have listed options. The OEX measures the performance of 100 of the largest stocks trading on the U.S. exchanges.

The S&P 500 ($SPX) is also a broad measure of the U.S. stock market. While the OEX includes 100 stocks, the S&P 500 consists of 500 different stocks. Meanwhile, the NASDAQ 100 ($NDX) is an index consisting of 100 of the largest nonfinancial stocks listed on the NAS-DAQ Stock Market. Therefore, it offers a gauge of the most important companies trading on the NASDAQ. More important, however, many traders prefer to trade the mini-NASDAQ 100 Index ($MNX) rather than the NASDAQ 100 Index. The mini-NASDAQ is equal to 1/100th of the NDX. Therefore, when the NDX is near 1,500, the mini-index will be trading near 15. The lower value has some important advantages when trading options (which were already mentioned in Chapter 1) with respect to the Dow and the Dow Jones Industrial Index ($DJX).

While the Dow and the S&P 500 are barometers for the performance of large companies, other indexes have been created to track the performance of smaller companies. The S&P MidCap 400 Index ($MID) is a popular tool for tracking medium-size companies. The Russell 2000 Index ($RUT) is the most widely watched barometer for the performance of smaller companies.

Keeping tabs on industry group leadership is another important key to analyzing the stock market as well. Again, there are too many sector indexes to list them all here for you. However, there are several that are actively traded and are worth watching for online options traders. Tables 2.2 and 2.3 provide a partial list. Note that the symbols have a dollar sign preceding the letters; this indicates that the security is an index.

All indexes can be studied using a combination of fundamental and technical analysis. Start by looking at the closing price. Next,

table 2.2   stock market indexes

Index	Symbol
S&P MidCap Index	$MID
NASDAQ 100 Index	$NDX
DJ Industrial Average	$INDU
S&P 500 Index	$SPX
S&P 100 Index	$OEX
Russell 2000 Index	$RUT

table 2.3   sector indexes

Index	Symbol
Amex Airline Index	$XAL
Cyclical Index	$CYC
Mini-NASDAQ 100 Index	$MNX
MS Commodities Index	$CRX
Natural Gas Index	$XNG
Oil Index	$XOI
AMEX Biotechnology Index	$BTK
AMEX Broker Dealer	$XBD
AMEX Morgan Stanley High Tech	$MSH
AMEX Pharmaceutical Index	$DRG
PHLX/KBW Bank Index	$BKX
PHLX Gold/Silver Sector Index	$XAU
PHLX Housing Sector Index	$HGX
PHLX Oil Service Sector Index	$OSX
PHLX Semiconductor Sector Index	$SOX
PHLX Utility Sector Index	$UTY
SIG Steel Producers Index	$STQ

check out the previous day's close as well as the percentage change between the two. Then take a look at the shift in price since the previous year and the overall change for the year to date. These four timeframes can help you to understand the index's current trend. Trends in the indexes tend to be similar to and often reflect the general mood of the economy.

exchange-traded funds

In recent years, the exchanges have launched options trading on a variety of new products; many of these new vehicles are exchange-traded funds (ETFs). While a lot exist, there are three that all options traders should know and understand.

First, the PowerShares NASDAQ 100 Index Trust (QQQQ), or "Qs," is one of the most actively traded investments today. Unlike an index, the Qs trades on the American Stock Exchange like a stock. In essence, the fund is a pool of money that invests in the same stocks, in the same proportion, as the NASDAQ 100 index. As we saw earlier, the NASDAQ includes the top 100 nonfinancial stocks that trade on the NASDAQ Stock Market.

Basically, the QQQQ is an investment vehicle known as a tracking stock because it tracks the performance of a specific index. In addition, the QQQQ is designed to equal 1/40th of the value of the NASDAQ 100 Index. For instance, if the NASDAQ 100 is near 1,500, QQQQ will trade for $37.50 a share (or 1/40th of $1,500). Like all ETFs, the Qs gives investors an opportunity to buy a basket of stocks in one transaction.

The Dow Jones Industrial Average index (DIA), or "diamonds," made its debut in 1998 and options on the fund started trading in 2002. Similar to the Qs, the diamonds trades on the exchanges like shares of stock. However, the DIA holds the same 30 stocks as the Dow Jones Industrial Average. Therefore, it is a tool for trading the Dow. Diamonds are designed to equal approximately 1/100th the value of the industrial average.

The S&P 500 (SPY), or "spiders," is an exchange-traded fund that holds the same stocks as the S&P 500 Index. The American Stock Exchange (AMEX) began trading the S&P Depositary Receipts in 1993. Each share of the SPY is equal to approximately to 1/10th the value of the S&P 500 Index. Therefore, when the SPX reaches 1,500, the spiders will trade near $150 a share.

Options on the DIA, QQQQ, and SPY are very actively traded and are a great way to trade the U.S. stock market. At the same time, a number of other ETFs exist. Some track the U.S. stock market; others focus on specific industry groups or international equities. So if you are looking to play a specific group of stocks, chances are there is an ETF or index out there that can make it possible.

a quick course in macroeconomics

The Federal Reserve was created following the panic of 1907 to help restore order to the financial system. Twelve very wealthy families actually stepped forward to bail out the U.S. government, and the Federal Reserve was officially created by Congress in 1913. Today, the Fed remains an important part of the financial landscape and essentially controls the flow of money in the United States economy.

The Federal Reserve is actually a conglomerate of 12 separate district banks governed by a seven-member Board of Governors. In many ways, the Fed works more like a government agency than a private corporation. It handles everything from the U.S. government's daily banking to receiving unemployment, withholding, and workers' compensation taxes. The Fed is also responsible for fulfilling the financial obligations of the U.S. government including providing Social Security and Medicare payments. The primary goals of the Federal Reserve are to stabilize prices, promote economic growth, and strive for full employment. These goals are accomplished through managing monetary policy, which is implemented by the Federal Open Market Committee (FOMC).

The Fed also controls the release of new money. Every six weeks, the Fed's Open Market Committee meets to regulate monetary policy by balancing the amount of money in circulation without creating inflation. It typically takes about six months for the economy to react to changes in monetary volume control. This delay causes the economy to have a life of its own, especially because many decisions do not trigger the originally intended impact. To further control the money supply, the Fed adjusts interest rates to balance out the rate of inflation while attempting to inspire national growth.

One of the Fed's primary tools for achieving balance in the economy is through changes in interest rates—the federal funds rate and, to a lesser extent, the discount rate. An interest rate is the annual percentage rate charged for the privilege of borrowing money. A change in interest rates can affect everything from bonds to the adjustable interest rate on your monthly mortgage payment. Subsequently, a relationship exists between interest rates, the prices of bonds, and the stock market. Bottom line: the Fed is responsible for maintaining economic stability, which is why the Fed was called to task when the worst banking crisis since the Great Depression hit Wall Street in September of 2008.

bonds, interest rates, and the market   A bond is a debt instrument issued by a government or corporation that promises to pay its bondholders periodic interest at a fixed rate (the coupon), and to repay the principal of the loan at maturity (a specified future date). Bonds are usually issued with a par or face value of $1,000, representing the principal or amount of money borrowed. The interest payment is stated on the face of the bond at issue. A bond's interest rate stays the same for the duration of the bond's maturity. That's why bonds have an inverse relationship to national interest rates. If interest rates rise, the value of a bond usually drops; if interest rates drop, the value of a bond usually rises in comparison.

For example, let's say that you decide you are going to lend me $1,000 for a five-year period. I agree to pay you interest at a rate of 8 percent each year, which happens to be the market rate for interest charges. Therefore, I will pay you $80 per year interest. The very next day, interest rates jump to 10 percent (I am exaggerating to make a point); you now could have lent the same $1,000 and received 10 percent interest, which would give you $100 per year. Did the value of the first loan go up or down with the interest rate rising? The value of the 8 percent loan went down because you do not have the opportunity to lend that money out at the higher rate of interest. Therefore, when interest rates go up, bond (loan) prices fall.

When interest rates go down, bond prices rise. If interest rates drop to 5 percent, an investor would receive only $50 on the same $1,000 investment. If you are already receiving $80, the value of your loan increases. That's how bonds are traded. As interest rates fluctuate, the value of a bond rises and falls in opposition. If a market is interest rate driven, this refers to a point in the business cycle when interest rates are declining and bond prices are rising. This is often enough to inspire a stock market rally as money shifts from interest rate instruments to equity-based instruments.

In general terms, this inverse relationship also holds for the stock market and interest rates. Hence, bond prices and the stock market move in tandem. Why? Let's assume your company has to buy $10,000 worth of equipment. You don't want to pay cash for the equipment; therefore, you finance the purchase. To finance anything, you pay interest. In this case, you pay 8 percent interest—$800 per year. Interest is an expense that gets subtracted from what you earn. Therefore, if you earn $20,000 before interest expenses, you will have earned $19,200 after interest is paid ($20,000 − $800 = $19,200). However, if interest rates are 10 percent, the same $10,000 loan costs $1,000 annually. Now your earnings are reduced to $19,000 ($20,000 − $1,000 = $19,000). In this way, the value of a stock is inversely linked to interest rates—the higher your interest rate, the less money flows to your earnings.

Since paying higher interest rates reduces earnings, a company's value will also decrease. This can seriously affect stock prices. Therefore, an increase in interest rates (or a fall in bond prices) should trigger a decrease in stock prices. This inverse relationship does not always hold. There are periods when a divergence will occur and a company's earnings will increase regardless of interest rates' direction. However, these divergences are generally short-term in nature.

In sum, the dynamic between stocks, bonds, and rates can be used as a guide to understanding market movement—bearish or bullish. Table 2.4 illustrates the typical interaction among interest

table 2.4   typical economic interrelationships

Interest Rates	Bonds	Stocks
Up	Down	Up or down
Down	Up	Up
Sideways	Sideways	Up

rates, bonds, and stocks. When interest rates rise, the stock market tends to react negatively because higher rates are not good for the economy. However, there will be times when the interest rates may increase and the stock market advances, or vice versa.

federal reserve system
established by Congress in 1913, the Federal Reserve System regulates the U.S. monetary and banking system by supervising, among other things, the quantity of new bills printed and interest rates; it keeps a watchful eye over member banks and acts as the government's bank.

interest rate
the charge for the privilege of borrowing money, usually expressed as an annual percentage rate.

Another voice to be listened to is that of the Federal Reserve chairman, currently Ben Bernanke. Traditionally when the Fed chairman speaks, the stock market hums with volatility. Twice a year, the Federal Reserve chairman officially speaks to Congress (Humphrey-Hawkins testimony) and stocks rally or descend in anticipation of what he'll say. In the wake of his testimony, the raising or lowering of interest rates may realign the course of the economy. This kind of information has a powerful effect on the markets.

The releases of several government reports also reflect the economics of the country and affect the stock market as well. The employment report is released on the first Friday of the month. It contains the current unemployment rate. A high unemployment rate speaks of more people looking for fewer jobs. This increase in competition can cause a decrease in wages. Less money for employment leads to lower production costs, tempering inflation. Ultimately this may lead to lower interest rates and turn the market from bearish to bullish.

The consumer price index (CPI) is another important report for the avid investor to review. The CPI directly measures inflation by studying the change in the cost paid by consumers for a standardized quantity of goods and services. A general increase in the CPI may lead to an increase in interest rates, which can have a bearish effect on the markets. A retail sales report released monthly by the Commerce Department has a similar message. An increase in retail sales shows a strong economy, as does a significant increase in new housing in the housing starts report. Prolonged increases may lead to higher interest rates to discourage inflation. A report on the gross national product (GNP) acts as a litmus test for the economy by taking everything into account.

A number of web sites provide daily economic analysis and related commentary. Just reading the news on Yahoo! Finance each morning (finance.yahoo.com) will tell you a lot about what the stock market is currently focused on. It could be interest rates, it could be oil, or it could be profits. Whatever it is, investors often get caught up in the news du jour. By taking a long-term view of the markets, it is sometimes possible to identify situations where investors have overreacted to short-term events. In short, it's important to understand the news and how it relates to the fundamentals of the stock market. However, it is very difficult to make money trying to play the short-term market swings that happen when investors react to the latest headlines.

psychological market indicators

Psychological market indicators can be thought of as criteria that analyze the subconscious of the marketplace. These indicators can be obtained by analyzing current market conditions and can tell you if the majority of investors are currently caught up in greed or fear. However, their utilization depends on your subjective interpretation of the facts. Keep in mind that some scenarios may inspire contrarian interpretations of the findings—that is, when everyone is bullish, it's time to get bearish, and vice versa.

You can start by comparing the number of bullish investment advisers to the number of bearish investment advisers. Although this information is relatively straightforward, this percentage can be interpreted to be contrarian in nature since a vast number of advisers are wrong a lot of the time. Therefore, more bulls than bears may indicate that the market is topping out, getting ready for a fall. The American Association of Individual Investors (www.aaii.com), Investors Intelligence (www.investorsintelligence.com), and Market Vane (www.marketvane.net) all provide weekly updates of investor sentiment in the stock market. Some are available for free, while others require a subscription.

Another way to gauge investment sentiment is to analyze options trading volume. Since buying puts is a bearish move and purchasing calls is a bullish move, the ratio between the two sometimes reveals how many investors are bullish and how many are bearish. However, since the majority of investors are wrong, investors often insist that this so-called put-to-call ratio actually indicates yet another contrarian point of view. Put-to-call ratios for the U.S. options market are available on the web sites of the International Securities Exchange (www.iseoptions.com), the Chicago Board Options Exchange (www.cboe.com), and the Options Clearing Corporation (www.optionsclearing.com).

Put-to-call ratios and investor sentiment surveys are not the only psychological indicators. Others are mentioned later in the book when we discuss volatility trading. However, a complete list of psychological indicators can be found at SentimenTrader (www.sentimentrader.com), which is another subscription-based site that provides a variety of tools for gauging the prevailing mood in the U.S. stock market.

riding the roller coaster

The global economy is a living, breathing entity. To understand it, you have to get to know it personally, and that takes time. Experience is earned, literally. If your experience culminates in effectual market knowledge, it's because you've found a way to tie all the loose ends together. Try to think of the market as a dynamic environment where sentiment and economic forces synergistically interact.

As online options traders armed to the nines with technology's latest and greatest, we've chosen to shed the protection of the more conventional full-service brokerages in order to pull ourselves up to the top—by our virtual bootstraps. But even with all that technology has to offer, the financial future of the market is still greatly affected by the whim of human emotion; this makes the business of forecasting market movement a subjective discipline. Human emotional reaction to market movement is a main motivating factor behind volatility. High volatility in a market triggers mass confusion and anxiety—emotions that tend to move a market even more erratically.

As market instability and resource scarcity continue to intensify worldwide, there is an even greater need for managed-risk options strategies. In recent times, this kind of activity has bordered on frenzy as commodity prices surge, a handful of technology stocks boom, and many major financial institutions crumble. These markets are the kind that options traders like me love to trade.

Offering unparalleled flexibility, options offer rights and confer obligations. They can be used alone or combined with one another to take advantage of specific market conditions. They can be used to hedge positions, offset the net cost of a trade, and limit the overall risk of the combined position. Options strategies take advantage of as well as curtail the losses associated with high volatility, and provide traders with straightforward mathematical equations to calculate a trade's maximum risk and reward. From there, it's easy to determine a trade's risk-to-reward ratio. You can also assess a trade's profit range by computing the trade's breakevens. Once this information has been determined, an informed decision can be made as to a trade's probability of profitability. The potential reward is either worth the risk or it's not.

In order to master complex options strategies, it is essential to have a thorough understanding of basic long and short stock and options strategies. There are six basic strategies: long stock, short stock, long call, short call, long put, and short put. These six strategies generate more than 20 advanced techniques that take advantage of a wide variety of market scenarios. We explore how to use these options strategies to profit from the stock market's wild swings in Chapters 4 through 9. First, however, our attention turns to some more of the specific resources available to the online options trader today. In Chapter 3, we break down the best and worst financial web sites.

conclusion

As a trader, you are also an analyst who needs access to financial market information to be able to form a picture of the current status and future prospects of individual stocks, industry groups, or the market as a whole. To determine the true growth prospects for any company, you'll need to gather a number of fundamental criteria and review the firm's competitors, as well as how the company's products are received by consumers. Unless you have a strong business background or are very familiar with a particular industry, this method of trading analysis will take time and energy to master.

As a technical analyst, you need to understand how to predict a price's future behavior by interpreting price and volume patterns. Sophisticated charting technology is widely available and will help. There are literally hundreds of sites that will instantly create a daily chart with historical prices. The best way to learn how to use charts is to visit these sites and experiment with the technical indicators. By looking at the graphs with the indicators overlaid, you can start to get a sense for what types of indicators are useful.

The debate on fundamental versus technical trading is an old one. Some traders swear by one and hold great disdain for the other. Other traders successfully integrate both methods. For example, fundamental analysis can be used to forecast market direction while technical analysis can trigger appropriate entrances and exits. Determining what works best for you will probably entail a period of experimentation. Ultimately, it depends on what kind of trading you wish to pursue. Perhaps you just want to buy stock and hold it until it makes a profit. Then you are looking for methods that help you determine when a stock is undervalued and on the move up.

However, finding a potentially profitable trading opportunity is only the beginning. Plenty of research needs to be done to verify the stock's capacity for price movement. Once you have established the trend within the market, you may want to analyze the industry group it belongs to as well as any psychological market indications of the bearish or bullish nature of the marketplace. If a company continues to look promising, there are software programs that can help you to find the most profitable strategy to employ. However, it is important to remember that the stock market is an uncontrollable force. Your ability to respond to the market's seemingly random impulsiveness will determine how much money you make or lose.

Whichever market analysis techniques you choose, make sure to test them over a sufficient period of time. You can do this by using current prices and watching market movement or by back-testing using trading software. Inevitably, as the markets change, suitable methods of analysis also will change. The key is to remain open-minded and flexible so that you can take advantage of whatever works. Although each of these trading methods deserves a chapter of its own, my purpose has been to briefly introduce them and inspire you to investigate them further by visiting sites that offer the best selection of trading tools. Speaking of sites, let's take a look at some of the best ones next.

chapter 3

online trading resources

surfing through the new datasphere

Efficiency is the key to successful online trading. One of the significant challenges is to cut through all of the information clutter and get to the stuff that is really valuable. It's not as easy as it sounds. In the past, most of the so-called research was available mostly through the major brokerage firms. The control of the information gave the brokers a decided advantage and justified paying them higher commissions in exchange for the competitive edge known as information. Today, however, the information is everywhere. It is literally overflowing.

To trade effectively, online options traders need to find a routine for sifting through the information that works for them. It could be on a weekly or daily basis. For example, a typical morning might involve reviewing the day's movers and shakers, comparing them to the overall economic numbers of the day, and then listening to what preferred analysts say about the news. Once a few promising stocks have been identified, the next step might be to spend time researching their price and volume potentials. If everything looks good, it's time to review a handful of option strategies in search of a strategically sound profit opportunity.

During the past decade, I have developed my own daily online rituals for collecting and analyzing investment information. However, my approach is unique to my needs. For example, trading guru Tom Gentile relies on an assortment of technical indicators to identify opportunities across a variety of markets (futures, stocks, and options). Meanwhile, I'm more focused on the fundamentals of specific companies and longer-term trading opportunities. Bottom line: no two traders share the exact same routine.

The research for this book involved exploring more than 200 investment sites and online brokerages. To simplify the investigative process for you, this chapter divides the sites into 14 separate categories: supersites, news, research, education, technical analysis, options, webzines, high technology, exchanges, advisory sites, specialty sites, weblogs, social networking, and fun and games. The following informal guide to the kinds of investment sites that are out there is designed to give you the a clear picture of the virtual landscape, which should help you develop your own concise routine for finding worthwhile information on the World Wide Web. A comprehensive list of sites can be found in Appendix D, while Chapter 12 discusses online brokerages in more detail.

before you surf   We will explore the specific sites that we, our instructors, and our students find most useful, but first let's consider ways of making the process of searching for information safer and more efficient. Keep in mind, it isn't unusual to multitask while researching and trading. For example, you might stop to look at a chart or graph while composing e-mail, reading a document, talking on the phone, or placing a trade. After all, this is the new millennium and the world is living online now. But if you are new to computers, this kind of multitasking can be hard going at first. Consequently, the following 11 rules might help put you in the right frame of mind.

1. If you plan on doing a lot of research and trading online, invest in a quick connection or satellite service, and a fast computer. Nothing is more frustrating than waiting for the next page to come into view.
2. Don't subscribe to more than a few e-mail services at a time. You'll be overwhelmed with e-mail alerts and junk mail.

Control your junk mail with spam killers to limit the number of useless e-mails.

3. Immediately bookmark the sites that strike you as useful so that you don't lose them.

4. Always have a plan B. Make sure you have a hard-copy master list of all portfolios (real or paper) and contact information for your broker. If your power goes out, you can always call an online broker, but you still need to know what's in which account. Keep that information easily available on your trading desk.

5. Paper (or pretend) trade any recommendations from an advisory source before putting your money on the line. That way you can verify the value of the information prior to risking any hard-earned cash. If the advisory service looks promising, check whether your broker offers *auto-trading*, which trades the recommendations for you. Auto-trading can save you a lot of time.

6. Don't waste time and money printing out too many research materials. Information gets old so fast that hard copies are usually a waste of paper (and trees).

7. Keep your fingers on the pulse of the mass psychology of the markets by consistently checking out a variety of resource sites and analyst commentaries.

8. Don't be afraid to subscribe to new services every once in a while to get differing perspectives. Take advantage of free trials, but make sure to cancel them before your credit card gets billed.

9. Get to know the E. F. Huttons of the Internet. If Warren Buffett or Ben Bernanke is talking, you can bet that a lot of people are listening and reacting.

10. Get in the habit of surfing a few select message boards or chat rooms to see what individual traders and analysts have to say concerning stocks you are interested in trading. However, recognize that a lot of message board chatter is useless and sometimes even harmful. There are plenty of people out there pursuing pump-and-dump scams, where they try to fill the stock with hot air based on rumors and then sell their position when the price has made a move higher.

11. Take all investment advice with a grain of salt. Always do your homework before allowing something that sounds too good

to be true to rob you blind. You might make some friends on-line, but there are very many dubious people as well. A recent study showed that 40 percent of all computers hooked to the World Wide Web are using or infected by bots—software designed to send e-mail, marketing messages, spyware, or malware. Protect yourself and your computer with the latest anti-virus technology.

kinds of sites

The number of financial-related sites on the Internet seems infinite. Sites come and go, redesigning their formats and upgrading their services as they strive to attract users in this highly competitive field. Some web sites offer stock and option quotes, news and commentary, fundamental and technical data, chat rooms and message boards, live interactive sessions, advisory e-mail services, and an endless assortment of investment ideas. These so-called *supersites* offer a one-stop place to get a variety of investment-related information. However, others are more specialized and focus on a specific area of finance like stocks, bonds, or options.

Although many sites are free, others charge a fee for additional services like research, data, portfolio tracking, e-mailed news, analysis, and advisory alerts. Trial subscriptions can help you to decide whether fee-based services will actually enhance your profit-making ability. So don't be surprised if you are constantly being asked to register or subscribe, even when sites are free. There are also the obligatory disclaimers that have to be formally acknowledged to complete registration. I have yet to read the legalese in any of these documents, but they basically want to make sure that subscribers absolve the sites of any wrongdoing. This process can become annoying, especially when the subscription form is less than user-friendly. As you skip from site to site, you will often be asked to choose a user name and password. By the time you die, you could have 10,000 passwords. Instead, it is a good idea to establish a consistent online identity so that no matter which site you visit, you can remember how to log on.

Since there is an abundance of investment-oriented sites, after a while, they may all start to look alike. One way to stay organized is to take notes as you go and bookmark sites that you find useful so that you can find them again. It also helps to visit sites that specialize in providing links to other financial web sites. This kind of convenient one-stop shopping can help you easily peruse a variety of sites. In that respect, two sites worth considering are Cyberinvest.com (www.cyberinvest.com) and InvestorLinks.com (www.investorlinks.com).

---

supersites
these comprehensive megasites have just about everything—from real-time quotes and interactive charts to news, commentary, and stock research capabilities. Most sites have a free area as well as subscription-based services. Subscriptions often include real-time or delayed quotes, recommendations, and daily e-mail newsletters containing quotes and news items on stocks in your portfolio.

news
most news services are spin-offs from the major news services, including television and print news media. ABC, NBC, CBS, Fox, CNN, Forbes, and Bloomberg all have web sites offering comprehensive investment coverage. Online news is often available with video and audio accompaniment, but you have to download the right software. The beauty of online news services is that they continuously update their information, unlike their print media cousins. Timely news is of utmost importance to the online trader, especially to option traders looking for volatile markets.

---

supersites   Supersites are comprehensive megasites that provide just about everything a trader or investor needs to monitor the markets (i.e., quotes, charts, news, commentary, and stock research). Yahoo! Finance (finance.yahoo.com) is an example of an investment supersite. It provides an abundance of stock market information including stock quotes, charts, news, options information, and fundamental data in one place. Other supersites include Google Finance (finance.google.com/finance), MarketWatch (www.marketwatch.com), and MSN Money (moneycentral.msn.com).

news   New information is the primary driver of prices in the stock market, and there are several sources online that provide great coverage of the happenings in the financial world. Most, but not all, require subscriptions. The *Wall Street Journal* (online.wsj.com), the *New York Times* (www.nytimes.com), *Investor's Business Daily* (www.investors.com), and the *Financial Times* (www.ft.com) are among the pillars of financial reporting.

Intraday news can be found in a number of other places at no cost. Examples include *Bloomberg* (www.bloomberg.com), the Associated Press (www.ap.org), Reuters (www.reuters.com), CNN Business (money.cnn.com/?cnn=yes), and Fox Business News (www.foxbusiness.com). These news sources have staffs of reporters who cover the stock market beat and provide intraday market updates online.

research Sites that specialize in market research provide a variety of analysis tools. The first two chapters of this book explored how research involves looking over a company's finances and management abilities and making sure operations are creating high cash flow, healthy earnings, and a strong balance sheet. In addition, I prefer companies with low overall debt, which translates into more operating cash for reinvestment in the business. Annual reports, company profiles, earnings estimates, and insider reports are available. To help you figure out which stocks are really moving, many sites include a section on price percentage winners and losers. Some of our favorite research sites include Hoover's (www.hoovers.com), VectorVest (www.vectorvest.com), and StockSmart Pro (www.stocksmartpro.com).

Hoover's also features an excellent free stock screening using up to 20 performance criteria. This screening service requires the input of specific detailed parameters. You can select everything from the type of industry you prefer to company size, rates of return, and volatility. Although there are many web sites that you can consult for fundamental data, Hoover's is definitely one of the best. It offers a cache of fundamental analysis tools, SEC filings, and company reports. You can also sign up for e-mails that make timely investment recommendations. MSN Money, the supersite, also offers a sophisticated stock screening research tool. It can be found at http://moneycentral.msn.com/investor/controls/finderpro.asp.

I also like VectorVest and StockSmartPro. Although the majority of their services are subscription-based, they do provide some free fundamental stock analysis. VectorVest has developed a unique system for evaluating a stock's actual value by analyzing a variety of fundamental indicators including earnings, earnings growth rate, dividend payments, dividend growth rate, financial performance, current interest, and inflation. It also provides additional indicators including relative value, relative timing, and VST-Vector. Its subscription services are comprehensive, including extensive historical data, recommendations, and the inherent values of call and put options.

education   Educational sites help traders get up to speed by providing innovative investment education through virtual stock exchanges, one-on-one online educational workshops, and investment games. I am completely biased here because my primary web site, www.optionetics.com, is one of the best sources for the novice looking for free information to learn how to trade options. Other educational sites worth looking at are Motley Fool (www.fool.com), Profit Strategies (www.profitstrategies.com) and the American Association of Individual Investors (www.aaii.com).

technical analysis   Sites that focus on technical analysis tools provide a variety of charts and graphs for the avid technical trader. This is where you can go to create charts with moving averages, stochastics, and momentum indicators. Some also offer chat rooms if you feel like discussing the ramifications of your research with the masses. Check out BigCharts (www.bigcharts. com), StockCharts (http://stockcharts.com), Investors Intelligence (www.investorsintelligence.com), and Daily Graphs Online (www.dailygraphs.com).

options   Some sites are completely dedicated to helping option traders get the customized information they need. Although a number of option services are advisory in nature, others offer real-time and delayed quotes, options calculators, historical option premiums and volumes, intraday and weekly charts, volatility and other Greek variables, and technical charts. The best option sites that I use include Optionetics (www.optionetics.com) and iVolatility.com (www.ivolatility.com).

webzines   Webzines are a relatively new concept that started taking off when I was writing the first edition of *Trade Options Online*. Basically, newspapers and magazines jumped onto the cyberbandwagon by developing online subscription services that mirror their newsstand issues. Some of the best webzines are *Kiplinger's* (www.kiplinger.com), *Forbes* (www.forbes.com), and *BusinessWeek* (www.businessweek.com).

exchanges These days every exchange has a web site. A tremendous amount of information about new and previously listed company data, annual reports, research, publications, and news and quotes is readily available along with daily market analysis. Check out the New York Stock Exchange (www.nyse.com), the Chicago Board Options Exchange (www.cboe.com), the NASDAQ (www.nasdaq.com), the American Stock Exchange (www.amex.com), the International Securities Exchange (www.iseoptions.com), and the Philadelphia Stock Exchange (www.phlx.com).

advisory sites Investment analysts are continually upgrading and downgrading stocks to strong buys, holds, or sells. Analysts can now download their recommendations through advisory sites. As this information leaks out into the public domain, it becomes the noise on the Street and it makes dollars and sense to pay attention to who is upgrading what and why. This is increasingly true as more and more financial sites use e-mail services to broadcast their picks and pans. Check out Avid Trader (avidtrader.com) and TheStreet.com (www.smartportfolio.com).

specialty sites A large number of sites target a particular audience or focus on a specific kind of market. Sites that target specific audiences include the GreenMoney Journal (www.greenmoney.com), which specializes in social and environmentally responsible companies; Morningstar (www.morningstar.com), which focuses on ETFs and mutual funds; and SmallCapInvestor.com (www.smallcapinvestor.com), a site dedicated to small cap stocks.

weblogs One of the newest categories for web sites is the so-called weblog, or blog. Some are similar to chat rooms, as many participants can post comments about specific subject matter. Other blogs, however, include only one author and generally focus on a specific subject matter. All blogs are rolling discussions and the frequency of the updates depends on the popularity of the blog and the number of participants involved. Some of the options-related blogs can be found at www.kirkreport.com, www.tradeking.com, and www.adamsoptions.blogspot.com.

social networking Have you ever seen the T-shirt that says, "You looked better on MySpace"? Social networking sites are among the fastest growing web sites out there today. IClub Central

(www.iclub.com) is an example of a site that brings investors together to form trading clubs.

fun and games   Who says investing has to be all work and no play?
The originators of these sites offer trading simulations, participa-
tory games, and educational guides that enable kids and adults alike
to venture forth into the investment arena. These sites are a wel-
come relief after too many hours of number crunching and corporate research. Get out of the rat race and into Stock Trak (www.
stocktrak.com) or WallStreetSports (www.wallstreetsports.com).

search engines   If you can't find what you're looking for, you've probably used a search engine to probe the Internet for appropriate sites.
Each search engine has its own site, and most offer a business and
finance section. Check out Lycos (www.lycos.com/business) or Yahoo! Finance (quote.yahoo.com), or just Google it!

e-mail newsletters

If you don't have time to go looking for the latest news updates and
analysts' reports, you might want to check out e-mail newsletters. Yet
another component of a diverse online trading experience, e-mail
newsletters are available from a variety of web sites, professional
analysts, and financial advisers. These convenient alerts are filled
with intraday summaries, customized portfolio news clippings, and
controversial counsel from numerous advisers who are more than
happy to deliver their advice right to your e-mail address.

Some newsletters are free and filled with distracting advertisements. Others require a subscription fee. Optionetics offers a variety
of timely newsletters with a variety of focuses. You can also set up a
portfolio and receive daily updates and news alerts concerning the
stocks you are watching. Some services have room for multiple portfolios while others may limit subscribers to a few at a time. To keep
track of things, it may be helpful to create two distinct portfolios:
stocks you are watching and stocks you are trading.

e-mail newsletters
publication seeking to provide financial advice including trade
recommendation and market commentary to their subscribers.

When it comes to advice, you should know that impartiality is *not* guaranteed. Some e-mail newsletters are advisory services accept compensation or have a financial interest in the companies they mention. It's a good idea to read the fine print (which can be tedious) or search the chat rooms for any consternation concerning newsletters with conflict of interest disorders.

---

zacks investment research
zacks investment research is a very popular financial site that offers a variety of free and subscription services. It provides access to research produced by thousands of analysts and hundreds of brokerage firms as well as a vast array of brokerage and equity research, screening, and advisory tools (www.zacks.com).

---

online routines

In order to help you get the most out of your online experience, the following section details possible online rituals. Your online workout will probably vary from day to day depending on your time availability and market dynamics.

As a trader, it's a good idea to start by looking at the day's news headlines to see if there is anything happening that could affect a possible or current investment. Although news of all kinds can affect the behavior of the stock market, bad news (as a rule) travels faster than good news. Therefore, you're looking for bad news opportunities and good news trends. If nothing jumps out at you, it's time to search for stocks that are up or down 30 percent (minimum) since yesterday's close. This task can be accomplished—as can most online research—at a number of different web sites.

You can start by going to MarketWatch (www.marketwatch. com) and scrolling down to "Top Gainers" and "Top Losers" in the web site's stock "Tools and Research" area. You can choose from lists directly from the New York Stock Exchange (NYSE), American Stock Exchange (AMEX), and NASDAQ. You might also look at the "Most Actives" and the day's analyst upgrades and downgrades to see what is moving and why.

volume
the number of shares bought and sold for a specific stock or option.

This initial process gives you the lay of the land. To find a serious contender, make sure to look for stocks (or options) with plenty of liquidity. A large number of buyers and sellers creates a high volume of trading activity that translates into high liquidity. Liquidity is imperative because it gives traders the opportunity to move in and out of a market with ease. Generally, I look for stocks that have a trading volume of at least 300,000 shares a day and preferably a million. Almost any site with fundamental data or delayed price quotes will show a stock's volume. I like BigCharts (www.bigcharts.com) because while I'm there I can also create a 12-month price and volume chart.

liquidity
the ease with which an asset can be converted to cash in the marketplace. A large number of buyers and sellers and a high volume of trading activity provide high liquidity.

If a stock passes the liquidity test, then I have to find out if the stock has options available. Checking for options involves searching for an option chain. You can accomplish this by surfing over to Optionetics (www.optionetics.com), entering a stock symbol into the quote box, and selecting "Option Chain." If a page of option quotes comes up, then you're in business. You can also get very accurate quotes at the Chicago Board Options Exchange (www.cboe.com).

Once you find a few stocks with options that fit these criteria, it's time to do some in-depth research. Next, create a chart and add a few indicators discussed earlier such as volume, stochastics, and MACD graphs. The interactive charts at Optionetics are free and provide a wide array of different indicators for analyzing a stock. To learn more about specific technical analysis tools, you may want to read some educational articles on the Optionetics site. Just click on Daily Articles in the green left-hand box and then type "Tool-box" in the Search box to find a host of archived articles that will help you to better understand how some of these indicators work.

---

macd
moving average convergence/divergence (MACD) refers to the crossing of two moving averages or the failure of two moving averages to confirm a trend.

Yahoo! Finance (finance.yahoo.com) is another site that offers a multitude of research tools. Enter a stock symbol and then click "Enter" to monitor everything from earnings to broker recommendations. If you want to do a little creative research, click on "SEC Filings" to read the last quarterly report filed with the Securities and Exchange Commission, or go to "Profile" to find the link to the company's web site. You can also check the stock's insider trading (select "Insider Transactions") or check the message board to see what other investors have to say.

TheStreet.com (www.thestreet.com) is another popular site that provides financial reports and informative commentaries throughout the day as the market moves. Published exclusively on-line, TheStreet.com has a reputation for objectivity and timeliness.

If that's not enough, you can also sign up for a free membership to Zacks Investment Research services (www.zacks.com). Zacks is an important site because it has earned the ear of the Street and therefore is quite an influence on the mass psychology of the marketplace. This site summarizes the current stock recommendations of thousands of analysts employed by hundreds of U.S. brokerage firms. These recommendations are translated into a number of subscription and free services geared for the avid investor. Check out the "Options Trader," which combines earnings information with options picks.

Once the research is accomplished and some promising stocks are identified, then the focus turns to the best options strategies, which are discussed in the following six chapters. I wrote this section with the intention of mentioning an array of sites that can be used to track down profitable stocks. Your own process may be much simpler. It just depends on the kind of analysis you like to do before making a trade. Developing your online trading procedure is an adventure—do it with gusto!

online quotes

Almost every investing site I've researched provides traders with the opportunity to get a snapshot quote on a specific stock, index, or ETF. Some of these quotes are real-time, but many more are delayed by at least 15 minutes. If you want to receive streaming real-time data on a portfolio of stocks, you must get it through a broker or be willing to pay for it. There are several companies that offer live stock and options market data for a fee. Examples include eSignal (www.esignal.com), PC Quote (www.pcquote.com), and Realtime Stockquote (www.realtimestockquote.com).

---

nasdaq level II
a NASDAQ Level II color-coded screen provides real-time information concerning who is buying and selling a specific stock and the volume of shares they are trading. Color-coding assists traders to determine which way the market should go. Yellow indicates the best quote or first tier of buyers, followed by green, then dark blue, and finally light blue.

---

trading software

Today's newest trading software enables traders to sift through thousands of positions to find optimal trading opportunities in a blink of an eye. This can include analyzing live data, getting alerts, and back-testing strategies using historical data. Perhaps the only drawback comes from the fact that having access to a myriad of technical indicators doesn't necessarily mean you know how to use them. Grasping the concepts underlying technical analysis methodologies can be extremely difficult. To gain an idea of just how big this area of expertise is, see the list of technical analysis systems in Appendix B.

To find out which program best fits your needs, you can use our own selection process. An example is included in Table 3.1. This system is the product of many years of investigation and experience. Before looking at your first program, you should create a comprehensive spreadsheet of preferred features—no matter how remote they may seem. Then, weigh how important each of your listed items is on a scale of 1 to 10, using 10 as the highest or most important rating. Next, decide on a scoring guide for each factor you review. I generally use a scale of 1 to 4, with 4 as the highest score. Finally, make sure

table 3.1 software scoring example

Factors	Weight 1–10	Scoring Guide	Score 1–4	Net Score (Weight × Score)
1. Graphing	8	1 Type 2 Types 3 Types 4 Types	3	24
2. Number of data vendors supported	5	1 Vendor 2 Vendors 3 Vendors 4 Vendors	4	20
3. Ability to test my own strategies	2	No Yes	4	8
4. Price	10	< $500 < $750 < $1,000 > $1,000	2	20
Total Score	25		13	72

you have everything on the list that interests you so that you can live with the selection even if it's not the program you originally wanted. You are now ready to review various software programs.

Some software companies will let you download the software directly from the Internet to review a beta version for free for a few weeks. Others will send you the program with a 30-day money-back guarantee. You'll have to pay for it up front, but if you don't like it you can send it back and ask for a refund. Others will make you pay for it up front with no refunds. Always read the fine print before ordering a product.

beta version software
software that is distributed to select users for testing before it is officially released to the public. Many software manufacturers will allow you to download beta version software directly over the Internet to try out a program before buying it.

How you gather your information is up to you. Once you have scored all of the factors, multiply the score by the weight and record that as the net score. Finally, add up the net scores to come up with the total score for each software program. Table 3.1 provides a demonstration on my selection process. Once you have the facts, you can decide whether to purchase the one with the highest score or the one that you simply enjoyed using the most.

In my opinion, ProfitSource, by Hubb Co. in Australia, (www.profitsource.com) is the best all-around software program for stock and options traders. It provides advanced charting features, options analysis, and the ability to use end-of-day or intraday data for global stocks, ETFs, indexes, and futures. I have worked closely with the software developers to make ProfitSource the most valuable trading software available to options traders today. I use it extensively!

ProfitSource also provides scanning tools that allow the trader to identify stocks with certain technical characteristics. As an example, the individual may want to further evaluate all S&P 500 stocks that have an increasing 50-day moving average to determine if a crossover with the 200-day moving average is imminent. Going one step further, the software can also be easily set up to back-test trading systems to determine how effective a moving average crossover approach would be on these stocks.

ValueGain is another excellent stand-alone software program. It makes use of a data feed to provide the most current financial metrics available. In addition to basic scans, the software provides users with precomputed scans based upon the fundamental approach used by some of the leading names in analysis. These scans are categorized by three investment styles: growth, value, and income. Additionally, ValueGain provides users with easy access to the second important comparison tool—the company's performance over time. This is accomplished by charting financial data for the firm so an analyst can readily see whether the reported value is improving or deteriorating.

ValueGain also includes calculators that provide the user with a theoretical value for a firm using current financial data and the selected valuation model (i.e., a Buffett Value Model). Results are provided in data and graphic formats, for ease of review. Similar to option pricing models, these calculators provide analysts with information about companies that may be overvalued or undervalued in the market.

profitsource
profitSource helps you identify profitable trading opportunities through precomputed scans, systems testing, personal scans, a complete suite of indicators, and more! Alerts, integration with Optionetics Platinum Software, and a complete portfolio help you to quickly and efficiently manage your trades as well! To order ProfitSource, contact Optionetics call (888) 366-8264.

valuegain
valueGain is revolutionary software that helps you make light work of analyzing the balance sheets and financial statements of companies by compiling all of the information that you could possibly need into one easy-to-use interface! To order ValueGain, go to www.valuegain.com.

conclusion

Finding profitable stocks is a matter of personal taste, combined with professional insights, hobbies, and interests. For some traders, finding the right stocks may be as easy as asking their 10-year-old child what the hottest games are on the market. For others, it's a matter of looking at television to decide who has the most compelling product and advertisements. Others simply look at which stocks are moving and have the ear on Wall Street.

This last category is where the online traders can really save some time. With the click of a few keys, you can instantly find out which stocks have had a sudden increase in price, a sharp rise in volume, or even major growth in insider buying activity. Most of the financial sites noted in this book can easily supply you with a quick list of the top 10 and bottom 10 stocks in any category. Some of the more specialized stock screening programs will give you a list of companies that meet your personal movement criteria.

The Internet's community nature also gives you the unprecedented opportunity to chat with other traders from around the world to hear what they think about specific stocks or stocks in a particular sector. There is a chat room for virtually every major stock, index, and market sector imaginable. Weblogs and social networking sites also let investors share information and strive for success together. It is no longer a "me against the world" mentality. The Internet has brought together many investors who share the same goals. Always keep in mind, however, that some people who post opinions in chat rooms have their own agenda in building up or tearing apart a stock, so be discriminating.

chat rooms
interactive online message boards where individual investors can post their own opinions on a multitude of subjects from online brokerages to specific stocks.

Once you figure out how you are going to pick your stocks, you need a way to stay on top of their activity. There are literally hundreds of sites that can give you the capability to track stocks through the use of portfolios. However, only a handful of online portfolios give you the ability to track option prices and positions. Good trading software and a reliable broker are really all you need to track your positions.

In sum, online trading is a bastion for independent thinkers. You have a wealth of resources at your fingertips that will engage your imagination and challenge your mental capacity. I look for sites that offer reliability and efficiency with as few screens as possible between me and my final destination. Most traders will do anything to speed things up. Luckily, technology has all kinds of gadgets and programs that can help you to do so. At the same time, however, good investment decisions often take some time. If you're new to the world of online trading, take some time to practice and place hypothetical trades using practice money. This process is often referred to as *paper trading*.

chapter 4

a primer for trading stocks and options

stocks around the clock

Today's equity market is a global affair. Each business day, trading starts in the Asia/Pacific region, then opens in Europe, and then North America. News, economic statistics, and happenings in one market quickly ripple through other markets across the globe. Often the events in the United States will set the tone for trading in other markets. However, that is not always the case. For example, in February 2007, the global equity markets experienced a sudden increase in volatility after stocks in Shanghai, China, suffered a short-term meltdown.

Yet, while the global financial market has become more complex, the fundamentals of investing in stocks and options have not changed much. Instead, the new era has created a variety of opportunities for individual investors to play with the biggest global banks and brokerage firms. For example, some U.S.-based online brokers offer the ability to trade in a variety of international markets. Meanwhile, with the help of new technology, foreign exchange or *forex*

(FX) trading has become easier than ever. Some traders like the FX market because it is open 24 hours a day, five days a week. Many futures markets also have overnight trading sessions.

forex
the simultaneous exchange of one country's currency for that of another. In its simplest form, an investor purchases or sells one currency, expecting to make a profit when the value of the currencies changes in favor of the investor. This dynamic global market, an acronym for the foreign exchange market, trades more than $1.9 trillion a day. A variety of market participants interact through the forex market including businesses, hedge funds, governments, banks, consumers, and, of course, individual investors and traders.

futures markets
the *futures market* refers to a continuous auction market where participants buy and sell commodities contracts for delivery on a specified future date. Trading is carried on through open outcry and hand signals in a trading pit or ring, as well as via electronic platforms.

One of the keys to success in any market, however, is an understanding of the fundamentals of that market. For example, trading foreign exchange involves a good understanding of how interest rates affect currency valuations. Conversely, successfully trading stock options hinges on one's knowledge of what drives stock prices and how the changes in those stock prices affect options prices.

Once an understanding of the fundamentals is in place, the investor is in a better position to identify opportunities to make profits via the options strategies (discussed in more detail in chapters 5 through 9). For now, however, let's dig into the fundamentals of stock, stock options, and index options.

Note: This chapter really covers the very basics, and if you've read our other books you probably have a good understanding of the information in the next few sections. So you may want to just skim over them and focus more time on the strategies chapters.

stock basics

In its most basic form, a stock market is an arena where investors gather to buy and sell stocks. A stock, also called a share, represents a unit of ownership in a company. Each share will reflect the total value of the company divided by the number of shares outstanding. A wide array of factors, like the company's earnings, debt, and products, will determine the value of the company. Analysts and investors are continually attempting to assess a company's future outlook and will buy and sell shares accordingly.

Not all companies have stocks outstanding, however. Some are privately held. Others become publicly traded through an initial public offering (IPO). The motivating force behind the company's initial sales of shares is the need to raise capital to grow the business.

---

initial public offering (IPO)
the first sale of common stock by a corporation to the public. Securities offered in an IPO are often, but not always, those of young, small companies seeking outside equity capital and a public market for their stock. Investors purchasing stock in IPOs generally must be prepared to accept very large risks for the possibility of large gains. IPOs by investment companies (closed-end funds) usually contain underwriting fees, which represent a load to buyers.

After the IPO, the shares begin trading on one or more of the stock exchanges and, with the help of a brokerage firm, the public can buy and sell shares during the trading day. Supply and demand economics will drive the short-term fluctuations in share prices. For instance, if there are substantially more buyers than sellers, prices will rise. If there are more sellers than buyers, prices will fall.

There are three ways to describe these movements or trends in share prices: bullish, bearish, and neutral. A market is bullish if prices are rising. To make money in a bull market, it pays to buy stocks with the goal of selling them after the price goes even higher. In a bear market, prices are falling and it can therefore be profitable to sell stock before prices drop too far. A neutral market continuously fluctuates between support and resistance zones (low and high points, respectively, beyond which the price doesn't tend to go). It basically moves sideways or in a range. Several combination option strategies can be employed to take advantage of a sideways-moving market. We explore strategies for a neutral market in Chapter 9.

How do you determine if a stock or market is going to move higher, lower, or sideways? There are scores of analysts, collectively known as "the Street," who study certain industries and companies in order to forecast movement. They typically issue earnings estimates and reports that assess a company's value.

Individual companies issue earnings reports quarterly. Prior to the release of a profit report, the Street expectation often drives stock prices. If investors feel a report will beat Street expectations, there will be more buyers compared to sellers and the price of the shares will be bid up. If the majority of the investors feel that the company's earnings will disappoint, then the price will decline. Then, when the actual numbers are released, the buying and selling can motivate big moves in the share prices. For that reason, there is often a noticeable increase in the volatility of a stock just before and after a quarterly earnings report.

---

volatility
a measure of the magnitude of price fluctuations of an investment, commodity, or market. Fast markets that see large price changes in short periods of time have high volatility. Slow or quiet markets that see little price movement from one day to the next have low volatility.

The size of a company is another determinant of price and risk. There are three unofficial size classifications: blue-chip, mid-cap, and small-cap. *Blue-chip* is a term derived from poker where blue chips hold the most value. Hence, blue-chip stocks symbolize stocks with the highest capitalization in the marketplace. Typically they enjoy solid value and good security, with a record of continuous dividend payments and other desirable investment attributes. Mid-cap stocks usually have a bigger growth potential than blue-chip stocks but they are not as heavily capitalized. Small-cap stocks tend to have more volatility and carry more risk. Often, small-cap stocks are emerging companies without a proven track record. However, these stocks, although quite risky, have above-average growth potential and big gains are possible. Some traders like to trade riskier stocks that have the potential for big price moves, while others prefer the longer-term stability of blue-chip stocks. In general, what stocks you choose to trade depends on your time availability, stress threshold, and account size. You need to strike a comfortable balance between risk and reward.

market capitalization
the total dollar value of all outstanding shares, computed as shares outstanding multiplied by the current market price. It is a measure of corporate size.

Regardless of whether the company is big or small, there are two kinds of stocks: common and preferred. A company initially sells shares of common stock through an IPO to help raise capital for expansion. If investors perceive that the company will do well in the future, the stock can immediately rise after the IPO due to strong demand, as many investors try to get in early. However, the long-term success of a company is often difficult to predict, and not all IPOs are a success. In fact, when reality doesn't live up to the hype, many stocks see substantial losses in the months after their IPO.

In the long run, investors make money by purchasing stock at a lower price and selling it at a higher price. You have probably heard the adage, "Buy low and sell high." The profit from buying and selling stocks is called a *capital gain*. However, if the company falters, the price of the stock may plummet and shareholders may end up holding stock that is practically worthless. In 2007 and 2008, many mortgage companies went bankrupt due to the problems in the housing market and the subsequent problems in the financial industry. Even one of the nation's biggest brokers, Bear Stearns, came to the brink of collapse in early 2008. The firm was eventually bought out by JPMorgan, but the final sales price was a fraction of what a share of Bear Stearns had fetched a year earlier. The collapse of Bear Stearns was then followed by a similar unraveling of Lehman Brothers (LEH), which also faltered amid hefty losses in mortgage-backed securities and a loss of confidence among its business partners. Not long thereafter, the government was forced to step in and rescue mortgage finance giants Fannie Mae (FNM) and Freddie Mac (FRE).

In September 2008, the FDIC moved in to seize control of Washington Mutual, which represented the largest bank failure in American history.

This chain of events was part of a massive meltdown in the financial industry on a global scale. Banks faltered, brokerage firms went under, and governments in the United States and Europe were forced to step in and save a number of major financial institutions. On Monday, September 29, fear reached an extreme after a government bailout intended to help solve the financial crisis was rejected by Congress. The Dow Jones Industrial Average fell 777 points for its largest one-day plunge ever.

Over time, investors expect to see the stock price rise and also be rewarded with dividends. Dividends represent a portion of the company's profits that are passed on to shareholders. Large, fully established companies can afford to pay dividends to their shareholders; hence, holders of common stock may or may not earn quarterly dividend payments depending on the history and financial strength of the company.

Holders of preferred stock receive guaranteed dividends prior to common stockholders, but the amount never changes even if the company triples its earnings. Also, the price of preferred stock increases at a slower rate than that of common stock. However, if the company loses money, holders of preferred stock have a better chance of receiving some of their investment back. All in all, common stocks are riskier than preferred stocks, but offer greater rewards if the company does well. When dealing in the options market and stock options, we are dealing with common stocks. Preferred stock rarely comes into play.

There is also a classification for stocks based on what companies do with their profits. If a company reinvests its profits to promote further growth, it is known as a *growth stock*. If it pays regular dividends to its shareholders, it is an *income stock*. Growth stocks are more risky than income stocks but have a greater potential for big price moves.

It is also important to determine whether a stock is *cyclical* in nature. Cyclical stocks closely reflect the general state of the economy. For example, if the economy is experiencing a slump, recreation and travel stocks are usually the first to feel the consumer pinch. Seasonal factors or events drive other stocks. For example, companies that produce natural gas often see better profits after the winter months when demand for home heating and natural gas has been strong. Other stocks, like grocery chains or pharmaceutical companies, tend to see more stable and predictable earnings. Traders practically need to grow antennas to keep up with all of the possible factors that contribute to price fluctuation.

However, many of the factors that will drive profits are related to trends in the industry. If you can get a good handle on industry trends, you will go far in understanding what influences the performance of an individual company's shares and, in particular, how volatile that stock is. For example, shares of major pharmaceutical companies will have similar levels of volatility. The same is true of semiconductor companies, airlines, food and beverage companies, retailers, and so on. So one starting point when looking for stocks is to gain a good understanding of the fundamentals of the industry and then establish bullish or bearish strategies on the strongest or weakest players in that industry.

exchanges

Stocks are traded on various organized exchanges all over the world 24 hours a day. In the United States, three main exchanges handle the majority of stock trades: the New York Stock Exchange (NYSE), the American Stock Exchange (AMEX), and the NASDAQ Stock Market. The first stock exchange was organized in Philadelphia in 1790. However, by 1817, the New York Stock Exchange was established on Wall Street and quickly became the most powerful center of financial exchange in the world. The original American Stock Exchange—originally called the New York Curb Exchange—was founded in 1842 and trading took place in the street until 1921.

exchange
a place where an asset, option, future, stock, or derivative is bought and sold. The most well-known exchange is the New York Stock Exchange.

Both the AMEX and the NYSE offer an auction-style trading floor where buy and sell orders are matched. However, over the years, the exchanges have updated and enhanced their electronic order routing capabilities, and many of the orders are now executed electronically rather than through specialists on the trading floor. In addition, the

NYSE announced in January 2008 that it would acquire the AMEX. The deal is expected to close in the second half of 2008.

In contrast, the National Association of Securities Dealers Automated Quotations System, or NASDAQ, is an all-electronic stock market. It facilitates the trading of stocks and options using a vast telecommunications network linking brokers all over the country. According to a January 15, 2008, press release, the NASDAQ became the largest U.S. stock exchange after trading 442 billion shares in 2007.[1]

Other regional exchanges, such as Los Angeles, Philadelphia, Chicago, Cincinnati, and Boston, also list stocks but play a much smaller role than the NYSE and NASDAQ. Some of the options exchanges have opened stock exchanges as well; examples include the ISE Stock Exchange and the CBOE Stock Exchange. In addition, a variety of international companies now trade in the United States, and a number of U.S. companies trade on exchanges outside of North America. In short, while the three biggest exchanges—NYSE, NASDAQ, and AMEX—handle most of the stock trading in the United States, the number of exchanges continues to grow and, thanks to advances in technology, to become more intertwined and efficient.

How does a company decide where to list its shares? Each exchange has its specific requirements. For example, as of this writing, to trade on the NASDAQ, a company must have earned more than $11 million over the past three years and issued at least 1.25 million shares of stock worth at least $70 million. To trade on the NYSE, the company must have earned more than $10 million over the past three years and issued at least a million shares of stock worth $100 million. I don't worry too much about where the stocks trade, so long as they have listed options. Options are listed on most actively traded stocks and, if it is a popular company worth trading, the options will become listed not long after the IPO.

option basics

As previously explained in Chapter 1, there are seven exchanges that list options in the United States alone: ISE, CBOE, AMEX, NYSE, NASDAQ, BOX, and PHLX. Each day, millions of contracts trade, and each year total volume sets new records. Many investors, both in the United States and abroad, have become savvier and are using

---

[1] "NASDAQ Becomes the Largest U.S. Stock Exchange in 2007," PrimeNewswire (www.primenewswire.com), January 15, 2008.

put and call options as part of their portfolios. But what exactly are puts and calls?

An option is a versatile trading instrument that can be used in a variety of different ways. Keep in mind that an option is actually a contract between two parties. There is a buyer or a seller. However, the contract is only valid for a specific period of time. It will eventually expire and become null and void. At that point, known as *expiration*, the option holder loses the rights afforded by the contract.

---

option
a security that represents the right, but not the obligation, to buy or sell a specified amount of an underlying security (stock, bond, futures contract, etc.) at a specified price within a specified time. The purchaser acquires a right to exercise the specifics of the contract, and the seller assumes a legal obligation to fulfill the contract if the purchaser chooses to exercise his/her right. It is interesting to note that options are a zero-sum game, meaning that if someone makes $10,000 on an option, the other person has lost out on that same amount.

Buying an option is done at a debit to the buyer (i.e., it costs money) and gives you the right, but not the obligation, to buy or sell a stock at a specified strike price. In contrast, selling an option brings in an immediate credit (you get money), but comes with an obligation to buy or sell the underlying stock if the option is assigned and exercised. Options are listed on a large number of stocks but certainly not every one.

---

leverage
using a smaller amount of capital or a small fixed cost in order to get a higher rate of return on an investment. Buying stocks on margin is an example. Using leverage can increase the rate of return. However, it also increases the risk associated with an investment.

There are two kinds of options: calls and puts. Calls give you the right to buy the underlying asset and puts give you the right to sell the underlying asset. The cost of an option is referred to as the option *premium*. All the options of one type (put or call) that have the same underlying stock are called a *class* of options. For example, all the calls on IBM constitute an option class. All the options in one class with the same strike price are called an option *series*. For example, the IBM 105 calls with various expiration dates constitute an option series.

Options are available with various strike prices depending on the current price of the underlying stock. For example, if IBM is currently trading at $105 per share, you may choose to buy a call option at 95, 100, 105, 110, or 115. If you decide to buy an August IBM 105 call, you would have the option to buy IBM at $105 per share until the third Friday in August. If the price of IBM rises to 120, you can profit from the 105 call either by exercising the option and buying IBM at the lower price or by selling the option for a higher premium. If the price of IBM falls below 105, your option's premium will also decrease in value.

Each option has a specific expiration date. All options are available in the current month, the following month, and several months throughout the year and beyond. There are three expiration cycles with four months in each cycle: (1) January, April, July, and October; (2) February, May, August, and November; and (3) March, June, September, and December. The options will expire on the Saturday following the third Friday of the expiration month. Some actively traded securities have weekly options, which are short-term options that expire each week. Others have quarterlies, which expire at the end of the calendar quarter.

---

monthly options expirations

options expire on the Saturday immediately following the third Friday of every month. The final hour or two of trading can bring some wild price gyrations to stocks that have a lot of options with open interest. If you like to trade options, this is perhaps the wildest time to do it because price swings can be dramatic. More than likely, it'll be back to business as usual by Monday. The so-called *quadruple witch* expiration can be especially volatile. It occurs quarterly when options, futures, futures options, and single stock futures expire simultaneously.

LEAPS (Long-term Equity Anticipation Securities) are long-term options that don't expire for at least nine months. Once an option's expiration gets closer than nine months, it becomes a plain option again with an entirely new ticker symbol. Be this as it may, LEAPS are in every way an option. Their expirations are a long way off, which makes them prime candidates for long-term plays and relatively secure bets for shorter-term trades.

Many new options traders use options merely as a leveraged way to play moves in the underlying stock. However, the value of the options contract will depend on numerous other factors as well. Option pricing is a process with seven main components that affect the premium of an option:

1. The current price of the underlying stock.
2. The strike price of the option in comparison to the current market price (intrinsic value).
3. The type of option (put or call).
4. The amount of time remaining until expiration (time value).
5. The current risk-free interest rate.
6. The volatility of the underlying stock.
7. The dividend rate, if any, of the underlying stock.

Each of these factors plays a unique part in the price of an option. The first four are easily deduced from the option itself. The last three are more complex. For example, higher interest rates can increase option premiums, while lower interest rates can lead to a decrease in option premiums. Dividends act in a similar way, increasing and decreasing an option premium as they increase or decrease the price of the underlying asset. Volatility not only contributes to an option's price, but it also helps to define which strategy can best be used to take advantage of specific market movement. High-volatility stocks usually have higher-priced options while low-volatility stocks offer lower-priced options. There are options strategies that can be applied to take advantage of either scenario.

call options

A call option gives you the right to purchase 100 shares of the underlying stock at a specified strike price until the third Friday of the expiration month. You may choose to buy (go long) or sell (go short) a call option. If you go long a call option, you are purchasing the right (but are under no obligation) to buy the underlying stock at the option's strike price until the expiration date. The premium of the long call option will show up as a debit in your trading account, and that debit represents the maximum loss you risk by purchasing the call. In contrast, the maximum profit of a long call option is unlimited, depending on how high the underlying stock rises in price (the upside). In general, you want to buy calls in bullish markets and sell calls in bearish markets.

---

call option
a call option is a contract that gives the owner the right to buy, or "call," the underlying asset at a specific price, called the *strike price*, for a specific period of time, ending in what is known as the *expiration date*. Hence, one January IBM call option @ 120 gives the buyer the right to purchase 100 shares of IBM at $120 until close of business on the third Friday in January.

Purchasing a call option is one of the simplest forms of options trading. A bullish trader purchases a call because he or she expects the underlying asset to increase in price. The trader will most likely make a profit if the market price of the underlying asset increases in the near future. Profits can be realized two ways. If the underlying stock increases in price before the option expires, the holder can exercise the call and purchase the underlying stock at the lower strike price. In addition, a rise in the price of the underlying asset increases the value of the call option, which can then be sold at a profit.

If you choose to sell or go short one call option, you are selling the right to buy 100 shares of the underlying stock at a specific strike price until the expiration date. A short call offers a limited profit—the price of the premium—and unlimited risk depending on how high the price of the underlying rises. In most cases, you are anticipating that the strike price of the short call will remain above the price of the underlying stock and will therefore expire worthless so you can keep the premium received. If the price of the underlying stock rises above the strike price, your short call may be assigned to an option buyer who exercises it. You are then obligated to deliver 100 shares of the underlying stock to the option buyer at the call's strike price. This entails buying the stock at the current (higher) price and selling

table 4.1	call option premiums with RIMM @ 120		
Strike Price	April	May	June
125	2.50	6.25	9.35
145	0.55	3.15	5.80
145	0.15	1.00	3.35

it back to the option holder at the (lower) call strike price, thereby creating a loss. This process can be expensive, which is why most brokerage firms allow what is known as *naked* call writing only to sophisticated options players with high net worth.

Strike prices are often spaced at 5- or 10-point increments, depending on the value of the underlying assets. Some of the more actively traded contracts have options at 1-point increments. Regardless, the premium of a call option will increase or decrease depending on the strike price and the time left until expiration. Table 4.1 shows a hypothetical variety of strike prices, expiration months, and call premiums for Research In Motion (RIMM), the underlying stock, priced at $120 per share. The numbers in the first column represent the strike prices of the RIMM calls. The months across the top are the expiration months. The numbers inside the table are the option premiums. For example, the price of a RIMM April 125 call is $2.50. Since each $1 in premium for a stock option is equal to $100 per contract, a price of $2.50 indicates that one contract would trade for $250 (2.5 × $100) plus commissions. If the price of RIMM rises above $125 per share, a 125 option will move into-the-money and, if it rises above $127.50 (125 plus the cost of the premium), the call can most likely be sold or exercised at a profit.

put options

Put options give the buyer the right to sell shares of stock. Just like call options, put options come in various strike prices with a variety of expiration dates. However, unlike with call options, if you are bearish (expecting market prices to fall), you might consider going long a put option. If you are bullish (expecting the market to rise), you might decide to go short a put option.

put option
a put option is a contract that gives the owner the right to sell, or "put," the underlying asset at a specific price, called the strike price, for a specific period of time, known as the expiration date. Hence, one January IBM put option @ 120 gives the buyer the right to sell 100 shares of IBM at $120 until close of business on the third Friday in January.

If you choose to go long one put option, you are purchasing the right to sell 100 shares of the underlying stock at the strike price until the third Friday of the expiration month. The premium of the long put shows up as a debit in your trading account and the cost of the premium is the maximum loss you risk. The maximum profit is virtually unlimited as the stock falls toward zero. As the underlying stock falls, the long put becomes more valuable because it gives you (or the person you sell it to) the right to sell the underlying stock at the higher strike price.

Table 4.2 shows some examples of put premiums for RIMM options. Notice that the short-term options with the lowest strike prices are the cheapest. They offer the most leverage, but also have the lowest probability of being in-the-money at expiration. (See the next section for an explanation of *in-the-money*.) Speculators often focus on the short-term options with strike prices just above or below the underlying stock price because they offer the most leverage. Buying extremely cheap options is kind of similar to buying lottery tickets; it's a gamble.

If you choose to go short one put option, you are selling the right to sell (or have 100 shares *put* to you) the underlying stock at a specific strike price until the expiration date. The premium is the

table 4.2   put option premiums with price of RIMM @ 120

Strike Price	April	May	June
115	2.40	6.00	8.80
105	0.60	3.00	5.15
95	0.10	1.20	2.85

maximum profit you can receive by selling a put option. It shows up as a credit in your trading account. However, the maximum loss is virtually unlimited depending on the price of the underlying stock as it falls toward zero. In most cases, you are anticipating that the underlying stock price will remain above the put strike price until expiration, leaving the put to expire worthless (so that you can keep the premium received). If, however, the underlying stock falls below the strike price of that put option, the contract might be assigned. You are then obligated to buy 100 shares of the underlying stock at the higher strike price from the option holder.

Some investors choose to sell puts in lieu of buying stock. That is, they sell puts and, if the stock falls, they get assigned the stock at the strike price of the option, which is okay because they were willing to buy the stock in the first place. Yet, while this form of put selling is common, I generally advise against it because it takes only one bad trade to create a substantial loss from selling naked puts.

To summarize, purchasing put options is a bearish move. An option holder who has purchased a put option benefits when there is a decrease in the price of the underlying asset. This enables the holder to exercise the option and sell the underlying asset at the higher price on the open market. A decrease in the price of the underlying asset also promotes an increase in the value of the long put's premium so that it can be sold for a higher price than was originally paid to purchase it. The purchase of a put option provides unlimited profit potential and limited risk based on the put option's premium and commissions. The sale of a put option provides limited risk as the underlying stock falls to zero; the maximum profit is limited to the credit received from the premium. Selling puts is a high-risk strategy that some investors use instead of buying stock. However, investors should carefully consider the risks from selling puts under the worst-case scenario (i.e., the company goes belly-up).

moneyness

The relationship between the price of the underlying asset and the strike price of the option is known as moneyness. The terms *in-the-money* (ITM), *at-the-money* (ATM), and *out-of-the-money* (OTM) are used in this context. Remember that call options give you the right to buy something at a specific price for a specific time. If the current market price is more than the strike price, the call option is in-the-money. If the current market price is less than the strike price, the call option is out-of-the-money.

table 4.3	option moneyness with price of IBM @ $100	
Strike Price	Call Option	Put Option
125	OTM	ITM
110	OTM	ITM
100	ATM	ATM
90	ITM	OTM
75	ITM	OTM

A put option is in-the-money when its strike price is higher than the market price of the underlying stock. A put option is at-the-money when the price of the underlying stock is equal or close to its strike price. A put option is out-of-the-money when the price of the underlying stock is greater than the strike price. Table 4.3 is designed to help investors make sense of whether an option is ITM, ATM, or OTM.

An option that is out-of-the-money by its expiration date expires worthless. If the current market price is the same as the strike price, the option is at-the-money. In general, I favor the ATM options for many strategies because they have the most liquidity. That is, most of the action occurs in options that have strike prices near the price of the underlying asset. However, the strike price rarely equals the stock's market price exactly. For that reason, the term *near-the-money* is sometimes used instead of ATM.

intrinsic value and time value   Intrinsic value and time value are two of the primary determinants of an option's price. *Intrinsic value* can be defined as the amount by which the strike price of an option is in-the-money. It is actually the portion of an option's price that is not lost due to the passage of time. The following equations will allow you to calculate the intrinsic value of call and put options:

- *Call options:* Intrinsic value = Underlying stock's current price − Call strike price
- *Put options:* Intrinsic value = Put strike price − Underlying stock's current price

Neither ATM nor OTM options have any intrinsic value because they have no real value. You are simply buying time value, which decreases as an option approaches expiration. The intrinsic value of an option is not dependent on the time left until expiration. *Time value* is the amount by which the price of an option exceeds its intrinsic value and is directly related to how much time the option has until expiration. For example, if a call option costs $5 and its intrinsic value is $1, the time value would be $4 ($5 − $1 = $4).

An option's intrinsic value tells you the minimum amount the option should be selling for and is therefore also called the *minimum value*—the cheaper the option, the less real value you are buying. The intrinsic value of an option is solely dependent on the price of the underlying stock and remains the same regardless of how much time is left until expiration. However, since theoretically an option with three months left till expiration has a better chance of ending up in-the-money than an option expiring in the present month, it is worth more.

There are two important elements of time decay that are worth noting. First, time value has a snowball effect. If you have ever bought options, you might have noticed that at a certain point close to expiration, the market stopped moving anywhere. That's because option prices are exponential—the closer you get to expiration, the more money you're going to lose if the market doesn't move. On the expiration day, all an option is worth is its intrinsic value. It's either in-the-money or it isn't. Second, an option has less time value and more intrinsic value as it becomes deeper in-the-money. Therefore, the option starts to move more like the underlying asset when it is deep ITM because very little of its premium is based on time value.

---

intrinsic value
the amount by which a market is in-the-money. Out-of-the-money options have no intrinsic value.

extrinsic value
the price of an option less its intrinsic value. An out-of-the money option's worth consists of nothing but extrinsic or time value.

---

liquidity

Most options strategies work in very specific market environments. Liquidity is one of the market conditions that I favor. Liquidity is the ease with which orders can be executed. A plentiful number of buyers and sellers usually boosts the volume of trading in a market, which in turn creates frenetic trading activity. Lots of activity produces a liquid market. Liquidity is an important factor in trading because it allows traders to get their orders filled easily as well as to quickly exit a position. In short, the more buyers and sellers, the better the market.

The best way to discover which markets have liquidity is actually to visit an exchange. The pits where you see absolute chaos are markets with liquidity. As long as there are plenty of floor traders screaming and yelling out orders as if their lives depended on it, you probably won't have a problem getting in and out of a trade. However, I have historically avoided the trading pits where the floor traders are falling asleep as they read the newspapers. These are obviously illiquid markets and it would not be a wise move to place an options-based trade there.

---

liquidity
the ease with which an asset can be converted to cash in the marketplace. A large number of buyers and sellers and a high volume of trading activity provide high liquidity.

If you don't have the ability to actually visit an exchange, that's okay. You can determine the liquidity of a market by reviewing the market's volume to see how many shares have been bought and sold in one day. Volume is a basic attribute that can easily be found by accessing a snapshot quote from most online financial sites. You can also assess a market's momentum by monitoring the change in volume to see if it is increasing or decreasing.

It's hard to quantify just how much volume is enough to qualify a market as one with liquidity. However, as a rule of thumb, I prefer to look for markets that are trading at least 300,000 shares every day. Since there are no absolutes, there are situations when this rule can be tossed out the window in exchange for common sense. But until you have enough experience, this may be a good rule of thumb to follow.

You can also gauge liquidity by looking at the spreads between the bid and offering price in the options market. The *bid* is the price at which a market maker is willing to buy the contract; it is the price at which you can sell the option. The *ask* is the price at which the market maker will sell, or the price at which you can buy. If you see a large spread between the bid and ask, chances are the options contract is not very liquid. In general, actively traded options will have spreads of $0.25 or less. If you see spreads of $1.00 or more, chances are the contract is not very liquid at all.

---

bid and ask
the quoted price in the financial markets includes the bid and the ask. The bid is an indication of willingness by an investor, a trader, or a dealer to buy a security—the price at which an investor can sell to a broker-dealer. The ask, or offer, is an indication of willingness by a trader or a dealer to sell a security—the price at which an investor can buy from a broker-dealer.

bid-ask spread
the difference between the bid and ask price in the financial markets is referred to as the *spread*. Narrow spreads generally indicate active interest and liquidity in the security while wide spreads generally indicate limited interest and liquidity in the security.

---

offsetting versus exercising

To exit a long option position, you can either exercise or offset it. If you want to exercise a long call option, you simply notify your broker, who will then notify the margin department. By the next day, you will own the corresponding underlying position. If you exercise a long put option, you will end up short the underlying stock. American options can be exercised at any time prior to expiration.

However, most options are closed out before expiration. To close out an existing options position, the strategist simply does the opposite of what he or she did when the trade was opened. For example, if I buy 10 January 90 Research in Motion (RIMM) calls to open, I can close the position at any time by instructing my broker (by phone or online) to sell 10 January 90 RIMM calls "to close."

Most traders offset an option when they decide they have made enough profit on the trade, or have lost as much as they can bear to lose. Offsetting must occur before the exercise date and, in the case of a short option, before it is assigned. It the option expires or has been assigned, it is too late to close the trade through an offsetting trade. Offsetting can be applied through the following procedures:

- If you bought a call, you have to sell the call.
- If you sold a call, you have to buy the call.
- If you bought a put, you have to sell the put.
- If you sold a put, you have to buy the put.

Buyers of options are the only ones who have the choice to exercise the option and purchase (call) or sell (put) the underlying stock at the strike price. Although the majority of all options with value are offset, there are various reasons why a trader might choose to exercise an option instead. Of those options that are exercised, 95 percent are exercised at expiration. If you neglect to offset your option, you have not exited the position. In this way, your option expires worthless. If you are shorting an option, this may be your strategy. But if you have purchased an option, you will lose the premium by letting it expire. However, if the option is ITM at expiration, it will be automatically exercised. This is a rule that brokers are required to implement on behalf of customers.

offset
to liquidate a position by entering an equivalent but opposite transaction. To offset an initial purchase, a sale is made; to offset an initial sale, a purchase is made.

exercise
to implement the right of the holder of an option to buy (in the case of a call) or sell (in the case of a put) the underlying security. When you exercise an option, you carry out the terms of an option contract.

auto-exercise
the process of automatically exercising in-the-money options at expiration. The rule, which was created by the Options Clearing Corporation (OCC), ensures that investors don't inadvertently leave money on the table by letting ITM options expire worthless. In some cases, the strategist might not want auto-exercise. If so, a request must be made to the brokerage firm before options expiration.

settling for cash

Options settle in one of two ways. While some settle for cash, others settle for shares. Stock options are an example of the latter. Specifically, an owner of a call option has the right to receive delivery of a physical asset—shares of stock. An owner of a put stock option, by contrast, has the right to sell 100 shares of stock per options contract. Exchange-traded funds also settle for the physical delivery of shares.

Index options, however, do not involve the physical delivery of an asset because it is not possible to buy or sell an index. Instead, cash-settled calls and puts give the owner the right to receive cash. To see how cash settlement works in real-world trading, let's consider an example using the PHLX Gold and Silver Mining Index ($XAU). Recall that the Gold and Silver Mining Index is one of the more actively traded sector indexes. It tracks a basket of gold mining stocks and is considered a tool for playing trends with respect to the price of gold.

Let's assume that we are bullish on the XAU and believe that it will rise above 95 by September. We buy five of the September 85 calls for $7.50 a contract. The cost of the trade is $3,750 ($7.50 × 100 × 5) plus commissions. The breakeven for the call position is 92.50 (85 strike price + $7.50). Therefore, at expiration (the Saturday after the third Friday of September), the exercise settlement value must be above 92.50 for the calls to yield a profit. If, at that point, the index options are exercised, the owner of the calls will receive cash equal to the difference between the strike price and the exercise settlement value. For instance, the XAU rises to 95 and therefore:

Exercise settlement value	95
Less strike price	−85
Difference/cash payment	10

The profit from the position would equal:

Amount received (5 contracts × 100 × $10)	$5,000
Less cost of calls	−3,750
Profit	$1,250

If the index fails to move above the breakeven (92.50), the position will not yield profits. The maximum loss will occur at 85 or less because, at that point, the call options will expire worthless.

It is important to know that XAU options can be exercised anytime prior to expiration. That is, XAU options settle American-style. (*Note*: It is one of only a few indexes that settle American-style.) However, just as with stock options, the options are not necessarily held until expiration and the position can be closed at any time by selling the same number of calls with the same strike price and expiration date—five XAU September 85 calls.

exercise settlement value
the value of the index at the time of expiration.

exercise settlement amount
the difference between the exercise price and the exercise settlement value of an index on the day the exercise notice is tendered, multiplied by the multiplier (100).

In order to determine the value of a cash-settled option at expiration, one must first consider the exercise settlement value and the strike price of the index option. The underlying asset price is, of course, simply the value of the index and can be found at any time by pulling up a quote. The exercise settlement value is generally determined on the last business day prior to expiration and is based on the first (opening) reported sale price for each component stock within the index.

Also, most index options settle European-style and therefore can only be exercised at expiration. The XAU is one of just a few exceptions. Stocks, ETFs, and a handful of index options settle American-style, and exercise or assignment can take place at any time prior to expiration. The European-style options have no early assignment risk, and therefore some traders prefer them when looking for opportunities to sell spreads (discussed later.)

american-style option
an option contract that can be exercised at any time between the date of purchase and the expiration date. Most exchange-traded options are American-style.

european-style option
an option contract that can only be exercised on the expiration date.

Finally, expiration is the Saturday following the third Friday of the expiration month, but, since settlement values of many indexes are based on closing prices from the Friday morning before option expiration, the last day to trade index options is often the Thursday prior to expiration. There are exceptions, however. For that reason, prior to entering a trade, the index strategist wants to carefully consider the contract specifications, including (1) how and when the index settlement value is computed; (2) the last day for trading the options (Thursday or Friday); and (3) whether the index options settle American- or European-style.

adjusting for splits and other adjustments

Sometimes options contracts are adjusted due to events that affect the price of the underlying security. For example, if the price of a stock gets too high, a corporation may choose to split the stock. A typical example is a two-for-one stock split. If, for instance, an investor holds 1,000 shares at $100 each and a two-for-one stock split is announced, he will now own 2,000 shares at $50 each. The value is the same, but the shares now cost much less; this makes it easier for additional investors to enter the market, driving the price back up. If a stock's price drops too low, a reverse stock split may occur. A one-for-two reverse stock split would mean that 1,000 shares at $100 apiece are reduced to 500 shares at $200 each. Splitting stocks often triggers heavy volatility.

When stock splits occur, the options contract must also be adjusted in a similar manner. In the previous example, two January 100 calls become four January 50 calls. Sometimes the adjustments are straightforward; other times they are not. Examples include mergers, bankruptcies, one-time special dividends, or unusual stock splits. When the contract adjustments are difficult to understand, ask your broker what is happening. Your broker is your most valuable resource. Also, the Options Clearing Corporation has informational memos about contract adjustments on its web site, www.optionsclearing.com.

---

stock split
an increase in the number of a corporation's outstanding shares that decreases the par value of its stock. The market value of the total number of shares remains the same. The proportional reductions in orders held on the books for a split stock are calculated by dividing the market price of the stock by the fraction that represents the split.

---

conclusion

If you have never traded options, the information in this chapter is essential. It represents the fundamentals of the options market; specifically, how options derive their values and why prices change in the market. The most important factor that determines the value of an option is the value of the underlying asset. That should come as no surprise. However, there are a number of other important factors to consider as well. For example, what is the relationship between the strike price and the underlying stock price? Is the option ATM, ITM, or OTM? How much time value remains? Does the option settle for cash or for shares? Is early assignment possible? To summarize, here are the key points to take home:

- *Call options.* Call options give traders the right to buy the underlying stock. A call option is in-the-money (ITM) if its strike price is below the current price of the underlying stock. A call option is out-of-the-money (OTM) if its strike price is above the current price of the underlying stock. A call option is at-the-money (ATM) if its strike price is the same as (or very close to) the current price of the underlying stock.
- *Buying calls.* If you are bullish (you believe the market will rise), buy (go long) calls. Buyers have rights. A call buyer has the right, but not the obligation, to buy the underlying stock at the strike price until the expiration date. If you buy a call option, your maximum risk is the money paid for the option—the debit. The maximum profit is unlimited depending on the rise in the price of the underlying asset. To offset a long call, you

have to sell a call with the same strike price and expiration to close out the position. By exercising your long call, you are choosing to purchase the underlying stock at the strike price of the call option.

- *Selling calls.* If you are bearish (you believe the market will fall), sell (go short) calls. Sellers have obligations. A call seller has the obligation to deliver the underlying stock at the strike price to the person to whom the option was assigned, if that person chooses to exercise the call. If you sell a call option, your risk is unlimited to the upside. The profit is limited to the credit received from the sale of the call. When selling calls, make sure to choose options with little time left until expiration. Call sellers want the call to expire worthless so that they can keep the whole premium. To offset a short call, you have to buy a call with the same strike price and expiration to close out the position.

- *Intrinsic value and time value of calls.* The intrinsic value of a call option is calculated by subtracting the call strike price from the current price of the underlying stock. The time value for a call option is calculated by subtracting the intrinsic value from the call premium.

- *Put options.* Put options give traders the right to sell the underlying stock. A put option is in-the-money (ITM) if its strike price is above the current price of the underlying stock. A put option is out-of-the-money (OTM) if its strike price is below the current price of the underlying stock. A put option is at-the-money (ATM) if its strike price is the same as (or very close to) the current price of the underlying stock.

- *Buying puts.* If you are bearish (you believe the market will fall), buy (go long) puts. Buyers have rights. A put buyer has the right, but not the obligation, to sell the underlying stock at the strike price until the expiration date. If you buy a put option, your risk is the money paid for the option, the debit. The profit is limited depending on the decrease in the price of the underlying asset (as it falls toward zero). To offset a long put, you have to sell a put with the same strike price and expiration to close out the position. By exercising your long put, you are choosing to go short the underlying stock at the strike price of the put option.

- *Selling puts.* If you are bullish (you believe the market will rise), sell (go short) puts. Sellers have obligations. A put seller has the obligation to buy the underlying stock at the strike price from the person to whom the option was assigned, if that person chooses to exercise the put option. If you sell a put option, your risk is limited as the underlying falls to zero. The profit is limited to the credit received from the sale of the put. When selling puts, make sure to choose options with little time left until expiration. Put sellers want a put to expire worthless so that they can keep the whole premium. To offset a short put, you have to buy a put with the same strike and expiration price to close out the position.

- *Intrinsic value and time value of puts.* The intrinsic value of a put option is calculated by subtracting the current price of the underlying stock from the put strike price. The time value for a put option is calculated by subtracting the intrinsic value from the put premium.

- *American verses European settlement.* Options that settle American style can be exercised at any time prior to expiration. Options that settle European style can only be exercised at expiration. Stock and ETF options settle American style. All but a handful of index options settle European style.

- *Settlement for cash versus shares.* Index options settle for cash. No shares trade hands when the options are exercised or assigned. Stock and ETF options settle for physical delivery of shares.

Put and call options can be used in a variety of ways. Many speculators use them to bet on the movement in a stock or index. For example, if you expect Research in Motion (RIMM) to perform well during the next two months, you might buy OTM call options that expire in three months. However, if you expect the stock to fall, you can buy puts. Buying puts and calls is one of the more popular ways to use options.

However, I don't buy puts and calls for our portfolios very often. Instead, I focus on strategies that combine options or that use options in combination with the underlying asset. For example, the collar strategy includes buying shares, selling calls, and buying puts. Why would this strategy work? The collar can be created as a way to profit from a gradual move higher in the stock price, but also limit risk thanks to the purchase of put options. The sale of the calls essentially pays for the protection from the put options.

Another strategy that works well in a market that is moving in a range involves selling at-the-money calls and buying both in-the-money and out-of-the-money calls. The so-called butterfly spread works because it takes advantage of the fact that options are wasting assets and lose value as time passes. The butterfly is a limited-risk approach that can produce nice returns over time.

If you are just starting out and this information seems a little confusing to you, don't worry. The next five chapters present detailed discussions of a variety of different strategies that have worked well for us over the years. I deliberately avoided entering into in-depth discussions of more advanced topics like the Greeks (which offer more advanced ways to measure the value of an options contract) and volatility (which also has an important effect on options prices). Instead, I am focusing on the practical knowledge that can help investors make profits using relatively low-risk strategies. For more advanced discussions of options pricing, readers are encouraged to look at *Options as a Strategic Investment*, by Larry McMillan (Prentice Hall Press Investment Analysis, 2002); *Option Volatility & Pricing: Advanced Trading Strategies and Techniques*, by Sheldon Natenberg (McGraw-Hill, 1994); or *The Volatility Course*, by Tom Gentile and George Fontanills (John Wiley & Sons, 2002).

chapter 5

basic option trading strategies

the balancing act

In many ways, your first trade is a rite of passage. To place it with confidence, you have to know how to play the game by cultivating your own resources in order to exploit market movement. Perhaps the attainment of effective market knowledge is the biggest creative challenge a trader has to face. In this way, the stock market is the greatest equalizer of our times. It doesn't matter how many degrees or how much money you have in your trading account. The Internet has leveled the playing field once and for all. The accumulation of profits depends on a trader's ability to place consistent winning trades while mitigating losses through the practice of risk management.

If you're going to enter the field of trading, you're going to become acquainted with risk. Trading stocks and options has potential rewards, but also risks. You must be aware of these risks and be willing to accept them in order to invest in the markets. As a rule, never trade with money you cannot afford to lose. There are no guarantees; as a trader, you'll have to settle for probabilities and potentials.

However, by predefining the risk you can afford to sustain, you can avoid making mistakes that jeopardize your whole trading career. But do not be fooled—investment risk is as inevitable as taxes. There are no free lunches.

Traders are constantly trying to find new investments that offer healthy returns with minimal risks. It is an ongoing balancing act to determine the amount of risk one is willing to take in order to obtain a potential reward. The more trading experience you have, the easier it becomes to assess the risk and reward of a particular market or a specific trade. However, one rule of thumb remains an essential key to successful trading: Never take the risk unless it's worth the return.

Risk comes in two varieties: the known and the unknown. Each time you make an investment, you are putting the cost of that investment on the line. This is a known risk because it involves a specific amount of money. The threat of unseen risk takes many forms. Unknown outside forces can exert relentless influence beyond anything market research may be able to decipher. Everything from changing interest rates to inflation and natural disasters has an effect on the markets.

It is also beneficial to think of evaluating risk in two ways: macroeconomic and microeconomic. Macroeconomic risks consist of uncertainties that affect entire groups of investment instruments. Interest rates, inflation, governmental regulations, and industry trends are all examples of macroeconomic risks. Microeconomic risks consist of fundamental and technical indicators that affect a specific company. Future earnings, management changes, P/E ratios, and the company's competitive position are all examples of microeconomic risks. Although an assessment of macro- and microeconomic risks is subjective, it can provide a rudimentary perspective from which informed investment decisions can be made.

To use an old cliché, trading is as much an art as a science. The art of trading requires *intuition, discipline*, and *imagination*. A trader who incorporates acquired knowledge with previous experience gradually develops trading intuition. Systematically attacking the markets each day creates a disciplined approach. Imagination is the soul of successful trading; it cannot be taught, but it can be enhanced. Eventually, these three variables form the basis of a trader's uniquely personal style.

Don't allow fear and doubt to stand in your way. Simply keep your eyes on the higher goal: to forge a new career as an online trader. At first, you will have to be satisfied with learning what may seem to be a series of abstract concepts and factual details. In time, these smaller units of information will merge together and you'll start to get a sense of the big picture. Learning to trade is a cumulative process; each piece of the puzzle may or may not have its place in your trading style.

risk profiles

The most helpful tool in understanding the risk and reward of a potential trade is a risk graph or payoff chart. The graph highlights three important variables—maximum risk, maximum profit, and breakevens—to help make sense of a trade's risks and rewards. The maximum risk of a trade estimates how much money can be lost if the worst-case scenario occurs. The maximum profit is the most you can ever hope to make on a trade. By comparing these two values, you can set up a risk-to-reward ratio that reveals whether the trade is worth placing. A breakeven point is the market price the underlying stock has to reach for the trade to break even (thus the name). Some trades have an upside breakeven because they offer unlimited profit to the upside. Others may have only a downside breakeven because they offer unlimited profit to the downside. A number of strategies require traders to calculate both the upside and downside breakevens to determine the profit range of the trade.

---

risk profile
a graphic determination of the risk and reward on a given trade at any given price. The vertical axis represents a trade's profit and loss and the horizontal axis represents a range of prices for the underlying asset.

---

maximum risk
the maximum loss a trade has the potential of incurring.

---

maximum profit
the maximum amount of profit that a trade has the potential to make.

---

breakeven
the stock price at which a trade breaks even. For example, a stock must reach a certain price for an option to avoid loss. For a call, the breakeven equals the strike price plus the premium paid. For a put, the breakeven equals the strike price minus the premium paid.

Knowledgeable traders can spot a good trade just by looking at its risk profile. In order to do so, however, the graph must first make sense. So, let's see how a risk graph is created by looking at the risk and reward of a trade in tabular format. For example, Table 5.1 considers call options on the Semiconductor HOLDRS (SMH). In this example, the SMH is the underlying asset. At the time of this example, shares of the fund are trading near $30 and one August 35 call can be purchased for $0.40, or $40 per contract. (Recall that the quoted prices are multiplied by 100 to arrive at the price for the call. In this case, one contract is quoted at $0.40 and therefore costs $40.)

Table 5.1 was created in order to see the risk and reward of buying and holding three SMH August 35 calls until expiration. The prices are those that would exist on the close of trading before expiration, or the third Friday in August. Notice that, if the stock falls at or below $35 a share, the position loses $120. In other words, the option expires worthless at or below $35 a share and the result is a loss of the entire premium. Conversely, if the stock climbs to $37.50, the options are worth $2.50 and the profit totals $2.10 per contract, or $630 for three contracts. At $40 a share, the profit equals $15 minus $1.20, or $13.80. The position breaks even at $35.40

---

table 5.1   risk/reward table of SMH

SMH @ Expiration	Aug 35 Call @ Expiration	Profit / Loss on 3 SMH Calls
$30.00	$0.00	$ –120.00
$32.50	$0.00	$ –120.00
$35.00	$0.00	$ –120.00
$37.50	$2.50	$ 630.00
$40.00	$5.00	$1,380.00

figure 5.1   **risk profile basics (long 3 August 35 calls @ $.40 each)**

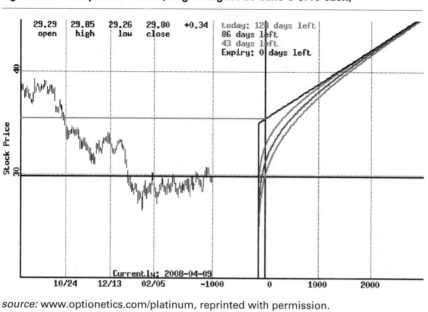

source: www.optionetics.com/platinum, reprinted with permission.

because the call is worth $0.40, or equal to the initial cost when purchased.

A second way to see the potential profit or loss from an option trade is by creating a risk profile or risk graph, which plots the profit from the option on one axis along with the price of the stock on the other axis. Figure 5.1 features an example of a risk graph using the same three SMH August 35 call options with the fund trading near $29.80 a share and 128 days left until expiration. It actually shows two charts. The first half is simply a stock chart similar to the charts discussed in Chapter 2. The risk profile is on the second half. As the graph moves to the right, it is showing a profit. When it falls to the left (below the zero line), it is showing a loss. In the case of the SMH August 35 calls, the graph slants up and to the right, which reflects the fact that the calls increase in value as the price of the SMH moves higher.

Looking at the risk graph, it is easy to see that the risk on this trade is limited to the price paid for the call option. The cost of the option is $0.40, or $120 for three contracts (consisting of 100 calls each). So the maximum risk is $120. The point where the profit/loss line crosses the vertical zero line is the breakeven. The breakeven of a long call is computed as the strike price plus the premium of the call option. In this example, the breakeven is $35.40 a share ($35 + $.40 = $35.40). The underlying asset has to rise above the breakeven to start making a profit. Beyond this point, the profit line continues to climb indefinitely as the price of the underlying stock rises—a graphic representation of the trade's unlimited profit potential. If SMH fails to rise above $35 a share, the calls expire worthless and the trade suffers its maximum possible risk, or $120.

The rest of this chapter strategically introduces examples of the six basic trading strategies along with their corresponding risk profiles. These examples are provided to teach you about the strategies and do not represent actual trades. The six basic strategies are as follows:

1. Long stock—unlimited profit/limited risk
2. Short stock—limited profit/unlimited risk
3. Long call—unlimited profit/limited risk
4. Short call—limited profit/unlimited risk
5. Long put—limited profit/limited risk
6. Short put—limited profit/limited risk

All subsequent options strategies are combinations of these six strategies. Likewise, the risk graphs of more complicated strategies are just combinations of the risk curves of these six basic strategies. So, although very basic, this chapter provides the fundamental building blocks for the more complex strategies explored in subsequent chapters.

long stock

It's a funny but sad fact that many traditional buy-and-hold investors never trade options because they consider options "too risky." The truth is, a wide array of options strategies are far less risky than buying and holding shares of stock. The risk of owning a stock is that if it falls to zero, the trade can result in a 100 percent loss of one's investment. Yet those risks are often overlooked and millions of investors each day buy stocks in order to profit from a rise in the price of the stock. So, although it is an inferior investment strategy, buying stock is widely understood and therefore serves as a good starting point for our discussion of basic options strategies.

> **going long the market**
> buying stocks, options, or futures contracts in order to profit from a directional move in the market price is referred to as *going long*.

An increase in the price of the stock obviously adds value to the investment. A profit is derived from the difference between the cost of the initial investment and the price received when the stock is sold. Timing is the key. To make a profit, investors must be able to identify a low and forecast an upcoming rise in price. Once a stock has been purchased, traders must watch for signs of a decline in price in order to sell off the shares before the decline hits. Developing a methodology that assesses a stock's fair value and determines price trends is the crux of making money as a traditional investor. Generally speaking, buy and sell decision making may be approached from two differing perspectives: assessing the overall mood of the market and analyzing characteristics of each individual stock.

According to *Investor's Business Daily*, a leading investment newspaper, three out of four stocks follow the general mood of the market. This means that if the market is experiencing a sharp decline, three out of four stocks will depreciate in value; if the markets are rising, three out of four stocks will go along for the ride. Many investors use this generalization to time their purchase of undervalued stocks or the selling of overvalued stocks. However, although many traders may follow the herd, one should never underestimate an individual stock's propensity to march to a different drummer. To successfully navigate the limitless sea of investment possibilities, an investor has to gradually develop a unique methodology that encompasses both fundamental and technical analysis.

Once a contender has been located, it's important to create a risk profile to assess the trade's profit and loss potential. As an example, let's create a hypothetical trade by tracking the purchase of 100 shares of Research in Motion (RIMM), as outlined in Table 5.2.

table 5.2   RIMM fundamentals

Research in Motion	
Last price	$118.16
Volume	16,000,000
52-week range	42.93 to 137.01
P/E ratio	51.21

The maximum risk for a long stock trade is limited to the price paid for the shares (plus commission fees). The maximum profit is unlimited as the price of the stock rises. If RIMM is trading for $118.16, 100 shares cost $11,816. Using a margin account, this trade would require 50 percent of the total price as a margin deposit, or $5,908. The breakeven on this trade is the exact price of the stock when the trade is initiated: $118.16.

The risk profile for the 100 shares of RIMM is provided in Figure 5.2. The left side shows the stock chart, while the right offers the

figure 5.2   long stock (long 100 shares of RIMM stock @ 118.16)

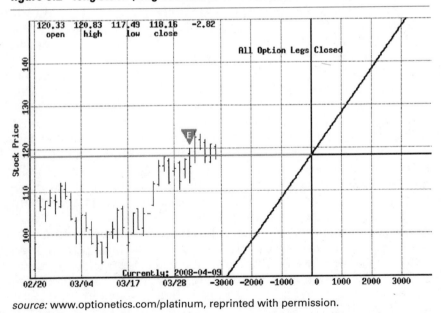

source: www.optionetics.com/platinum, reprinted with permission.

table 5.3   long stock (hypothetical) strategy results

Long 100 Shares of RIMM				
Price at Initiation	Price at Exit	Days in Trade	Profit / Loss	Return on Investment
$11,818	$13,000	60	$1,182	10%

risk profile. Notice how the profit/loss line slopes upward from left to right, visually graphing the trade's ability to make a profit as the price of the RIMM stock rises. If the price of the stock falls, money is lost on a dollar-for-dollar basis.

Notice that shares of RIMM have been in a steady uptrend. If you expect the move higher to continue, you might want to set a profit objective of $130 a share. After 60 days, RIMM trades at your target price and you can sell the 100 shares at $130 to garner a profit of roughly $1,180 (minus commission costs). This translates into a 10 percent return on investment—a modest yet tidy profit (see Table 5.3).

rule of thumb
look for stocks that have hit their low and look poised to trend up again.

short stock

If an investor believes the price of a stock is heading into a bearish decline, it may be profitable to sell short. This technique has a limited profit potential (as the price falls to zero) and unlimited upside risk. To short a stock, an investor borrows the shares from his or her brokerage firm to be sold in the market. The investor's account receives a credit for the total selling price of the stock. If the stock price declines, the investor can buy the stock back at the lower price and pocket the difference as profit. If the stock price rises, the investor may be required to place an additional margin deposit to stay in the trade. Buying the stock back is known as *covering the short*.

---

selling short
selling stocks, options, or futures in order to profit from a
directional move in the market price is referred to as *selling short*.

If you are interested in shorting stock as a means of investing,
consider these important points before jumping in headfirst:

- Margin requirements for shorting stocks differ from long stock
  positions. Most brokerage firms require the full price of the
  stock plus 50 percent or more as margin on a short stock
  trade. Additional margin may be required if the stock price
  rises dramatically.
- If the stock pays a dividend, the short seller is responsible for
  the payment.
- Holding a short position in the stock for over one year does not
  constitute a long-term capital gain. Capital gain tax shelters
  are for long stockholders, not short sellers.

---

dividend
a sum of money paid out to a shareholder from a stock's profits
at the behest of the company's board of directors.

---

capital gain
the profit received when a trade makes money, minus any
commission costs. Capital gains are subject to being taxed.

To illustrate this strategy, we have to find a company that seems
poised for a move lower. After searching the news for clues, we
stumbled on Valero (VLO), a leading oil refining company that has
been seeing its profit margins compressed due to higher costs for
crude oil. We find the stock at $67.66 per share, and coming down
from the upper end of its 52-week range (see Table 5.4). The chart

table 5.4   VLO fundamentals

Valero (VLO)	
Last price	$67.66
Volume	14,000,000
52-week range	44.94 to 78.68
P/E ratio	46.18

(Figure 5.3) shows the stock beginning to set some lower lows and lower highs. Given the outlook for profits and the breakdown on the chart, another move lower may be in the offing.

In this example, let's sell short 100 shares of VLO at $67.66 per share to receive $6,766 upon placing the trade. The maximum reward is limited to the price of the stock at initiation, or $6,766. The price of Valero must decline below that price level for the investor to make a profit. The maximum risk of a short stock strategy is unlimited as

figure 5.3   short stock (short 100 shares of VLO stock @ 67.66)

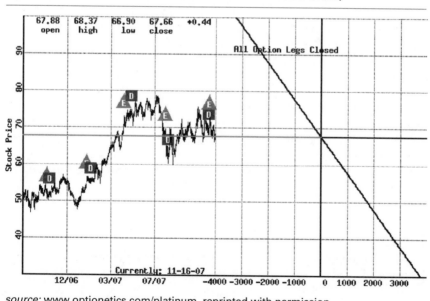

source: www.optionetics.com/platinum, reprinted with permission.

table 5.5 **short stock strategy results**

Short 100 shares of VLO @ 57				
Price at Initiation	Price at Exit	Days in Trade	Profit / Loss	Return on Investment
$6,766	$5,490	60	$1,276	19%

the price of the stock rises—as the price rises, the investor starts to lose money on a dollar-for-dollar basis.

Once again, the investor can break even on the trade by exiting the trade when the stock is at the same price it was when the trade was initiated. The risk profile for this trade (see Figure 5.3) shows a profit/loss line that slants downward from left to right, revealing the trade's propensity to lose money as the price of the stock rises.

After 60 days, the stock has lost considerable ground and it seems a real possibility that the bottom is in, at least in the short term. So when Valero declines to $54.90, it's time to buy the shares back at that price, or $5,490 for 100 shares, for a gain of $1,276—a 19 percent profit on investment (Table 5.5). Not bad, but never forget that short selling has its pros and cons. In addition, remember that commissions or fees for brokerage services will affect this trade. They have been ignored for the sake of simplifying the discussion.

We do sometimes sell stocks short, but it is not a strategy we teach to our students. In general, we recommend short selling as a means of hedging risk, preferring to mitigate the unlimited risk associated with going short by combining short shares with options. We don't recommend short selling options, either. Even if you have a large trading account, putting yourself in a position of unlimited risk is simply not advisable when there are so many limited-risk alternatives. The risks of selling options short are discussed in greater detail a bit later.

rule of thumb
look for a bearish market that is ready to make a sharp move down. The short stock strategy is best used in tandem with options to limit risk.

long call

Many investors become interested in options because of the leverage associated with call buying. As with buying shares, the objective of buying calls is to make profits if the stock price moves up. Calls can be purchased for a fraction of the cost of buying the underlying stock. However, the risk of large percentage losses from straight call buying is also quite high.

> **leveraging**
> the utilization of available funds in order to increase the quantity or magnitude of investments and thereby magnify investment returns.

Remember that the purchase of a call option gives the holder the right, but not the obligation, to buy 100 shares of the underlying stock at the option's strike price at any time until the option's expiration date. The holder pays a specific price or premium for the call option, which is the maximum risk of the trade. Profits develop when the price of the underlying stock rises above the breakeven, which is computed as the strike price of the option plus the premium for the call.

If the stock moves considerably higher, a trader can exercise his right to buy the underlying stock at the lower strike price and then sell it at the higher current price, pocketing the difference as profit. However, many call buyers are not really interested in owning the stock. Instead, a large percentage of calls that are bought as a way to speculate are offset with the sale of a call option at a higher premium. The value of the premium increases due to a rise in price of the underlying stock. If the price of the underlying stock declines in value, the premium of the option also falls. In this case, the option may expire worthless and the holder loses the premium paid for the call.

Using our previous RIMM scenario from the long stock example, let's create an example of a long call trade. Options, as with stocks, are quoted using a bid and an asking price, or offer. As previously mentioned, the bid is the highest price a prospective buyer (in the market) is prepared to pay for a specified time for a trading unit of a specified security. The ask is the lowest price acceptable to a

long call strategy
the purchase of a call option with the expectation that the underlying asset's price will rise—a bullish strategy with limited risk and unlimited reward.

strike price
all options have strike prices. The strike price represents the price at which the underlying stock can be purchased (call) or sold (put) at any time prior to the option's expiration date if the option is exercised.

expiration date
the last day on which an option may be exercised. American-style options can be exercised at any time before the expiration date. European-style options can be exercised only on the expiration date.

prospective seller of the same security. Together, the bid and ask prices constitute a quote, and the difference between the two prices is the bid-ask spread. If there is a high demand for the underlying asset, the prices are bid up to a higher level. In contrast, a low demand for a stock translates to the market being "offer down" to the lowest price at which a person is willing to sell.

As an off-floor trader, you will typically buy at the ask and sell at the bid, or you can place a limit order somewhere between the two. Your order will be displayed in the market and will be executed when another buyer or seller comes along. Meanwhile, the floor trader typically makes his money by purchasing from off-floor traders at the bid and selling to someone else at the ask. Since we are talking about buying a call option, Table 5.6 shows the bid prices of RIMM call options with various strike prices and expiration dates.

Using these prices, let's buy one RIMM call with a strike price of 130 and a June expiration date. The premium for this call is $6.60 or $660 (100 × 6.60 = $660). The maximum loss of this trade is the premium paid, or $660. The maximum potential reward is unlimited depending on the rise in the price of RIMM.

To derive the price at which the trade breaks even, simply add the premium to the option strike price. In this example, the breakeven is $136.60 (130 + 6.60 = 136.60). For this trade to make money, the price of one share of Research in Motion must rise above $136.60 by

table 5.6   call option premiums with RIMM @ 118.16

Price of RIMM = 118.16 (04/09/08)

Call Strike Price	May	June	September
100	20.40	22.75	28.40
110	12.95	16.00	22.55
120	7.25	10.60	17.55
130	3.50	6.60	13.45
140	2.00	3.85	10.10

the June options expiration day for the trade to show a profit. Figure 5.4 shows the risk profile of this trade.

After 60 days, RIMM rises to $130, but the premium for the call option is only $6.00. The call has decreased in value despite a 10 percent increase in the stock price. How is this possible? The main reason is time decay. Although the stock moved higher, the option now has only 12 days of life remaining. Time decay is an important risk to consider when buying deep out-of-the-money call options.

figure 5.4   long call (long 1 June RIMM 130 call @ 6.60)

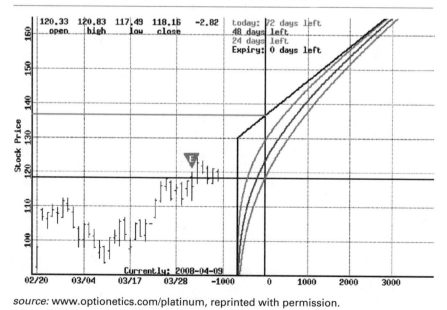

source: www.optionetics.com/platinum, reprinted with permission.

table 5.7   long call results

Long 1 RIMM June 100 Call

Price at Initiation	Price at Exit	Days in Trade	Profit / Loss	Return on Investment
$2,275	$3,000	60	$725	32%

Long 1 RIMM June 130 Call

Price at Initiation	Price at Exit	Days in Trade	Profit / Loss	Return on Investment
$660	$600	60	−$60	−9%

Consider what would happen if the June 100 call was purchased for $22.65 instead. After 60 days, when RIMM hits $130, the call option would have intrinsic value of at least $30, which would translate into a 32.5 percent return on investment. Table 5.7 summarizes the results for both of these options. Clearly, buying in-the-money or near-the-money is a less aggressive strategy than buying deep out-of-the-money calls. However, buying in-the-money options requires more capital, which is also placed at risk should the stock fall.

Traders can use the long call strategy to make a profit in two scenarios. The more basic technique is to buy a call in a rising market and then selling it when the premium increases. Another scenario involves buying a call to protect profits on a short stock. If you sell a stock short and then the price of the stock declines, there is a chance that the stock may reverse direction and wipe out the profit. For example, if you sell RIMM for $100 a share and it then falls in price to $80, you can protect your $20 profit by purchasing a RIMM 80 strike call option. If the price of RIMM starts to rise, you can exercise the 80 call and use the shares to cover the short stock. If the stock continues to fall instead, the premium on the long call will decrease, but at a slower rate than the short stock will be gaining.

rule of thumb
buy call options in a bullish market with at least 45 days until expiration.

short call

Selling a call option—commonly known as *writing* a call option—is a bearish strategy that offers limited profit potential and unlimited risk. When a call option is sold to open, the writer receives a credit in his account in the amount of the option premium. As long as the price of the underlying stock falls below the strike price of the call, the call writer keeps the credit received. If the price of the underlying stock rises above the call strike price, then the short call option is in danger of being assigned to an option holder and subsequently exercised. If the option is exercised, the writer of the short call is obligated to deliver the underlying stock to the assigned option holder at the strike price of the short call. The handling of assignment involves buying the underlying stock at the current market price and delivering it to the option holder at the strike price. The difference between the current market price and the strike price comprises the loss on the trade. While I don't recommend selling calls naked, it's important to learn the mechanics of a short call so you can combine it with other option strategies.

---

short call strategy
the sale of a call option with the expectation that the underlying asset's price will fall—a bearish strategy with unlimited risk and limited reward.

assignment
the decision by an option holder to exercise a long option results in an assignment to an option seller. In the case of the assignment of a call, the option seller must deliver the underlying stock to the option holder at the short call option's strike price regardless of the current price of the underlying asset. In the case of an assignment of a put, the option seller must purchase and take delivery of the underlying asset from the option holder at the short put option's strike price regardless of the current price of the underlying asset.

Let's explore what Valero (VLO) has to offer us in the way of short call prices. Table 5.8 shows the call premiums at the ask price for various VLO options. Since the profit on a short call option depends on the option expiring worthless, less time until expiration increases a trader's chance of keeping the short option's

table 5.8   call option premiums with VLO @ 67.66

Price of VLO = $67.66 (11/16/07)

Call Strike Price	November	December	January
62.50	5.20	6.10	7.20
65	2.70	4.40	5.60
67.50	0.10	2.90	4.20
70	0	1.90	3.00
72.50	0	1.20	2.15
75	0	0.70	1.55

premium. We generally prefer to sell options with less than 45 days until expiration. However, if you are selling a call, it is essential to find a balance between the time left until expiration and the premium received from the sale. If you are going to take on a position with unlimited risk, the payoff should be worth it (but it almost never is).

Using the prices in Table 5.8, let's create an example by going short two VLOW January 67.5 call options at $4.20 a contract. Upon initiation of the trade, the option writer receives a credit of $840. This is the maximum profit available on this trade. The maximum loss is unlimited as the price of the underlying stock rises above the breakeven, which is derived by adding the call premium to the strike price of the option.

This trade breaks even when the price of VLO equals 71.70 (67.5 + 4.20= 71.70). Figure 5.5 shows this trade's risk profile; notice how the profit line improves as the stock price falls.

After 60 days, VLO is at $54.90 a share and the January calls are offered at only a nickel. There is an extremely good chance that they will expire worthless, but the prudent approach at this point is simply to close the position by buying back two VLO January 67.5 calls to close. The cost to close the trade is therefore $10 (2 × $.05 × 100), which is subtracted from the initial credit of $840, and the profit from the trade is $830. (See Table 5.9.)

Traders can write calls to profit from a declining market or to protect profits on a long stock position. In the latter scenario, known as a *covered call* strategy, a purchase of underlying stock is offset by selling a call option against it. A covered call strategy is best

figure 5.5   short call (short 2 January VLO 60 calls @ $4.2)

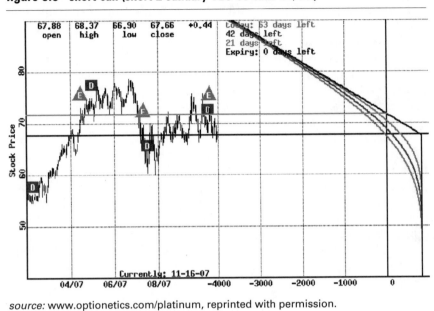

implemented in a bullish to neutral market where a slow rise in the market price of the underlying asset is anticipated.

> **rule of thumb**
> sell a call option with less than 45 days until expiration in a bearish market and monitor the market carefully for signs of a reversal. Consider hedging the sale with the purchase of a deep out-of-the-money call. This so-called *credit spread* is discussed in more detail in Chapter 6.

table 5.9   short call results

Short 2 VLO January 67.5 Calls			
Price at Initiation	Price at Exit	Days in Trade	Profit/Loss
$840	$10	60	$830

long put

A long put option offers limited risk and limited profit potential as the stock falls to zero. The purchase of a put option gives the holder the right, but not the obligation, to sell 100 shares of the underlying stock at the option's strike price at any time until the option's expiration date. Profit is achieved when the underlying stock falls below the breakeven. Risk is limited to the price paid for the option premium—an amount substantially less than the unlimited risk that accompanies shorting a stock.

Traders have two basic methods of collecting a profit on a long put in a declining market. If the price of the underlying stock falls, traders can exercise their right to short the underlying stock at the higher strike price and then buy back the shares at the lower market price, pocketing the difference as profit. Most traders, however, prefer to offset the position by selling a put option at a higher premium. If the price of the underlying stock rises in value, the premium of the put option generally decreases and could potentially expire worthless, leaving the put owner out the money paid for the contract.

---

long put strategy
the purchase of a put option with the expectation that the underlying stock's price will fall—a bearish strategy with limited risk and limited reward.

Since a long put strategy works best in a bearish market, let's find a trade using Valero, which was used in two previous examples on short selling and short call selling. Remember, when purchasing options, it is important to buy enough time so that the option has a better chance of being in-the-money by expiration.

Using quotes in Table 5.10, let's buy three VLO January 65 puts at $2.70. With the stock at $67.66, the puts with the 65 strike are just out-of-the-money and therefore offer a lot of leverage. This is an aggressive play on a move down in the stock price.

The maximum loss of this trade is the premium paid, or $810 (100 × 3 × 2.70). The maximum reward seems potentially unlimited, depending on the fall in the price of VLO. However, the potential profits are not really unlimited—a stock can't fall below zero.

table 5.10   put option premiums with VLO @ 67.66

Price of VLO = $67.66 (11/16/07)

Put Strike Price	November	December	January
62.50	0.05	0.95	1.85
65	0.05	1.65	2.70
67.50	0.05	2.65	3.80
70	2.55	4.00	5.10
72.50	5.10	5.80	6.80
75	7.60	8.00	8.60

To compute the price at which the trade breaks even, simply subtract the premium from the option strike price. In this example, the breakeven is 62.30 (65 − 2.70 = 62.30). Hence, the stock price must fall below $62.30 a share for this trade to make money. The risk profile of this trade is shown in Figure 5.6.

figure 5.6   long put (long 3 VLO January 65 puts @ $2.10)

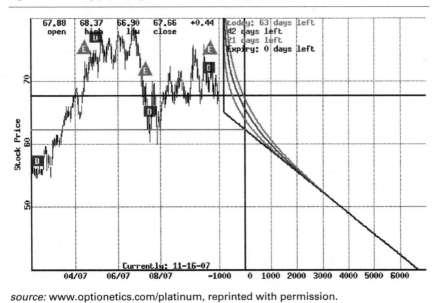

table 5.11   long put results

Long 3 VLO January 65 Puts				
Price at Initiation	Price at Exit	Days in Trade	Profit / Loss	Return on Investment
$810.00	$3,000	60	$2,190	270%

After 60 days, only three days remain until expiration and shares of Valero have fallen below $55. The long put has intrinsic value of $10, for a whopping profit of $730 a contract—a 270 percent return on investment (see Table 5.11). This scenario demonstrates how an option strategy can be used to leverage trading funds in order to consistently build your account. If you had gone short 100 shares of VLO, you could have made a profit of $1,276. But a short stock trade would have required a hefty margin whereas a long put strategy does not require any margin beyond the debit of the put option's premium.

There are two basic ways to make money by purchasing puts. Traders can simply buy a put in a declining market and follow the previous example or buy puts to lock in profits on a long stock position. The latter technique is a form of hedging. If the price of the stock continues to rise, then the trader may lose the put premium. However, if the price of the stock starts to fall, the money lost on the long stock position is offset by the rise in the put premium. In addition, long puts are used in a variety of spreads and delta neutral trading strategies.

rule of thumb
buy puts with at least 45 days until expiration in a bearish market.

short put

Selling a put option—also known as writing a put option—offers limited profit potential and limited risk as the stock falls to zero. When a short put trade is placed, the writer receives a credit in his account in the amount of the option premium. As long as the price of the underlying stock rises above the put strike price, the put writer may keep the credit received. If the price of the underlying stock falls below the put strike price, then the short put option is in danger of being assigned to an option holder. If the option holder exercises the option, the writer of the short put is obligated to buy the underlying stock from the assigned put holder at the strike price of the put option. The put writer then owns the stock at a higher price than the current market price at which it can be sold. Once again, while I don't recommend selling puts naked, it's important to learn the mechanics of a short put so you can combine it with other option strategies.

---

short put strategy
the sale of a put option with the expectation that the underlying stock's price will rise—a bullish strategy with limited risk (as the underlying asset falls all the way to zero) and limited reward.

In a short put strategy, the maximum profit occurs if the option expires worthless. Therefore, it is best to sell options with 45 days or less until expiration. They will lose value at a faster rate than longer-term options. However, for this example, we will use options with 72 days of life remaining. To be specific, looking at Table 5.12, we focus on one RIMM June 120 put @ 11.85. Upon initiation of the trade, this rather greedy option writer receives a credit of $1,185—the maximum profit available on this trade. The maximum loss is limited as the price of the underlying stock falls below the strike price of the option to a price of zero.

To derive the breakeven of a short put, simply subtract the put premium from the strike price of the option. This trade breaks even when the price of RIMM hits $108.15 (120 − 11.85 = 108.15). Figure 5.7 features the risk profile of this trade.

table 5.12   put option premiums with RIMM @ 118.46

Put Strike Price	April	May	June
100	0.15	1.00	4.20
110	1.00	4.60	7.50
120	4.60	10.00	11.85
130	12.30	15.00	17.85

figure 5.7   short put (short 1 RIMM June 120 put @ $11.85)

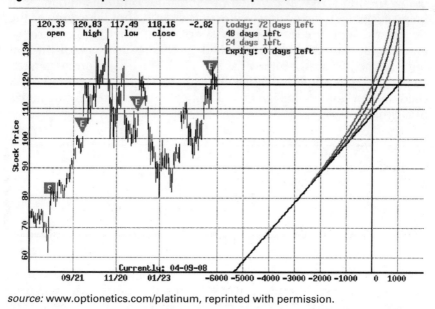

source: www.optionetics.com/platinum, reprinted with permission.

If the market continues to rise, the short put will not be assigned to the writer at expiration. In this example, if shares trade higher and move above the 120 strike price, the put option expires worthless and we get to keep the $1,185 credit we received upon entering the trade (see Table 5.13).

Traders can profit from a short put position in two basic ways. They can simply sell an uncovered (naked) put in a rising market. Technically this strategy comes with limited risk as the underlying asset can only fall as far as zero. But the term *limited* is misleading in this context. A significant loss can occur if the underlying asset falls heavily. In the RIMM example, the strategist stands to lose up to

table 5.13   short put results

Short 1 RIMM June 120 Put @ $11.85			
Price at Initiation	Price at Exit	Days in Trade	Profit / Loss
$1,185	0	73	$1,185

$10,815 for selling one put contract! The risk-reward ratio is almost 10-to-1 negative. That's why a short put strategy should be used with extreme caution, even when the writer is willing to take delivery of the stock at the strike price. The risks are the same.

The other technique is to write a covered put by selling the underlying stock and selling a put option against it—a strategy best implemented in a bearish to neutral market where a slow fall in the market price of the underlying stock is anticipated. If the underlying stock rises, the put will be assigned and when it is exercised the resulting shares that are purchased from the option buyer can be used to cover the losing short.

---

rule of thumb
sell puts in bullish markets with less than 45 days to expiration.

---

conclusion

The strategies in this chapter are very basic. In fact, for options traders with a year or two of experience, there isn't much new here. Nevertheless, it would be impossible to write a book on trading options online without exploring these basic strategies. They form the foundation for many advanced strategies discussed in later chapters.

I don't use these basic strategies very often. Sometimes I do buy stocks or straight puts and calls; however, a variety of other strategies offer more compelling risk and rewards. For example, a straddle combines the purchase of both a put and a call. It makes money from big moves higher or lower in a stock price. A butterfly involves selling and buying puts or calls. The butterfly can make nice profits when a stock remains rangebound.

In the options market, there is definitely more than one way to go. I didn't invent any of the basic strategies, but over the years I, along with a host of Optionetics instructors and students, have found ways to modify them and use them in a variety of innovative ways. In short, there is no right or wrong way to trade and, while I am trying to set forth some clear guidelines, there are really no hard, fast rules. However, an understanding of the fundamentals of the options market is essential to successful trading. Hopefully, these first few chapters have helped lay that foundation.

chapter 6

vertical spreads

introduction to vertical spreads

All markets have the potential to fluctuate beyond their normal trend; hence, it is essential to your success to employ strategies that can limit your losses to a manageable amount. A variety of options strategies can be employed to hedge risk and leverage capital. Each strategy has an optimal set of circumstances that will trigger its application in a particular market. Vertical spreads are basic limited-risk strategies and that's why I tend to introduce them first. These simple hedging strategies enable traders to take advantage of the way option premiums change in relation to movement in the underlying asset.

Vertical spreads offer limited potential profits as well as limited risks by combining long and short options with different strike prices and like expiration dates. The juxtaposition of long and short options results in a net debit or net credit. Either way, vertical spreads generate profits when the underlying stock moderately moves in the anticipated direction. Hence, a bullish spread makes money if the price moves higher; bearish spreads generate profits if the underlying market falls. Consequently, correctly forecasting the nature of a directional trend is the key to making a profit on these strategies. Trending directional markets can often be located by observing increases in volatility. Vertical spreads offer limited risks and limited rewards. Low risk makes these strategies inviting, especially for beginners.

There are two kinds of *debit spreads*: the bull call spread and the bear put spread. As their names imply, a bull call spread is placed in a bullish market using calls, and a bear put spread is placed in a bearish market using puts. Debit spreads use options with more than 45 days till expiration. The maximum risk of a debit spread is limited to the net debit of the trade—far less than what it would cost to trade the underlying instrument.

There are two kinds of *credit spreads*: the bull put spread and the bear call spread. The bull put spread is placed in a bullish market using puts, and a bear call spread is placed in a bearish market using calls. In contrast to debit spreads, the maximum profit of a credit spread is limited to the net credit of the trade. In general, credit spreads have lower commission costs than debit spreads— additional commissions are avoided by simply allowing the options to expire worthless.

---

vertical spread
a spread in which one option is bought and one option is sold, where the options have the same underlying asset and expiration date but have different strike prices.

debit spread
an options spread in which the difference between the long and short options' premiums results in a net debit—the maximum risk on the spread.

credit spread
an options spread in which the difference between the short and long options' premiums results in a net credit—the maximum profit on the spread.

In general, vertical spreads combine long and short options with the same expiration date but different strike prices. The key is to find a market with option premiums that create a spread with high potential reward and low risk. This enables traders to take advantage of the way option premiums respond to changes in the price of the underlying asset. Traders should decide on an exit strategy in advance. I usually look for a 50 percent profit or we exit the position before a 50 percent loss. We also recommend doing two contracts at once. Try to exit one of the spreads with enough profit to cover the cost of the double contracts. The other trade will become a virtually free trade, allowing you to take more of a risk and accumulate a bigger profit.

One of the keys to understanding these managed-risk spreads comes from grasping the concepts of intrinsic value and time value—variables that provide major contributions to the fluctuating price of an option. Although changes in the underlying asset of an option may be hard to forecast, there are a few constants that influence the values of options premiums. The following constants provide the key to why vertical spreads offer a healthy alternative to traditional bullish and bearish stock trading techniques:

- Time value continually evaporates as an option approaches expiration.
- Out-of-the-money (OTM) and at-the-money (ATM) options have no intrinsic value. They are all time value and therefore lose more premium as expiration approaches than in-the-money (ITM) options.
- The premiums of ITM options have minimum values that change at a slower pace than OTM and ATM options.
- Vertical spreads take advantage of these differing rates of changes in the values of options premiums.

Vertical spreads are excellent strategies for small investors who are getting their feet wet for the first time. Low risk makes these strategies inviting. Although they combine a short and a long option, the combined margin is usually far less than what it would cost to trade the underlying instrument. If you are new to the options game, I highly recommend taking the time to learn these four strategies by paper trading them first.

bull call spread

A bull call spread consists of buying a lower strike call and selling a higher strike call in a proportion of one-to-one with the same expiration date. This strategy is implemented in a bullish market and when prices are expected to rise. Like the long call, the bull call spread provides high leverage and the total investment is usually far less than the amount required to purchase the stock outright. However, as you will see, the spread requires less capital than straight call buying.

At the same time, the bull call spread offers limited profit potential and limited downside risk. No matter how high the underlying climbs, a bull call spread offers a limited reward. Conversely, no matter how low the underlying falls, this strategy offers a limited loss. The maximum risk is limited to the net debit paid for the spread and occurs when the underlying stock closes at or below the strike price of the long call. The maximum reward is limited to the difference in strike prices minus the net debit (per spread), times the multiplier. The maximum reward occurs when the price of the underlying stock closes at or above the strike price of the short call. The breakeven of a bull call spread is calculated by adding the net debit to the lower call strike price.

A bull call spread is best used when you are moderately bullish. If you were extremely optimistic about a major move in the market, you may want to use a bullish strategy that offers an unlimited reward. As an example, let's create a hypothetical bull call spread using the U.S. Oil Fund (USO), using the numbers shown in Table 6.1. The fund is an exchange-traded fund (ETF) and not a stock. In addition, unlike most other ETFs, which were discussed in Chapter 2, the USO doesn't hold shares of specific companies. Instead, it holds crude oil futures contracts and is designed to track the price of crude oil.

In this case, it is October 2007, and we are bullish on crude oil prices. Since the USO is expected to perform well, let's create a bull call spread. With the USO sitting near $62.61, Table 6.2 shows a variety of call options contracts that could be use to create the spread. Since bull call spreads involve a net debit, it is best to use options with 45 days or more until expiration to give the trade enough time to make a profit. Therefore, let's create a bull call spread by going long three January 65 calls at $4.00 a contract and selling three January 70 calls for $2.50. This is a relatively aggressive play since

table 6.1   U.S. oil fund fundamentals

U.S. Oil Fund (USO)	
Last price	$62.61
Volume	4,680,000
52-week range	$43.23 to $64.25

---

table 6.2   call option premiums with USO @ 62.61

Price of USO = $62.61 (10/4/07)

Call Strike Price	October	November	January
55	8.20	9.10	10.30
60	4.20	5.50	7.00
65	1.65	2.80	4.00
70	0.65	1.50	2.50
75	0.20	0.50	1.50

---

both options are out-of-the-money. It is a bet that the USO will make a substantial move between now and the end of the year.

> **bull call spread**
> a debit spread involving the purchase of a lower strike call and the sale of a higher strike call with the same expiration date—a bullish strategy with limited profit and limited risk.

As Table 6.3 shows, the maximum loss on this trade is limited to the net debit, which is $450 for the three bull call spreads [(4 − 2.5) × 3 × 100 = $450]. To calculate the maximum profit, multiply the number of spreads times the multiplier times the difference in strike prices and then subtract the net debit. In this trade, the maximum profit is $1,050: [3 × (70 − 65) × 100] − 450 = $1,050. This trade risks $450 to make a maximum profit of $1,050—that's more than 200 percent return on investment, if successful.

---

table 6.3   bull call spread trade calculations

Long 3 USO 65 Calls @ 4.00 and Short 3 USO 70 Calls @ 2.50

Maximum risk = net debit	$450
Maximum reward = (strike difference × 100) − net debit	$1,050
Breakeven = long strike price + net debit	66.50
Return on investment = reward/risk	230%

figure 6.1   bull call spread (long 3 USO January 65 calls @ 4.00, short 3 USO January 70 calls @ 2.50)

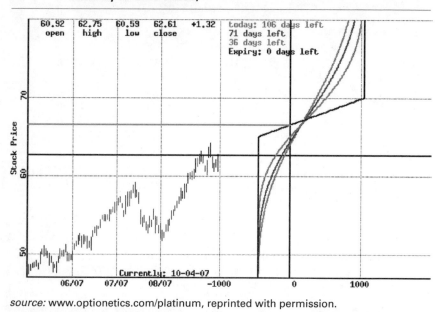

source: www.optionetics.com/platinum, reprinted with permission.

The breakeven is derived by adding the net debit divided by the number of spreads (divided by 100) to the long call strike price. In this example, the breakeven is 66.50 [66 + (450 ÷ 100/3) = 69.50]. USO needs to make a move above $66.50 by expiration in order to start making a profit. At the same time, the profit doesn't max out until USO reaches 70. Luckily, the January expiration gives the trade three months to get there. Figure 6.1 shows the risk profile of this example.

After 100 days, January expiration is approaching, and the price of U.S. Oil Fund sits near $77 a share. Both options are now deeply ITM. At this point, you can exercise the 65 call and then sell those shares to the assigned option holder for $70 a share for the maximum profit of $1,005 (Table 6.4). Or you can simply instruct the broker to close the spread for a credit, which should be approaching $5 per spread.

To find a market that is appropriate for placing a bull call spread, look for stocks, indexes, or ETFs that are trending up nicely or have reached their support level and are poised for a rebound. The goal is for the market to rise as high as the strike price of the short call.

table 6.4 bull call spread results

Long 3 USO January 65 Calls @ 4.00, Short 3 USO January 70 Calls @ 2.50

Debit at Initiation × 3 Contracts	USO Price at Initiation	USO Price at Exit	Days in Trade	Credit at Exit × 3 Contracts	Profit	Return on Investment
$450	$62.61	$76.76	80	$1,455	$1,005	123%

That way, if it's exercised early, you can make the maximum return on the trade by exercising the long call and pocketing the difference.

rule of thumb
buy the ATM options and sell the OTM options. Look for markets that are trending up and then use options with 45 days or greater until expiration. The greater the strike spread, the higher the profit potential.

bear put spread

A bear put spread is a debit spread created by purchasing a higher strike put and selling a lower strike put on a one-to-one basis with the same expiration date. This strategy works best in a bearish market when prices are falling. Like the bull call spread, the bear put spread provides high leverage over a limited range of stock prices. The profit on this strategy can increase by as much as one point for each one-point decrease in the price of the underlying asset. However, the total investment is usually far less than the amount required to sell stock short. The strategy has both limited profit potential and limited downside risk.

bear put spread
the sale of a lower strike put and the purchase of a higher strike put with the same expiration date—a bearish strategy with limited risk and limited reward.

---

table 6.5   hovnanian enterprises fundamentals

Hovnanian Enterprises (HOV)

Last price	$25.26
Volume	2,100,000
52-week range	$38.66 to $23.63
P/E ratio	Negative

Let's create an example using the homebuilder Hovnanian Enterprises (HOV) in May 2007. The housing industry is suffering a slump, and in many of the homebuilder's key markets, homes just aren't selling. We are certainly seeing more for-sale homes in our neighborhood and the industry is expected to get hit hard in the second half of the year. Hovnanian is already losing money on a per share basis (see Table 6.5). Let's set up a bear put spread and have several expiration months and strike prices to choose from (Table 6.6). Since bear put spreads involve the net purchase of options, it is best to use options with 45 days or more until expiration to give the trade enough time to make a profit.

In this situation, we create a bear put spread by going long five HOV July 25 put options @ $1.50 and short five HOV July 20 puts @ $0.25 (see Table 6.7.) The maximum risk of a bear put spread is limited to the net debit of the spread. In this example, the maximum risk is $625 [5 × (1.50 − .25) × 100 = $625]. The maximum profit of a bear call spread is calculated by multiplying the number of contracts times the difference in strike prices by the value per point

---

table 6.6   put option premiums with HOV @ 25.26

Price of HOV = $25.26 (05/31/07)

Put Strike Price	June	July	August
17.5	0.05	0.10	0.10
20	0.05	0.25	0.35
25	0.85	1.50	1.85
30	4.75	5.00	6.00
35	9.75	10.00	10.25

---

table 6.7 HOV July 25/20 bear put spread trade calculations (five contracts)

Bear Put Spread Using HOV @ $25.26

Maximum risk = net debit	$625
Maximum reward = (strike difference × 100) − net debit	$1,875
Breakeven = long strike price − net debit	$23.75
Return on investment = profit/risk	300%

---

and then subtracting the net debit. This trade offers a maximum profit of $1,875, a 300 percent return on investment: [5 × (25 − 20) × 100] − $625 = $625.

To calculate the breakeven for a bear put spread, you simply subtract the net debit divided by the number of contracts divided by 100 from the higher strike price. The breakeven for this trade is 23.75 [25 − (625/5 ÷ 100) = 23.75]. HOV must drop below $23.75 to start making a profit—just slightly lower than the current market price at the trade's initiation. This trade has two months until expiration—plenty of time for the trade to move in-the-money. The risk profile for this example is shown in Figure 6.2.

The best way to exit a bear put spread is for the underlying market to move below the strike price of the short option in hopes that the short put will be assigned. You will then have to purchase the underlying stock from the option holder at the lower short put strike price and, by exercising your long put, sell it at the higher price to garner the maximum profit. In this example, HOV has been falling precipitously, as expected, and is trading near $17.50 a share by mid-July. Both contracts are now deep in-the-money and the spread can be closed for a credit, which will probably be close to $5.00

---

rule of thumb
buy the puts at-the-money and sell the puts out-of-the-money. Look for markets that are trending down or have reached 52-week lows; then check the fundamentals (look a little deeper; when a company goes down it happens quickly). Make sure you have at least 45 days or more until expiration.

figure 6.2   **bear put spread (long 5 July 25 puts @ 1.50, short 5 July 20 puts @ 0.25)**

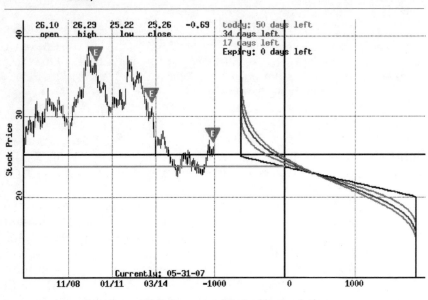

26.10   26.29   25.22   25.26   −0.69   today: 50 days left
open   high   low   close   34 days left
17 days left
Expiry: 0 days left

Currently: 05-31-07

source: www.optionetics.com/platinum, reprinted with permission.

per spread (see Table 6.8). Or, as noted earlier, the strategist can anticipate assignment and then cover with the exercise of the long put. This should yield the maximum profit from the spread, minus commissions. However, make sure your broker is on the same page with a phone call or an e-mail. In other words, once you get the assignment notice, inform the brokerage firm to exercise your long put in order to honor the assignment.

table 6.8   **bear put spread results**

Long 5 July 25 Puts @ 1.50, Short 5 July 20 Puts @ .25

Debit at Initiation	Days in Trade	Credit at Exit	Profit/Loss	Return on Investment
$625	50	$2,400	$1,775	284%

bull put spread

A bull put spread is a credit spread created by purchasing a lower strike put and selling a higher strike put on a one-to-one basis. It is called a *credit spread* because the put with the higher strike price will bring in more premium when compared to the cost of the put option with the lower strike. The result is a net credit. In any case, both options have the same expiration date. This strategy is implemented in a bullish market when prices are expected to rise. Like the debit spreads, the bull put spread provides limited profit potential and limited downside risk. The profit on this strategy can increase by as much as one point for each one-point increase in the price of the underlying asset. However, the total investment is usually far less than the amount required to buy the stock outright.

Since a bull put spread makes the maximum profit when the short put expires worthless, options with 60 days or less give the underlying stock less time to move into a position where the short put will be assigned; 45 days or less is even better. In the best scenario, the underlying stock moves and stays above the higher strike price by expiration. Like selling puts, the goal is to see time decay eat away at the options contract. However, unlike selling naked puts, there is a hedge, namely, the long put is protecting the trader from a big drop in the stock price. Let's consider an example using the same options discussed in Chapter 5 in the short put sale on RIMM. Table 6.9 gives us the fundamentals.

---

bull put spread
a credit spread involving the sale of a higher strike put and the purchase of a lower strike put with the same expiration date—a bullish strategy with limited risk and limited reward.

---

table 6.9   research in motion fundamentals

Research in Motion	
Last price	$118.16
Volume	16,000,000
52-week range	$42.93 to $137.01
P/E ratio	51.21

table 6.10   put option premiums with RIMM @ 118.16

Price of RIMM = 118.16 (4/9/08)

Put Strike Price	April	May	June
100	0.15	1.00	4.20
110	1.00	4.60	7.50
120	4.60	10.00	11.85
130	12.30	15.00	17.85

Using the option premiums in Table 6.10, let's create a bull put spread using the RIMM May 120 and May 100 puts. To be specific, let's sell one May 120 put for $10 per contract and hedge that bet by purchasing a May 100 put for $1.00. The net result is a credit in the account equal to $9.00 per spread, or $900 for one bull put spread.

In this example, RIMM is near $118 and therefore both the short and the long puts are out-of-the-money. The profit on this trade depends on both puts expiring worthless at expiration. So RIMM needs to rise above $120 a share between now and the third Friday in May. Since the stock's 52-week range is $42.31 to $137.01, this certainly is not a difficult feat in a bullish market. In other words, the stock is clearly capable of making big moves and, since it is already at $118.16, a move to $120, or less than 2 percent, is clearly a reasonable expectation. Since the trade clearly has a bullish bias, the stock is expected to move higher and not lower.

To exit this trade with a profit, RIMM would need to close at $120 or more on the third Friday in May. If so, all options expire worthless and the strategist keeps the premium of $950 earned from selling the spread (Table 6.11). The maximum profit is limited to the net credit received on the trade, or $950 [(10.5 − 1) × 100 = $950]. The maximum risk is calculated by multiplying the difference in strikes

table 6.11   bull put spread trade calculations

Bull Put Spread Using RIMM @ 118.16

Maximum risk = (strike difference × 100) − net credit	$1,050
Maximum reward = net credit	$950
Breakeven = short strike price − net credit	110.50
Return on investment = reward/risk	90%

figure 6.3   bull put spread (long 1 May RIMM 100 put @ 1.00, short 1 May RIMM 110 put @ 10.50)

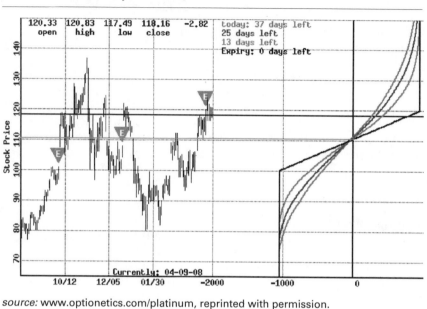

source: www.optionetics.com/platinum, reprinted with permission.

times the value per point and then subtracting the net credit. The maximum risk of this trade is $1,050 {[(120 − 100) × 100] − $950 = $1,050}.

The breakeven of a bull put spread is calculated by subtracting the net credit divided by 100 from the higher strike put. In this example, the breakeven is 110.50 [120 − (950 ÷ 100) = 110.50]. This trade makes a profit when RIMM stays above 110.50. Its risk profile is shown in Figure 6.3.

After 37 days, RIMM is well above $120 a contract and both puts are now well out-of-the-money. The strategist can do nothing and lets the options expire. Importantly, however, the last day to trade the options is the Friday before expiration. News on Friday afternoon can cause the stock to move in the after-hours trading session. Consequently, bad news could potentially send the stock reeling Friday afternoon and, if so, the strategist could face the unpleasant news that the short put has been assigned during Saturday's options expiration. For that reason, even when the credit spread is deep out-of-the-money, it makes sense to close it out on Friday rather than

table 6.12 RIMM bull put spread results

Long 1 RIMM May 100 Put @ 1.00, Short 1 RIMM May 110 Put @ 10.50

Credit at Initiation	Stock Price at Initiation	Stock Price at Exit	Days in Trade	Profit
$950	$118.16	$120+	37	$940

simply let the options expire. Assuming that the OTM puts are closed for a nickel each on the day before expiration, Table 6.12 summarizes the results.

> **rule of thumb**
> a bull put spread is a credit spread in which the profit depends on the underlying stock remaining above the strike of the short put so that the options expire worthless. Look for a wide range between premiums and use options with fewer than 45 days until expiration.

bear call spread

A bear call spread is a credit spread created by purchasing a higher strike call and selling a lower strike call on a one-to-one basis. Once again, both options have the same expiration date. As the name implies, this strategy is appropriate in a bearish market and when the price of the underlying asset is expected to fall. Like the bull put spread, the bear call spread has both limited profit potential and limited downside risk. Profit increases as the underlying asset falls below the strike price of the lower strike short call.

> **bear call spread**
> a credit spread involving the sale of a lower strike call and the purchase of a higher strike call with the same expiration date—a bearish strategy with limited risk and limited reward.

table 6.13   PHLX gold and silver mining index fundamentals

PHLX Gold Index ($XAU)	
Last price	192.27
Number of components	12
52-week range	$120.41 to $209.27

When I was fishing for a bearish market, the PHLX Gold and Silver Mining Index ($XAU) displayed an interesting chart The index, which was mentioned in Chapter 2, tracks the performance of a dozen gold and silver mining companies. It is very sensitive to the price of gold, and in March 2008, gold prices looked to be at historically high levels as economic growth slowed and fears of inflation subsided.Is there a way to profit from this view about the macroeconomic outlook? Indeed there is. Let's create a bear call spread using the XAU. Table 6.13 provides the fundamentals of the index, and Table 6.14 details various call option premiums.

Remember that a credit spread's success depends on the short option losing value and possibly expiring worthless at expiration. Therefore, it's best to focus on options with less than 60 days until expiration. In addition, since the short call must expire worthless, it's best to choose a short strike price that the underlying stock has a low probability of reaching.

In this case, the XAU is at 192.27 and we don't expect it to return to its previous highs of more than 200 (see Figure 6.4). So we create a

table 6.14   call option premiums with XAU @ 192.27

Price of XAU = 192.27 (3/18/08)			
Put Strike Price	March	April	May
180	13.50	19.50	22.30
190	9.00	13.10	17.50
200	1.00	8.00	12.50
210	0.30	5.30	9.50
220	0.05	3.00	5.00

figure 6.4   bear call spread (long 1 May XAU 220 call @ 5.00, short 1 May XAU 200 call @ 12.50)

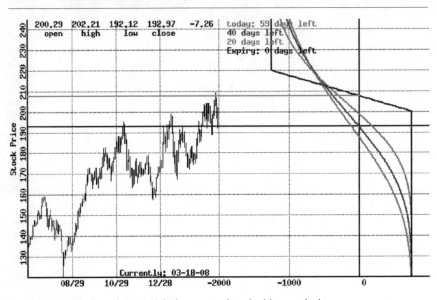

source: www.optionetics.com/platinum, reprinted with permission.

bear call spread by going long one May XAU 200 call @ 5.0 and short one May XAU 220 call @ 12.50. The options have 59 days of life left.

The maximum profit on a bear call spread is limited to the net credit received on the trade. In this example, the maximum profit is $750 [(12.50 − 5) × 100 = $750]. (See Table 6.15.) The maximum risk is calculated by multiplying the difference in strikes by the value per point and then subtracting the net credit. This trade's maximum risk is $1,250 {[(220 − 200) × 100] − $750 = $1,250}.

table 6.15   bear call spread trade calculations

Bear Call Spread Using XAU @ 192.27

Maximum risk = (strike difference × 100) − net credit	$1,250
Maximum reward = net credit	$750
Breakeven = short strike price + net credit	207.50
Return on investment = reward/risk	60%

---

table 6.16 bear call spread results

Long 1 May XAU 220 Call @ 5.00, Short 1 May XAU 200 Call @ 12.50

Credit at Initiation	Price at Entry	Stock Price at Exit	Days in Trade	Profit
$750	192.97	200 or less	58	$730

The breakeven for a bear call spread is calculated by adding the net credit divided by 100 to the lower strike call. This trade breaks even at 207.50 [200 + (750 ÷ 100) = 207.50]. For this trade to make a profit, the PHLX Gold and Silver Mining Index must stay below 207.50. Figure 6.4 shows the risk profile for this example.

When the options expire on the Saturday following the third Friday of May, XAU is trading well below 200. Letting the options expire worthless enables the trade to keep the maximum profit of $750 received at the trade's initiation. (See Table 6.16.) Since the index dropped below the short strike and stayed there until expiration, the short 200 option was not in danger of being assigned. Importantly, if XAU had risen above 200 and the short option had received notice of assignment, the strategist would have had to deliver cash equal to the difference between the strike price of the options and the value of the index.

Additionally, the XAU is one of a handful of indexes that settles American-style, which means that assignment can also occur before the options expiration. For that reason, when the calls are out-of-the-money and the spread has a nice profit as expiration approaches, it makes sense to bank the profit rather than run the risk of seeing a reversal and facing the risk of assignment at or near expiration. Assuming both contracts were closed out for a dime apiece, the result of the trade is detailed in Table 6.16.

---

rule of thumb
look for a moderately bearish market—the smaller the spread, the lower the risk. Use options with fewer than 45 days until expiration with a wide premium range to enhance limited profits.

conclusion

Vertical spreads are best used when moderate price action is the forecast. Once you have discovered a directional trend, play around with a couple of strategies and various strike prices and expiration dates to find the trade with the best probability of profitability. The key is to find option premiums that create high potential reward without risking an arm and a leg. Since adjustments cannot be made to increase profits once the trade is placed, traders should determine their exit strategy in advance.

These strategies are quite popular because many trades can be placed without risking more than $500. In addition, as you are learning these strategies, try to keep the difference between strikes relatively small. You may want to place two contracts at a time and then exit one contract when you reach 50 percent of the maximum reward. The other contract becomes a free trade and you can try to make a higher profit by letting it ride.

You can practice this strategy by studying market movement and paper trading markets that seem appropriate. A paper trade is a hypothetical position using real prices for the benefit of learning how a strategy works. Once you have initiated a paper trade, you can study how the passage of time and price movement affect the trade firsthand.

Many online financial research sites and brokerages offer portfolio services to make this process of paper trading easier than ever before. Many of them will e-mail you automatic updates using end-of-day prices. In addition, pay close attention to how to exit these strategies and keep notes on your successes and failures. Any fictitious losses can be chalked up to experience rather than costing out-of-pocket cash, and all winning trades will inspire confidence. As you become familiar with these strategies, using a computer to help you make your next decision will become second nature.

chapter 7

delta neutral strategies

introducing delta neutral trading

Greed and fear are often at work in the financial markets, creating aggressive buying and selling, and triggering periods of mind-boggling volatility. These two emotions can spread like wildfire as markets soar to new highs or plunge into hopelessness and despair.

To avoid getting caught up in these emotion-driven markets, experienced traders rely on trading plans. Part of the plan is to know when to enter a trade and when to exit. These parameters are set out before the trade is ever created. Another part of a sound long-term plan is to develop an arsenal of different strategies that work in a variety of different markets, including the ones that turn out to be very volatile and chaotic.

Delta neutral trading is a powerful approach that can help traders make money regardless of which way the underlying asset moves. But what is the delta of an option? *Delta* is a Greek letter used in options to indicate the price sensitivity of an option's premium with respect to a $1.00 change in the price of the underlying stock.

For example, a call option with a delta of +.50 would have risen $.50 as a result of a $1.00 rise in the price of the underlying stock. Hence, a delta neutral trade is composed of trading instruments with a combined position delta of zero (i.e., the sum of all the deltas of the instruments in the strategy has a net position of zero). A stock has a fixed delta; no matter how the price of the stock fluctuates, a stock's delta never changes. For example, buying 100 shares of stock has a fixed delta of +100 while selling 100 shares has a fixed delta of −100. In contrast, a variable delta changes as the price of the underlying stock moves. All options have variable deltas. The combination of fixed and variable deltas can create trades that offer traders profit potentials in both directions.

option greeks
a set of measurements that explore the risk exposures of a specific trade. Options and other trading instruments have a variety of risk exposures that can vary dramatically over time or as markets move. Each risk measurement is named after a different letter in the Greek alphabet.

delta
the change in the price of an option relative to the change of the underlying security.

delta neutral
a combination option/options or option/stock trade in which the sum of all the deltas equals zero. Delta neutral trades have the capacity to make money regardless of market direction.

Another way to think of an option delta is the degree of probability that an option will close in-the-money (ITM) by expiration. An at-the-money (ATM) option has a 50-50 chance of closing in-the-money. Therefore, an ATM option has a delta of plus or minus 0.50.

An out-of-the-money (OTM) option has a lower probability of closing in-the-money; therefore, OTM options have delta values lower than 0.50. An ITM option has a greater than 50 percent chance of closing in-the-money and therefore boasts a delta greater than 0.50. As options go deeper and deeper in-the-money, their deltas approach 1.00 and they begin to act more like the underlying stock.

To facilitate delta neutral trading, it is essential to be well acquainted with the deltas of options and how they change. In general, the following rules always apply to delta neutral trading:

- Buying stock or calls creates a positive delta.
- Selling stock or calls creates a negative delta.
- Buying puts creates a negative delta.
- Selling puts creates a positive delta.

at-the-money
when the strike price of an option is the same as the current price of the underlying instrument.

out-of-the-money
a call option is out-of-money when its strike price is above the current market price of the underlying asset. A put option is out-of-the-money when its strike price is below the current market price of the underlying asset. An out-of-the-money option has no intrinsic value and expires worthless.

in-the-money
a call option is in-the-money when its strike price is less than the current market price of the underlying asset. A put option is in-the-money when its strike price is greater than the market price of the underlying asset. If you were to exercise an in-the-money option, it would generate a profit.

Delta neutral trading involves combining stocks with options, or options with options, in such a way that the sum of all the deltas in the trade equals zero. A zero position delta enables a trade to make money within a certain range of prices regardless of market direction; as the price of the underlying stock moves, the overall delta changes. Before placing a trade, the upside and downside breakevens must be calculated to gauge the trade's profit range. A trader also needs to calculate the maximum potential profit and loss in order to assess the viability of the trade. In some cases, additional profits can be made by adjusting the trade back to delta neutral through buying or selling more options or shares of stock.

---

zero position delta
the sum total of all deltas in a combination trade equal zero—the trade is delta neutral.

Matching the right strategy to the right set of circumstances takes training, skill, and practical experience. The strategies examined in this chapter are based on the more basic option strategies explained in Chapter 5. For example, we will see that a straddle is simply the combination of a long put and a long call. However, while the straddle is a great strategy, market conditions will dictate whether it is an appropriate strategy at any given time. In short, by studying the examples in this chapter closely, you will be well on your way to a successful delta neutral trading career.

volatility

Volatility is a complex and often misunderstood concept. Mathematically, volatility is defined as a statistical measurement of a stock's price change (regardless of direction), represented by a percentage. We prefer to think of it as the speed of change in a market. A stable market moves slowly, but a volatile market is fast. An option has a better chance of ending up in-the-money in a high-volatility market. For that reason, options on assets with high volatility will have higher premiums than those assets that have lower levels of volatility.

> **volatility**
> the amount by which an underlying instrument is expected to fluctuate in a given period of time. Options often increase in price when there is a rise in volatility even if the price of the underlying doesn't change.

To take it a step further, options traders generally look at two different kinds of volatility: *historical* volatility and *implied* volatility. Historical volatility (sometimes called *statistical* volatility) is based on a stock's past price action during a specific time period. It can be calculated by using the standard deviation of a stock's price changes from close to close of trading, going back a specific number of days (10, 20, 100, and so on).

Implied volatility, by contrast, is a computed value that measures the underlying asset's volatility based on the prevailing option premiums. That is, it takes the value of an option and, using an options pricing model, reflects the current level of volatility that is implied by that option's price. Although it is computed using a model, many web sites and brokerage firms offer implied volatility data.

Many more experienced traders compare the current market price of an options contract to its fair value. The *fair* value of an option is calculated by entering the historical volatility of the underlying asset into an options pricing model. The computed fair value may differ from the actual market price of the option. Implied volatility is the volatility needed to achieve the option's actual market price. In basic terms, historical volatility gauges price movement in terms of past performance and implied volatility approximates how much the marketplace thinks prices will move.

Both kinds of volatility are valuable tools for finding profitable trading opportunities. A stock's historical volatility is often significantly impacted by scheduled and breaking news, including unexpected earnings, management reorganizations, newly released products and services, and news regarding industry competitors.

Implied volatility is very cyclical—it tends to move back and forth within a given range. It can also act as a guide to avoiding the purchase of overpriced options and the sale of underpriced options. Many great trades have been found online by searching for an abnormality in the price of an option compared to the movement of the underlying stock. An abnormality is created when the market price of an option increases without a change in the price of the underlying stock. This situation triggers an increase in the implied volatility of the option. When the theoretical option price and the current market price differ significantly, an abnormality occurs, causing the overpricing or undervaluing of an option's premium.

To determine whether an option is undervalued or overpriced, you can calculate 20-day or 90-day volatility ratios. The 20-day volatility ratio is calculated by dividing 1-day implied volatility by 20-day statistical volatility. The 90-day volatility ratio is calculated by dividing 1-day implied volatility by 90-day statistical volatility. If the implied volatility of a stock's options moves below or above the actual statistical volatility of the stock, it may create a *volatility crush*.

When implied volatility moves above statistical volatility, a high-volatility ratio is created. If this condition arises in a stock you are tracking, it is safe to assume that the options are overvalued. In this scenario, if the price of a stock increases but the implied volatility of the option decreases, you may lose money even though the stock moved in your favor. This is a sign to sell options. If implied volatility falls below statistical volatility, the volatility ratios are low and the options are likewise undervalued. If the price of the stock falls and the implied volatility increases, option premiums will increase. This is a good time to buy options.

Option traders must learn to integrate the use of implied and statistical volatility ratios into finding optimal trading opportunities. If you locate a stock with underpriced options, you may want to try placing a long straddle. In contrast, a stock with overvalued options may be ripe for a short straddle. Specific volatility scenarios can also be used to implement ratio spread and ratio backspread strategies (see Chapter 8). At first, volatility may seem complex, but it's well worth your while to get comfortable using it because it can alert you to profitable markets.

rule of thumb
buy underpriced options during periods of low volatility; sell overpriced options during periods of high volatility.

long straddle

A long straddle is a nondirectional trading strategy that involves buying both a call and a put with identical strike prices and expiration dates. *Nondirectional* simply means that the strategist isn't anticipating or betting that the stock or market will move in one direction. Instead, the straddle is best placed in a market with low volatility where a sharp volatility increase is anticipated. Keep in mind that a straddle can be quite expensive because the strategist is buying both put and call premiums. However, the maximum risk is limited to the net debit of the double premiums and there is no need to worry about margin requirements. Nevertheless, since the strategist needs to make enough profit to cover the double premiums, this strategy requires the underlying stock price to move sharply in either direction beyond the breakevens by anticipating a period of increased volatility.

Let's create a long straddle using BiogenIdec (BIIB), a leading biotechnology company with a historically volatile share price (Table 7.1). Since a long straddle involves buying options, it is best to use options with 60 days or more until expiration to give the trade enough time to move into the trade's profit range. In the case of BIIB, the stock is trading for $79.29 and has a wide 52-week range between $43.16 and $84.75.

It is October 16, 2007, and the stock has made a big gap higher (see Figure 7.1). Volatility is picking up and is expected to continue rising. The direction that the stock is going to move, however, is unknown. So let's create a long straddle position by going long one BIIB January 80 call @ $6.00 a contract and long one BIIB January 80 put @ $5.75 (from Table 7.2). This is very close to delta neutral because a long ATM call has a delta of +0.52 and a long ATM put has a delta of −0.48, thereby creating a net delta of +0.04, or almost zero.

The maximum risk of a long straddle is equal to the net debit of the trade (Table 7.3). In this example, the maximum risk is the net debit of $1,175 [($6.00 + $5.75) × 100 = $1,175]. Since the maximum

table 7.1   biogenidec quick facts

BiogenIdec (BIIB)	
Last price	$79.29
Volume	2,709,600
52-week range	$43.16 to $84.75

figure 7.1 **long straddle (long 1 BIIB January 80 call @ $5.75, long 1 BIIB January 80 put @ $6.00)**

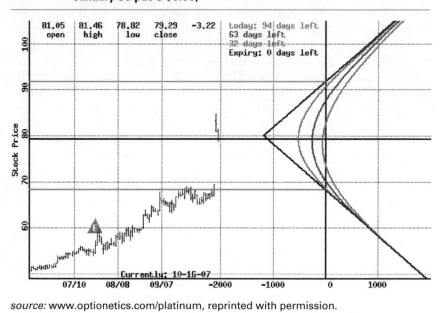

source: www.optionetics.com/platinum, reprinted with permission.

profit is unlimited in both directions, a long straddle's range of profitability is determined by deriving the upside and the downside breakevens. The upside breakeven at expiration is simply the strike price of the options, plus the net debit (per contract), or $91.75 ($80 + $5.75 + $6.00 = $91.75). The downside breakeven is the strike price minus the debit, or $68.25 ($80 − $11.75 = $68.25).

table 7.2 **option premiums for BIIB @ 79.29**

Price of BIIB = $79.29 (10/16/07)

Expiration Date	Call Premium	Put Premium
January 70	12.00	2.10
January 80	6.00	5.75
January 90	2.00	12.00

---

table 7.3   long straddle trade calculations

Long Straddle Using BiogenIdec @ $79.79

Maximum risk = net debit	$1,175
Maximum reward = Unlimited above and below breakeven	Unlimited
Downside breakeven = long strike price − net debit	$68.25
Upside breakeven = long strike price + net debit	$91.75

Therefore, BIIB has to move above 91.75 or below 68.25 for this trade to make a profit at expiration. However, if it makes a sudden move higher shortly after the trade is initiated, then profits can develop sooner—the faster the move, the better. If it makes a substantial move higher or lower over the following few days or weeks, the strategist can often close out the winning side and simply hold the losing side or close it out for a loss.

> **long straddle strategy**
> a delta neutral options strategy that is best placed in a highly volatile market and involves the simultaneous purchase of equal numbers of ATM puts and calls with the same expiration date.

Figure 7.1 shows the risk profile of this trade. As previously defined, a long straddle is the purchase of a call and a put with the same strike price and the same expiration date. Since risk profiles are combinations of other risk curves, a long straddle's risk profile is the combination of a call and a put risk curve. Together they create a U-shaped curve, which signals limited risk and unlimited profit potentials beyond the breakevens.

Two months later, BiogenIdec has fallen back below $56 a share. Assuming that the trade is closed when the stock is at that level, the put can be sold for $24 a contract; the profit from that side of the trade is $18.25 per contract. A 100 percent loss occurred on the calls because nobody is willing to buy those January 80 calls when BIIB is down at $56. So we subtract $6.00 per contract from the profit, and the total gain is $12.25 per straddle, or $1,225 (Table 7.4).

When looking for a market that is appropriate for placing a long straddle, it is imperative to seek markets with the capacity to make big moves. Look for stocks that are listed in the daily percentage

table 7.4   long straddle spread results

Long 1 January BIIB 80 Call @ $5.75, Long 1 January BIIB 80 Put @ $6.00

Debit at Initiation	Call Price at Exit	Put Price at Exit	Days in Trade	Profit/Loss	Return on Investment
$1,175	$0	$24	60	$1,225	104.25%

winners and losers on web sites like MarketWatch, the interactive *Wall Street Journal*, or *Investor's Business Daily* (see Chapter 3). Most likely you'll find the press will be talking them up, as well as the chat rooms. Then check the fundamentals and find out what's going on with the company. If you understand the fundamentals, it might give you more confidence to stick with the trade if the stock doesn't make a big move right off the bat.

---

rule of thumb
look for markets that have the capacity to make large moves in either direction with 60 days or more until expiration.

---

short straddle

A short straddle involves selling a put and a call with identical ATM strike prices and expiration months. This strategy is attractive to the aggressive strategist who is interested in selling large amounts of time premium in hopes of collecting all or most of this premium as profit if the underlying stock remains fairly stable. This is a higher-risk strategy than the long straddle because both options are uncovered. I do not suggest that any trader ever place a short straddle that is uncovered, but there are methods that can be utilized to substantially reduce the risks associated with this strategy.

---

short straddle strategy
a delta neutral options strategy that is best placed in a stable market and involves the simultaneous sale of the same number of ATM puts and calls with the same expiration date.

**table 7.5 select sector technology
quick facts**

Select Sector Tech Fund (XLK)

Last price	$22.58
Volume	5,670,000
52-week range	$22.84 to $28.39

Let's create a short straddle using the Select Sector Technology Fund (XLK). This exchange-traded fund holds all of the technology companies from the S&P 500 (Table 7.5). It makes sense, if you really want to sell straddles, to do it on an exchange-trade fund (ETF). It is very unlikely that an ETF will make a one-day 30 or 50 percent move higher or lower, which is certainly possible when dealing with individual stocks. In any event, Table 7.6 lists some quick facts about the XLK. It is very actively traded and currently has a relatively narrow 52-week range between $22.84 and $28.39 per share.

Since a short straddle involves the selling of options, it is best to use options with less than 45 days till expiration. In this case, it is early February and we are looking at the options that expire in 44 days, or in March (see Table 7.6). Let's create a short straddle by selling three XLK March 23 calls @ $0.75 and also shorting three XLK March 23 puts for $1.30. The maximum reward for this trade is limited to the net credit, or $615. The maximum risk is unlimited to the upside and downside beyond the breakevens, which makes this trade potentially dangerous. This trade will require a substantial margin deposit to place.

---

table 7.6 select sector technology option premiums

Price of XLK = $22.58 (2/5/08)

Expiration Date	Call Premium	Put Premium
March 21	2.00	0.40
March 22	1.30	0.70
March 23	0.75	1.30
March 24	0.35	1.85

---

figure 7.2   short straddle (short 3 XLK March 23 calls @ 0.75, short 3 XLK March MSFT 23 puts @ 1.30)

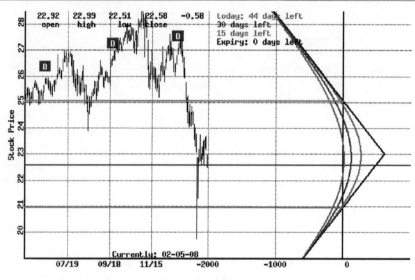

source: www.optionetics.com/platinum, reprinted with permission.

The risk profile for a short straddle combines a short call and a short put to create an upside-down U-shaped curve. This clues us in to the fact that short straddles have limited profit potential and unlimited risk. The risk profile for this trade is shown in Figure 7.2. Notice that, since the strike prices are not exactly at-the-money, this trade has a bias. That is, it will make better profits if the share price moves higher. Specifically, if XLK rallies from $22.58 to exactly $23 a share, both the puts and the calls expire worthless.

When you sell straddles, it is extremely important to calculate the profit range to determine the point at which potential losses begin (see Table 7.7). The upside breakeven occurs when the underlying asset's price equals the strike price plus the net credit per straddle. In this example, the upside breakeven is $25.05 (23 + 1.30 + 0.75 = 25.05). The downside breakeven occurs when the underlying asset's price equals the strike price minus the net credit per straddle. In this case, the downside breakeven equals $20.95 (23 − 2.05 = 20.95). In sum, the Select Sector Technology Fund must remain stable and move in a range between $20.95 and $25.05 per share for this trade to remain profitable. Although at expiration only one side can be

table 7.7   short straddle trade calculations

Short Straddle Using XLK @ $22.58

Maximum risk = Unlimited above and below breakeven	Unlimited upside; limited to stock falling to zero on the downside.
Maximum reward = Net credit	$615
Downside breakeven = Long strike price − net debit	$20.95
Upside breakeven = Long strike price + net debit	$25.05

wrong, the options also run the risk of being assigned if they move too far in-the-money. Since short straddles offer unlimited risk, it is vital to keep a close watch on the market and move quickly at the first sign of trouble.

By expiration on the Saturday after the third Friday of March, the Select Sector Technology Fund is priced at $22.39 a share (Table 7.8). The short put is $.61 in-the-money and the short call is out-of-the-money. At expiration, the three short puts will be assigned to the straddle seller, who will be required to buy 300 shares at $23 apiece. However, the seller sold those puts for $1.30 and also sold calls for $.75. Therefore, the net profit relies on the gain from the puts (assuming the assigned shares are sold in the market for the market price of $22.39) of $1.30 minus $.61 plus the profit from the calls, or $1.44 per straddle. For three straddles, the profit is $432: $[1.30 − (23 − 22.39) + .75] \times 3 \times 100$.

Obviously, the most advantageous price at which the market could have settled would have been the strike price at 23. All of the options would expire worthless and the trader would get to keep the net credit. Before placing a trade, you have to assess just how likely it is for a market to close on the exact strike price of your short options. Review past price action by checking a stock's historical

table 7.8   short straddle results

Short 3 XLK March 23 Calls @ .75, Short 3 XLK March MSFT 23 Puts @ 1.30

Credit at Initiation	Stock Price at Initiation	Stock Price at Exit	Days in Trade	Profit/Loss
$615	$22.58	$22.39	44	$432

table 7.9 biogenldec option premiums		
Price of BIIB = $79.29 (10/16/07)		
Expiration Date	Call Premium	Put Premium
January 70	12.00	2.10
January 80	6.00	5.75
January 90	2.00	12.00

prices. Shorting straddles is a risky trade unless you find markets that are not likely to move away from a centerline.

---

rule of thumb
look for stable markets and use options with 45 days or less until expiration and with enough premium to make the trade worthwhile.

---

long strangle   A strangle is similar to a straddle, except OTM options are used instead of ATM options. A long strangle is created by purchasing an OTM call and an OTM put with the same expiration month (see Table 7.9). There are both drawbacks and advantages to this strategy over straddles. A long strangle costs less than a straddle because OTM options are less expensive than ATM options. Unfortunately, long strangles also require the underlying stock to make even larger moves to make a profit.

---

long strangle strategy
a delta neutral options strategy that is best placed in an extremely volatile market and involves the simultaneous purchase of equal numbers of OTM puts and calls with the same expiration date.

Let's set up a long strangle using BiogenIdec by going long one BIIB January 90 call @ $2.00 and long one BIIB January 70 put @ $2.10 (see Table 7.10). The maximum risk of a long strangle is equal to the cost of the double option premiums. In this example, the maximum risk is $410 [($2.00 + $2.10) × 100 = $410]. Beyond the breakeven, the

table 7.10   long strangle trade calculations

Long Straddle Using Biogenldec @ $79.79

Maximum risk = Net credit	$410
Maximum reward = Unlimited above and below breakeven	Unlimited to the upside. Limited to the stock falling to zero on the downside.
Downside breakeven = Put strike price − net debit	$65.90
Upside breakeven = Call strike price + net debit	$94.10

maximum profit is unlimited to the upside and limited to the stock falling to zero to the downside. The upside breakeven occurs when the underlying asset equals the call strike price plus the net debit per strangle, or $94.10 (90 + $2.10 + $2.00). The downside breakeven occurs when the underlying asset equals the put strike price minus the net debit per strangle (70 − $4.10 = $65.90).

Figure 7.3 shows the risk profile for this trade. Once again, we see a U-shaped risk curve indicating a trade with unlimited profit

figure 7.3   long strangle (long 1 BIIB January 90 call @ $2.00, long 1 BIIB January 70 put @ $2.10)

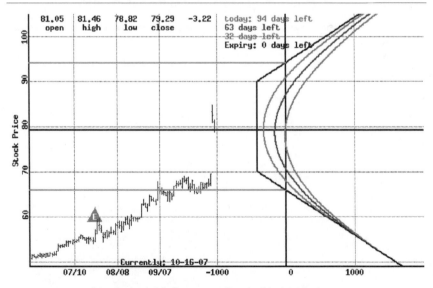

source: www.optionetics.com/platinum, reprinted with permission.

potential and limited risk. Profit depends on a large move in the underlying stock. In this example, the stock must be lower than $65.90 or higher than $94.10 at expiration to yield a profit. However, as with the straddle, if the stock makes a significant move in the near term, profits can begin to accumulate sooner. In fact, we don't recommend holding straddles or strangles until expiration because that period (the last 30 days) is when the options suffer the fastest rate of time decay.

To exit a long strangle, you have to sell options with the identical strike prices and expiration dates. As we saw in the straddle example, BIIB fell below $56 per contract by mid-December. At that time, the January 70 put has intrinsic value of at least $14 per contract. Recall that the strangle cost $4.10. The January 90 call will be worthless, but by selling the put, the strategist banks a $9.90 profit (minus commissions and slippage). Table 7.11 shows the results. Notice that while the straddle produced greater profits ($1,225), the percentage return on the strangle is higher. Always keep in mind, however, that the breakevens are much wider for the strangle compared to the straddle.

> **rule of thumb**
> look for a high-volatility market with the capacity to make a very large move using options with at least 45 days until expiration.

short strangle

Shorting an OTM call and an OTM put with the same expiration date creates a short strangle. Short strangles are profitable only in stable markets that continue to trade between the breakevens of the trade.

table 7.11   long strangle results

Long 1 BIIB January 90 Call @ $2.00, Long 1 BIIB January 70 Put @ $2.10

Debit at Initiation	Call Price at Exit	Put Price at Exit	Days in Trade	Profit/Loss	Return on Investment
$410	$0	$14	0	$990	125%

Just like the short straddle, the short strangle's maximum profit is limited to the net credit received from the double option premium. However, short strangles have even more limited profit potential because the OTM options are less expensive than the premium of ATM options. Risk is thereby reduced accordingly.

---

short strangle strategy
a delta neutral options strategy that is best placed in a stable market and involves the simultaneous sale of the same number of OTM puts and calls with the same expiration date.

Since the profit on a short strangle depends on the options expiring worthless, use options that do not have a lot of time until expiration. Let's use the Select Sector Technology Fund, which we also considered in the discussion about short straddles.

This time, instead of shorting the March 23 puts and calls, we short three XLK March 23 calls @ $.75, and short three XLK March 22 puts @ $.70. (See Table 7.12.) Both contracts are out-of-the-money. The maximum reward is limited to the net credit of the option premiums, or $435 [3 × (.75 + .70) × 100 = $435]. The maximum risk is unlimited in both directions beyond the breakevens. The upside breakeven occurs when the underlying equals the call strike price plus the net credit per strangle. In this example, the upside breakeven is equal to $24.45 (23 + 1.45 = 24.45). To calculate the downside breakeven, subtract the net credit per strangle from the put strike

---

table 7.12   option premiums with Select Sector Technology Fund @ 22.58

Price of XLK = $22.58 (2/5/08)

Expiration Date	Call Premium	Put Premium
March 21	2.00	0.40
March 22	1.30	0.70
March 23	0.75	1.30
March 24	0.35	1.85

table 7.13   short strangle trade calculations

Short Strangle Using XLK @ $22.58

Maximum risk = Unlimited above and below breakeven	Unlimited upside; limited to stock falling to zero on the downside.
Maximum reward = Net credit	$435
Downside breakeven = Put strike price – net debit	$20.55
Upside breakeven = Call strike price + net debit	$24.45

price. In this trade, the downside breakeven is equal to 20.55 [22 – 1.45 = 20.55]. XLK has to stay between $20.55 and $24.55 for this trade to be profitable. (See Table 7.13.)   Figure 7.4 shows the risk profile of this trade.

On March 17, when these options expire, the XLK sits at $22.39 a share (see Table 7.14). Both options are out-of-the-money and expire

figure 7.4   short strangle (short 3 XLK March 23 calls @ $.75, short 3 March MSFT 22 puts @ $.70)

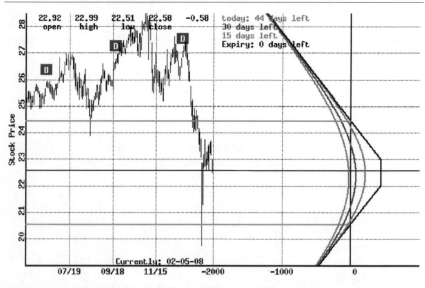

---

table 7.14   short strangle results

Short 3 XLK March 23 calls @ $.75, Short 3 March MSFT 22 Puts @ $.70

Credit at Initiation	Stock Price at Initiation	Stock Price at Exit	Days in Trade	Profit/Loss
$435	$22.58	$22.39	44	$435

worthless. In this case, the strategist can do nothing and lets the options expire. However, there is a risk in doing nothing. For example, if some news comes out after the close of trading Friday, which is the last day to trade the XLK March puts and calls, shares can make an adverse move in the after-hours market and the strategist can face assignment Saturday morning. For that reason, some traders prefer to buy back the contracts to close, even if they are quoted for only a few pennies or a nickel.

rule of thumb
look for a wildly volatile market where you anticipate a drop-off into a very stable market with low volatility. Look for overpriced options with less than 45 days until expiration.

conclusion

Delta neutral trades offer a divergence from traditional directional strategies. I usually allow the cost of the trades to inspire me to choose one position over another. Some brokerages simply do not allow their clients to short the market using uncovered options. Others require expensive margin deposits of more than $50,000. Either way, it is imperative to execute paper trades before using real money in order to recognize the subtle dynamics of each strategy.

Options at different strikes will have different deltas and will change as the underlying security changes. The object of the game is to keep your trade as close to zero deltas as possible. When the next uptick changes the market you are trading, you are no longer neutral. You may be able to make an additional profit by making an adjustment by purchasing or selling options to get the trade back to delta neutral again. This is especially true of trades that use multiple contracts.

When you are trading delta neutral, it's a good idea to think of one side of your straddle as your hedge and the other side as your directional bet. If you are 100 percent wrong, you still can profit. It doesn't matter which way the trade goes because, theoretically, you are going to make a comparable amount on either side. When you start factoring in things like time decay and volatility, that figure may change. To find an appropriate market for a delta neutral trade, just surf the Net to a site that provides real-time or delayed quotes and see what you can find.

chapter 8

ratio spreads and backspreads

nondirectional spreads with a bias

The previous chapter explored straddles and strangles, nondirectional strategies that make money whether a stock makes a significant move higher or lower. The idea is to find a stock or market that is ready for an explosive move and then buy both puts and calls to profit from the increase in volatility. However, if the stock or market fails to move, losses can result due to the negative impact of time decay. Strangles are especially vulnerable to the effects of time decay as both the puts and calls are out of the money. They have no intrinsic value and consist only of time value.

In this chapter, let's explore a few more nondirectional strategies that involve both the purchase and the sale of options. These strategies can make money whether the market moves higher or lower, but they clearly have a bias. That is, they will make a lot more money if the market moves in a certain direction. For example, the call ratio backspread, one of our favorite longer-term strategies over the years, will make a lot more money if the stock moves higher rather than lower. However, as we will see, it is also possible to make profits using a call ratio backspread if the market moves to the downside.

introducing ratio spreads

Just as I don't recommend trading short straddles and short strangles, I don't particularly recommend call or put ratio spreads. However, I present them in this chapter for educational purposes and to help set the table for the discussion of ratio backspreads. Like the short straddles and strangles, ratio spreads carry a substantial amount of risk that just doesn't make sense for most individual traders. The backspreads, however, have a predetermined amount of risk and the potential for significant rewards when the market makes a substantial move higher (for a call ratio backspread) or lower (put ratio backspread).

ratio call spread

Unlike straddles and strangles that use an equal proportion of options on either side of a trade, ratio spreads offset an uneven number of different types of options with the same expiration. A ratio call spread involves buying a lower strike call option and selling a greater number of OTM higher strike call options with the same expiration date. This technique is also called a long ratio spread and can be thought of as a bull call spread with an extra short call (or two or three depending on the trade specifics). In general, it has an overall position delta of zero and is best placed in a bearish market. The maximum profit is realized when the market is at the higher strike price, but not above it, at expiration.

---

ratio spread
a strategy involving disproportionate numbers of puts and calls with the same expiration date to create a trade that offers limited risk and unlimited profit potential.

ratio call spread strategy
a bearish or stable strategy in which a trader buys two higher strike calls and sells a greater number of lower strike calls.

**table 8.1   semiconductor HOLDRS
quick facts**

Semiconductor HOLDRS (SMH)

Last Price	$27.91
Volume	7,538,500
52 Wk Range	$27.53 to $41.41

There are many different ways to set up a ratio call spread. For example, you can buy one OTM call option and sell two call options that are even further out-of-the-money. You can also use a different ratio than one-to-two. For instance, you might buy one ATM option and sell three OTM options. A ratio call spread is useful when a trader sees a slight rise in a market followed by a sell-off or a slight decline. If this trade is placed at a net credit, you have an increased chance of success. Unlimited risk exists to the upside due to the extra short calls, and therefore a large margin is required to place a trade using this strategy.

Referring to the quick facts for the Semiconductor HOLDRS (SMH) in Table 8.1, and using the values in Table 8.2, let's create a ratio call spread using SMH as our underlying security by going long one SMH May 25 call @ $4.00 and short three SMH May 35 calls @ $.50. The net debit of this trade is $250: $[(3 \times .50) - (1 \times 4)] \times 100 = -250$. The maximum profit of a ratio call spread is calculated by multiplying the number of long contracts times the difference in strike prices by the value per point, plus the net credit received

---

table 8.2   call premiums with SMH @ 27.91

Price of SMH = $27.91 (1/16/08)

Call Strike Price	April	May
22.5	5.50	5.90
25	3.20	4.00
27.5	1.40	2.30
30	0.40	1.50
32.5	0.10	0.75
35	0.05	0.50

---

table 8.3   ratio call spread trade calculations

Ratio Call Spread Using Semiconductor HOLDRS @ $27.91

Net debit = Net short call premium − net long call premium	$250
Maximum risk = Unlimited above upside breakeven	Unlimited
Maximum reward = (strike difference × 100) − net debit (or + net credit)	$750
Upside breakeven = {[# of short calls × (short call premium + short call strike price) − # of long calls × (long call premium + long call strike price)] / (# of short calls − # of long calls)}	$38.75
Downside breakeven = Lower strike price plus net debit	$27.50

(or minus the net debit). In this example, the maximum profit is equal to $750: $[1 \times (35 - 25) \times 100] - 250 = \$750$. (See Table 8.3.)

The maximum risk is unlimited to the upside above the breakeven. To calculate the upside breakeven of a ratio call spread, multiply the number of short calls times the sum of the short call premium plus the strike price of the short call, and then subtract the number of long calls times the sum of the premium plus the strike price of the long call. Finally, divide this number by the number of short calls minus the number of long calls. In this trade, the upside breakeven is equal to 38.75 $\{[3 \times (.5 + 35) - 1 \times (4 + 25)] / (3 - 1) = 38.75\}$. The risk to the downside is the debit. The downside breakeven is computed as the lower strike price plus the net debit, or $27.50 (25 + 2.50). At that point, the short calls expire worthless and the long call can be sold for $2.50 to recover the cost of the trade. The risk profile for this trade is found in Figure 8.1.

Closing this trade profitably has several possibilities depending on what happens in the underlying market. For this strategy to work well, the price of the underlying stock needs to rally sharply. The best profits occur at the strike price of the short call. In other words, if SMH is at $35 a share at expiration, the long call has intrinsic value of $10 and the short options expire worthless. Since the trade consists of one long call, the profit from the call equals $6. In addition, the strategist keeps the premium from selling three calls at $.50 each. So at $35 a share, the total profit is $600 plus $150, or $750.

In late April, SMH has rallied to $31.05 a share. The May 25 and May 35 calls, which have 17 days of life remaining, are quoted at $6.10 and $.02, respectively. At this point, the strategist might want to close out the position, as the options have very little time value remaining.

figure 8.1   **ratio call spread (long 1 SMH May 25 call @ 4,00, short 3 May 35 calls @ $.50)**

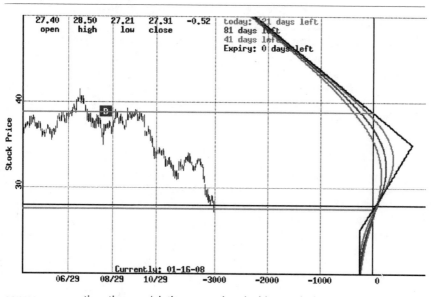

source: www.optionetics.com/platinum, reprinted with permission.

If so, the May 25 call produces a $2.10 profit and the May 35 calls can be bought to close for $.02, which equals a profit of $.48 per contact, or $144 for the three. The total profit is $354 (see Table 8.4).

---

rule of thumb
Look for highly volatile markets with a bearish bias and options with a forward volatility skew.

---

table 8.4   **ratio call spread results**

Long 1 SMH May 25 call @ $4.00, Short 3 May 35 calls @ $.50

Debit at Initiation	Days in Trade	Price of 25 Call	Price of 35 Call	Profit/Loss
$250	104	$6.10	$2.00	$354

ratio put spread

A ratio put spread can be implemented when a slight fall in the market is anticipated followed by a sharp rise. Although it resembles a bear put spread with an extra short put (or two or three), a ratio put spread should be implemented in a bullish market, preferably one with a reverse volatility skew. This strategy works well in the stock market, as stocks generally want to move up in price. However, it is important to place this trade only on stocks that are high-quality stocks. If the company has reported lower than expected earnings or bad news is released, exit the position.

---

ratio put spread strategy
a bullish or stable strategy in which a trader buys a higher strike put and sells a greater number of lower strike puts.

reverse volatility skew
markets in which lower strike options have high implied volatility and are therefore overpriced, and higher strike options have low implied volatility and are often underpriced.

A ratio put spread consists of going long a higher strike put and going short a greater number of OTM lower strike puts with the same expiration date. The maximum profit is realized when the market is at the lower strike, but not below that strike price at expiration. Note that the short options are not covered by long options, which is where the downside risk exists. For example, if you bought one and sold three, two of the short puts would be at risk. If you are doing an uneven number, you will have expensive margin requirements on the uncovered short options.

Table 8.5 displays some quick facts about ConocoPhillips (COP), a very actively traded energy company. COP's options have considerable activity day in and day out. The stock has been in a range between $71 and $91 a share over the past 52 weeks, but shares are expected to drift lower to $80. The stock is currently trading near $85.

Using the numbers in Table 8.6, let's create a ratio put spread by going long one COP January 95 put @ 10 and short three January 80 puts @ 1.50. The maximum profit of a ratio put spread is limited

---

table 8.5   conocophillips quick facts

ConocoPhillips (COP)

Last price	$85.56
Volume	10,747,600
52-week range	$71.18 to $90.84

---

to the number of long puts times the difference in strike prices times 100, plus the net credit (or minus the net debit). This example has a net debit of $550 [(10 − 3 × 1.5) × 100] and a maximum reward of $950: [(1 × 15) × 100 − $550] = $950. (See Table 8.7.)

The maximum risk is unlimited to the downside beyond the breakeven. However, in the worst-case scenario, the losses can be substantial. To be specific, if the stock falls to zero, the trade will see a considerable profit on the long 95 put, but big losses on the short puts. The downside breakeven is calculated by multiplying the number of short puts times the short put strike price minus the short put premium, and then subtracting the number of long puts times the long put strike price minus the long put premium. Then divide this number by the number of short puts minus the number of long puts. In this example, the downside breakeven is $75.25: [3 × (80 − 1.50) − 1 × (95 − 10)] / (3 − 1) = 75.25. The upside breakeven is the long put strike minus the net debit, or $89.50 (95 − 5.50). At that point, the short puts expire worthless, but the long put has a $5.50 profit, which offsets the cost of the trade. The risk graph for this trade is shown in Figure 8.2.

---

table 8.6   put premiums with COP @ 85.56

Price of COP = $85.56 (1/4/08)

Put Strike Price	January	February
70	0.05	0.20
75	0.40	1.75
80	1.50	3.10
85	4.85	6.00
90	10.00	11.50
95	14.20	16.00

---

table 8.7   ratio put spread trade calculations

Ratio Put Spread Using ConocoPhillips @ $85.56

Net debit = Net short put premium − Net long put premium	$550
Maximum risk = Limited below downside breakeven (to zero)	$15,050
Maximum reward = [# of long contracts × (strike difference × 100) + net credit (or − net debit)	$950
Downside breakeven = {[# of short puts × (short put strike price − short put premium) − # of long puts × (long put strike price − long put premium)] / (# of short puts − # of long puts)}	$75.25
Upside breakeven = long put strike price − the net debit	$89.50

figure 8.2   ratio put spread (long 1 COP 95 put @ 10, short 3 COP 80 puts @ 1.50)

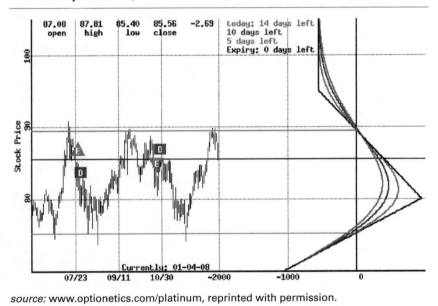

source: www.optionetics.com/platinum, reprinted with permission.

table 8.8   ratio put spread results

Long 1 COP 95 Put @ 10, Short 3 COP 80 Puts @ 1.50						
Debit at Initiation	Days in Trade	Stock Price at Initiation	Stock Price at Exit	Price of 80 Put at expiration	Price of 95 Put at Expiration	Profit/Loss
$550	14	$85.56	$80.60	0.05	$14.40	$875

Closing a ratio put spread profitably depends on the price movement of the underlying stock. In the best scenario, COP would have closed at the strike price of the short puts, or $80 a share. The short options would have expired worthless so that the trader can keep the credit while the long put could have been sold at a relatively high premium. The risk to the upside is limited to the net debit. In some cases, the ratio spread can be initiated for a credit, which makes it possible to make a profit regardless if the market moves higher or lower.

In this example, COP traded down to $80.60 a share at January expiration. In that case, the short puts can be closed out (buy to close) for a nickel or $1.45 profit (the initial credit, or $1.50, minus the current price to close, or $.05) and the long put has intrinsic value of $14.40 a share. The total profit is therefore $435 for the short puts ($1.45 × 3 × 100) and $440 on the long put [($14.40 − $10) × 100]. The total profit is $875 over 14 days (see Table 8.8). The full $950 maximum reward was not realized as (1) the short puts were closed out rather than allowed to expire worthless, and (2) the stock did not fall all the way to $80 and therefore the maximum potential profit from the long put was not achieved.

---

rule of thumb
use highly volatile markets with a bullish bias and options with a reverse volatility skew.

---

ratio backspreads

Ratio backspreads have become a popular nondirectional trading strategy. One reason is because backspreads offer unlimited profit potential and limited risk. Like the ratio spread, this is a volatility-based strategy that involves buying one leg and selling another at a disproportionate ratio. If the markets move, you make money; if they don't move, you can still make money. That's one of the reasons why ratio backspreads are also called *vacation trades*. They do not need to be monitored very closely as long as the options have 30 days of life or more remaining. In many cases, traders can place a ratio backspread and then turn their attention elsewhere as the trade continues to make money. This is partially due to the fact that correctly forecasting market direction is not essential to profit making. However, having a good feel for volatility is important. Let's take a closer look at both the put and the call ratio backspread.

---

ratio backspread
a delta neutral spread where an uneven number of contracts are bought and sold. Optimally no net credit or net debit occurs.

There are two kinds of ratio backspreads: call ratio backspreads and put ratio backspreads. Call ratio backspreads are best placed in markets where a move higher in the underlying stock and a rise in volatility are anticipated. When substantial movement lower in the underlying stock is expected, the situation is ripe for a put ratio backspread. In order to place either kind of ratio backspread, the following seven rules are generally observed:

1. Choose markets with high volatility.
2. Avoid markets with consistent low volatility. If you really want to place a ratio backspread in a market that does not move, pay close attention to rule 4.
3. Do not use ratios of options greater than .67—use ratios that are a multiple of 1:2 or 2:3.
4. If you choose to trade a slow market, a .75 ratio or higher is acceptable only by buying the lower strike and selling the higher. However, there is more risk.
5. To create a call ratio backspread, sell the lower strike call and buy a greater number of higher strike calls.
6. To create a put ratio backspread, sell the higher strike put and buy a greater number of lower strike puts.
7. Avoid debit trades. If you do place a ratio backspread with a debit, you must be willing to lose this amount.

One way to figure out the most effective ratio is to accurately calculate the net credit of a trade. This can be accomplished by calculating the full credit realized from the short options and dividing it by the debit of one long option. You then use up as much of the credit as you can to make the most profitable ratio.

Credit = # of short contracts × short option premium
× $ value of each point

Debit = # of long contracts × long option premium
× $ value of each point

It can be difficult to find ratio backspread opportunities in highly volatile markets when stock options have very rich premiums. Try to focus on stocks with prices below $100 or look for opportunities among the ETFs. Locating the right markets can be frustrating at first. Learn to be persistent. They're out there; you just have to keep looking.

call ratio backspread

Call ratio backspreads are created by simultaneously selling a lower strike call and purchasing a greater number of higher strike calls with the same expiration date in a ratio less than two to three. Call ratio backspreads are best placed in bullish markets when a significant move higher in the share price is expected to occur. Sometimes you can find reverse volatility skews in these markets, or a situation where the lower strike options (the ones you want to sell) have higher implied volatility and may be overpriced. The lower strike options (the ones you have to buy) enjoy lower implied volatility and are often underpriced. By trading the reverse volatility skew, you can capture the implied volatility differential between the short and long options.

---

call ratio backspread strategy
an option combination trade that involves the simultaneous sale of lower strike calls and the purchase of a greater number of higher strike calls with the same expiration date.

---

table 8.9   apple computer quick facts

Apple Computer (AAPL)	
Last price	$125.02
Volume	35,450,000
52-week range	$89.83 to $202.96

Let's introduce the delta to this situation. As previously discussed, the delta is the probability of an option closing in-the-money at expiration. Obviously an option that's already in-the-money has a higher probability of closing in-the-money than an option that's out-of-the-money. Therefore, the delta for an ITM option is higher than the delta for the ATM option or an OTM option. The higher the probability an option has of closing in-the-money, the higher its premium. Ratio backspreads take full advantage of this relationship by enabling a trader to create trades that are virtually free of charge.

Table 8.9 shows some quick facts about Apple Computer (AAPL), a leading maker of computers, cell phones, and digital music players. The stock has been absolutely raging in the past several years, especially right before its quarterly earnings reports are released. However, the stock is now well off its 42-week high and the decline is an excellent opportunity to create long-term bullish trades on Apple.

Using the values in Table 8.10, and keeping in mind that ratio backspreads, unlike ratio spreads, offer unlimited profit, let's create a call ratio backspread by going short two AAPL January 130 calls @ $21.50 and long three AAPL January 150 calls @ $14. The net credit

---

table 8.10   call premiums with AAPL @ 125.02

Price of AAPL = $125.02 (2/29/08)		
Strike Price	July	January 09
120	15.10	26.00
125	12.90	NA
130	11.00	21.50
135	9.20	NA
140	7.75	18.00
145	6.50	NA
150	4.50	14.00

table 8.11   call ratio backspread trade calculations

Call Ratio Backspread Using Apple Computer @ 125.02

Net Debit/Credit = Net short call premium − net long call premium	$100
Maximum risk = [(# short calls × difference in strikes) × 100 − net credit (or + net debit)]	$3,900
Maximum reward = Unlimited to the upside and limited to the net credit on the downside (if any)	Unlimited
Upside breakeven = {[Long call strike price + [(difference in strikes × # of short calls) − (net credit / 100)} or + [(net debit / 100) / (# of long calls − # of short calls)]	$189
Downside breakeven = If the trade has a net debit, breakeven = {short call strike price − [(net debit/100) / # of short calls]}. If the trade has a net credit, then breakeven = {short call strike price + [(net credit / 100) / # of short calls]}	$130.50

on this trade is $100: [(2 × 21.50) − (3 × 14)] × 100 = −$100. (See Table 8.11.) The maximum risk is calculated by multiplying the number of short calls by the difference in strike prices by the value per point and then subtracting the net credit (or adding the net debit). The maximum risk on this trade is $3,900: [2 × (150 − 130) × 100] − 100 = $3,900. The upside breakeven is calculated by adding the strike price of the long calls to the following number: Take the difference in strike prices times the number of short calls minus the net credit divided by 100 (or plus the net debit divided by 100) and divide this number by the number of long calls minus the number of short calls. In this example, the upside breakeven is $189: 150 + {[(150 − 130) × 2 − 100/100] / (3 − 2)} = 150 + 39 = 189. Hence, this trade has an unlimited profit potential above 189.

The downside breakeven is the lower strike price plus the net credit per contract divided by the number of short contracts, or $130.50 (130 + 1.00/2 = 130.50). At that point, the long calls expire worthless, but the short calls have fallen enough in value to offset the cost of the long puts. With any move below $130 a share, all of the options expire worthless and the strategist keeps the premium from selling the backspread. (See Figure 8.3.)

As I write these words, this trade is still open; so far, so good. Apple Computer has increased from roughly $125 a share to $178.60 in two months. On the last day of trading in April, the January 130s are offered at $58 per contract and the 150s bid for $43.90. At this

figure 8.3   call ratio backspread (short 2 AAPL January 130 calls @ 21.50, long 3 AAPL January 150 calls @ 14)

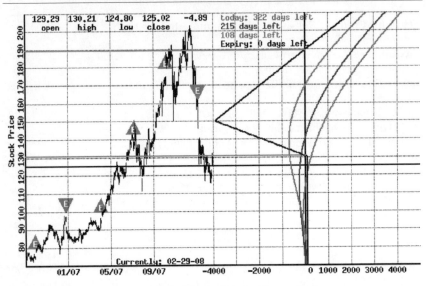

source: www.optionetics.com/platinum, reprinted with permission.

point, the delta of both options is .75 and there is still some profit opportunity in the spread. However, if I decide to close it out now, I can buy to close the January 130s for a loss of $36.50 per contract, or $7,300 total [(58 − 21.5) × 2 × 100 = 7,300] and sell to close the January 150 calls for a profit of $29.90 per contract, or $8,970 total [(43.90 − 14) × 3 × 100 = 8,970]. The total profit is therefore $1,670 (see Table 8.12). However, the options still have 261 days of life remaining, so there is still plenty of time and profit potential remaining in this call ratio backspread.

table 8.12   call ratio backspread results

Short 2 AAPL January 130 Calls @ 21.50, Long 3 AAPL January 150 Calls @ 14.00

Credit at Initiation	Price of Long Call	Price of Short Call	Days in Trade	Profit/Loss
$100	14.00	21.50	60	$1,670

> **rule of thumb**
> use highly volatile markets with a bullish bias and options with a
> reverse volatility skew.

put ratio backspread

A put ratio backspread is basically the opposite of a call ratio backspread. In a put ratio backspread, the higher strike put is sold and
simultaneously a greater number of lower strike puts is purchased. In
a call ratio backspread, you want the market to go up; however, you
don't necessarily lose money if it goes down. With a put ratio backspread, you want the market to go down (bearish). In addition, put
ratio backspreads are best placed in markets with a forward volatility skew. In these markets, the higher strike options (the ones you
want to sell) have higher implied volatility and are therefore overpriced. The lower strike options (the ones you have to buy) enjoy
lower implied volatility and are not quite so expensive.

> **put ratio backspread strategy**
> an option combination trade that involves the simultaneous sale
> of higher strike puts and the purchase of a greater number of
> lower strike puts with the same expiration date.
>
> **forward volatility skew**
> a market in which higher strike options have high implied
> volatility and are therefore overpriced, and lower strike options
> that have low implied volatility and are often underpriced.

The key to finding a profitable ratio backspread is to arrange options premiums that create a downside breakeven that fits the stock's
profile. Using the values for Lehman Brothers (LEH) in Table 8.13,
note how the stock is coming off the upper end of its 52-week range.
The stock is expected to fall amid ongoing turmoil in the brokerage industry. So, in early 2007, using the numbers in Table 8.14, let's create
a put ratio backspread by going short two LEH January 08 85 puts
@ 8.00 and long three LEH January 08 75 puts @ 4.00. The net credit
is equal to 400 [(2 × 8) − (3 × 4) − × 100 = 400]. (See Table 8.15.)

---

table 8.13   lehman brothers quick facts

Lehman Bros. (LEH)	
Last price	$83.29
Volume	9,535,000
52-week range	$59.42 to $86.12

The risk is limited, but the reward potential is substantial. The maximum risk is equal to the number of short puts times the difference in strike prices multiplied by the value per point (100) minus the net credit or plus the net debit. In this trade, the maximum risk is $1,600: [2 × (85 − 75) × 100] − 400 = 1,600. The upside breakeven is the higher strike put option minus the net credit divided by 100 and then divided by the number of short puts. In this case, the upside breakeven is 83 [85 − (400/100)/2 = 83]. The maximum profit is limited to the stock falling to zero to the downside below the downside breakeven. The downside breakeven is calculated by multiplying the number of short contracts times the difference in strike prices, and subtracting the net credit divided by 100 or adding the net debit divided by 100. Then divide that amount by the number of long puts minus the number of short puts. Finally, subtract that amount from the lower strike price. In this trade, the downside breakeven is 59: 75 − [2 × (85 − 75) − 400/100] / (3 − 2) = 59. This trade will make money as long as the price of Lehman Brothers falls below $59. The risk profile for this example is shown in Figure 8.4.

---

table 8.14   put premiums with LEH @ 83.29

Price of LEH = $83.29 (2/15/07)		
Strike Price	July	January
65	0.80	2.05
70	1.40	3.00
75	2.35	4.00
80	3.80	5.90
85	5.90	8.00

---

table 8.15   put ratio backspread trade calculations

Put Ratio Backspread Using Lehman Bros. @ 83.29

$400 Net Debit / Credit = Net short put premium − net long put premium	$400
Maximum risk = [(# short calls × difference in strikes) × 100 − net credit (or + net debit)]	$1,600
Maximum reward = Unlimited to the downside below the breakeven, to the stock falling to zero. Limited to the upside to the net credit (if any).	$5,900
Upside breakeven = If the trade has a net debit, breakeven = {short put strike + [(net debit / 100) / # of short puts]}. If the trade has a net credit, then breakeven = {short put strike price − [(net credit / 100) / # of short puts]}	$83
Downside breakeven = Long put strike price − {[(# of short puts × difference in strikes) − net credit/100 or + (net debit/100)] / (# of long puts − # of short puts)}	$59

figure 8.4   put ratio backspread (short 2 LEH January 85 puts @ 8.00, long 3 LEH January 75 puts @ 4.00)

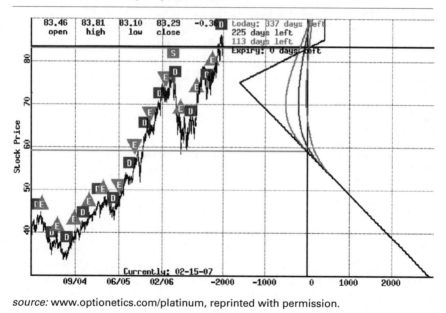

source: www.optionetics.com/platinum, reprinted with permission.

table 8.16   put ratio backspread results

Short 2 LEH January 85 Puts @ 8.00, Long 3 LEH January 75 Puts @ 4.00

Credit at Initiation	Days in Trade	Price of 85 Put at Entry/Exit	Price of 75 Put at Entry/Exit	Profit/Loss
$400	337	8.00/32.00	4.00/22.00	$600

By tracking this trade, we find that at the January options' expiration, LEH had fallen to $53.25 a share and below the breakeven. To exit the trade, simply buy back the short 85 puts at $32 per contract and sell the 75 puts for $22 each. The strategist loses $4,800 on the short side of the trade [2 × (32 − 8) × 100] but sees a profit of $5,400 on the long side [3 × (22 − 4) × 100] for a total net profit of $600 (see Table 8.16). If the options are held until expiration, the short puts will be assigned and long puts exercised because they are in-the-money. If so, Monday morning, the account will be net short 100 shares at $75 and can be sold in the market Monday morning. Depending on the price Monday morning, there is the potential for nice profits either way. Nevertheless, it might make sense to close out the trade before expiration and avoid the risk of seeing the stock move against the strategist in the after-hours market.

> **rule of thumb**
> use highly volatile markets with a bearish bias and options with a forward volatility skew.

conclusion

The best markets for ratio backspread trades have high volatility. Before placing a call or put ratio backspread, I spend a lot of time analyzing the overall risk of the trade. Once a trade is executed, patience is required to let the trade do what it was constructed to do. Sometimes it's the hardest thing in the world to just leave a ratio backspread alone. It's a good practice to monitor the trade once a day, but get in the habit of allowing it to mature to profitability.

This is especially difficult for those traders who spend the entire day poring over real-time quotes.

For example, Apple Computer is a super high-flying stock. What can you do to take advantage of Apple's sharp price movement? If it moves up quickly over a three-day period, you have two choices. You can certainly follow the upward trend and do a put ratio spread or a call ratio backspread, or you could bet on a correction and place a call ratio spread or a put ratio backspread. It's a tough choice. Sometimes a contrarian trade is a good idea. Other times it's best to just go ahead and follow the trend. Only personal experience can guide you when it comes to making these kinds of critical choices.

To arrive at a decision, try investigating the host of economic information sources that are available. In the pre-Internet era, I could get the big picture and pay attention to details just by picking up the *Wall Street Journal* and *Investor's Business Daily*. Now I jump online and the information is right there. Anyone can buzz from site to site in seconds. If you learn that stocks are going up, interest rates are going down, the commodities markets are stable, and the dollar is going down, which one of these facts worries you? Everything is betting for an up move in stocks, except for the dollar going down. Why? Because the Federal Reserve at one point may say the dollar's too weak. Since the Fed is in the business of trying to support the dollar, I translate the Fed's comments as meaning that the dollar will be okay for a little while, but sooner or later the dollar is going to be killed again. This may be a simple way of looking at the markets, but it's also a good example of intermarket analysis. You have to keep a close eye on the circle of money flow both within the United States and internationally.

When I investigate individual stocks, I focus on volatility skews. As previously discussed, volatility measures the speed of change in the price of a market. High volatility leads to inflated stock prices. A volatility skew exists when different options with the same expiration and the same underlying instrument have substantially different implied volatilities. Higher implied volatility leads to inflated option premiums. Don't let the imposing nature of volatility intimidate you. Recognizing volatility skews is a viable method of finding markets with profitable option premium interrelationships.

If a stock's options have lower strikes with high implied volatility, a reverse volatility skew exists. This is recognizable when lower strike options are priced higher in comparison to the premiums of higher strikes. In these kinds of markets you should aim to buy the higher strike options and sell the lower strikes. This works in your favor when looking for profit-making price quotes for call ratio backspreads or ratio put spreads. A forward volatility skew exists when higher strikes have high implied volatilities and lower strikes are less expensive in comparison. Markets with forward volatility skews are ripe for placing a put ratio backspread or a ratio call spread, since you want to sell the higher priced strikes and buy the lower priced strikes.

The method of locating volatility skews is easier than ever. Although there are several option analysis software programs that enable traders to calculate implied volatilities, you can just as easily access implied volatility data at various financial web sites. Monitor the implied volatility of options with the same expiration date but differing strikes with an eye for abnormalities.

chapter 9

sideways strategies

trading sideways markets

Many stocks do not trend up or down but do move sideways between two prices for a few months or even years. The minimum time frame I generally look at is two months, although a longer time frame can mean a more stable sideways market. Although sideways markets may not be the most appropriate for aggressive buy-and-hold investors, there are limited-risk options strategies that can take advantage of and profit from the price consistency of rangebound markets.

The two price caps of a sideways market are commonly referred to as support and resistance. Hence, if every time IBM declines to $100 per share, the market rebounds, this would establish the *support* level. If IBM trades up in price to reach $130 and then sells off again, this would establish the *resistance* level. These two levels can then be used to create an effective options strategy that enables traders to collect time premium.

Remember that the primary determinants of an option's premium are intrinsic value, time value, and volatility. Time value is lost due to the *theta decay* of the option. Options lose the most time value in the last 30 days of the life of the option; the closer the expiration date comes, the faster the theta decay. Therefore, on the last day there will be the greatest loss of value due to time. Options lose value over time if markets do not move. This basic option characteristic can be used to create strategies that work in markets that are moving sideways.

Charts are essential when looking for nontrending markets. You can scan daily price and volume charts and basically just eyeball them for the support and resistance levels. If I spot a market that looks like it is going sideways, I take a ruler and see if I can draw support and resistance lines. Once this is accomplished, I look for the most effective option strategy to take advantage of the circumstances of the chosen market. Let's take a look at seven of my favorite sideways strategies: covered call, collar, calendar spread, diagonal spread, long butterfly, long condor, and iron butterfly.

---

sideways markets
stable markets that tend to trade in a range, fluctuating between specific support (low) and resistance (high) levels. Resistance is a historical price level of a market at which rising prices have a hard time breaking through to the upside. Support is a historical price level at which falling prices generally stop falling and either move sideways or reverse direction.

---

covered call

The covered call strategy is one of the more widely used and popular options strategies. It is sometimes called the *buy write* because it involves buying shares and writing calls. For investors with stock brokerage accounts and the desire to trade options for the first time, this strategy is a good starting point because most brokers allow investors to use the covered call even if they don't have any other previous options trading experience. So if you already own shares, you can probably move into options trading by selling calls against those shares. Keep in mind, however, that all firms require the investor to submit an account approval form. So that's the first step.

But let's go back to the strategy discussion. The covered call is relatively easy to understand. Let's consider an example using eBay

---

table 9.1   eBay quick facts

---

eBay (EBAY)

Last price	$28.75
Volume	15,784,500
52-week range	$25.64 to $40.63

(EBAY). Some quick facts about the stock appear in Table 9.1. On January 4, 2008, the stock is trading for $28.75 a share. Shares of the online auctioneer are seeing steady trading activity and daily volume often surpasses 10 million shares. The options are also actively traded. Meanwhile, the stock has a 52-week range of $25.64 and $40.63. At $28.75, it is expected to continue to move off its 52-week low and head gradually higher.

In order to profit from our expectations for a gradual move higher, the strategy of choice is a covered call consisting of 500 EBAY shares and 5 short calls. Table 9.2 shows some possibilities. Since the stock is at $28.75 and a gradual move higher is expected, let's focus on the calls with strike prices above the current market price (i.e., out-of-the-money calls). In-the-money options could be used if your goal is to capture time value from selling calls. However, the strike price serves as a ceiling over potential profits from the stock price. That is, the calls will be assigned at expiration and the stock price sold at the strike price of the option. A call with a $30 strike price, by contrast, allows room for upside profits. If the stock moves up to $30, our profit from the stock alone is $1.25 per share or $625 for 500 shares ($5 \times 125 = 625$).

---

table 9.2   call premiums with EBAY @ 28.75

Price of EBAY = $28.75 (02/04/08)

Call Strike Price	February	March	April
25	3.90	4.30	5.00
27.5	1.75	2.50	3.00
30	0.45	1.25	1.75
32.5	0.10	0.45	0.95
35	0.05	0.15	0.50

We also want to sell calls and possibly make profits from both the long stock and short calls. The chosen expiration month depends on the strategist's outlook for the stock. Also, since the idea is to take advantage of time decay, and time decay occurs faster with short-term options, it's best to look for options with 60 days or less until expiration; 45 is even better. In Table 9.2, let's focus on the March contract, with 42 days left until these options expire.

Looking at the prices in Table 9.2, let's create the buy write with 500 shares at $28.75 and short five March 30 calls for $1.25 per contract. The shares are purchased for a total of $14,375. Five March 30 calls are sold for $1.25 a contract, or $625, which offsets the cost of the shares. The total cost of the trade is therefore $14,375 minus $625, or $13,750, which is also our maximum risk. In fact, the covered call carries the same risks as owning shares, minus the premium from the call writes.

Unlike owning shares, however, the maximum profit is limited. It is computed as the strike price of the calls plus the premium received, minus the stock price, all multiplied by the number of shares. The maximum reward for this example is $1,250 [(30 + 1.25 − 28.75) × 500 = $1,250].

The downside breakeven for the trade is the purchase price minus the premium received, or $27.50 ($28.75 − 1.25 = $27.50 a share.) So, ideally, the stock will stay above $27.50 and the best-case scenario is a move up to $30 a share. At $30 the stock can be assigned and the strategist keeps the premium for the short calls and the profit from the stock. Table 9.3 and Figure 9.1 show the risk/reward dynamics of the EBAY covered call.

In the EBAY example, the stock didn't move much. At March expiration, the stock drifted down about 15 cents to $28.60. The

---

table 9.3   covered call trade calculations

Covered Call Using EBAY @ 28.75

Maximum risk = Stock price × number of shares − options price minus # of contracts	$13,750
Maximum reward = (Strike price + premium − stock price) × # of shares	$1,250
Breakeven = Purchase price − premium	$27.50

figure 9.1   covered call or buy write (long 500 EBAY shares @ 28.75, short 5 EBAY March 30 calls @ 1.25)

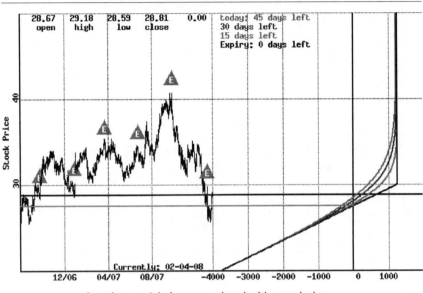

source: www.optionetics.com/platinum, reprinted with permission.

short calls expire worthless and produce a $1.25 per contract profit, or $625. Meanwhile, the stock is showing a $.15 per share loss, or $75 total ($.15 × 500 shares). The net profit at $28.60 per share is therefore equal to $550 and equal to the premium received for the calls minus the loss on the stock trade: ($1.25 × 5 × 100) − [($28.75 − $28.60) × 500] = $550. (See Table 9.4.)

table 9.4   covered call results

Long 500 EBAY Shares @ 28.75, Short 5 EBAY March 30 calls @ 1.25

Closing Price of EBAY Stock	Days in Trade	Price of 30 Call	Profit/Loss	Return on Investment
$28.60	45	0	$550	4%

collar

The collar is a lot like a covered call, but with a twist. As with the buy write, the strategist buys or own shares and sells calls. In addition, however, the strategist also buys put options. It can be thought of as the combination of a buy write and a protective put. The puts limit the downside risk of the share price. The sale of calls finances all or part of the purchase of the puts.

> **buy write**
> the term *buy write* is another name for a covered call. It stems from the fact that the strategy involves buying shares and writing calls against those shares.
>
> **protective put**
> the protective put is a simple strategy that combines long stock and put options. The puts protect the value of the shares.

Table 9.5 shows put and call premiums for EBAY in early February 2008. The March calls are the same premiums used in the covered call example (Table 9.2), and the March puts are also listed. EBAY is expected to move gradually higher between now and the options' expiration, but this time there is also concern about an adverse move to the downside. Again, let's focus on the options with the 30 strike price.

table 9.5   put and call premiums with EBAY at 28.75

Price of EBAY = $28.75 (02/04/08)

March Strike Price	Calls	Puts
25	4.30	0.35
27.5	2.50	0.90
30	1.25	2.10
32.5	0.45	4.00
35	0.15	6.30

table 9.6   collar trade calculations

Collar Using EBAY @ 28.75	
Maximum risk = (Stock price − call option premium − strike price of put + put option premium) × # of shares	$450
Max Reward = (Net premium − stock price + call strike price) × # of shares	$800
Breakeven = Stock price − call premium + put premium	$28.40

To create the collar, let's buy 500 shares at $28.75, sell 5 March 30 calls for $1.25 a contract, and buy 5 March 27.5 puts for $.90. The options part of the trade yields a credit of $.35 per contract ($1.25 − $.90). Therefore, the cost of the trade is equal to the cost of the stock minus the credit times the number of shares, or $14,200 [(28.75 − .35) × 500].

As with the covered call, the potential reward for the collar is limited because of the short call. In the event of a dramatic move higher, the calls will be assigned. In this case, the profits max out when EBAY moves up to $30 per share. For example, at $30 per share at expiration, both the puts and call expire worthless and the strategist will keep the credit of $.35 per contract. Shares can be sold for $30 and produce profit of $1.25 a share. The total profit is then $175 for the options (.35 × 5 × 100) plus $625 for the shares (1.25 × 500) for a total profit of $800, which is the maximum profit potential (see Table 9.6). If the stock moves above $30 and the options are assigned, then the profit is the same $800 because the shares are assigned at $30 and the strategist keeps the net credit from selling the calls minus the puts. The breakeven is simply the cost of the shares minus the net credit, or $28.40 (28.75 − .35 = 28.40). Figure 9.2 shows the risk profile for this trade.

In this example, the stock drifted down about $.15 to $28.60 at March expiration. The short calls and long puts expire worthless and produce a net profit of $175 [(1.25 − .9) × 5 × 100). However, the stock is showing a $.15 per share loss, or $75 total ($.15 × 500 shares). The net profit at $28.60 a share is therefore equal to $100 and equal to the premium received for the calls minus the cost of the puts minus the loss on the stock trade: ($.35 × 5 × 100) − [($28.75 − $28.60) × 500] = $100. The results are summarized in Table 9.7.

figure 9.2 collar spread (long 500 EBAY shares @ 28.75, short 5 EBAY March 30 calls @1.25, and long 5 March 27.5 puts @ .90)

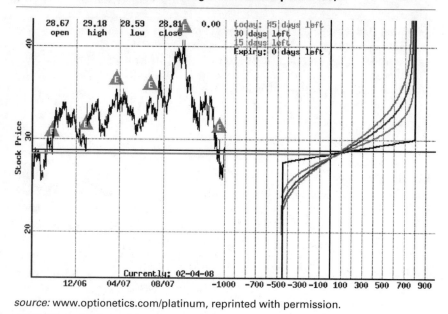

source: www.optionetics.com/platinum, reprinted with permission.

calendar spread

A calendar spread is another strategy that works well in range-bound markets. The strategy involves buying longer-term calls (or puts) and then selling shorter-term ones. When using call options, a calendar spread is similar to covered calls, but instead of using shares, the strategist buys longer-dated call options. The strategy

table 9.7 collar results

Long 500 EBAY Shares @ 28.75, Short 5 EBAY March 30 Calls @ 1.25, and Long 5 March 27.5 Puts @ .90

Closing Price of EBAY Stock	Days in Trade	Price of 30 Call	Price of 27.5 Put	Profit/Loss	Return on Investment
$28.60	45	0	0	$100	.5%

table 9.8 mcdonald's quick facts

McDonald's (MCD)	
Last price	$57.05
Volume	7,160,800
52-week range	$46.64 to $63.69

works because of the nonlinear nature of time decay and the fact that short-term options see a faster rate of decay when compared to longer-term options. However, it is important for the stock to remain rangebound. Big moves higher or lower will generally result in losses for calendar spreads. Let's consider another real-world example.

McDonald's (MCD) is an actively traded stock on the New York Stock Exchange. Some recent stats about MCD appear in Table 9.8. Daily volume of the shares is in the millions. At that time, in early 2008, we see the stock trading for $57.05 a share and roughly at the midpoint of its 52-week range. We expect the stock to stay rangebound and perhaps trend modestly higher from here.

Looking at the options contracts for McDonald's, we find some quotes similar to those in Table 9.9. This example uses calls, but calendars can also be created using put options. In fact, some strategists prefer to use puts because there is less risk of early assignment. Remember that call options on stocks with high dividend yields have a greater chance of assignment because of the dividends. If the call holder wants to exercise the option to collect the dividend, the short call will be assigned and the calendar spread is no longer a calendar

table 9.9 MCD call option premiums

Price of MCD = $57.05 (01/04/08)

Call Strike Price	January	February	June
52.5	4.70	5.40	7.60
55	2.50	3.50	6.00
57.5	0.95	2.00	4.25
60	0.20	0.95	3.00
62.5	0.05	0.35	2.15

spread. Instead, it will be a position in short stock and long calls. At that point, the strategist has been taken out of the calendar spread and will need to make an adjustment, such as closing the position entirely or buying back the shares and selling another short call. It usually doesn't make sense to exercise the long call to honor the assignment of the short call because there will be time value remaining in the longer-term contract. If the option is exercised, the time value is lost. To make a long story short, when faced with assignment on a calendar spread, the strategist will want to make an adjustment other than exercising the long call to satisfy the assignment.

In this example, MCD is not scheduled to make a dividend payment during the next two months, so let's create a calendar spread using the June and February 57.5 calls. Since the stock is trading for $57.05, the spread has a modestly bullish bias because the stock price is below the strike price of the call option.

In order to enter the spread, we buy five of the June 57.5 calls for $4.25 per contract and sell five of the February 57.5 calls for $2.00 per contract. The net debit to enter the trade is $2.25 per spread, or $1,125 total [(4.25 − 2.00) × 5 × 100]. The debit is at risk in the calendar spread. If, for example, the stock falls and never recovers to $57.50 and the strategist does nothing, both the call options will expire worthless and the premium is lost. In this case, the strategist is putting $1,125 at risk (see Table 9.10). Figure 9.3 outlines the risk profile for this trade.

The maximum profit potential of the trade varies depending on the adjustments made during the life of the June options contract. If the idea is to sell a series of calls against the longer-term contract, the risk/reward profile will be much different than if the strategist intends to sell only one call. In addition, after the short call expires, the strategist can close the position altogether, simply hold the call, or make an adjustment such as entering a bull or bear call spread.

In this example, the calendar spread was held until one week before the February options expiration, or for 35 days. By that time,

table 9.10   calendar spread trade calculations

Calendar Spread Using McDonald's @ 51.50

Maximum risk = Limited. Use software to calculate.	$1,125
Maximum reward = Limited. Use software for calculation.	$845
Downside breakeven = Use software for calculation.	$53.58
Upside breakeven = Use software for calculation.	$62.26

figure 9.3   **calendar spread (long 5 MCD June 57.5 calls @ 4.25, short 5 MCD February 57.5 calls @ 2.00)**

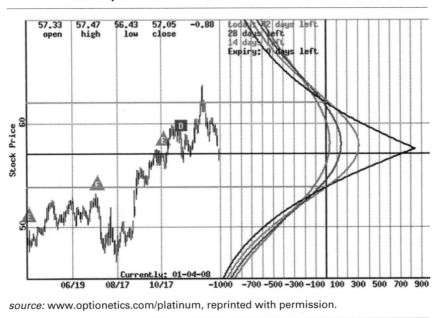

57.33 open	57.47 high	56.43 low	57.05 close	-0.88

Today: 42 days left
28 days left
14 days left
Expiry: 0 days left

Currently: 01-04-08

source: www.optionetics.com/platinum, reprinted with permission.

shares of McDonald's had fallen to $55.64. On the surface, this might seem like bad news. However, since the decline was not dramatic, only 2.5 percent, the calendar spread yields a profit nevertheless. The June calls are currently bid for $3.00 and the February calls for $.15. Since the strategist paid $4.25 for the June calls, the loss is $1.25 per contract or $625 total [(4.25 − 3) × 5 × 100]. However, the profit of the short calls is greater. Since the February calls were sold for $2.00, they can be purchased to close the trade for $.15 or a profit of $1.85 per contract, or $925 [(2 − 0.15) × 5 × 100]. The total profit is therefore $300 (925 − 625), which is a 26.7 percent return on investment (see Table 9.11).

diagonal spread

Like the calendar spread, a diagonal spread involves buying longer-term options and selling short-term ones. However, in the diagonal spread, the strike prices are different. In general, the strategist using put options will buy longer-term options with a lower strike price

table 9.11   calendar spread results

Long 5 MCD June 57.5 Calls @ 4.25, Short 5 MCD February 57.5 calls @ 2.00
(First Expiration)

Closing Price of MCD Stock	Days in Trade	Price of June Call	Price of February Call	Profit/Loss	Return on Investment
$55.64	35	3.00	0.15	$300	26.7%

and sell shorter-term options with a higher strike price. A diagonal spread with calls involves selling shorter-term options with a lower strike price and selling longer-term options with a higher strike price.

Using the same quotes from Table 9.9, let's create a calendar spread with the purchase of (instead of June 57.5 calls) five June 60 calls for $3.00 per contract and sell the same 5 February 57.5 calls for $2.00 a contract. The net debit to enter the trade is $1.00 per spread, or $500 total [(3.00 − 2.00) × 5 × 100]. In this case, the strategist is putting more than the initial debit at risk. Since the long call has a higher strike price than the short call, it doesn't fully cover the risk associated with writing the call. For example, if the stock rallies to $60 and the short calls are assigned, the strategist must sell the stock for the strike price, or $57.50 a share. Since he doesn't own the stock, he must either buy it in the market for $60 or exercise his long call. Either way, he is forced to buy at $60 a share. (However, it makes more sense to buy in the market and sell the long call because it will have time value remaining and can help to offset some of the losses from the stock trade.)

Buying for $60 and immediately selling for $57.50 a share results in a loss of $2.50 a share, and doing it 500 times equals a loss of $1,250. Since the net debit of $500 for the options is also lost (with the exception of any time value remaining in the June call), the total risk is $1,750. (See Table 9.12.) In short, the diagonal spread generally carries more risk than the calendar spread. (See Figure 9.4.)

While the diagonal spread carries more risk, it also requires less capital and holds the possibility for a greater return on investment. In this example, the diagonal spread was held until one week before the February options expiration, or for 35 days. As noted earlier, shares of McDonald's had fallen to $55.64 by that time. The June

table 9.12   diagonal spread trade calculations

Diagonal Spread Using McDonald's @ 51.50

Maximum risk = Limited. Use software to calculate.	$1,750
Maximum reward = Limited. Use software for accurate calculation.	$865
Downside breakeven = Use software for accurate calculation.	$51.97
Upside breakeven = Use software for accurate calculation.	$61.10

calls are now bid for $2.00 and the February calls for $.15. Since the strategist paid $3.00 for the June calls, the loss is $1.00 per contract or $500 total [(3.00 − 2) × 5 × 100]. However, the profit from the short calls is greater. Since the February calls were sold for $2.00, they are bought to close for $.15 or a profit of $1.85 per contract, or $925 [(2 − 0.15) × 5 × 100]. The total profit is therefore $425 (925 − 500), which is an 85 percent return on investment (see Table 9.13).

figure 9.4   diagonal spread (long 5 MCD June 60 calls @ 3.00, short long 5 MCD February 57.5 calls @ 2.00)

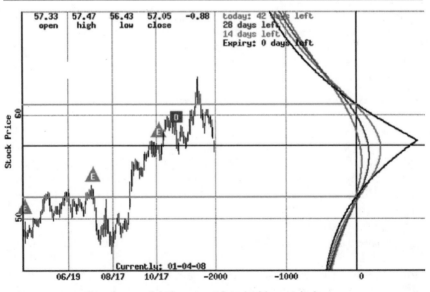

source: www.optionetics.com/platinum, reprinted with permission.

table 9.13   diagonal spread results

Long 5 MCD June 60 Calls @ 3.00, Short 5 MCD February 57.5 Calls @ 2.00

Closing Price of MCD Stock	Days in Trade	Price of June Call	Price of February Call	Profit/Loss	Return on Investment
$55.64	35	2.00	0.15	$425	85%

long butterfly

The butterfly spread, a combination of a bull and a bear credit spread, is one of the most popular option strategies for a rangebound market. There are two basic long butterfly scenarios: one uses calls and the other uses puts. Both consist of three different strikes—the body and the two wings. The body contains an option with the strike price between the support and resistance levels. The wings are composed of options with the strike prices at both ends of the trading range.

---

long butterfly strategy
a complex option strategy where two identical options are sold or bought together with the purchase (sale) of one option with an immediately higher strike, and one option with an immediately lower strike. All options must be the same type, have the same underlying asset, and have the same expiration date.

To create a long butterfly, you go long the wings and go short the body (the middle strike options) by purchasing as many option contracts as you sell. The trick is to sell more value in the body than in the wings. This trade offers a limited profit in a sideways-moving market when the underlying stock closes in between the upside and downside breakevens.

Table 9.14 shows some quick facts about Hewlett-Packard Company (HPQ). It is a very actively traded stock with very liquid options. In addition, as shown in Figure 9.5, the stock has been grinding higher, but seems to have found some support around $50 and $51 a share. With the stock trading at $51.50, we expect this support level

table 9.14 hewlett-packard quick facts

Hewlett Packard Company (HPQ)

Last Price	$51.50
Volume	2,073,500
52 Wk Range	47.06 to 82.38

to hold and for the stock to continue its quiet trading for the next few weeks.

Looking at the prices in Table 9.15, let's create a long butterfly spread using options with 60 days or less so that the short options have a better chance of expiring worthless. However, the November prices may not create enough of a profit to make the trade

figure 9.5 long butterfly spread (long 2 HPQ December 50 calls @ 3.35, short 4 HPQ December 52.5 calls @ 2.00, long 2 HPQ December 55 calls @ .85)

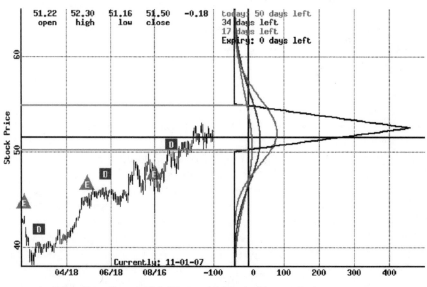

source: www.optionetics.com/platinum, reprinted with permission.

table 9.15   call premiums with HPQ @ 51.50

Price of HPQ = $51.50 (11/01/07)

Call Strike Price	November	December	January
45	6.60	7.20	7.60
47.5	4.25	5.20	5.70
50	2.10	3.35	3.95
52.5	0.75	2.00	2.50
55	0.15	0.85	1.45

worthwhile, so let's go long two HPQ December 50 calls @ 3.35, short four HPQ December 52.5 calls @ 2.00, and long two HPQ December 55 calls @ 0.85. The maximum risk of a long butterfly spread is the net debit paid for the trade. In this example, the net debit is $40: $[(2 \times 3.35) + (4 \times 2) - (2 \times 0.85)] \times 100 = \$40$.

The maximum profit potential of the trade is calculated by taking the difference in the strike prices of the middle and lower strikes times the number of lower strike options times the value per point, minus the net debit paid. The maximum reward for this example is $460: $[(52.5 - 50) \times (2 \times 100)] - \$40 = \$460$.

The downside breakeven for the trade is calculated by adding the lowest strike price to the net debit of the trade divided by the number of lowest strike options times 100, or $50.20: $50 + [40 / (2 \times 100)] = 50.20$. The upside breakeven is calculated by taking the highest strike price minus the net debit divided by the number of highest strike contracts times 100, or $54.80: $55 - [40 / (2 \times 100)] = 54.80$. Therefore, the breakeven range for this trade is between $50.20 and $54.80. (See Table 9.16.) The risk profile for this trade is shown in Figure 9.5.

Although you can leg out of the trade, it is important to monitor the market as a spread every day until the prices enable you to exit the trade with a good profit. Table 9.17 shows the results of the trade. After 49 days, one day before the December options expiration, Hewlett-Packard is trading at $51.16. The 50 call is priced at 1.15. Meanwhile, the 52.5s and the 55s are offered at a nickel. They are set to expire worthless. The trade has a profit equal to the premium remaining in the long call minus the debit, or 190: $[(1.15 \times 2) - 40] \times 100 = \$190$.

table 9.16   long butterfly trade calculations

Long Butterfly Spread Using Hewlett Packard Company @ 51.50

Maximum risk = net debit	$40
Maximum reward = (# lower strike options) × (strike difference × 100) − net debit	$460
Downside breakeven = Lowest strike price + [net debit / (# of lowest strike options × 100)]	$50.20
Upside breakeven = Highest strike price − [net debit / (# of highest strike options × 100)]	$54.80

Why wasn't the full profit realized? If the stock had closed at exactly $52.50, the trade would have earned the maximum possible gain. At that point, the HPQ December 50 calls would be closed at $2.50 each, or $500. The 52.5s and 55s expire worthless. So the strategist pockets $500 for the long call minus the debit paid and the total profit is $460. However, even if the stock closes near $52.50, the strategist runs the risk of being assigned on the four December 52.5 calls at expiration. For that reason, it can make sense to close the successful butterfly before expiration to avoid the risk of an adverse move in the after-hours market before the Saturday morning options' expiration.

The long butterfly trade is a very popular strategy that captures time premium as the market trades back and forth between the wings. Since the premise for this trade is to capture time premium, it's best to use this strategy in the optimal time decay zone (i.e., the last 30 days of the life of the option). However, if you find a market that has been going sideways for a long time, the options premium you receive

table 9.17   long butterfly results

Long 2 HPQ December 50 Calls @ 3.35, Short 4 HPQ December 52.5 Calls @ 2.00, Long 2 HPQ December 55 Calls @ .85

Closing Price of HPQ Stock	Days in Trade	Price of 50 Call	Price of 65 Call	Price of 75 Call	Profit/ Loss	Return on Investment
$51.16	49	1.15	0.05	0.05	$190	375%

may be very low due to a decreased volatility premium attached to the options. Therefore, when you sell short the body of the butterfly you will receive less of a premium for time than in a market that has higher volatility. You will likely have to go out at least another 30 days in the expiration cycle to make the trade reasonably profitable.

rule of thumb
look for sideways-moving markets with option prices that make the limited profit of this strategy worthwhile.

long condor

The long condor is one of my favorite nontrending market strategies. It can be thought of as a butterfly spread with an extra short strike price or a combination of a bull and bear (all call or all put) spread. In a long condor, the trader needs to go short the two inner option strikes that make up the body of the condor and buy the wings. You are shorting the middle options to collect time premium as the underlying stock continues to trade in between the wings. This strategy usually creates a net debit, which is also the maximum risk.

long condor strategy
the sale or purchase of two options with consecutive exercise prices, together with the sale or purchase of one option with an immediately lower exercise price and one option with an immediately higher exercise price. All options must be the same type and have the same underlying asset and the same expiration date.

Like the butterfly, the condor will make money with the passage of time as long as the price of the underlying stock stays between the wings. Using the prices in Table 9.15, let's create a long condor by going long two December 47.5 calls @ 5.20, short two December 50 calls @ 3.35, short two December 52.5 calls @ 2.00, and long two December 55 calls at $.85. The maximum risk for the trade is equal

---

table 9.18   long condor trade calculations

Long Condor Spread Using Hewlett Packard @ $51.50

Maximum risk = Net debit	$140
Maximum reward = [# of lowest strike contracts × difference in strikes) × 100) − net debit	$360
Downside breakeven = Lowest strike price + [net debit / (# of lowest strike options × 100)]	$48.20
Upside breakeven = Highest strike price − [net debit / (# of highest strike options × 100)]	$54.30

---

to the net debit, or $140: $[-(2 \times 5.20) + (2 \times 3.35) + (2 \times 2.00) - (2 \times .85)] \times 100 = 140$. (See Table 9.18.)

The maximum reward is equal to the number of lowest options times the difference in the strike price of the lower short option and the lower long option, multiplied by the value for each point, less the net debit paid (or plus the net credit taken, if any). In this case, the maximum reward is $360: $[2 \times (50 - 47.5) \times 100] - 140 = \$360$.

The upside breakeven is equal to the highest strike price minus the net debit divided by the number of highest strike options multiplied by 100. In this example, the upside breakeven is $54.30 $[55 - (140 / 2 \times 100) = 54.30]$. The downside breakeven is equal to the lowest strike price plus the net debit divided by the number of lowest strike options times 100. In this example, the downside breakeven is equal to $48.20 $[47.5 + (140 / 2 \times 100) = 48.20]$. The profit range is therefore between $48.20 and $54.30. The risk profile of this example is shown in Figure 9.6.

To exit a condor, the long options are sold to close and the short options are bought back to close. Since timing is critical, a condor must be monitored daily so that you can strike while the iron is hot. In this example, after 49 days, HPQ is at $51.16. The December 47.5 calls are bid for $3.60, the 50s are offered for $1.20, and both the 52.5s and 55s are a nickel. The result is a loss on the long calls but gains on the short calls. To be specific, the strategist loses $310 on the 47.5s $[(5.20 \times 2 - 3.6 \times 2) \times 100 = 310]$ and $160 on the 55s $[(0.85 \times 2 - 0.05 \times 2) \times 100 = 160]$. However, those losses are offset by gains of $430 on the December 50 calls $[(3.35 \times 2 - 1.20 \times 2) \times 100 = 430)$ and $390 on the 52.5 calls $[(2 \times 2 - 2 \times 0.05) \times 100 = 390)$. The net result is a profit of $350. (See Table 9.19.)

figure 9.6   long condor (long 2 HPQ December 47.5 calls @ 5.20, short 2 HPQ December 45 calls at 3.35, short 2 HPQ December 52.5 calls @ 2.00, long 2 HPQ December 55 calls @ 0.85)

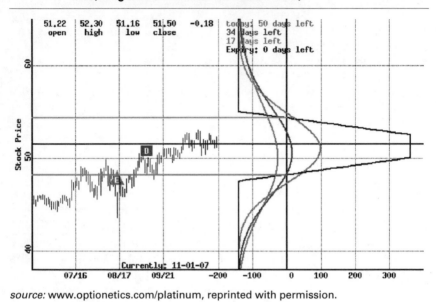

source: www.optionetics.com/platinum, reprinted with permission.

A long condor trade can use strikes that are farther apart as long as you sell the body and buy the wings. You can also use puts instead of calls. In most cases, the option premiums will determine the optimal trade to place. Make sure you have enough time premium to make the trade worthwhile. In addition, it can be interesting to leg out of this trade to cover the net debit and wait to see if the other half of the trade makes a free profit. This is easily accomplished because

table 9.19   long condor results

Long 2 HPQ December 47.5 Calls @ 5.20, Short 2 HPQ December 45 Calls at 3.35, Short 2 HPQ December 52.5 Calls @ 2.00, Long 2 HPQ December 55 Calls @ 0.85

Closing Price of HPQ Stock	Days in Trade	Price of 47.5 Call	Price of 50 Call	Price of 52.5 Call	Price of 55 Call	Profit/ Loss	Return on Investment
$51.16	49	$3.60	$1.20	0.05	0.05	$350	150%

a condor is the combination of a bull call spread and a bear call spread. You can simply close one and wait to see what happens to the other. In this example, however, the strategist waited until a day before expiration and exited the trade.

---

rule of thumb
look for a market that has been trading in a range for at least three months with option premiums that make the limited nature of the strategy worthwhile.

---

long iron butterfly

The long iron butterfly spread is the third strategy that can be used in a sideways market. It combines two more basic option strategies: the bear call spread (short lower call and long higher call) and the bull put spread (long lower put and short higher put). It is similar to a long condor but has a particular twist. This shift is illustrated in Table 9.20. As you can see, the long iron butterfly is created by using a combination of calls and puts instead of all calls or all puts.

---

long iron butterfly strategy
an options strategy that combines two more basic option strategies: the bear call spread (short lower call and long higher call) and the bull put spread (long lower put and short higher put). All options must have the same underlying asset and the same expiration.

---

table 9.20   long iron butterfly strategy shift

Strike Price	Condor Calls	Iron Butterfly Calls	Puts
135	Buy 1	Buy 1	
125	Short 1	Short 1	
115	Short 1		Short 1
105	Buy 1		Buy 1

table 9.21	call and put premiums with HPQ @ 51.50	
Price of HPQ = $51.50 (11/1/07)		
Call Strike Price	December Calls	December Puts
45	7.20	0.25
47.5	5.10	0.50
50	3.35	1.00
52.5	2.00	1.70
55	0.85	2.80

Let's create a long iron butterfly using the prices in Table 9.21 for Hewlett-Packard by going long two HPQ December 47.5 puts @ $.50, short two December 50 puts @ $1.00, short two December 52.5 calls @ $2.00, and long two December 55 calls at $.85. The maximum reward is equal to the net credit of the spread. In this example, the maximum reward is $330: [(1.00 + 2.00) × 2 − (0.50 + 0.85) × 2] × 100 = $330.

The maximum risk is equal to the number of lowest strike options times the difference between the long and short strike prices times the value per point, minus the net credit received. In this case, the maximum risk is $170: [2 × (50 − 47.5) × 100] − 330 = $170. The upside breakeven is equal to the highest short strike plus the net credit divided by the number of highest strike options times 100.

In this example, the upside breakeven is $54.15: 52.5 + [330 / (2 × 100)] = 54.15. The downside breakeven is equal to the lowest short strike minus the net credit divided by the number of lowest strike options times 100. The downside breakeven is $48.35: 50 − [330 / (2 × 100)] = 48.35. Therefore, the profit range for this trade is between $48.35 and $54.15. (See Table 9.22.) The risk graph for this trade is shown in Figure 9.7.

To exit this trade, you need to monitor the underlying market daily. In the best of all possible scenarios, the underlying stock continues to move sideways between the strikes of the short options so that neither one is assigned. In this example, HPQ generally moves sideways to $51.16 at expiration and in between the two short strike prices, leaving the options to expire worthless. Hence, the trader gets to keep the net credit of $330 (Table 9.23).

---

table 9.22   long iron butterfly trade calculations

Long Iron Butterfly Using Hewlett Packard Company @ $51.50

Maximum risk =[(# of lowest strike options × the difference in strikes) × 100] − net credit	$330
Maximum reward = Net credit	$330
Downside breakeven = Lowest short strike − (net credit / # of lowest strike options × 100)	$48.35
Upside breakeven = Highest short strike + net credit / # of highest strike options × 100)	$54.15

It's amazing how each strategy's profit margin fluctuates slightly using primarily the same premiums. (See Table 9.24.) As a rule, look for the trade with the best reward-to-risk ratio and the least risk. In general, if your calculations show an increased reward-to-risk ratio, it's best to place an iron butterfly instead of a condor. This often

---

figure 9.7   long iron butterfly (long 2 HPQ December 47.5 puts @ 0.50, short 2 HPQ December 45 puts at 1.00, short 2 HPQ December 52.5 calls @ 2.00, long 2 HPQ December 55 calls @ 0.85)

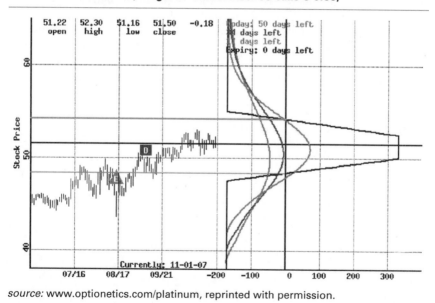

table 9.23   long iron butterfly results

Long 2 HPQ December 47.5 Puts @ 0.50, Short 2 HPQ December 45 Puts at 1.00,
Short 2 HPQ December 52.5 Calls @ 2.00, Long 2 HPQ December 55 Calls @ 0.85

Closing Price of HPQ Stock at Expiration	Days in Trade	Price of 47.5 Put	Price of 50 Put	Price of 52.5 Call	Price of 55 Call	Profit/ Loss
$51.48	50	0	0	0	0	$330

Note: Options with a strike price less than 60 expire worthless.

happens when the puts and calls have different implied volatilities, but finding the right markets for these strategies is quite difficult if you are searching manually. This is where options trading software really comes in handy.

For example, in Optionetics Platinum you can customize the filter to search for only bullish, limited-risk butterfly trades. In seconds you'll have your choice of a variety of trades as well as each trade's maximum risk, maximum reward, and theoretical profit and loss. If you find one you like, you can then set up the trade's risk profile, calculate the breakevens, and even run a probability check to ascertain the trade's probability of ending up in-the-money. These kinds of tools are invaluable as you cascade from market to market looking for trading opportunities. Perhaps this is the real crux of the business: Trading online increases your capacity to sift through all the numbers looking for that winning opportunity. When you unleash

table 9.24   comparison of sideways spread results

Trade	Maximum Risk	Maximum Gain	Breakevens	Days in Trade	Profit at Exit	Return on Investment
Long butterfly	($40)	$460	$50.20 to $54.80	49	$190	375%
Long condor	($140)	$360	$48.20 to $54.30	49	$350	150%
Long iron butterfly	($170)	$330	$48.35 to $54.15	50	$330	Depends on margin

the power of your computer to hunt down optimal opportunities for making money, you have the competitive edge necessary to make money in the markets.

---

rule of thumb
look for a sideways market and then try out a variety of put and call premiums until an optimal trade is located.

---

conclusion

Generally, most people believe the market is going to move higher over the long term, so they structure positions to take advantage of that market assumption. However, a disciplined approach to play the shorter-term trends in a market can provide additional returns, reduce stress, and make trading more enjoyable. There are many different ways to capture option premium in the short term; taking multiple approaches to your trading seems to be the right thing to do. However, keep in mind that the most important aspect of exploiting sideways trading opportunities is to implement a strategy with limited risk.

Since no search or system will ever be 100 percent accurate when it comes to predicting the future direction of a security or whether a current trend will continue, it's imperative for traders to use limited-risk strategies to preserve capital just in case they're wrong. Luckily, markets go sideways the majority of the time; hence, understanding how to profit from rangebound markets might just be your ticket to creating success.

The examples in this chapter show seven of these sideways strategies that make money by capturing time premium in a neutral environment. For your convenience, Table 9.24 details the results of each trade so that you can easily compare them.

If I find a really stable market, the numbers tell me which strategy to apply. But to keep it simple, I usually start by running the numbers on a butterfly strategy. If the numbers look good, then I look at the difference when the spread is expanded into a condor. If this looks unusually promising, I'll do the calculations for an iron butterfly and see which has the optimal numbers.

Butterflies and backspreads are techniques that professional floor traders use all the time to hedge their risk. In addition, there are many ways to modify butterflies and condors to create great risk/reward opportunities. These are successful strategies to use because the risks are not as great as they might appear to be. These spreads are always hedging themselves one way or the other and do not require adjustments. Sometimes the hardest part of trading is to believe that you have a good trade in your hands and simply leave the trade alone.

chapter 10

the futures market

back to the futures

Many options traders don't deal with stocks and options, but focus on futures options instead. For example, the market for S&P 500 Index futures is a vibrant one and options on the S&P futures see robust trading activity. In addition, many of the strategies discussed in the previous four chapters can be applied in the futures market. However, before launching into futures trading, strategists should first develop a good understanding of the futures market.

There are two general types of futures: commodities for hard assets, such as agricultural products, metals, and livestock; and commodities for financials, such as currencies, interest rates, and market indexes. Commodities are derivative products whose price is based on the spot price for the underlying asset plus the cost of carry to the contract date. Cost of carry includes things like interest and storage, while the contract date is the point in time at which the underlying physical asset is exchanged. A trader who does not want to take possession of the asset must close out his position by a date prior to actual expiration (this date can be as early as the month prior to the contract date).

Futures contracts trade on one of eight commodity exchanges, including Chicago, New York, Kansas City, and Minneapolis, as well as cyberspace. Each exchange offers a unique set of commodity contracts and establishes its own rules, subject to the oversight of the Commodity Futures Trading Commission (CFTC). The CFTC is a federal regulatory agency with responsibilities that parallel the rules administered by the Securities and Exchange Commission (SEC) over stock markets. In addition, an industry self-regulatory body—the National Futures Association (NFA)—handles the registration and testing of professionals involved in the execution of futures trades (www.nfa.futures.org).

Since futures are regulated under a separate authority, they require a separate type of brokerage account. It isn't possible to trade both stocks and futures in the same account. Similarly, trading stock options and options on futures requires two different trading accounts. However, some firms, like OptionsXpress and Interactive Brokers, offer both. If trading options on futures is important to you, make sure to ask your broker or prospective broker if they offer futures accounts when you sign up.

straight facts about futures

The Chicago Board of Trade (CBOT), the world's first modern futures exchange, was formed in 1848. In the early years, trading consisted of forward contracts. The first corn contract was written in 1851, and in 1865 standardized futures contracts were introduced.

The futures markets today have easily outgrown their agricultural origins. With the addition of the New York Mercantile Exchange (NYMEX) and the Chicago Mercantile Exchange (CME), which acquired the CBOT in 2008, trading of financial products using futures dwarfs the traditional commodity markets. These products play an extremely important role in the global financial system, trading trillions of dollars each day.

Despite the growth in the numbers and types of futures products traded, none would exist without standardization, one of the important innovations wrought by the CBOT. To attract traders, contracts were transformed from customized vehicles into readily tradable investments. By standardizing contract sizes and specifications, the CBOT created fungible or interchangeable instruments. The fungibility of futures contracts allows them to be readily offset, or closed out, before delivery. In addition, with standardization, traders know, for example, that each wheat contract calls for the delivery of 5,000 bushels of No. 2 Red Winter or Northern Spring grain through selected warehouses in Illinois, Indiana, and Ohio. Delivery dates are also standardized to provide contract lengths that suit buyers' and sellers' time frames.

Less than 4 percent of all futures contracts actually result in deliveries. The vast majority are offset prior to the delivery month. For example, buyers of futures contracts simply sell their contracts to close. Likewise, contract sellers can relieve themselves of the obligation to make delivery by purchasing the same contract that they had sold.

Futures are closed through offsetting transactions similar to unwinding an options position. Selling a contract previously bought or buying a contract that had been sold leaves the trader *flat* (i.e., devoid of any contract). Some futures day traders are flat at the end of each trading session. Realizing a profit or loss is based on the difference between the contract's purchase and sale prices. If I short S&P 500 futures and the market falls, I can bank a profit by buying the futures contract back at a lower price.

Margin is another aspect of futures trading that attracts speculators to the market. In the early days, forward contracts were formed with a handshake and the promise of payment upon delivery of the commodity. When futures are traded, however, both buyers and sellers post good faith deposits. Unlike the margin used in stock trading, deposits don't represent down payments. Instead, the margin requirements are performance bonds that guarantee that the contracts will be honored by each side. They allow traders to control a large amount of an asset with relatively little money down. Margin requirements are sometimes reduced for hedgers who have physical ownership of the commodity or spread traders who have offsetting contracts.

hard asset commodities   There are several different categories for commodities, as well as various contracts within each category. For example, major categories include agricultural, livestock, metals, and energy. Within the agricultural category there are various soybean, wheat, oats, and corn contracts, as well as cocoa, coffee, and sugar contracts. Each product has unique specifications (i.e., the quantity that the underlying represents) that must be reviewed and understood prior to entering the market.

financial futures   The financial futures markets serve to hedge risks of large participants. For instance, you may have a global corporation that manufactures products in one currency and sells them in other currencies. As the rates change across markets, that corporation has both competitive concerns as well as foreign exchange concerns. The financial futures markets allow corporations, among others, to hedge currency risk. Again, contract specifications provide information about the contract timing, underlying deliverables, and quantity represented.

Major financial futures categories include interest rates, foreign currencies, and market indexes (Dow, Financial Times Stock Exchange, S&P 500, commodity groups, etc.). The market for all of these products is global in nature—don't look at them merely in a domestic context.

more on margin   In the futures market, margin is used to minimize credit risk to the exchanges. In general, traders must post margin or a performance bond of between 5 and 15 percent depending on the contract. The futures exchanges and futures brokerage firms post the specific margin requirements on their web sites. There are different types of margin in the futures market.

- *Customer margins* are the financial guarantees that both buyers and sellers of futures contracts as well as sellers of options will fulfill their contract obligations. Also referred to as *performance bond margin*, the customer margins are determined on the basis of market risk and contract value.

- *Initial margin* is paid by both buyer and seller and represents the loss on that contract that is unlikely to be exceeded during a normal day of trading. The initial margin requirement is set by the futures exchange.

- *Maintenance margin* is the minimum margin per outstanding futures contract that a customer must maintain in the account. If the margin drops below the margin maintenance requirement, a margin call will be issued to bring the account back up to the required level. A futures account is marked to market daily.

- *Clearing margin* requirements are separate from the requirements imposed on individual investors. They are financial safeguards to ensure that firms perform on their customers' open futures and options contracts.

Understanding the risks of trading in the futures market requires knowledge of customer margin requirements and how that leverage impacts the risk/reward potential of going long and short. For example, in early 2008, the initial margin requirement for trading a 10-year Treasury bond, with a value of $100,000, was less than $500. However, due to increasing volatility, that requirement was gradually raised to roughly $1,200. Exchanges will raise and lower margin requirements based on the price action of the underlying asset. Nevertheless, even at $1,200, the margin on the 10-year Treasury bond was less than 2 percent of the value of the futures contract, which can translate to large percentage gains and losses if the trader is buying and selling the contract using only minimum margin requirements.

spot market versus futures

Without a spot market, a futures contract wouldn't exit. The spot or cash market represents the price of a product in the market today. It is the cash price for a commodity today and the face value of that commodity for delivery on the spot. The futures price is based on all the costs associated with holding that commodity for future delivery. Gold, for example, can be purchased by a bullion dealer at the spot price today. If, however, you buy bullion through the futures market, you have to wait for the delivery month to get your gold. In the time you wait for delivery, your gold must be stored, insured, and financed. These so-called carrying costs explain why futures often trade at higher prices compared to the spot market.

Let's consider an example. It's early August and gold is trading for $850 per ounce. If you want to lock in today's price of gold for delivery in, say, September—a month from now—the dealer might ask you to pay $852.60 per ounce. The extra $2.60 per ounce premium over the spot price is the dealer's cost for holding the gold till September. If you want the dealer to carry until December, a premium of $10.00 per ounce might be levied to cover the additional storage charges. The greater the time left in the futures contract, the greater the cost of carry. For any given commodity, several delivery months trade simultaneously. Each month will have a different value or price level depending on the carrying costs for each delivery.

The near-term market for gold on the COMEX division of the New York Mercantile Exchange, for example, might look like Table 10.1. In a normal market such as this, the prices of nearby delivery months are less than the deferred deliveries. The spot month—in this case, August—typically has the lowest prices. In sum, the prices of commodities typically increase over delivery months due to carrying costs such as storing, insuring, and financing the commodity.

table 10.1   gold futures prices

NYMEX CMX Gold (100-ounce Contracts, Dollars per Ounce)

Month	Last
August	850.50
September	852.60
October	855.50
December	862.00
February	869.60

In Table 10.1, all of the contracts call for the delivery of the same quantity and quality of metal: 100 ounces of .995 fine (24-karat) gold, which currently sells in the cash market for $850 per ounce. The closer a contract is to expiration, and to the cash market, the lower the carrying charges. At the end of a contract's delivery period, the cash or spot market and the expiring futures converge in price. They are equal.

Arbitrage players, or arbitrageurs (often called *arbs*), ensure that the spot and futures price align at expiration. If the alignment of futures and cash market prices are significantly out of whack, arb players step in to capitalize on pricing disparities. For example, if the futures prices trade too far above the spot (reflecting abnormally high carrying charges), sharp-eyed arbs could sell the overpriced futures, buy an equivalent amount of spot gold, store it, and then deliver the gold against the short futures in the delivery month. The inflated carry premium would thus be captured as a profit. Conversely, sales of overpriced futures exert downward price pressure in the contract market as spot metal prices are bid up by offsetting purchases.

arbitrageurs (arbs)
players who attempt to profit from price differences between two substantially equal assets. This might involve, for instance, buying a commodity on one exchange and simultaneously selling a similar commodity on another exchange in order to profit from the price difference between the two.

If futures markets don't reflect full carrying charges for some reason, arbs can also exploit the mispricing by doing a reverse version of this trade. The discount would be corrected when underpriced futures are purchased and spot metal is sold (the gold received at delivery against futures offsets the arbs' short cash market sales). This often happens in the stock market when the S&P 500 futures are out of line with the cash equities market. In that case, buy-and-sell programs hit the equity market and attempt to make a risk-free profit from arbitrage.

The mere fact that arbitrage occurs keeps prices from getting out of line most of the time. At times, however, arbitrage players miss opportunities and different delivery months can move out of step within a normal or carrying charge market. A normal market reflects ample supplies across all delivery months. Not all markets appear that way. There are times when large disparities occur because of inherent differences in supply and demand for storable commodities.

Winter wheat is an example. It is planted in late fall, dormant during the winter (hence its name), and then harvested in early summer. Nearby delivery months before the summer harvest in May or June reflect the old crop, but more distant delivery months reflect a market with new crop supplies. A surplus or shortage in old crop months, therefore, is not necessarily reflected in new crop months. In fact, it's not unusual to see new crop months trade at a relative discount to old crop months, reflecting ample quantities of new wheat. In short, bullish or bearish movements in old crop months might not be reflected in new crop months.

Depending on the contract, some delivery months will attract more interest than others. December gold is another example. It attracts more commercial interest at the end of the year because jewelry manufacturers hedge their holiday sales. Meanwhile, prices in other, more thinly traded delivery months may be more volatile, allowing for more persistent price disparities between December and other months. Understanding the fundamentals of the commodity in question is the key to knowing why divergences occur and how to profit from abnormal price action.

inverted markets   Normal markets reflect normal supplies of a commodity. Shortages, however, can cause a market to invert. Inverted markets develop as spot or near-term supplies are hoarded. Inverted

---

table 10.2 crude oil futures prices

NYMEX Crude Oil (1,000-barrel Contracts, Dollars per Barrel)

Month	Last
July	111.24
August	110.78
September	110.23
October	109.89
November	109.77

---

markets reflect consumer unwillingness to wait for delivery of a commodity. They don't want it later, they want it now!

---

inverted markets
a situation where prices in the spot market are greater than in the futures market. Inverted markets can occur when there is strong present demand for a commodity.

The energy markets are particularly prone to inversion because the sometimes whimsical OPEC controls a great deal of supply. As you can see in Table 10.2, the (hypothetical) prices of deferred deliveries are lower than those of nearby deliveries in an inverted market. The spot month, July in this case, is priced highest.

While the numbers in Table 10.2 are hypothetical, it isn't unusual to see inverted markets in crude oil futures. They can change over time, because shifts in supply and demand cause markets to move in and out of inversion. For example, if supplies increase or demand falls, or both, an inverted market can return to normalcy.

hedgers and speculators

A hedger is a player in the futures market who depends on contracts to lock in prices. For example, a farmer looking to lock in historically high wheat prices might sell futures. Stock investors might hedge with stock index futures, banks can hedge using financial futures, and gold producers can hedge prices with gold futures.

hedger
an investor who uses the futures market to minimize the risk in his business. Hedgers may be manufacturers, portfolio managers, bankers, farmers, and so on. Hedging can help lock in existing profits and/or reduce the overall risk of loss to fluctuating prices.

speculator
a trader who hopes to benefit from a directional move in the underlying instrument, attempts to anticipate price changes, and, through buying and selling futures contracts, aims to make a profit. The speculator does not use the futures market in connection with the production, processing, marketing, or handling of a product, and thus has no interest in making or taking delivery.

Speculators supply liquidity to the futures market. Somebody, after all, has to take the other side of the hedging trades made by commercial users. Speculators look for profits by correctly forecasting price changes. They don't plan on taking ownership of the physical commodity. For example, a speculator might bet that December cocoa will rise to $1,800 per ton by purchasing futures at the current $1,600 price. That trader has no intention of actually taking delivery of the cocoa in December. They don't need 10 tons of cocoa beans! Instead, the speculator expects to offset the futures position before the delivery period.

Let's say cocoa's price rises to $1,820 per ton by October. The speculator who went long at $1,600 can take $2,200 in profits ($220 per ton times the 10-ton contract size) by selling the contract. Conversely, if prices move southward to $1,470 per ton as December approaches, the speculator might be forced to liquidate the position at a $1,300 loss ($130 times the 10-contract size) to avoid the risk of delivery, or being forced to buy the cocoa.

Speculators are attracted to the futures market because of leverage. The initial margin required for your cocoa trade might be only $1,700, for instance, but the speculator is trading cocoa with a

---

table 10.3   profit from hypothetical cocoa trade

	Price per Ton	Margin
Bought 1 contract		
December cocoa	$1,600	$1,700
Sold 1 contract		
December cocoa	$1,820	
13.8% price gain	$ 220	
Contract = 10 tons	× 10	
Gross profit	$2,200	
Divide profit by margin	$2,200 ÷ $1,700	
Return	129.4%	

---

total contract value of $16,000 ($1,600 per ton × 10 tons). The leverage is nearly 10 to 1. In other words, the speculator puts up only 10.6 percent of the commodity's value, but profits and losses are the same as those of someone who had paid the full cash price for a wholesale lot of cocoa.

Calculating the profit and loss potential in the scenarios we've described, let's see how this leverage works for or against you (see Table 10.3).

The attraction of a $2,200 gain on a $1,700 investment is obvious. Notice that the underlying commodity had to move less than 14 percent to produce a 129 percent return. This is similar to the leverage offered by buying a put or call. Leverage, however, is a two-edged sword that can cut deeply. Losses, too, can pile up dramatically on small moves (see Table 10.4).

In either case, whether the trade yields a profit or a loss, the transactions are limited to the futures market and the speculator never intends to touch the actual commodity. Speculators avoid deliveries because of the substantial costs associated with the transfer and storage of the underlying commodities. In fact, many futures brokerage firms frown on trading after the first notice date (FND), which is when a speculator might receive a delivery notice. Unlike options, the delivery notice can occur at any time during the trading day. Assignment notices in the options market only occur at the end of the day. In the options market, if the position is closed before the end of day, assignment won't occur. However, that isn't true for the futures market.

---

table 10.4   loss from hypothetical cocoa trade

	Price per Ton	Margin
Bought 1 contract		
December cocoa	$1,600	$1,700
Sold 1 contract		
December cocoa	$1,470	
8.1% price decline	−$ 130	
Contract = 10 tons	× 10	
Gross loss	$1,300	
Divide loss by margin	$1,300 ÷ $1,700	
Return	−76.5%	

What if price expectations take a little longer than expected to materialize? As an example, let's say December cocoa reaches only $1,760 on the eve of the delivery period and the speculator believes there's room for a further price advance. If he wants to maintain a long position, the next step is to execute a rollover of the long position to the next available delivery month. To do so, the investor sells the December contract and simultaneously buys March futures, the following contract month.

rolling
closing out a position in one month and opening a similar position in a subsequent month.

A short position is established by opening your futures trade with a sale instead of a purchase. How do you sell a commodity you don't already own? Remember that you're selling futures, not the actual cocoa. Futures are obligations to make or take delivery, secured by margin. A short sale is simply a wager that prices will decline before the contract's last trading day. Offsetting the short sale with a purchase before delivery precludes the need to actually own the commodity. For example, a speculator can bet on a decline in cocoa's price. If he expects a drop to the $1,500 level, he might sell December cocoa short at $1,600.

If December cocoa declines to $1,470 per ton, a $1,300 profit ($130 per ton × 10 tons) could be generated by buying back the December contract to close out the short position. This is the exact reverse of the loss in the long position described previously. Since the margin is the same for a short position as it is for a long position, the speculator makes (instead of loses) 76.5 percent. Then, if the speculator thinks there is further softening in cocoa's price ahead, he could roll the short position forward by buying back December futures while simultaneously shorting March cocoa.

This is the same process in any futures market. If prices are expected to move higher, traders can go long one or more futures contracts. Conversely, if they expect prices to fall, they short one or more futures contracts. There are more advanced futures strategies, called spreads, which lie outside of the scope of this book. Readers interested in more information in this area of finance are encouraged to read another of my books, *Getting Started in Commodities* (John Wiley & Sons, 2007).

conclusion

When building asset allocation models, futures are the third major asset class considered, along with stocks and bonds. The correlations among these three markets serve to diversify portfolios and offset downdrafts in one market by realizing gains in another.

There are two areas of risk in the commodities market that differ from those in the stock market. The first risk is the possibility of providing or taking possession of a physical asset, which may result in a large unwanted cash transaction. While you would not actually have a truck stopping by your house to unload bushels of corn, there could be a substantial amount of cash required to satisfy your long or short obligations under the futures contract. The bottom line: Be sure you understand your obligations and the last trade date required for you to exit those obligations for your specific contracts.

The second area of risk involves margin. While you can purchase stocks on margin, the requirements for stocks are higher and rarely change through the holding period for the stock. Commodity and futures contracts have a very low margin requirement (5 to 10 percent) but are impacted by volatility in the underlying. These markets are *marked to market* each trading day and participants are required to add money to the position if it goes against them. With such low margin and the potential for large moves, these daily amounts can be sizeable. It's vital to really understand market and account dynamics so that you can be prepared to effectively manage your risk. These two products (commodities and futures) cannot be passively managed to the extent that some stock portfolios are managed.

The commodity markets were developed in the Midwest to address the risks of farmers, then those of large-quantity consumers. Farmers wanted to lock in prices before harvest so they could be certain that the season would be worthwhile economically and cash flows could be projected. On the consumer side, large-quantity users also had the opportunity to lock in major costs and to price product accordingly. As a result of this dynamic, there are market participants in both the commodities and financial futures markets who are there just to hedge their risks. The markets serve a distinct business goal of forecasting future costs or income based on current conditions. Additionally, there are market participants who will accept some of the future risk for the hedgers for a price. They seek to earn profits on their dollars. Both of these types of participants significantly impact supply and demand in the markets.

Many futures contracts also have listed options. To trade them requires an account that is approved to trade futures. Some, but not all, of the brokerage firms listed in Chapter 12 offer futures accounts. Many of the strategies discussed in Chapters 5 through 9 can also be applied in futures options. However, keep in mind that, unlike the stock and index options discussed in earlier chapters, futures options don't settle into shares or cash. Most settle into the underlying futures contract.

The commodities and futures markets also offer equity investors the opportunity to diversify into other assets including grains, energy, or metals. These commodities can go through bull or bear markets when the equity market is doing just the opposite. Active participation in the commodities and futures markets is not for everyone; however, these remain important asset classes. But many of the new futures contracts have been created with the smaller investor in mind. That is, the exchanges have created smaller contracts, called *minis*, that trade electronically. Hence, it's easier than ever to get into futures trading. The key to your success is to develop a solid understanding of the fundamentals.

chapter 11

online trading
from A to Z

streamlining your approach

Since it's now time to pull everything together, this chapter is designed to walk you step-by-step through a series of online sites to help find the most promising trading opportunities. Rather than surfing from web site to web site, I prefer to concentrate on a few select sites with the most useful information. So let's get started on our final cyber-tour into the online trading matrix.

First things first: The following step-by-step process has been designed to help you pick profitable trades—regardless of whether the markets are bullish, bearish, or sideways-moving. It includes some of the same steps that we have developed and refined over the past two decades. Each step will be followed by a breakdown of how it can best be used. The steps are as follows:

1. *Charting:* Looking at chart patterns and indicators.
2. *News:* Looking at the fundamental picture.
3. *Strategies:* Developing an options strategy.
4. *Tracking:* Tracking open positions.

charting

Many people start trading options with a dart-throwing mentality. It is amazing to see just how many people trade options without any knowledge about the underlying asset. In my system, I don't even look at the options until the third step. I prefer to start by looking at charts to determine whether a stock or market is in an uptrend, downtrend, or moving sideways. Is volatility high or low? Is it a slow or a fast market? Without an understanding of the technicals and fundamentals of the underlying asset, it is impossible to identify the optimum options strategy. We need to put the horse before the cart.

As explained in Chapter 2, a wide variety of types of charts can be created to analyze and assess a stock's movement. For example, I rely heavily on charting software such as ProfitSource, which allows us to view real-time and historical charts. However, since this book is about trading options online, the discussion is limited to the charting tools that are available in cyberspace—some free and others available for a modest subscription. Also keep in mind that many online brokers offer charting tools. Chapter 12 takes a closer look at a dozen brokers and the kinds of tools and services they offer.

Generally, if you are a new trader, you want to review a few chart services and then find the one that seems the most valuable to you. It could be on a web site, through your broker, or in a premium software package. The ideas presented here are not all-inclusive. Talk to other traders and get a feel for what is out there today. Then make a decision based on the amount of trading you want to do. For example, if you are trading daily, you probably want to pay for a more advanced software package. However, if you trade only once a month, free charts available online will probably do.

First, let's do a short review of charting basics. A chart is a series of data and numbers that consist of price (or volume) and time. Charts give investors a visual survey of a stock's price movement and volume activity in order to identify patterns and trends that aid in forecasting future price movement. An abundance of charting techniques and even more technical analysis methods can be used to analyze price fluctuations.

Charts for individual stocks are as unique as a person's fingerprints. However, all bar charts, which are the most commonly used types of charts, include four pieces of information: opening price, high for the day (or for the hour, week, etc.), low for the day (hour, week, etc.), and closing price. The four parts of a simple bar chart, which is sometimes called an open-high-low-close (OHLC),

figure 11.1　**bar chart basics**

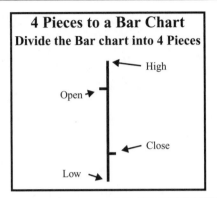

show the price change of a market over a specific time period. (See Figure 11.1.) As time passes, other bars are created that start to form the chart pattern. Patterns can be up, down, sideways, or a combination of one or more. Once you put enough of the bars together, you have the makings of a historical chart.

Bar series can range from minutes to months. It all depends on the time interval you choose. If you're a day trader, then looking at monthly bar charts is a waste of time. Looking at five-minute bar charts will better suit you. As an options trader, I spend most of my time reviewing daily and weekly bar charts. An abundance of sites offer charting services, but some of my favorites are Optionetics (www.optionetics.com), StockCharts.com (www.stockcharts.com), and BigCharts (www.bigcharts.com).

day trader
an active trader who limits his or her trading to intraday positions by entering and holding positions from a few minutes to hours and exiting or offsetting these positions by the end of the day.

Let's consider a simple example using the charting tools on StockCharts.com to look at Dell Computer (DELL). When you visit the StockCharts.com home page you will see a box similar to Figure 11.2. Type in the symbol "DELL" at the home page and then click on "Go."

---

figure 11.2   **create a chart on StockCharts.com**

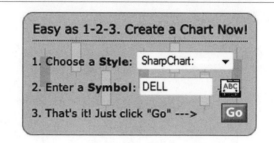

source: www.optionetics.com/platinum, reprinted with permission.

Within a few seconds, a new screen appears with a chart similar to Figure 11.3. On this site, the price action is not an OHLC or bar chart. It includes Japanese candlesticks. Many traders prefer to use the candlesticks because they are larger and it is easier to view price action. For example, in Figure 11.3, the bars are solid on days when the stock is moving lower but are clear on up days. The bar is created by the open and close of the day. The day's range (high and low) is reflected by the lines above and below the bar. Figures 11.4 and 11.5 show sample bars for down days and up days, respectively.

candlestick charts
a technical analysis charting method that shows the high, low, open, and close over a specified period of time. It adds dimension and color, by shading the bars white or green for an up move and black or red for a down move. Price moves outside of the range of opening and closing prices are shown as lines that reach to the high and the low. More advanced technical analysis based on candlesticks lies outside the scope of this book. For a more complete discussion, readers are encouraged to visit www.japanesecandlesticks.com.

Traders can change the charts with a few simple clicks. Figure 11.6 shows some of the charting tools available at StockCharts.com. For example, the time frame can be modified from daily to weekly. Users can change from candlesticks to OHLC or line charts. Volume can be added or removed. In addition, a number of computer-based indicators can be applied to study the price action

figure 11.3   candlestick chart of dell computers with indicators

source: www.stockcharts.com, reprinted with permission.

in more detail. In the current default setting on StockCharts.com, charts include volume, moving averages, the relative strength index (RSI), and moving average convergence/divergence (MACD). Let's take a look at these four indicators in more detail to better understand what the DELL chart is telling us.

figure 11.4 comparison of OHLC and candlestick charts (down day)

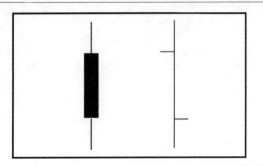

tick charts
typically used by day traders, tick charts feature incremental price and volume movement over a time span of your choice that enables you to watch price changes as they happen.

line charts
a simple graph that appears as a line based on the closing prices of the day, week, month, and so on.

point and figure charts
a graph that reveals a stock's significant upward and downward moves using closing prices through a pattern of Xs and Os.

figure 11.5 comparison of OHLC and candlestick charts (up day)

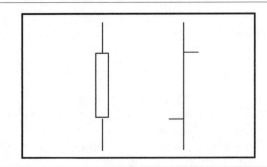

figure 11.6 stockcharts.com charting tools

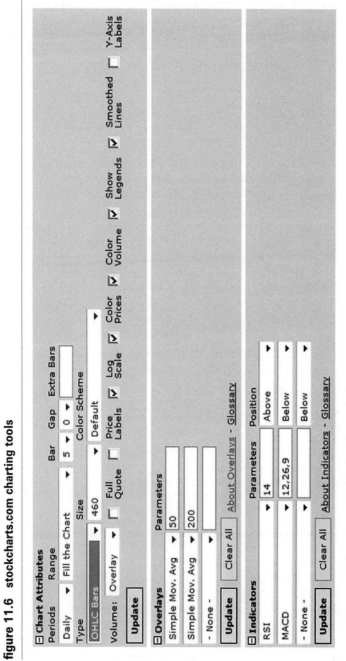

source: www.stockcharts.com, reprinted with permission.

239

volume as an indicator Volume can be used in a variety of ways. The volume part of the chart is located at the bottom of the screen beneath the price chart. Figure 11.3 shows some excellent volume indicators for Dell. Notice the volume spikes that occurred during the month of April. At that time, volume increased to twice its average daily volume and the price of Dell had a big move downward. However, by consulting the day's closing price on the day of extra volume, you'll find that buyers came rushing in before the close and pushed the price off the low. A week later the stock was rallying again.

Note: Don't try to use volume spikes with short-term, intraday price bars. This can spell disaster because most of the volume in a stock usually comes in the first and last trading hours of the day.

While volume spikes are good indicators of reversals in price, volume is also used to confirm longer-term trends. In general, during a healthy market advance, volume is used to confirm the move higher by increasing on the up days and declining on the down days. Then, when prices have risen to a point of exhaustion, volume will diminish during advances, which could be a sign that the uptrend is running out of gas and it's time to bank profits. The opposite can also happen. For example, after the big volume spike in DELL in April, the stock fell two more times on diminishing volume. This was a sign that the selling pressure was easing, and then the stock saw a rather dramatic one-month rebound.

volume spike
an extreme rise in a market's volume—the number of shares bought and sold—often resulting in a big price movement in either direction. Spikes sometimes occur at panic lows, or when investors capitulate. These episodes can lead to dramatic reversals.

simple moving average A moving average (MA) is one of the best technical analysis tools available. Most institutional traders and newspapers use both a 50-day and a 200-day moving average and you should, too, since it will give you an idea as to what the people with the real money are going to do. For example, a strong stock will tend to stay above its 50-day moving average. In Figure 11.3, DELL is spending most of its time below its 50-day moving average before making a break above it in May. That break signals the beginning of a new trend.

Many traders use two or more moving averages together. For example, if a stock breaks below its 50-day moving average, it had better bounce off its 200-day moving average. This is often accompanied by a large increase in volume (a volume spike) that drives the price back up to its 50-day moving average. If a stock closes below this number, it tells us that there is a possible trend change and that we should avoid this market due to uncertainty in the trend. Bearish stocks react in the opposite way. When a stock is breaking down it may fall to its 50-day average, encounter a volume spike, and then try to climb back up to its 200-day moving average. If it can't break through, it is probably headed back down to its 50-day moving average. As you can see in Figure 11.6, adding and removing multiple moving averages on StockCharts.com is easy.

---

moving averages
a mathematical procedure employed by adding together a stock's closing prices (usually for the previous 50 days or 200 days) and then dividing that number by the number of days in the period. The result is noted on a chart. The next day the same calculations are performed with the new result being connected (using a solid or dotted line) to yesterday's, and so forth.

---

relative strength index Figure 11.3 also includes the relative strength index (RSI) indicator, which is another type of oscillator. Developed by Welles Wilder, RSI is common on almost any computer trading software program available today and, therefore, does not require manual computation. Instead, the RSI is generally viewed on a stock chart above or below the price chart. In Figure 11.3 the RSI is at the top.

There are basically three ways to use the RSI. The first is to identify overbought and oversold conditions. The RSI will fluctuate between 0 and 100. On the DELL chart, the RSI has been between, roughly, 30 and 70 percent, which is the normal range. Conversely, when the indicator rose above 70 percent in late May, it was a sign of deeply overbought conditions and hinted at a possible pullback. The stock suffered a three-day decline shortly thereafter.

---

oscillator
a type of chart indicator that moves above and below a zero line. When it reaches extremes, it can hint at overbought or oversold conditions. For example, if an oscillator reaches an extreme low, the stock or market might be oversold and due to bounce higher. Other examples of oscillators include stochastics, accumulation/distribution, and on balance volume.

The second way to use oscillators is as a confirmation tool. When looking at trends, the RSI should be setting new highs or new lows along with the index. For instance, Dell Computer shares fell to a new low in mid-March, but the RSI did not—it was trending higher. These types of divergences are often followed by a move in the opposite direction. So if a stock or market moves to new highs, but the RSI does not, watch out! A reversal lower could be in the cards.

Finally, when looking at the relative strength index, also consider the slope of the indicator. An upward-sloping RSI is the sign of a healthy advance and a downward sloping RSI is evidence of a strong decline. Most oscillators are used in the same fashion as the RSI, but each is unique in its own way and must be considered individually.

moving average convergence/divergence (MACD)   The MACD is another popular chart indicator. It appears along the bottom of Figure 11.3. The MACD falls into a category of indicators known as trend followers. It can help to determine if a trend in a stock is healthy and likely to continue, or set for a reversal instead. The MACD is viewed on a stock chart either as lines or as a histogram, or both.

---

trend-following indicator
a group of indicators that are used to identify the strength and sustainability of a trend. Volume and moving averages form the foundation for many trend-following indicators.

When plotted using two lines, the MACD consists of a fast line and a slow line. The fast line is computed as the difference between two moving averages with different time periods. One is the average over a relatively short period of time, such as 12 days, while the second is the average price change in a stock over a longer period of time, such as 26 days. The 26-day MA is subtracted from the 12-day MA to create the MACD. The slow line (sometimes called the *signal* line) is simply the 9-day moving average of the MACD. (The number of days used in this computation is indicated in parentheses at the top of the MACD graph—in this case 12, 26, 9.)

When a stock or market is rising, the line that tracks the shorter-term moving average will rise more rapidly than the slow line. During times when one line changes faster than the other, the difference between the two lines will increase. In a downward trending market, the fast line will drop below the slow line. The fast line reacts faster to the most recent price changes and moves quicker than the slow line. Traders watch this divergence between the two lines.

In addition, the crossovers between the two lines generate trading signals. When the fast line is below the slow line and then rallies above it, the crossover triggers a buy signal. If the fast line is above the slow line, then moves lower, and crosses below the slow line, the move triggers a sell signal. A bearish crossover occurred in Figure 11.3 in early April when the fast line started falling and moved below the slow line.

MACD is plotted as a histogram as well. When the fast line is above the slow line, the bars on the histogram are positive and sit above the zero line. Conversely, if the fast line is below the slow line, the bars on the histogram are negative and below the zero line.

The histogram can be used as a confirmation tool for a stock's trends higher and lower. When the fast line is moving up at a faster pace than the slow line, the MACD histogram rises into positive territory and is confirming the move higher in the stock or index. If the stock or index is rallying and the MACD histogram is not moving higher, the rally is not confirmed and is likely to prove short-lived. The same kind of analysis is used during market declines.

In fact, there are ways to use MACD alone and along with other indicators. So many indicators have been created in recent years that there are too many to use because it creates too many conflicting trading signals. The purpose here is only to discuss a few and to help the reader understand the logic behind some of the more popular trend-following indicators and oscillators. More in-depth discussions of technical analysis tools such as these are available at stockcharts.com, metaquotes.com, investopedia.com, and the article archives at optionetics.com.

the kiss principle: keep it simple, stupid   Although a wide variety of additional indicators can be applied to any one chart, using too many crowds the chart with too much data and leads to trading indecision. There are probably more than 1,000 indicators available. If you applied all of them to one chart, half would be telling you that the chart is bullish, and the other half would be telling you that the chart is bearish. You can even create your own custom indicators. But the point I am trying to make here is that simple indicators are sometimes the best.

So what do I look for in an uptrend? I tend to look for a strong stock, preferably one that has made a 52-week high recently. I also look for a pullback off the highs, but not below a 200-day moving average. When it comes to time entry, I look for a volume spike, which lets me know that the majority of the selling in that stock has been done and it's time to move back up. I prefer to identify at least two of these criteria to be met before continuing to the next step: news.

news

News plays a quintessential role in the business of trading. The effect of news is constantly reflected in the price of a stock. For instance, if you were online and saw that a stock you were tracking had a change of +10 points on the day, there is probably some news behind why that stock moved up so much. News is categorized into two different types: breaking news and scheduled news.

breaking news   Spontaneous news that comes with little or no warning to the public is considered breaking news. Examples of breaking news include tragedies, violent weather, pre-earnings announcements, the death of world leaders, and accounting irregularities. Most of these newsworthy events have very little correlation to one another, but they all contribute to market movement. Since breaking news comes as a surprise, we cannot use it to anticipate price movement. But once an event occurs, we can ride the trend that the news inspires.

> **breaking news**
> spontaneous news regarding sudden changes, including management shake-ups, mergers and takeovers, or international crises.

If you're looking for the quintessential market news site, check out MarketWatch (www.marketwatch.com). Designed to keep traders and investors in the know, this site features top-notch journalists, insightful commentary, and superior news reporting. Another good source of aggregated financial news is Yahoo! Finance (finance.yahoo.com). Figure 11.7 shows the home page. A market recap and the top stories of the day appear first. Readers can also link to a list of popular stories and investing ideas articles. Finally, by typing the ticker symbol into the quote box, investors can pull up quotes and news stories for individual companies. Google recently launched a similar site (Figure 11.8), with a lot of the same features and information (finance.google.com/finance).

scheduled news   Scheduled news can be anticipated and is easily accessible. Examples include government reports, company earnings releases, product announcements, and weather reports. Scheduled news is important because it can help you determine the right time to get into or out of a market. Learning to prioritize information is an important part of a trader's training since some facts are more useful than others. Knowing how a company's last quarter's numbers look may be important, but not as crucial as knowing when an earnings report will be released. Many traders buy options just before earnings reports are released, hoping to get in prior to a big breakout.

Perhaps the biggest benefit you can derive from receiving scheduled news is the ability to enter, adjust, or exit a trade immediately before a big report is announced. Keeping track of stocks that are on your watch list or that you are trading is easier than ever before. Various financial web sites will e-mail you scheduled and breaking news on the stocks of your choice. Check out MarketWatch (www.marketwatch.com), WhatsTrading.com (www.whatstrading.com), CNN Money (money.cnn.com), or INO (www.ino.com) to avail yourself of this kind of free service. Once you have what you need, it's on to step 3.

figure 11.7   yahoo! home page

source: www.yahoo.com, reprinted with permission.

---

scheduled news
news that can be anticipated for release, including earnings
reports, stock splits, and government reports.

---

strategies

Finding the right strategy depends on how well you've done your
homework using steps 1 and 2. The right options strategy is

figure 11.8 **latest news from google finance**

source: www.google.com, reprinted with permission.

determined by whether you're bullish, bearish, or neutral on a specific stock. Having a good base of options knowledge will help you here. If you're a novice to options trading, I suggest a visit to the Optionetics web site (www.optionetics.com), where you can find a wealth of information designed specifically to help options traders locate the tools needed to compete in the marketplace (Figure 11.9). If you are new to options trading, click on "Options Education" and you'll find an abundance of educational information.

To determine the right options strategy to use in a particular market, it helps to have some software dedicated to options trading. Some brokerage firms have developed advanced options analysis software for customers. We, along with the help from hundreds of other options traders, have developed Optionetics Platinum, which we will use to explain one approach to identifying trading opportunities (Figure 11.10). It is a subscription-based product, but readers can sign up for a 14-day free trial to work through an example similar to the one covered in this chapter.

figure 11.9   optionetics.com home page

source: www.optionetics.com, reprinted by permission.

When looking for strategies, there is more than one way to begin the search. One is to identify the stock you want to trade and then, if it looks bullish, find the strategy with the best risk and reward based on your expectations for the stock price. Another is to screen the market for unique trading opportunities. For example, with Optionetics Platinum Software, you can screen the market for stocks that have options with high implied volatility levels. High levels of implied volatility generally mean that the market expects the stock to move. I like stocks that are showing some movement

figure 11.10 optionetics platinum sign in

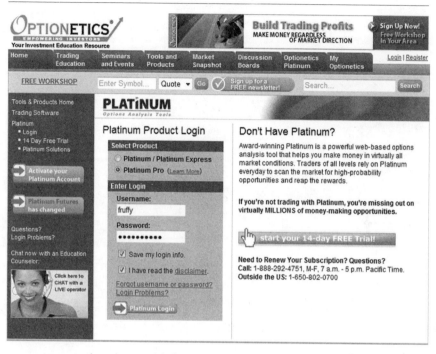

source: www.optionetics.com/platinumpro, reprinted with permission.

and getting investor interest. Figure 11.11 shows a recent screen for stocks with high levels of implied volatility. Intel (INTC), Oracle (ORCL), and Dell Computer (DELL) are at the top of the list. These are actively traded stocks with vibrant options markets—the kind of stocks I like to look for.

Oracle (ORCL) is a leading software company, and let's say our technical and fundamental research indicates that the stock should trend higher over the next few months. Next, click on the company name in the table and look at the option's historical premium levels, otherwise called implied volatility (IV). A chart (Figure 11.12) appears and shows the implied volatility over the past 20 months. The 30- to 60-day volatility, which reflects the July and August options (as this chart was created during the month of May), is quite elevated compared to the implied volatility of the short- and longer-term options. In addition, at more than 40 percent, it is also much higher

figure 11.11 implied volatility ranker

| Precomputed Rankings: Expensive: 1 mo | |

You can save over 1000+ Implied and Statistical Volatility preranked stocks into a list. Enter the number of stocks to Replace or Add in the text boxes shown.

Edit list name: My Stock List **REPLACE**

Add/Replace 250 stocks in list: My Stock List ▼ **ADD**

Click a Stock Symbol to find trades or Click an Option Symbol to begin analysis (if present)
Only the top 50 stocks or top 20 Options are shown below.

Option Rankings

STATISTICAL VOLATILITY
Explosive
Quiet

IMPLIED VOLATILITY
Expensive: 1 yr
Cheap: 1 yr
Breakout Hi
Breakout Low

OPTION PARAMETERS
Highest Volume
Highest Open
Unusual Hi Vol

Historical stock rankings NOT found for **2008-05-22**.
Precomputed Rankings are computed after each End Of Day Data Update.

Online historical stock rankings start at 2004-01-02.
Stock rankings shown below are for latest available date:.

High Percentile 1MO Implied Volatility Last Updated 05-21-08, 4:00PM EDT

Stock	High IV	Low IV	Current IV	IV Chg
1) Intel Corporation (INTC)	33.07%	27.21%	33.07%	+ 1.79%
2) Oracle Corporation (ORCL)	32.72%	27.51%	32.72%	+ 1.60%
3) Dell Inc (DELL)	35.41%	30.38%	35.41%	+ 1.42%
4) Broadcom Inc. (BRCM)	48.83%	38.74%	48.83%	+ 2.59%
5) General Electric Company (GE)	25.15%	20.34%	25.15%	+ 2.68%
6) eBay Inc (EBAY)	37.33%	28.65%	37.33%	+ 1.83%
7) Nokia Corporation ADR (NOK)	37.45%	31.99%	37.45%	+ 3.21%
8) International Business Machin (IBM)	23.25%	12.86%	23.25%	+ 1.25%
9) Exxon Mobil (XOM)	27.70%	21.81%	27.70%	+ 3.90%
10) Texas Instruments Incorporate (TXN)	28.88%	24.61%	28.88%	+ 1.00%

source: www.optionetics.com/platinumpro, reprinted with permission.

than May of the preceding year. So in this situation, we are bullish on the stock and implied volatility is high.

---

implied volatility
volatility computed using the actual market price of an option and a pricing model (Black-Scholes). For example, if the market price of an option rises without a change in the price of the underlying stock, implied volatility will have risen.

Our attention now turns to the Strategy Matrix, which allows us to pick a bullish, bearish, or neutral strategy within a variety of volatility periods. For example, if volatility is low and we are bullish,

figure 11.12   **implied volatility ranker**

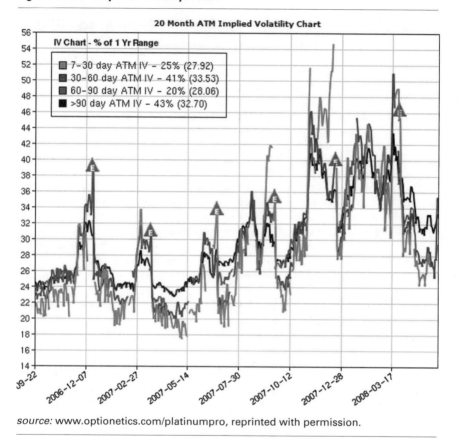

source: www.optionetics.com/platinumpro, reprinted with permission.

we might buy puts or use a bear put spread. In this case, since IV is high and the stock looks bullish, let's try an out-of-the-money call butterfly. If we check the box and click "Search," we find the information found in Figure 11.13.

The next step is to scan the list of potential trades for the ones that seem to offer the best risk/reward ratio. The table in Figure 11.14 provides a variety of useful information.

- *Stock price:* The current market price for the underlying asset.
- *Cost:* The combined trade cost in dollars. A negative means a credit to your account.

figure 11.13   strategy matrix

Select Option Strategies

IV	Price		
	Bullish	**Neutral**	**Bearish**
Low	☐ Buy Call ☐ Buy Stock, Buy Put ☐ Call Vertical Spread (DB) ☐ Put Vertical Spread (CR) ☐ Sell ITM Call ButterFly ☐ Sell OTM Put ButterFly ☐ Buy OTM Call Calendar Spd ☐ Buy ITM Put Calendar Spd ☐ Low IV Call Diag Calendar ☐ Low IV Put Diag Calendar	☐ Buy Straddle ☐ Long Synthetic Straddle ☐ Buy Strangle ☐ Sell ATM Call ButterFly ☐ Sell ATM Put ButterFly ☐ 1x2 Call Backspread (Bullish) ☐ 1x2 Put Backspread (Bearish) ☐ 2x3 Call Backspread (Bullish) ☐ 2x3 Put Backspread (Bearish) ☐ 1x2 Call Calendar Backspread ☐ 1x2 Put Calendar Backspread ☐ 2x3 Call Calendar Backspread ☐ 2x3 Put Calendar Backspread ☐ Sell ATM Call Calendar Spd ☐ Sell ATM Put Calendar Spd ☐ Debit Box Spread	☐ Buy Put ☐ Sell Stock, Buy Call ☐ Call Vertical Spread (CR) ☐ Put Vertical Spread (DB) ☐ Sell OTM Call ButterFly ☐ Sell ITM Put ButterFly ☐ Buy ITM Call Calendar Spd ☐ Buy OTM Put Calendar Spd ☐ Low IV Call Diag Calendar ☐ Low IV Put Diag Calendar
Mixed	☐ Long Call, Short Put	☐ Do Not Trade	☐ Long Put, Short Call
High	☐ Sell Put ☐ Covered Call ☐ Call Vertical Spread (DB) ☐ Put Vertical Spread (CR) ☑ Buy OTM Call ButterFly ☐ Buy ITM Put ButterFly ☐ Sell ITM Call Calendar Spd ☐ Sell OTM Put Calendar Spd ☐ Forward Hedge Wrapper (Collar) ☐ Hi IV Call Diag Calendar ☐ Hi IV Put Diag Calendar	☐ Sell Straddle ☐ Short Synthetic Straddle ☐ Sell Strangle ☐ Buy ATM Call ButterFly ☐ Buy ATM Put ButterFly ☐ Iron Butterfly ☐ Iron Condor ☐ Long Condor ☐ 1x2 Call Ratio Spread ☐ 1x2 Put Ratio Spread ☐ 2x3 Call Ratio Spread ☐ 2x3 Put Ratio Spread ☐ 1x2 Call Ratio Calendar ☐ 1x2 Put Ratio Calendar ☐ 2x3 Call Ratio Calendar ☐ 2x3 Put Ratio Calendar ☐ Buy ATM Call Calendar Spd ☐ Buy ATM Put Calendar Spd ☐ Credit Box Spread	☐ Sell Call ☐ Covered Put ☐ Call Vertical Spread (CR) ☐ Put Vertical Spread (DB) ☐ Buy ITM Call ButterFly ☐ Buy OTM Put ButterFly ☐ Sell OTM Call Calendar Spd ☐ Sell ITM Put Calendar Spd ☐ Reverse Hedge Wrapper ☐ Hi IV Call Diag Calendar ☐ Hi IV Put Diag Calendar

Your selected Strategies

Buy OTM Call ButterFly

source: www.optionetics.com/platinum, reprinted with permission.

figure 11.14   possible butterfly spreads

Rk	Stock	Click trade below for Options Analysis	Stock Price	Cost	Max Profit	Max Risk	Prob Of Profit	Odds	Days
1 ☐	ORCL	Buy 1 JAN09 35 Call@ 0.10 Sell 2 JAN09 30 Call@ 0.30 Buy 1 JAN09 25 Call@ 1.35	21.98	$85.00	$413.49	$-85.00	23.33%	0.8 to 1	238
2 ☐	ORCL	Buy 1 JAN10 35 Call@ 0.80 Sell 2 JAN10 30 Call@ 1.45 Buy 1 JAN10 25 Call@ 3.30	21.98	$120.00	$378.49	$-120.00	18.38%	0.4 to 1	602
3 ☐	ORCL	Buy 1 DEC08 25 Call@ 1.20 Sell 2 DEC08 23 Call@ 1.85 Buy 1 DEC08 21 Call@ 3.00	21.98	$50.00	$148.85	$-50.00	18.81%	0.4 to 1	210
4 ☐	ORCL	Buy 1 DEC08 26 Call@ 0.95 Sell 2 DEC08 24 Call@ 1.45 Buy 1 DEC08 22 Call@ 2.45	21.98	$50.00	$148.80	$-50.00	17.51%	0.3 to 1	210
5 ☐	ORCL	Buy 1 JUL08 26 Call@ 0.15 Sell 2 JUL08 25 Call@ 0.20 Buy 1 JUL08 24 Call@ 1.25	21.98	$25.00	$73.75	$-25.00	11.46%	0.2 to 1	56
6 ☑	ORCL	Buy 1 JUL08 26 Call@ 0.15 Sell 2 JUL08 24 Call@ 0.40 Buy 1 JUL08 22 Call@ 1.25	21.98	$60.00	$138.80	$-60.00	27.33%	0.5 to 1	56
7 ☐	ORCL	Buy 1 DEC08 24 Call@ 1.55 Sell 2 DEC08 23 Call@ 1.85 Buy 1 DEC08 22 Call@ 2.45	21.98	$30.00	$68.85	$-30.00	8.83%	0.1 to 1	210

source: www.optionetics.com/platinum, reprinted with permission.

- *Maximum profit:* The greatest amount of money you can make from this trade. Some trades are unlimited. This number should be positive. If it is negative, this means you can't win!
- *Maximum risk:* The probable greatest amount of money you can lose from this trade. Some trades have unlimited risk.
- *Probability of profit:* The probability that the predicted stock price falls within the option trade's profit zones.
- *Odds:* A ratio found by dividing the predicted average profits by the predicted average losses.
- *Days:* The number of days remaining in the trade. For calendar spreads, the near-month leg is used for days until expiration.

Recall from Chapter 9 that, since this is a butterfly spread, we are looking for time decay to work in our favor. We want options with less than 60 days until expiration; 45 days or less is even better. In this case, we pick the July 22/24/26 call butterfly (see Figure 11.14). There are 56 days remaining before the July options expire. Once we click on the trade, we find the risk curve in Figure 11.15. The strategy is indeed a bullish one. It makes its best profits if the stock moves up to the 24 strike price and the short calls expire worthless.

figure 11.15   ORCL July 22/24/26

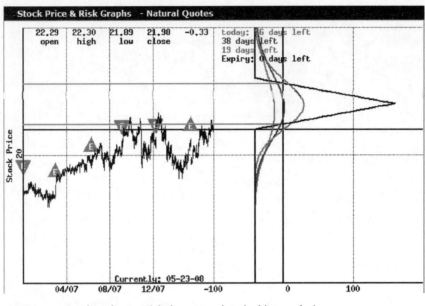

source: www.optionetics.com/platinum. reprinted with permission.

The risk/reward ratio is a little more than two to one. That is, the strategist is risking $60 per spread to make $138.80.

tracking

One of the best ways to learn how to trade is to use online portfolio trackers to monitor strategies that seem profitable. A tracking service will enable you to study what happens to these trades as the market prices fluctuate. This is an excellent way to learn and experience the effects that various events and news can have on a market. Several web sites offer portfolio tracking without making you invest a penny. Some online brokerage firms offer great virtual trading, which allows you to track hypothetical trades in real time!

To backtest a trading strategy or set of parameters using real-market prices, check out Optionetics.com Platinum. You can create trades and backtest them. You can also save trades and track the profits and losses over time (see Figure 11.16). You can then track forward to determine certain criteria and patterns in specific stock options. This is an excellent tool for garnering experience without risking any cash.

online trading approaches

While we are each, as traders, unique in our trading approaches, the advent of the Internet has leveled the playing field considerably. That said, regardless of account availability, time constraints, or market preferences, the Internet provides traders with an infinite number of ways to enhance their trading approaches. In order to help you develop your online style and give you a taste of daily trading modes, this section outlines the following three trading approaches: basic fundamental/technical, growth stock, and hedging strategies.

fundamental/technical trading approach   One of my favorite trading approaches that has been quite profitable over the years focuses on selecting stocks that have superior fundamentals and have recently experienced a pullback establishing a solid support area. In addition, I look for stocks that have options available. To best illustrate just how to trade this methodology, let's walk through an example of how a trade is selected and implemented. This will include the fundamental information typically used, the technicals analyzed, as well as the best option strategy to employ given the projected trading opportunity.

fundamental criteria used   Choosing which fundamental criteria to use is a subjective decision at best, but there are a few constants. For example, *free cash flow* is an important fundamental variable to analyze when selecting solid fundamental stocks as it is closely linked to profitability. It allows companies to internally finance new product lines and helps fuel future growth. *Return on equity* is another big factor when identifying fundamentally superior stocks. This fundamental variable tells us how well a company is managing its resources. *Earnings momentum*, which measures whether a company's earnings are accelerating or decelerating, is also a very important piece of information when screening for stocks that continue to have some price appreciating potential.

Earnings growth is another crucial fundamental variable that helps traders to identify explosive stocks. It informs traders of just

figure 11.16 profit/loss tracking

P/L	Trade Name	Stock Symbol	Open Date	Current Stock Close	Open Cost ($)	Current Cost ($)	Delta (Shares)* Close ($)	Delta (Shares)	Gamma (δDelta/ δStock)	Vega ($/%IV)	Theta ($/day)	Commission ($)	Pct. Change (%)	Profit/ Loss ($)	Profit/Loss w/Comm ($)
☑	AAPL Jan09 130-150 Call (Backtest)	AAPL	02-29-08	181.17	100.00	-1660.00	10509.67	58.01	0.69	68.30	-7.11	0.00	1760.00	1760.00	1760.00
☑	BIIB Jan08 80 Call Put (Backtest)	BIIB	10-16-07	61.02	-1175.00	-2009.00	0.00	0.00	0.00	0.00	0.00	0.00	70.98	834.00	834.00
☑	HOV Jul07 20-25 Put (Backtest)	HOV	05-31-07	7.69	-625.00	-2500.00	0.00	0.00	0.00	0.00	0.00	0.00	300.00	1875.00	1875.00
☑	LEH Jan08 75 Put (Backtest)	LEH	02-15-07	36.11	400.00	-175.00	0.00	0.00	0.00	0.00	0.00	0.00	143.75	575.00	575.00
☑	ORCL Jul08 22-24-26 Call (Backtest)	ORCL	05-23-08	21.98	-40.00	-25.00	98.03	4.46	-2.64	-1.07	0.44	0.00	-37.50	-15.00	-15.00
☑	RIMM Jun08 120 Put (Backtest)	RIMM	04-09-08	131.64	950.00	0.00	0.00	0.00	0.00	0.00	0.00	0.00	100.00	950.00	950.00

source: www.optionetics.com/platinumpro. reprinted with permission.

how robust a company's earnings have been in the past four quarters, as well as year after year. It is typically measured in earnings per share. Finally, *sales growth* is a key filter in helping identify stocks with some upward potential. Sales growth measures a percent change in a company's sales this quarter versus the same quarter in the previous year.

technical criteria used   One of the most consistent techniques of determining a good entry point (from a timing perspective) is by accurately identifying whether the stock is currently in an Elliot Wave-4 or Wave-5 buy pattern and is above its 200-day moving average. In addition, if the stock is making new 52-week highs, the trader can look at the relative strength oscillator to see if there is divergence to confirm whether the stock is topping out.

option strategies used   Three of the best option strategies to use with a bullish directional approach include out-of-the-money (OTM) bull put credit spreads, in-the-money (ITM) bull call debit spreads, and in-the-money (ITM) calls. The OTM bull put spreads and ITM bull call spreads are higher-probability trades giving some downside cushion. If the stock is less than $30 per share or has an options market that is not particularly liquid, then an ITM call could be implemented. An ITM call has a high delta, allowing it to move much like the underlying stock.

software tools used

- *Optionetics Platinum:* An excellent Web-based options analysis tool that can be used on a daily basis to select the best option trades to implement. In addition, Platinum provides a very revealing picture of a trade's risk-to-reward profile by analyzing the generated risk graphs.
- *ProfitSource:* ProfitSource is a financial market analysis program that can be used for most of your technical analysis work, particularly when identifying Elliott Wave-4 and Wave-5 buy setups.
- *ValueGain:* ValueGain helps traders identify strong fundamental stocks and is a seamless interface with ProfitSource. It will enable you easily to implement whatever fundamental/technical systems approach you have.

financial web sites used

- **www.stockTA.com** This site provides a variety of technical analysis filters to the stocks that are currently on your watch list.

- **www.valueline.com** An excellent site to help traders evaluate a stock's fundamentals including sales growth, earnings growth, and return on equity.

- **www.finance.yahoo.com** Good site to quickly get stock profiles, quotes, and earnings information.

- **www.tradethenews.com** This site provides live audio breaking market analysis and news. It allows traders to get a good feel for how the broader markets are currently behaving.

- **www.earningswhisper.com** Use this site for the latest earnings news as well as to see the current earnings calendar for a particular stock.

sample trade analysis and implementation The first step is to identify a fundamentally superior stock. For this example, the Monsanto Company (MON) was selected due to its impressive sales growth, terrific earnings growth, and outstanding return on equity (but not its environmental record). To start, it's important to see how the stock looks technically and assess if this is a good time to initiate a bullish position. As depicted in Figure 11.17, Monsanto is exhibiting an Elliot Wave-4 buy pattern and is still in a solid uptrend trading well above its 200-day moving average.

Since Monsanto's stock price is relatively high, let's look at implementing either an ITM bull call spread or OTM bull put spread. The easiest way to compare the two spreads is to use Optionetics Platinum. A simple comparison shows us that the ITM bull call spread is the most promising. Hence, let's construct a trade by purchasing 1 April 2008 90 call and selling 1 April 2008 100 call for a total net debit of $620. (See Figure 11.18.)

This position generates profits if Monsanto's stock stays above the 96.20 (90 + 6.20) breakeven by the April expiration date. Also, looking at the trade's risk graph (see Figure 11.19), notice how profits on this trade can be garnered earlier than the April expiration date if the stock surges to the upside in a rapid fashion. Another very important point about using the ITM bull call spread is that with the current stock price at 105.75, this trade provides a nice $9.55 per share cushion before any losses are incurred (105.75 − 96.20 = 9.55).

figure 11.17 elliott wave-4 buy pattern for monsanto

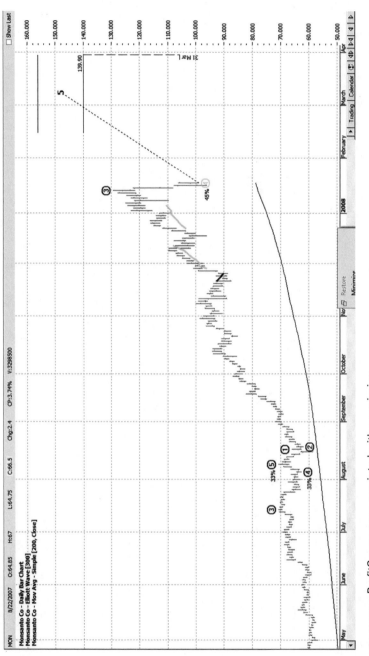

source: www.ProfitSource.com, reprinted with permission.

figure 11.18   trade summary for monsanto's ITM bull call

| | | | | MON - <u>Stock News</u> | | Dividend: | 0.6 % | (2008-04-02) | | | | | |
| | | | | MONSANTO CO | | Sector: | Agricultural Chemicals | | | | | | |

Leg Date	Position	Num	OptSym	Expire	Strike	Type	Entry	Bid/Ask	Model	IV %	Vol	OI	Days
2008-01-18	Bought	1	<u>MONDU</u>	APR08	90	Call	21.6	21.4/21.9	21.531	62.1	43	1494	91
2008-01-18	Sold	1	<u>MONDC</u>	APR08	100	Call	15.4	15.1/15.5	15.280	57.0	1021	6324	91

Entry Debit (Cost)	Profit	Max Profit	Max Risk	Delta (Shares)	Gamma	Vega	Theta
$620.00	$-30.00	$380.00	$-620.00	11.53	-0.286	$-3.20	$0.51

Downside Breakeven	Upside Breakeven	Max Profit/Max Risk	Max Profit/Cost
96.20	96.20	61%	61%

figure 11.19   **price chart and risk graph for MON's in-the-money bull call spread**

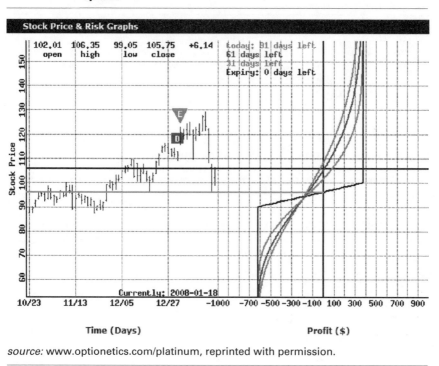

source: www.optionetics.com/platinum, reprinted with permission.

Hence, this is a high-probability trade with a very respectable risk-to-reward profile.

the growth stock trading routine

In many ways, the daily routine of a person focused on growth stock trading isn't all that different from that of someone investing in options—both are looking at more familiar household and typically larger-cap names that represent perceived value situations. In both camps, traders/investors need to stay informed of pending stock-specific situations such as an earnings release, product introductions, litigation, mid-quarter updates, or even the results of a clinical study if you're looking at a biotech or drug company. Additionally, closely watched economic reports that can affect the broader market, as well as any breaking news or reports from sector peers associated with the growth stock position, need to be accounted for as well as possible.

---

trader
an individual who buys and sells investment instruments frequently with the objective of short-term profit and is prepared to accept calculated risk in the hope of making better-than-average profits.

investor
an individual whose principal concern in the purchase of a security is the minimizing of risk for long-term profits.

Growth stocks generally move faster and react harder to news. For the option trader specializing in this market segment, this means liquidity in the derivatives can be an issue, particularly during times of heightened volatility. That said, while preparation is a necessity for all traders, being proactive rather than reactive is critical for executing successfully with options on growth stocks. Bearing this in mind, now let's move into some of the specifics as to what a daily trading routine might look like and take a look at some resources that should be of use to the options trader focused on growth stock investing.

premarket   The opening bell might not ring until 9:30 ET each business day, but traders versed in the markets realize strong opportunities can often be found during the premarket hours. Economic data like the jobs report and the consumer price index are a couple of the more important and likely market-moving catalysts always released in front of the opening bell. Luckily, resources used for staying on top of the economic calendar are widely available for free on the Internet. Bloomberg (www.bloomberg.com) is an excellent site to visit to obtain this information; it offers consensus estimates for the data, as well as a description of the statistic itself.

Now it gets tricky. While options cannot be traded during the premarket period, hedging with the underlying is possible depending on a trader's position type, such as a long curve/gamma position. Due to the nature of said reports and quite often exaggerated price moves immediately following their release, stock purchases may soar to levels not tested during normal trading hours in the trading accounts of those prepared in front of the report.

During the premarket, turning on CNBC is a fast way to get a feel for many of the day's top stories and which stocks are potentially setting the tone for the start of trade. The NASDAQ web site also breaks down the early leaders, laggards, and most active issues. If it's earnings season, Yahoo! Finance, MarketWatch, and CNBC.com are three sites where you can find out which companies are reporting. For a well-packaged and comprehensive look at both earnings, stories, and recent analyst notes on a particular stock, Briefing.com, a subscription service, does an excellent job at keeping traders informed.

If you are in a position and any of the aforementioned catalysts are influencing your underlying stock, or you can reasonably expect an abrupt opening move once the bell rings, putting in orders to hedge or adjust with options during the premarket is another important part of the morning ritual. By using an options calculator and/or pulling up a risk-to-reward position profile from software such as Optionetics Platinum, traders can place orders in a more meaningful way than can those traders surprised by any lightning-fast opening moves and quite often equally fleeting opportunities in the options market.

regular hours   The opening hour of trade is typically an important one. It's important to be concerned with existing orders that hedge or adjust an already established position. As well, it's often during this period that a readjustment of expectations and/or prices is made. During this important trading window, it's also commonplace that the growth stocks you've been tracking (or have yet to become familiar with) quickly move into the spotlight.

Checking out *Investor's Business Daily's* web site (investors.com) and the tool "Stocks on the Move" is one way to quickly obtain a list of growth stocks that are finding strong moves on equally impressive volume. The IBD 100 list and New America page are also excellent resources for finding growth stocks that may just be gaining a following among institutional traders or are already established and possibly afford strong technicals and fundamentals. Stock screeners found on Yahoo! Finance or MSN.com are another means to cultivate watch lists, an integral part of any stock trader's arsenal. ValueGain in conjunction with the Profit-Source charting software is another excellent tool for obtaining stocks with many of the characteristics necessary to fit the growth profile.

Monitoring and updating watch lists comprised of growth stocks is typically where much of a trader's daily efforts will be found. For growth traders who are keying off of Elliott Wave and/or like to set up other technical parameters to locate potential trade candidates, ProfitSource can reduce some of the workload. For those seeking flat bases, cup with handles, or ascending bases that fit the criteria of classic base structures poised for breakouts, more time will likely be spent physically scrolling through the watch list and updating it as candidates fall from technical grace and others move into position.

As a stock moves up the proverbial radar, a trader looking to use the options market to secure a position will need to spend time qualifying that situation. Using a service such as Optionetics Platinum in conjunction with a broker's services is the next logical step. What needs to be determined is which strategies might fit well with the objectives and risk tolerance levels of the trader, as well as the constraints of the options market and the underlying asset in question. Going through this process, a trader can systematically reach a conclusion as to how an option position can or can't be approached. Being familiar with the current liquidity, implied volatilities, and how a stock has behaved in the past at certain technical levels should result in better plan of attack or the realization that better opportunities are likely found elsewhere.

the final hour   CNBC heralds the last hour as the most important one, as volume levels generally pick up and it becomes clearer whether investors are willing to commit to overnight positions. It's during this time that a trader's own preparation for the next day begins. The question of whether you're comfortable with outstanding position risk needs to be addressed. As discussed earlier, economic and earnings releases, either overnight or in the premarket, always have the ability to move prices away from the closing levels. While a hedge or adjustment with stock may exist, the inability to use options and the potential for gap risk with no out until the next day's opening are factors to consider in making a more informed decision regarding your positions.

hedging strategies using technical analysis

Following a core belief that no one knows what will happen the next week or even the following day in the markets, I believe that options are ideal for hedging both investments and trades. This view was solidified while reading Nassim Taleb's *Fooled by Randomness* (W. W. Norton, 2001). After using technical analysis to identify possible trades, positions are established using exchange-traded funds (ETFs), Long Term Equity Anticipation Securities (LEAPS), and option straddles. Relatively longer-term directional positions are created, and the positions are hedged with shorter-term options as different technical conditions emerge.

the technical analysis process   Technical analysis is used to identify strong trending moves and potential reversals in the broad markets and sectors by applying, among others, the following short list of tools:

- Price and volume.
- Regression channels.
- Exponential moving averages.
- Relative strength comparisons.
- Bollinger bands.
- Rate of change (ROC) indicator with moving averages.
- Moving average convergence/divergence (MACD).
- Relative strength index or stochastics.
- Average directional index (ADX) and/or directional movement indicator (DMI).
- Time segmented volume (TSV).
- Balance of power (BOP).
- Market breadth tools.

Two charting packages used for analysis and various data downloads are HUBB Financial Group's ProfitSource (www.hubb.com) and Worden Brothers, Inc.'s TeleChart (www.worden.com).

Regression channels and moving averages (MAs) provide unbiased trend information that can be confirmed using volume behavior as prices move toward channel or MA lines. Different momentum, directional, and other volume-based indicators are also used to confirm that a trend is on track. Longer-term positions (months) are placed in the direction of the trend. When key price areas are reached, the probability of the trend continuing becomes less certain and a relatively shorter-term hedge is applied.

Momentum, directional, and market breadth tools are also used at this time to help provide insight on potential continuations or reversals. This helps weight the hedge (partial to full). The hedge is closed for a profit or loss when signs of a trend continuation appear. If an intermediate or long-term reversal in the trend emerges, the longer-term position is exited. It's not uncommon for this to result in a relatively short period of time (weeks) when trading accounts have larger cash allocations.

the exchange-traded funds process   Exchange-traded funds (ETFs) are used to establish longer-term market and sector positions. When there is a strong trend in place, leveraged ETFs such as the ultra long and ultra short funds from ProShares (www.proshares.com) may also be used. Other sources used for ETF information include:

- The American Stock Exchange (www.amex.com).
- Google search (www.google.com).

Once potential ETFs are selected, the following items are checked:

- ETF liquidity.
- ETF movement relative to the target index (correlations).
- Availability of options.
- ETF option liquidity.

At times, ETFs with less liquid options may be used, providing longer-term strategies are anticipated. In this case additional trading costs are accepted (slippage) if the ETF represents a unique sector or asset.

ETF closing price data is downloaded along with index or individual stock data to check the correlations for paired data sets (ETF-index, ETF-stock, stock-index). This helps to confirm that the security traded serves as a good proxy for the index (well correlated) or serves to diversify holdings (either negatively correlated or not correlated).

A final step may include checking the index and index construction methodologies from sources including:

- Dow Jones (www.djindexes.com).
- Standard & Poor's (www.standardandpoors.com).
- Goldman Sachs (www2.goldmansachs.com/services/securities/products).
- Google search using the index name and the keywords "construction methodology."

Using a technical signal, a long ETF position is established (it may be on a short-oriented ETF). The need for a hedge is also evaluated and may be applied immediately after the purchase. More typically, it is completed within days of the purchase and evaluated on an ongoing basis using technical tools and market-timing models.

Occasionally a purely directional trade is put in place using ETF options to reduce the total assets at risk. Again, technical tools and market-timing models are analyzed to identify potential trades. Smaller positions are established as a money management guideline.

individual stocks   Using a smaller number of familiar stocks (four to five), LEAPS contracts may be purchased when a strong uptrend is in place or after upward moves from long basing patterns. Hedges using long puts are created and removed throughout the LEAPS holding period.

Occasionally, more volatile moves are sought when a strong upward or downward trend is in place. At these times, directional trades in less familiar stocks may be taken using short-term option trades. These stocks are selected from popular names of the day given news stories from Google or Yahoo! Finance.

As an alternative approach for stocks less frequently traded, a straddle may be established when a consolidation precedes a scheduled event expected to move the stock strongly up or down. Straddles can also be established on ETFs.

the options analysis process   Options analysis is performed using Optionetics Platinum with a focus on implied volatility (IV) charts, historical volatility (HV) charts, and the options calculator. This is especially useful for trading in less familiar names since IV levels are relative to the specific security. Current IV is obtained with the options calculator and compared to previous IV and HV levels using the volatility charts. The goal is to create new long option positions when IV is relatively low.

Buying relatively low IV can't always be accomplished when the markets are declining, so relative IV levels may dictate how in-the-money (ITM) the option is. In addition, pure speculative positions (out-of-the-money options) may still be established without relatively low IV; however, position size is reduced as part of a money management guideline.

In addition to these uses, different find-a-trade tools are used to search specific strategies for a group of stocks or ETFs. New strategies are also explored using find-a-trade, system searches, and risk graphs.

the market timing process As part of a broad market analysis, different tools are used for market timing. These help identify directional bias for positions and warn of potential reversals for both stock and bond markets. The models currently included in the assessment process include those referenced by a variety of sources: Gerald Appel; Martin Zweig; Timothy Hayes, CMT; Ned Davis Research; and Nelson Freeburg. A smaller group of indicators will eventually be used pending results from real-time testing.

By monitoring interest rates and other economic indicators, along with breadth and momentum indicators for asset and sector indexes, points are generated for the model. Cumulative point levels are then used to help identify allocation percentages for holdings.

Sources for the models include the following:

- Gerald Appel, *Technical Analysis: Power Tools for Active Investors* (FT Press, 2005).
- Martin Zweig, *Winning on Wall Street* (Grand Central Publishing, 1997)
- Timothy Hayes, *CMT, The Research Driven Investor* (McGraw-Hill, 2000).
- Ned Davis, *Being Right or Making Money* (Ned Davis Research, Inc., 2000).
- Nelson Freeburg, *Timing Models and Proven Indicators for Today's Markets* (Marketplace Books, 2005) (audio CD).

An outstanding source of economic data is the FRED economic database from the St. Louis Federal Reserve Bank (research. stlouisfed.org/fred2/). Occasionally Yahoo! Finance is also used for data downloads by obtaining a quote for the specific security and accessing historical data.

a sample trade scenario In June 2007 the U.S. equity markets began to lose upward momentum as the very first indications of subprime mortgage problems started to impact the markets. Two longer-term charts are displayed to provide insight on the initial conditions and analysis performed for what resulted in a six-month trading period. Shorter-term charts are provided to display conditions during the trading period.

technical analysis process Starting with the long-term trends in place, Figures 11.20 and 11.21 display monthly and weekly charts for the S&P 500 SPDR ETF (SPY), respectively. Specifications for each chart follow.

Monthly
- A 3.5-year linear regression channel (from October 2006 to March 2007) extended to the right.
- A 10-month exponential moving average (EMA).
- Stochastic (12, 5, 5).
- Moving average convergence/divergence (MACD: 6, 13, 4).

Weekly
- A 3.5-year linear regression channel (from October 2006 to March 2007) extended to the right.
- Both 10-week and 40-week exponential moving averages.
- Stochastic (12, 5, 5).
- On balance volume (OBV).

Regression channel techniques rely on expectations for price to move between the upper channel line and middle channel line or between the lower channel and the middle channel line. Any movement outside of the channel represents either a potential acceleration or change of the trend. It is not uncommon for price to return to the price channel. When price is near any of the channel lines, momentum and volume indicators are monitored to gauge the likelihood of movement in one direction or the other, away from the line.

Since a line chart is used in these figures, each period's high and low levels (which are used to create the upper and lower channel

figure 11.20 SPY monthly chart with lagging and leading indicators (6/30/2007)

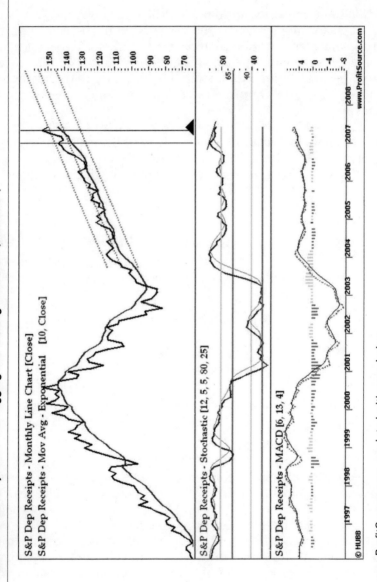

S&P Dep Receipts - Monthly Line Chart [Close]
S&P Dep Receipts - Mov Avg - Exponential [10, Close]

S&P Dep Receipts - Stochastic [12, 5, 5, 80, 25]

S&P Dep Receipts - MACD [6, 13, 4]

© HUBB

www.ProfitSource.com

source: www.ProfitSource.com. reprinted with permission.

figure 11.21 SPY weekly chart with lagging and leading indicators (July 6, 2007)

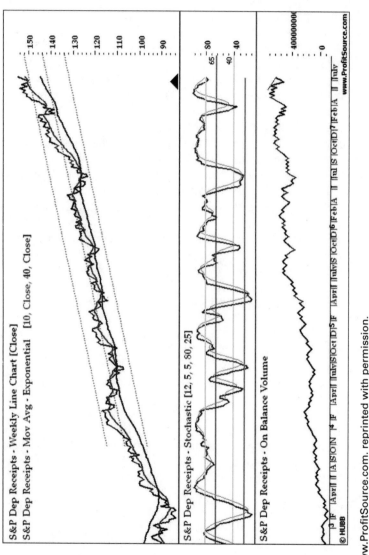

S&P Dep Receipts - Weekly Line Chart [Close]
S&P Dep Receipts - Mov Avg - Exponential   [10, Close, 40, Close]

S&P Dep Receipts - Stochastic [12, 5, 5, 80, 25]

S&P Dep Receipts - On Balance Volume

© HUBB

www.ProfitSource.com

source: www.ProfitSource.com. reprinted with permission.

271

lines) are not visible. The monthly chart includes two momentum tools, a stochastic indicator and an MACD indicator. In late spring 2007, price accelerated upward out of the channel; however, by June the move seemed potentially unsustainable as stochastic momentum diverged from price action.

Using channel principles, the stochastic divergence, and volume data (not displayed here), a potential downturn in SPY seemed to be setting up. In order to take advantage of this bearish view for SPY, short ETFs and SPY options were initially analyzed. Since the monthly chart represents longer-term trends, a longer-term position was anticipated (held for months if conditions persist) using SDS, the ProShares UltraShort S&P 500 ETF.

Periodic hedges were anticipated for the position using similar channel, momentum, and volume principles, along with other potential support or resistance analysis (i.e., exponential moving averages). These are focus areas since movement away from each area had the potential to be strong. The use of option straddles on SPY is a second strategy employed that could also capitalize on this outlook.

For the week ending July 6, both stochastics momentum and on balance volume (OBV) diverged from price, with the fast stochastic line dropping below 80, signaling an alert used to establish a small initial bearish position in SDS on July 11 (50 shares at $52.64 per share). Since the position was small and early in the trend, a 10 percent stop loss (to $47.38) was identified. Alerts using SPY were identified for closes at $154.40 and $155 on the weekly chart, indicating price may remain above the upward channel. A return to the channel (at approximately SPY = 150.46) would provide an alert to add to the position. Figure 11.22 provides the daily chart through mid-August.

Price ended the week at $154.85 and had one close above $155 on a daily basis. However, the weekly close of $153.50 failed to exceed previous highs and technical indicators continued to display weakness. Rather than hedging the position, the potential for continued downward movement had to be confirmed. Otherwise the position would be exited.

Weakness continued and the following week an additional 50 shares were purchased on July 23 at $50.31. A stop at $47.38 was maintained. The scaling-in process resulted in a lower price for the second purchase as price followed weakening signals from the indicators. By the end of the week, prices closed within the regression channel. A final 100 shares were added at $54.46 on July 31, as the 200-day EMA was tested for support.

figure 11.22   SPY daily chart with lagging and leading indicators through mid-August

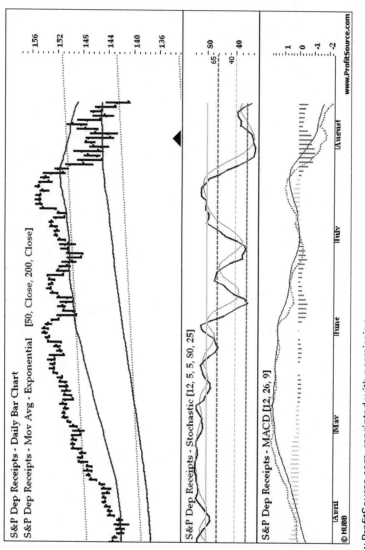

source: www.ProfitSource.com, reprinted with permission.

Prices closed the week on August 3 below the 200-day EMA with weekly and daily momentum remaining weak. Prices rebounded to the 50-day EMA the following week. Three actions were taken on August 9:

1. Partial profits were taken for 100 of 200 shares in the SDS position.
2. The SDS position was replaced with a small SPY put option position.
3. An in-the-money strangle on SPY was established.

With the EMA lines converging and price moving in the upper channel region, partial profits were taken since travel was on the docket later the following week. A short-term ITM strangle was created since two potential resistance or support areas could be violated, including the more widely followed 50-day and 200-day EMAs. A partial bearish SPY position was maintained (SDS) since technical indicators remained weak. Additional puts were purchased at the strangle strike prices to add modestly to the bearish view. Prior to the planned travel, prices weakened further and all positions were closed for a net profit.

Upon returning, two additional SDS positions were established using the same technical principles, along with a longer-term at-the-money straddle (October SPY options). SPY remained below the stop level, but due to a pending Fed meeting with expectations for interest rate cuts (bullish), hedges were initiated for the SDS position. Hedges were created and removed based on (1) technical conditions, (2) economic events, and (3) profit-taking.

One hedge is described here; the remaining ones appear on the partial trading sheets at the end of this example. On September 18 a hedge was created for SDS in anticipation of a Fed interest rate cut. At that point, 200 shares of SDS were held so next-month at-the-money options were used to create a relatively delta neutral position (see the partial trading sheets provided later in this section). A quick exit was also planned for a portion of the hedge in anticipation of a sharp initial move; these exits are also shown in the partial trading sheets for this example. Figure 11.23 displays the daily chart through early December when the final hedge described here was removed.

the ETF process   In order to capitalize on a broad market view using ETFs, the ETFs must be compared to the index being analyzed.

figure 11.23   SPY daily chart with lagging and leading indicators through early December

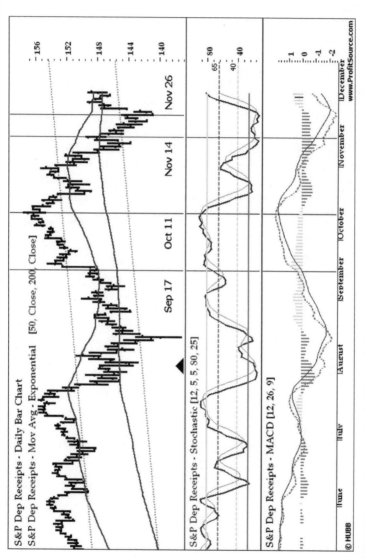

Although an overlay chart can be used to approximate the relationship, a better method is to perform a statistical analysis on the returns for the index versus the ETF. Returns are used rather than prices because returns are normally distributed, allowing the use of correlation analysis, while prices are not normally distributed (they are bounded below by 0).

The S&P 500 Index (SPX) is a commonly used benchmark index for U.S. stocks and is used to assess broad market conditions. One of the most widely traded ETFs, SPY has a strong positive correlation with SPX so it serves as a reasonable bullish proxy for the index.

Checking the ProShares web site, it was noted the fund family offers other ETFs that are intended to track SPX positively or negatively. The objective of SDS is to inversely track SPX in a leveraged manner (two times the index). This means a strong negative correlation is expected. Rather than just taking fund objectives at face value, a correlation analysis is performed to see if there is a negative correlation and the ETF can be used as a bearish proxy for both SPX and SPY.

To perform a correlation analysis, the following three steps were completed:

1. Download daily closing data from Worden Brothers' TeleChart2007 for SPX, SPY, and SDS into Excel.
2. Calculate daily returns for each.
3. Use the "=correl(data1,data2)" formula to calculate correlation values.

Correlation calculations are performed on paired data sets of the same size. Since SDS began trading in 2006, approximately 242 data points were available which represents a little less than one year of daily closes. Paired correlations were as follows:

- SPX-SPY: +0.969 (strong positive)
- SPX-SDS: −0.975 (strong negative)
- SPY-SDS: −0.974 (strong negative)

The conclusions are that SPY serves as a good proxy for the S&P 500 and SDS serves as a good inverse proxy for SPY. This also means SPY call options, which are more liquid than SDS put options, can be used for an imperfect hedge on SDS.

The September 18 hedge was created as follows:

- SDS position delta: 200 shares × −2.0 delta = −400 delta.
- SPY October 149 call: 8 contracts × 52.8 delta = 424 delta.
- Net delta = +24.

On the same day, two contracts were exited after the announcement when an initial price spike upwards occurred (from 148.86 to 150.60). Profit-taking on three contracts was completed the following day (from 148.86 to 153.80), leaving a 50 percent hedge on the position since the delta for the remaining three contracts had moved up to 72.1 (net delta = −184.0).

Although SPY was trading above the upper channel line, weakness returned the following day, which eventually led to price movement back within the channel by week's end. On September 20 the remaining hedge was removed when SPY was trading at $153.21. Price remained near the upper channel line so a new hedge was established on October 1.

options analysis process   The correlation analysis for SPX-SPY concluded that call options can be used to capitalize on a bullish view for SPX, and SPY put options can be used to capitalize on a bearish view. The strong negative correlation between SPY and SDS also allows a trader to use the more liquid SPY call options to hedge SDS, rather than the less liquid SDS options that will add to trading costs (slippage).

When strangles and hedges were initiated on a short-term basis, they were in-the-money, and when more time to expiration was available, the straddle or hedge was generally slightly out-of-the-money. This was done to minimize the impact of accelerated time decay on the long option.

Hedges were partial or full with a bullish directional bias depending on conditions. This was accomplished by analyzing delta values for the SPY options. Although each SDS share represents approximately −1.95 SPY share based on correlations, for ease of calculation it was assumed each SDS share had a −2.0 delta.

partial trading sheets   Due to space constraints, only a portion of the columns appearing on the trade management spreadsheet are provided here. (See Tables 11.1 and 11.2.) Columns omitted include

table 11.1   entry points

Position	Date	Strategy	Option	Qty	Price	Stop	Value
SDS ETF	7/11/07	Channel, MO	SDS stop	50	52.64	47.38	2,640
	7/23/07	Channel, MO	SDS stop	50	50.31	47.38	2,523
	7/31/07	Channel, MO	SPY stop	50	54.46	150.7	5,454
	8/20/07	Channel, MO	SPY stop or hedge	50	57.06	151.18	5,714
	8/22/07	Channel, MO		50	55.85	151.18	5,593
SPY Options							
Straddle	8/9/07	S/R	Aug 152 p	3	5.20	Short-Term, time	1,566
SPY @ 147.0			Aug 143 c	3	5.29		1,597
Straddle	8/24/07	Low Volatility	Oct 148 c	4	4.60		1,763
SPY @ 147.6			Oct 148 p	4	4.40		1,851
Single position	8/9/07	Channel, MO	Aug 152 p	2	5.20	150.7	1,046
Hedges							
SPY @ 148.86	9/18/07		Oct 149 c	8	3.90	Hedge	3,116
SPY @ 153.50	10/1/07		Oct 154 c	4	2.16	Hedge	875
SPY @ 154.90	10/8/07		Oct 154 c	4	2.39	Hedge	967
SPY @ 147.55	11/8/07		Nov 150 c	5	1.17	Hedge	597
SPY @ 143.45	11/26/07		Dec 150 c	6	1.20	Hedge	733

market and position trends, along with some position values such as commission, which are incorporated in the final tallies.

Both the strangle and straddle yielded losses when you separate out the single bearish put that was initiated with the strangle. The put was actually established in combination with the strangle and exited later for a net profit on the whole position. The net result for these positions was a loss of $225 on $7,823 traded, or 2.9 percent.

One of five hedges was exited for a loss and the remaining hedges and ETF positions were exited for profits as follows: hedges $2,258 on $6,287, or 35 percent; and ETFs $1,966 on $21,885, or 9.0 percent.

conclusion

In this chapter, we try to help you make sense of what it's like to go online and search for a moneymaking trade. As you become more

table 11.2   exit points

Position	Date	Strategy	Option	Qty	Price	Value	Net
SDS ETF	8/9/07	Part. profits		50	54.38	2,715	129.3
	8/9/07	Part. profits		50	54.38	2,715	241.9
	8/15/07	Travel		50	57.68	5,760	363.0
	1/15/08	SPY support		50	60.04	5,996	281.9
	1/17/08	Fed	w/div	50	63.50	6,342	950.1
SPY Options							
Straddle	8/9/07	Eod	Aug 152 p	2	5.40	1,071	20
SPY @ 147.0		Eod	Aug 143 c	2	4.80	950	(118)
	8/10/07	Risk	Aug 152 p	1	6.70	662	(169)
		Risk	Aug 143 c	1	3.68	360	142
Straddle	8/29/07	TRIN	Oct 148 p	2	6.6	1,310	380
SPY @ 144.11	8/29/07	TRIN	Oct 148 c	2	3.3	650	(233)
SPY @ 146.71	9/11/07	Channel, MO	Oct 148 c	1	3.8	372	(68)
SPY @ 151.00	9/18/07	Fed	Oct 148 c	1	5.6	551	111
SPY @ 154.30	10/15/07	Time	Oct 148 p	2	0.14	20	(900)
Single position	8/9/07	Channel, MO	Aug 152 p	2	8.3	1,650	610
Hedges							
SPY @ 150.60	9/18/07	Fed	Oct 149 c	2	4.6	910	116
SPY @ 153.80	9/19/07	Profits	Oct 149 c	3	6.4	1,910	748
SPY @ 153.21	9/20/07	Channel	Oct 149 c	3	5.84	1,741	582
SPY @ 155.37	10/5/07	Profits	Oct 154 c	4	2.72	1,077	202
SPY @ 156.03	10/11/07	Volatility	Oct 154 c	4	3.6	1,429	462
SPY @ 146.85	11/7/07	Rally	Nov 150 c	3	0.68	194	169
SPY @ 149.00	11/14/07	Time	Nov 150 c	2	0.71	134	100
SPY @ 147.20	11/29/07	TSV	Dec 150 c	4	1.98	781	289
SPY @ 148.29	12/5/07	Resistance	Dec 150 c	2	1.88	366	127

comfortable, each of these steps will become second nature to you. But in the beginning, it can be of great help to keep an online journal so that you can remember where you've been and what you've learned. Let's review the steps for researching a trade:

1. *Charting*. Monitor chart patterns of specific stocks for signs of impending runs. Look for stocks that are approaching 52-week highs. If they have pullbacks, make sure they don't pull back below the 200-day or 50-day moving average. Keep an eye on volume and make sure that during pullbacks,

volume has spiked to double its average daily volume before confirming a stock as bullish. A volume spike often washes out most of the sellers and is a clear sign that the stock is hitting the bottom.

2. *News.* Look at the fundamental picture. Watch scheduled news and be ready when surprises happen. Read company reports as well as outlooks of earnings reports to come. Be careful getting into a trade just before an earnings report is released because that's what the crowd does and the crowd isn't always right.

3. *Strategies.* Once you've located a promising market, find a strategy that fits the market's profile. Check out options premiums to find a position with the best probability of profit. Use implied volatilities to locate abnormal patterns in option premiums.

4. *Tracking.* Track your open positions on a day-to-day basis, rather than minute-by-minute. Using a longer time frame gives you the opportunity to use a variety of research tools. Plenty of web sites and online brokerages will also send you nightly e-mails summarizing your open portfolio positions.

The most important part of trading is to do your homework on a stock. It doesn't take long to develop a consistent procedure using a few web sites to research a stock's profit-making potential. I've developed this four-point process for evaluating and tracking trades over my past few years as an online trader. Feel free to integrate my process into your own plan. Execute this plan just like a business.

A lot of people think that we trade just for the fun of it or that we treat it like a game. We do like to say that trading is like grown-up Nintendo, but it's no laughing matter. Money is the bottom line for trading, and generating profits is the reward for all of your hard work, knowledge, and discipline.

chapter 12

the quest for the ultimate online brokerage

taking the plunge

The final link in a cyber-trader's world is the online brokerage firm. Twenty years ago, there were only a handful of brokerages bold enough to take their business online. It was considered a risky strategy because of security issues and the high costs of developing the technology needed to provide investors with the tools to buy and sell online. Important questions were raised. How many investors would actually trade online? What about system outages and the risk of lost data? Is this whole Internet thing a passing fad?

Today, those questions have been answered. The Internet is real and online trading is here to stay. In fact, huge numbers of individual investors have turned to online brokers as their preferred method of trading. Not only is the technology reliable and efficient these days, but the costs of trading have come down amid heavy competition among online brokers. In 2008, the average commission for a 500-share online stock trade was between $5.00 and $7.00.

Keep in mind that an enormous difference exists between the kinds of brokers out there, and your specific needs will determine which broker is right for you. For example, traders focused on international markets will have a different set of needs compared to investors focused only on U.S. small-cap stocks. In addition, some firms are large and offer a wide range of financial services like banking, insurance, and retirement planning. Others are focused on very specific types of investments like futures, foreign exchange, or options.

In addition, for some investors, online trading is not necessarily the right avenue. Some need the help of a full-service broker. Clients at full-service firms deal with live brokers—actual people. While they generally pay higher prices for trading services, they also have the opportunity to ask for research, information, and advice. Many online traders, however, are self-directed and are quick to scorn the stale advice of the traditional big brokerages. Some investors use both full-service brokerage firms for longer-term planning needs and online brokerage firms for short-term trading. Some firms have responded to this demand by offering both.

A few online brokerage firms stand out because of their size and marketing clout. Chances are you have heard of big firms like Charles Schwab, TD Ameritrade, and E*Trade Financial. They are probably the most prominent online brokerages today. Charles Schwab is a longtime discount broker and therefore had an infrastructure of accounts from which to draw when it opened up its online services in 1996. E*Trade, by contrast, started from scratch and has become an online brokerage empire. TD Ameritrade started offering online trading in 1996 through eBroker, an Internet-only division of All American Brokers. It has since grown, partly through its merger with TD Waterhouse in 2005, into another online trading powerhouse.

In recent years, a number of new firms that specialize in options trading have come onto the scene. OptionsXpress, ThinkorSwim, and OptionsHouse are taking online options trading to the next level with a combination of advanced tools and low commissions. The trend is a boon for individual options traders because option trading is different from traditional stock trading. It requires customized services and the ability to deal with more advanced orders. The complexity of putting on an options trade requires brokers to install a series of complicated mechanisms in order to understand what the strategist is trying to do, and then to take that order to the market for execution at good prices.

In fact, just the basic task of providing options quotes requires a complex infrastructure. There are thousands of optionable stocks, ETFs, and indexes trading today. The options quotes on each underlying instrument are known as options chains, and each individual chain may contain 100 individual options contracts. Remember that options symbols are denoted using a base code combined with a code for the strike price and another code for the expiration month. Strike price codes use the 26 letters of our alphabet. Since there are sometimes more strike prices than there are letters, you sometimes have to switch base codes. For example, the letter A denotes the strike prices of 5, 105, 205, and 305 (see Appendix A). Usually, the strike price is the one closest to the current stock price. The problem is that the options codes can change very quickly. Since many (but not all) online firms require the symbols, keeping pace with the changes requires some very clever programming.

---

option ticker symbol
a system of alphabetical symbols that represent option strike prices used to describe an option when actually placing an order through an exchange.

Options traders represent a niche market for online brokerage firms. Many brokers may not want to cater to this smaller group when they have the onslaught of the stock trading masses to deal with. In addition, offering options trading puts the brokerage firm under closer regulatory scrutiny because it requires a different set of licenses and more advanced understanding of the derivatives market. The point that they may have missed, however, is that options trading volume is growing much faster than stock trading volume and options traders trade more frequently, generating greater commissions.

Of the hundreds of the online brokerage firms in existence today, many do not have the capacity to handle option spreads directly online. Unlike stocks, options are often bought in combinations with specific pricing relationships between the different parts of the trade. This means that multiple trades have to be placed simultaneously, and only under certain conditions. Most brokers are set up to handle single transactions—simply buying or selling one trading instrument at a time. In short, buying and selling options online is a common occurrence, but employing option spread and combination strategies online is limited to a relatively small number of firms that have invested in the technology to do so. All of the firms discussed in this chapter have online options trading capabilities in one form or another.

On the bright side, there is little to fear from cyber-snoopers, since major online brokerages have developed superb security systems. Due to an increase in the use of wireless modems and portable Web devices, a number of firms offer the tools to trade with cell phones and PDAs. That means you can get a price alert, check the activity of your favorite stocks and options, and place a trade all from a beach in Maui. But before you go online to check out the best prices on tickets to Hawaii, let's take an in-depth look at online brokerages and what makes one better than the other.

criteria for brokerage reviews

A *conundrum* is defined as a brain-teasing enigma. Finding the best broker has always been and continues to be a conundrum of the highest degree. Obviously *best* means the ultimate combination of brokerage attributes: low commissions, swift executions, and reliability. Since this book focuses on options trading, we also looked for online brokerages to provide the customized features that option traders need to compete in the marketplace. Therefore, before launching into the reviews of the 12 best online brokerages, let's clarify the 10 qualities we looked for in assessing the hundreds of brokerage firms available. Keep in mind, there might be some very good brokers that did not make the rankings for a number of different reasons. Nevertheless, the list should be a good starting point to help you find the broker that's right for your particular trading needs.

1. *Stock and options experience.* Not all brokerages handle options, so it is important to make sure that the brokerage you choose to work through not only handles options, but has an interest in catering to option traders' needs. Your broker must have an extensive background in options trading to be able to get your complex option orders filled and exited at a profitable price. In addition, brokerages that offer stock and options screening services are a real plus. You should also be able to easily track several portfolios in order to monitor

your investments and observe the movement of stocks and options for potential future trades.

2. *Low commission rates.* From the start, online brokerages have been able to offer much lower commission rates than conventional full-service brokerages. Online rates for 100 shares of stock are as low as $5, whereas conventional discount brokers start at around $30 and go as high as $150. Option orders usually have a minimum commission per trade plus a per contract fee. Some firms, however, have started offering a flat fee. Lower rates are especially important to option traders because combination spread orders consist of multiple contracts. Since the maximum reward on many spread trades is limited, profits can be severely reduced by high commission rates. However, low commissions also mean bare-bones services, while traditional brokers offer a variety of money management services including investment advice. Look out for hidden costs.

3. *Margin.* You can trade stocks on margin, but not options. Margin for stocks is 50 percent. When margin is offered, traders are charged interest on the loan. This amount of interest is referred to as the margin rate. Margin rates vary from brokerage to brokerage. In addition, many brokerages require high margin deposits (up to $100,000) to be held on account if you want to trade spreads and naked options. Straightforward debit spreads and straddles should not require more than the maximum risk for the trade. Also, some firms have started offering portfolio or risk-based margin to some investors. To qualify, investors are generally required to have a certain number of experience and a certain account size like $100,000 or $250,000, depending on the firm. Once approved for portfolio margin, the amount of margin is computed based on the true risk of a position. For example, in a protective put the margin is normally 100 percent deposited for the put options (all long option strategies require 100 percent margin) and 50 percent for the shares. However, the portfolio or risk-based margin will be much less. It will be based on a formula that considers the underlying stock price minus the strike price of the option, which is the true risk of the position.

4. *Trading account size.* Many brokerages require a minimum amount of money to establish an account. This number

varies from nothing at all to $15,000. Low minimums have undoubtedly inspired more new traders than ever before to jump into the fray.

5. *Option spreads.* Many online brokerages charge a higher commission fee for placing a trade using a broker. As the infrastructure of online trading progresses, placing spread orders online has become more commonplace. Some firms are accomplishing this feat by switching from a third-party clearing firm to a self-clearing organization. In any event, if the brokerage firm requires that spread and advanced orders be sent to a live broker, they might also charge higher fees compared to simple online buy and sell orders. This can add up to a lot of money. Therefore, for active online options traders, it is important that their firm's trading platform handle advanced orders. The capabilities vary. Some handle a few strategies, others can handle almost all.

6. *Order execution.* Order execution is based on a brokerage's ability to buy at the lowest price or sell at the highest price once your order has been placed. If you place a market order, especially in a fast market, there is a good chance that you won't get the price on your screen. You can eliminate this problem by placing a limit order. Although limit orders are not always filled, at least if they are filled you get the price you want. Reliable order execution is by far the most important link in your chain to making money in the markets. Unfortunately, this area is very hard to rate until you actually have an account. Conversations with thousands of traders have made us realize that for every trader who relates a bad experience there are many more who never have a problem. Therefore (although I have made it a point to keep track of the complaints I've heard over the years), this part of the review has been restricted to the following areas:

   - A broker's ability to issue all types of orders online, including short sales, contingent orders, all-or-none (AON) orders, trailing stops, and stop orders.
   - Additional fees for processing orders other than market orders.
   - Customer comments as to the consistency of a firm's ability to get good fills.

7. *Quotes.* There are two basic kinds of quote services: real-time and delayed. A few firms offer unlimited streaming real-time quotes. Others offer a limited amount of free real-time access when someone opens up a new account plus a certain number of real-time snapshot quotes per executed trade. Some companies automatically supply delayed quotes and charge a monthly fee for a link to a dynamic real-time quotes system. However, most do offer some type of real-time data these days. Some also offer real-time options chains with Greeks and implied volatility data. These firms definitely have options traders in mind.

8. *Customer service.* There's nothing like really needing to talk with your broker and not being able to get through, especially when you have a problem getting online. No matter how automated trading may become, nothing will ever take the place of having a knowledgeable and courteous person available to talk to when you have a question. Good customer service is in everyone's best interest. Many firms offer customer service only through e-mail. Others have started adopting live chat. Quick response is the key, especially if the question is about an order, assignment, or other issue that will directly affect your profits and losses.

9. *Reliability.* Reliability of service is a key issue. System failure is simply unacceptable when it creates losses that could have been avoided if service was functioning properly. Online brokerages have steadily increased capacity to meet demands, but we're not out of the woods yet. In judging a brokerage, it is important to note the alternative methods for reaching the brokerage in case there is a system failure. What is their contingency plan and is their data secure? Most brokerages provide this information on their web site.

10. *User-friendliness.* Finally, web design is more than a matter of creativity. Although creative sites filled with exotic and colorful designs are wonderful, we are mainly interested in efficiency. Time is the bottom line. If it takes five screens to get you to your account information, that's too many. How long does it take to cough up a stock's various options premiums? Does your service offer 24-hour order entry? Do you have fast access to charts, news, and research information? Regardless of whether you are looking for a trade or placing one, an online brokerage needs to be easy to

use and fast. At the same time, for some firms, the web design doesn't matter. Some offer software-based rather than web-based trading platforms, which can range from very simple to highly advanced. In the past, these software-based programs were mostly for very active traders. Not anymore. Capabilities have been converging and some firms are now offering multiple ways to access your trading account.

These 10 criteria were used to narrow down the hundreds of brokerage firms offering online trading to the best of the bunch for options traders. What follows is an in-depth review of our favorite (top 12) picks.

the dynamic dozen

Speculations aside, I have spent a considerable amount of time investigating online options trading services. Since options traders have very different needs from stock traders, this top 12 list is probably not the same as those of other rating services found in other publications. To create this list, I looked at the set of criteria detailed in the previous section and used the following three points to make the final decisions:

1. Resources—options tools and information.
2. Usability—the ease of entering options orders online.
3. Site design—how easy or difficult to navigate the site.

The list in Table 12.1 represents my personal opinions, which can change quickly depending on how each company evolves. So please keep in mind that in the tremendously dynamic environment of the Internet, some of the information published in this book may have changed by the time you read it. To keep up with this evolutionary process, we will be continually updating this list at our web site (www.optionetics.com). Please feel free to visit the site and our message boards to talk to us about ongoing changes in the industry. After all, thanks to the Internet, freedom of speech has never been so free.

In the following pages, you'll find detailed information regarding the services and costs of each of the brokerages in our top 12 list. You need to be aware that the account minimum required to open an account and the minimum amount required for spread trading are not always the same. And sometimes the difference is staggering! For example, one firm might require an initial deposit of only $2,000 to open an account, but that minimum jumps up to $20,000 if you want to do spread trading. Where the brokerages were willing to provide the information to us directly, I used their information. In other cases, I pulled the information off their web sites. Here, however, are the highlights of my list-making thought process.

The number one spot goes to optionsXpress because the firm has clearly made a concerted effort to create a brokerage firm for options traders. The tools and research are helpful and the order entry screen is straightforward and easy to navigate. The system also offers tools for screening

Two relative newcomers tied for second. Both TradeKing and OptionsHouse have high rankings due to innovative site design and options usefulness, which includes low commissions. TradeKing has been gaining popularity with help from its vibrant community. Meanwhile, OptionsHouse, which was launched by the institutional options firm Peak6, has developed a wide array of advanced options trading tools and trading capabilities.

Interactive Brokers took third overall. The firm's advanced trading platform makes it very useful for options traders. Interactive Brokers also offers low commissions and the ability to trade a variety of different financial products in one account. Traders interested in international markets might also want to take a closer look at this firm. However, the complexity of its trading system makes it less than ideal for novice options traders and, for that reason, more experienced and active traders form the majority of its clientele.

We ran into a four-way tie for fourth place, but each firm ranked highly for somewhat different reasons. ThinkorSwim has developed a state-of-the-art software-based options trading system that is extremely popular among options traders today. Commissions are low by industry standards and the general feedback about the firm's customer service has been good. ChoiceTrade, meanwhile, also ranks high, thanks to low trade costs and ongoing improvement in its options trading tools and capabilities. Two of the powerhouses in the online industry are also vying for fourth: TD Ameritrade and E*Trade received high marks due to their range of offerings, the ease of use of their sites, and ongoing improvement to trading capabilities.

The remaining four firms, Charles Schwab, eOption, Wall-Street*E, and Newedge USA, are all strong in certain areas, but also had some noticeable weaknesses in others. For example, Charles

table 12.1 online brokerage top 12 list

Top 12 Online Brokerage Comparison Table

	Online Brokerage	Option Tools	Usability	Site Design	Overall Rank	Stock Commission	Option Commission*	Account Minimum
#1	**OptionsXpress** www.optionsxpress.com	10	9	10	9.67	$14.95	$15.00	None
#2	**TradeKing** www.tradeking.com	9	9	9	9	$4.95	$11.45 ($4.95 + $.65 per contract)	None
#3	**OptionsHouse** www.optionshouse.com	9	9	9	9	$4.95	$9.95	$1,000
#4	**Interactive Brokers** www.interactivebrokers.com	9	8	8	8.33	$1.00 (penny per share)	$10.00 ($1.00 per contract)	$10,000
#5	**E*Trade Financial** www.etrade.com	8	8	8	8	$6.99 to $12.99 depending on platform	$14.99 ($6.99 + $.75 per contract)	$1,000
#6	**TD Ameritrade** www.tdameritrade.com	7	8	9	8	$9.99	$17.49 ($9.99 + $.75 per contract)	$2,000

#7	**ThinkorSwim** www.thinkorswim.com	9	7	NA	8	$.015 per share ($5.00 minimum)	$21.35	$3,500
#8	**Choice Trade** www.choicetrade.com	8	8	8	8	$5.00	$9.90 ($.99 per contract)	None
#9	**Charles Schwab** www.schwab.com	8	7	8	7.67	$9.95 (30 or more trades per month)	$9.95 + $.95 per contract (30 or more trades per month)	$10,000
#10	**WallStreet*E** www.wallstreete.com	7	8	8	7.67	$21.95 ($19.95 + $.02 per share)	$50 ($25.00 + $2.50 per contract)	$2,500
#11	**eOption** www.eoption.com	7	8	7	7.33	$5.00	$7.50 ($5.00 + $.25 per contract)	None
#12	**newedge USA** www.preferredtrade.com	7	7	8	7.33	$10.90 ($9.95 + $.0095 per share)	$9.95 ($.95 per contract or $9.95 min.)	$5,000

*Commissions assume 10 contracts or 100 shares.

Schwab is a powerful broker with the ability to handle many types of orders, but the account minimums are high and the tools for options traders are not as robust as some of the other firms. WallStreet*E, which took top spot in the first edition of *Trade Options Online*, has slipped because its commissions are high relative to its peers and the online trading capabilities aren't keeping pace, either. Nevertheless, the firm offers a range of financial planning products and, for options traders looking for the ability to trade options online as well as the benefits of a full-service broker, WallStreet*E is worth a closer look.

Newedge USA offers low commissions, but the online trading tools have not developed as fast as its competitors. However, the firm also led the way in the development of portfolio margin accounts, and for strategists looking to trade using risk-based margin, Newedge USA might be worth talking to. Finally, we haven't had much feedback on eOption yet, as this is a relatively new player in the field. With its low commissions and an obvious focus on the options market, this firm will certainly be worth watching in the future.

That's it for the highlights. The following list details each of the top 12 brokerages so that you can do your own comparison. Remember, if you are paying a premium for the services of a live broker, make sure that they are knowledgeable enough to earn that premium. And don't be afraid to interview a long list of brokers before making your final choice. Brokerages are the intermediaries of trading. To effectively compete in the new online trading arena, make sure you choose the firm that gives you what you need at a fair price.

1. optionsxpress

> **web site:** http://www.optionsxpress.com
>
> **address:** 311 W. Monroe Street, Suite 1000, Chicago, IL 60606
>
> **toll-free:** 888-280-8020
>
> **direct:** 312-629-5455
>
> **e-mail:** info@optionsxpress.com
>
> **category:** Low-cost online options broker
>
> **slogan:** "Online Options, Stock & Futures Brokers"
>
> **option tools** $= 10$
>
> **usability** $= 9$
>
> **site design** $= 10$
>
> **overall** $= 9.67$

- **general description:** For options traders, OptionsXpress stands out above the rest. As the firm's name implies, it is an options trading specialist and continues to develop new products and tools with the options community in mind. David Kalt, James Gray, and Ned Bennett came together to form optionsXpress in late 1999, pouring their 30 years of option industry experience into the firm. The firm is publicly traded and its shares trade under the symbol OXPS.

- **features:** Custom order entry screens for options, spreads, covered calls, stocks, bonds, futures, futures options, or mutual funds, including contingent orders, one-cancels-other, and advanced orders. Most complex options combinations and spread orders can be processed online. OptionsXpress then directly routes them to the exchange floor to be traded as spreads, not legged into.

- **additional services:** Screeners, Xtrends, Dragon, Strategy-Scan, Pricer, Trade Calculator, and Virtual Trading help traders identify and analyze simple and complex trading opportunities. Auto-trading with option advisers gives traders the ability to automatically trade the suggestions of their favorite analyst or newsletter writer. OptionsXpress also offers cash management services and cash sweeps, Schaeffer's Research, Optionetics commentary, along with Briefing.com news, data, and analysis. Volatility and stock charts are available at no additional charge. OptionsXpress also offers free educational webinars.

- **options:** $1.50 per contract for 10 or more contracts, or $14.95 minimum per trade (examples: 5 contracts = $14.95, 10 = $15, 20 = $30). No hidden fees. E-mail them at info@optionsxpress. com to find out how you might qualify for a special rate as low as $1.25 per contract. Each leg of a spread represents a trade. (See Table 12.2.)

- **stocks:** $14.95 up to 1,001 shares less $.015 per share for 1,001 shares and above. Margin rates as low as 3.75 percent (subject to change).

- **account minimum:** There are no minimum account requirements at OptionsXpress.

- **quotes:** Free unlimited real-time quotes, including real-time option charts, news, and pricing chains. Streaming quotes, charts, and news are available at no additional cost.

table 12.2 optionsxpress

Trade [Apple Computer (AAPL) @ $172]	Margin	Commission
Long Stock 100 Shares	$8,600 (50 percent of stock)	$14.95
Long Call AAPL January 175 call @ $5.00	$500.00 (100 percent of options)	$14.95 (minimum)
Long Straddle Long 1 AAPL January 175 call @ $2.50 Long 1 AAPL January 175 put @ $5.00	$750.00 (100 percent of options)	$14.95
Short Straddle Short 1 AAPL January 175 call @ $5.00 Short 1 AAPL January 175 put @ $2.50	$4,190 (100 percent of options premiums plus 20 percent of the underlying stock)	$14.95
Bull Call Spread Long 1 ΛAPL January 175 call @ $5.00 Short 1 AAPL January 180 call @ $2.0	$300 (net debit or risk of spread)	$14.95
Butterfly Spread Long 1 AAPL January 170 call @ $8.50 Short 2 AAPL January 175 calls @ $5.00 Long 1 AAPL January 180 call @ $2.00	$50 (net debit)	$14.95
Portfolio Margin	**Available (yes/no)**	**Minimum Account**
	NA	NA

2. tradeking

web site: http://www.tradeking.com

address: 5455 N. Federal Hwy, Suite E, Boca Raton, FL 33487

toll-free: 877-495-5464 (877-495-KING)

e-mail: service@tradeking.com

category: Online discount broker

slogan: "An Online Options and Stock Broker. Power to the Individual Investor."

option tools $= 9$

usability $= 9$

site design $= 9$

overall $= 9$

- **general description:** TradeKing is a straightforward, no-nonsense online broker. The browser-based trading platform is easy to use and the firm offers a variety of tools and information to help make the decision-making process easier. The commissions on stocks and options orders are among the lowest in the business, and *SmartMoney* and *Barron's* have consistently given the firm top ratings for its tools and customer service. These are the main reasons many traders are turning to TradeKing.

- **features:** The TradeKing web-based platform features powerful online equity, options, and fixed-income trading tools including real-time portfolio information; advanced order entry; customized charting and alerts; free research and integrated news; stock, option, and mutual fund screeners; volatility charts; a pricing probability calculator; enhanced option chains; and interactive educational information. TradeKing also features innovative community networking capabilities to help connect like-minded traders for enhanced strategy development and information sharing.

- **additional services:** TradeKing gives traders a complete online trading system that allows efficient, smart-router order entry and tracking. Their powerful charting tools are provided by Recognia and can automatically identify many technical analysis trends and chart patterns. TradeKing also boasts a large collection of educational material including articles, options-focused instructional blogs from options experts, videos, and podcasts.

- **options:** TradeKing offers options trades for the low rate of only $4.95 per trade plus $0.65 per contract. It costs $0.95 for exercise of a contract. The firm offers online trading of both simple and complex strategies including straddles, butterflies, covered calls, and collars. (See Table 12.3.)

---

table 12.3   tradeking

Trade [Apple Computer (AAPL) @ $172]	Margin	Commission
Long Stock 100 Shares	$8,600 (50 percent of stock)	$4.95
Long Call AAPL January 175 call @ $5.00	$500.00 (100 percent of options)	$5.60
Long Straddle Long 1 AAPL January 175 call @ $5.00 Long 1 AAPL January 175 put @ $2.50	$750.00 (100 percent of options)	$6.25
Short Straddle Short 1 AAPL January 175 call @ $5.00 Short 1 AAPL January 175 put @ $2.50	$4,190 (100 percent of options premiums plus 20 percent of the underlying stock)	$6.25
Bull Call Spread Long 1 AAPL January 175 call @ $5.00 Short 1 AAPL January 180 call @ $2.00	$300 (net debit or risk of spread)	$6.25
Butterfly Spread Long 1 AAPL January 170 call @ $8.50 Short 2 AAPL January 175 calls @ $5.00 Long 1 AAPL January 180 call @ $2.00	$50 (net debit)	$7.55
Portfolio Margin	**Available (yes/no)** Yes	**Minimum Account** $250,000

- **stocks:** $4.95 per trade on Internet, broker-assisted, market, or limit orders.
- **account minimum:** There are no minimum account requirements at TradeKing.
- **quotes:** Unlimited real-time quotes to customers who are actively trading.

3. optionshouse

web site: http://www.optionshouse.com
address: 303 E. Wacker Drive, Suite 700, Chicago IL 60601
toll-free: 877-653-2500
direct: 312-676-8801
e-mail: customerservice@optionshouse.com
category: Online discount brokerage
slogan: "Flat Fees. Sharp Tools."
option tools = 9
usability = 9
site design = 9
overall = 9

- **general description:** OptionsHouse is one of the newer players on the options trading scene. Developed with institutional options market-making firm Peak6 Investments, LP, the OptionsHouse site was created using web technology so traders don't need to flip from page to page to execute a trade. It's all in one place.
- **features:** The web-based trading platform makes it easy to check quotes, create and analyze advanced options strategies, then send orders using easy point-and-click technology. A sophisticated order ticket gives strategists the ability to enter every combination of stock and options order, up to four legs. Orders are executed electronically using a professionally developed smart router to attempt to secure the best price in the market.
- **additional services:** The OptionsHouse web site offers order entry from every logical place on the site. For example, traders can enter trades using context-sensitive menus from the

option chain, orders pane, portfolio pane, and quote look-up. Covered Call Investigator gives potentially interesting covered call (or collar) ideas from your watch list, portfolio, or the market at large. The Risk Viewer is used to track a portfolio by monitoring P&L, market risk, and the greeks; you can also trade from it to modify your risk exposure. The Hotlist

table 12.4   optionshouse

Trade [Apple Computer (AAPL) @ $172]	Margin	Commission
Long Stock 100 shares	$8,600 (50 percent of stock)	$4.95
Long Call AAPL January 175 call @ $5.00	$500.00 (100 percent of options)	$9.95
Long Straddle Long 1 AAPL January 175 call @ $2.50 Long 1 AAPL January 175 put @ $5.00	$750.00 (100 percent of options)	$19.90
Short Straddle Short 1 AAPL January 175 call @ $5.00 Short 1 AAPL January 175 put @ $2.50	$4,190 (100 percent of options premiums plus 20 percent of the underlying stock)	$19.90
Bull Call Spread Long 1 AAPL January 175 call @ $5.00 Short 1 AAPL January 180 call @ $2.00	$300 (net debit or risk of spread)	$19.90
Butterfly Spread Long 1 AAPL January 170 call @ $8.50 Short 2 AAPL January 175 calls @ $5.00 Long 1 AAPL January 180 call @ $2.00	$50 (net debit)	$29.85
Portfolio Margin	**Available (yes/no)**	**Minimum Account**
	Yes	$250,000

tool shows interesting activity in the options market. Finally, the Execution Report shows you (with one click) how a trade did relative to the National Best Bid and Offer (NBBO) at the time and how long it took.

- **options:** $9.95 flat-rate commission, unlimited contracts. (See Table 12.4.)
- **stocks:** $4.95 commission, unlimited shares.
- **account minimum:** $1,000 for cash and $2,000 for a margin account.
- **quotes:** Free stock quotes and options chains.

4. interactive brokers

web site: http://www.interactivebrokers.com
address: One Pickwick Plaza, Greenwich, CT 06830
toll-free: 877-442-2757
phone: 312-542-6901
e-mail: help@interactivebrokers.com
category: Direct access broker
slogan: "The Professional's Gateway to the World's Markets"
option tools = 9
usability = 8
site design = 8
overall = 8.33

- **general description:** Interactive Brokers is one of the bigger online firms. It has offices in Chicago, Switzerland, Montreal, Hong Kong, London, Sydney, and now India. It is the best firm for traders who are looking for tools and capabilities to trade multiple financial markets in one location. It is also well suited for active do-it-yourself traders who want a one-stop shop for direct access trading in multiple financial markets at deeply discounted commission rates. Interactive Brokers' shares trade on the NASDAQ under the symbol IBKR.
- **features:** The IB Universal account allows traders to buy and sell stocks, options, exchange-traded funds, single stock futures, futures, mutual funds, bonds, and forex within the same account. In addition, the system allows trading in a wide

array of international markets from one Trader Workstation screen (TWS). Options traders use Interactive Brokers' TWS system to create combination limit orders for options and spread orders for futures. TWS also provides several modules dedicated to traders solely focusing on specific markets. The FX Trader offers currency trading in 12 major currencies.

table 12.5   interactive brokers

Trade [Apple Computer (AAPL) @ $172]	Margin	Commission
Long Stock 100 Shares	$8,600 (50 percent of stock)	$1.00
Long Call AAPL January 175 call @ $5.00	$500.00 (100 percent of options)	$1.00
Long Straddle Long 1 AAPL January 175 call @ $2.50 Long 1 AAPL January 175 put @ $5.00	$750.00 (100 percent of options)	$2.00
Short Straddle Short 1 AAPL January 175 call @ $5.00 Short 1 AAPL January 175 put @ $2.50	$4,190 (100 percent of options premiums plus 20 percent of the underlying stock)	$2.00
Bull Call Spread Long 1 AAPL January 175 call @ $5.00 Short 1 AAPL January 180 call @ $2.00	$300 (net debit or risk of spread)	$2.00
Butterfly Spread Long 1 AAPL January 170 call @ $8.50 Short 2 AAPL January 175 calls @ $5.00 Long 1 AAPL January 180 call @ $2.00	$50 (net debit)	$4.00
Portfolio Margin	**Available (yes/no)** Yes	**Minimum Account** $100,000

exchange for that, traders have all of the services available in ChoiceTrader Select plus advanced charting, bracket orders, position and order management, as well as other analytical tools.

- **additional services:** Education, third-party research, and ChoiceTrade Investment Community (CTIC).
- **options:** Online orders for 1 to 20 contracts are $0.99 per contract ($8.95 minimum, no trade fee). Online orders of 21 or more contracts are only 0.75 per contract. There is a $25 surcharge for broker-assisted trades, $15 for exercise and assignment. (See Table 12.9.)
- **stocks:** $5.00 for online trades; $5.00 or $.005 per share all-in on Direct Pro; $25 surcharge for broker-assisted trades.
- **account minimum:** No account minimum.
- **quotes:** Real-time streaming quotes (free with five trades per month, regular price $14.95) and Level II. (eSignal subscription is necessary for ChoiceTrader Select.)

9. charles schwab

web site: http://www.schwabat.com

address: 101 Montgomery Street, San Francisco, CA 94104

toll-free: 888-245-6864

e-mail: Visit their web site.

category: Full-service discount broker

slogan: "Schwab gives Active Traders an edge in today's markets."

option tools = 8

usability = 7

site design = 8

overall = 7.67

- **general description:** Schwab is the largest brokerage of them all and therefore has the resources to offer one of the most advanced information retrieval systems and technology available. Traders using Schwab have access to the very latest news, research, and investment information concisely analyzed and tailored to fit specific needs. The firm is well suited for long-term investors who need a variety of investment-related products and services under one roof. In addition, with 374 branches all over the country, it's not hard to find customer service and help. Commissions run a little higher than their competitors, but that is not unusual given the range

---

table 12.10   charles schwab

Trade [Apple Computer (AAPL) @ $172]	Margin	Commission
Long Stock 100 Shares	$8,600 (50 percent of stock)	$9.95
Long Call AAPL January 175 call @ $5.00	$500.00 (100 percent of options)	$10.90
Long Straddle Long 1 AAPL January 175 call @ $2.50 Long 1 AAPL January 175 put @ $5.00	$750.00 (100 percent of options)	$5.90
Short Straddle Short 1 AAPL January 175 call @ $5.00 Short 1 AAPL January 175 put @ $2.50	$4,190 (100 percent of options premiums plus 20 percent of the underlying stock)	$21.80
Bull Call Spread Long 1 AAPL January 175 call @ $5.00 Short 1 AAPL January 180 call @ $2.00	(net debit or risk of spread)	$21.80
Butterfly Spread Long 1 AAPL January 170 call @ $8.50 Short 2 AAPL January 175 calls @ $5.00 Long 1 AAPL January 180 call @ $2.00	$50 (net debit)	$33.65
Portfolio Margin	**Available (yes/no)**	**Minimum Account**
	NA	NA

of products and services Schwab offers. Schwab is a public company with shares trading under the ticker SCHW.

- **features:** Schwab is really a full-service firm and offers execution on options, equities, exchange-traded funds, mutual funds, corporate bonds, and Treasuries. Investors also use Schwab for stock screening, portfolio management, and planning for long-term goals such as retirement, tax planning, and college education funds.

- **additional services:** Schwab has several service centers for non-English-speaking investors. The firm also offers life insurance, CDs, and money markets. In the event of web site outages or Internet connection problems, investors can turn to alternate contacts through other channels like Telebroker, live broker, and local branch broker.

- **options:** Traders who make any combination of 30 or more equity and options trades per quarter, or who have assets of more than $1 million, pay $9.95 plus $.95 per contract. (See Table 12.10.)

- **stocks:** $9.95 flat fee for 30 or more trades, and $9.95 to $19.95 (depending on household balances) for 29 or fewer trades.

- **account minimum:** $10,000

- **quotes:** Free real-time quotes.

10. wallstreet*e

web site: http://www.wallstreete.com

address: 7242 S.W. 42nd Terrace, Miami, FL 33155

phone: 305-669-3026

toll-free: 888-WALL-STE (925-5783)

fax: 305-661-7402

e-mail: info@wallstreete.com

category: Online stock and options broker

slogan: "Where Money Meets Technology"

option tools = 7

usability = 8

site design = 8

overall = 7.67

- **general description:** WallStreet*E offers a wide array of services including traditional banking services, insurance, long-term investments, and trading of both stocks and options. The firm is best suited for those investors looking for a variety of solutions to longer-term financial planning needs and also tools and research necessary to trade various options strategies.

- **features:** The firm offers three distinct service levels for trading: do-it-yourself deep discounted brokerage, full brokerage online advisers, and valet brokerage service. The deep-discount service is geared for independent-thinking, self-directed investors who want to research and manage their own accounts using online interactive services. They have access to all the usual electronic bells and whistles—from online research and analytical tools to real-time quotes and news alerts. The full advisory service provides novice traders or experienced traders with limited time availability with professional investment guidance and assistance in developing a wide range of investment strategies. The final valet service is in between the two previous alternatives and enables traders to personally trade and manage a variety of products and seek help from an adviser.

- **additional services:** WallStreet*E also offers newsletters, portfolio trackers, article archives, free unlimited access to real-time corporate data filed with the Securities and Exchange Commission (SEC Edgar Reports), the ability to search, and screen and bond quotes. Traders also have access to free money market sweep; free checkbook; cash and asset allocation account with a Visa card; checking account; money market account; trust services; investments in fixed-income instruments including CDs, corporate bonds, emerging market sovereign debt, and Brady bonds; retirement accounts, IRAs, SEPs, and 401(k)s. Trading in major markets outside the United States is available.

- **options:** $25 plus $2.50 per contract

- **stocks:** NASDAQ OTC market orders are $14.95 per trade ($.02 per share above 1,000 shares). All other orders, NYSE listed, limit, stop, and GTC are $19.95 per trade plus $.02 per share plus frequent trader bonuses. (See Table 12.11.)

- **account minimum:** $2,500.

- **quotes:** Real-time streaming quotes.

table 12.11   wallstreet*e

Trade [Apple Computer (AAPL) @ $172]	Margin	Commission
Long Stock 100 Shares	$8,600 (50 percent of stock)	$16.95 ($14.95 + $.02 per share)
Long Call AAPL January 175 call @ $5.00	$500.00 (100 percent of options)	$27.50
Long Straddle Long 1 AAPL January 175 call @ $2.50 Long 1 AAPL January 175 put @ $5.00	$750.00 (100 percent of options)	$55.00
Short Straddle Short 1 AAPL January 175 call @ $5.00 Short 1 AAPL January 175 put @ $2.50	$4,190 (100 percent of options premiums plus 20 percent of the underlying stock)	$55.00
Bull Call Spread Long 1 AAPL January 175 call @ $5.00 Short 1 AAPL January 180 call @ $2.00	$300 (net debit or risk of spread)	$55.00
Butterfly Spread Long 1 AAPL January 170 call @ $8.50 Short 2 AAPL January 175 calls @ $5.00 Long 1 AAPL January 180 call @ $2.00	$50 (net debit)	$85.00
Portfolio Margin	**Available (yes/no)**	**Minimum Account**
	NA	NA

11. eOption

web site: http://www.eOption.com

address: 950 Milwaukee Avenue, Suite 101, Glenview, IL 60025

toll-free: 888-793-5333

direct: 847-375-6080

fax: 877-367-8466

e-mail: support@eOption.com

category: Online discount broker

slogan: "Exercise Your Option to Save."

option tools = 7

usability = 8

site design = 7

overall = 7.33

- **general description:** Supported by over 30 years of options experience, eOption was established in 2007 as a division of Regal Securities, Inc., member FINRA/SIPC, a Chicago area broker/dealer since 1975. eOption offers execution capabilities on all major exchanges, simple order entry, and ultra low per contract pricing.

- **features:** eOption has simplified the process of complex order entry with tools like strategy scanners and one-click closeout of multileg orders. A web-based platform allows traders to trade up to four legs from a single screen and displays a real-time quote on each leg of the order, as well as on the overall strategy. Direct-access trading and multiple platforms for active traders are also available. Strategy scanner can search the markets for the best covered calls, spreads, and straddles based on several search functions and criteria such as underlying stock price, volatility, expiration, estimated return, probability of trade success, and option price range. Screener features include customized search options by exchange, share value, performance, moving average, trading volume, valuation, or fundamentals.

- **additional services:** As a diversified financial services firm, eOption offers stocks, mutual funds, fixed income products, and no-fee IRAs.

- **options:** $5 plus $.25 per contract. (See Table 12.12.)

table 12.12   eOption

Trade [Apple Computer (AAPL) @ $172]	Margin	Commission
Long Stock 100 Shares	$8,600 (50 percent of stock)	$5.00
Long Call AAPL January 175 call @ $5.00	$500.00 (100 percent of options)	$5.25
Long Straddle Long 1 AAPL January 175 call @ $5.00 Long 1 AAPL January 175 put @ $2.50	$750.00 (100 percent of options)	$10.50
Short Straddle Short 1 AAPL January 175 call @ $5.00 Short 1 AAPL January 175 put @ $2.50	$4,190 (100 percent of options premiums plus 20 percent of the underlying stock)	$10.50
Bull Call Spread Long 1 AAPL January 175 call @ $5.00 Short 1 AAPL January 180 call @ $2.00	$300 (net debit or risk of spread)	$10.50
Butterfly Spread Long 1 AAPL January 170 call @ $8.50 Short 2 AAPL January 175 calls @ $5.00 Long 1 AAPL January 180 call @ $2.00	$50 (net debit)	$15.75
Portfolio Margin	**Available (yes/no)** Yes	**Minimum Account** $250,000

- **stocks:** $5 unlimited shares, market or limit.
- **account minimum:** No minimum to open an eOption account.
- **quotes:** Real-time, multichannel quote module for access to comprehensive stock quotes, research and expanded analytics, option chains, stock screener, mutual fund profiles, and Level II/Depth.

12. newedge USA

web site: http://www.preferredtrade.com
address: 220 Bush Street, Suite 650, San Francisco, CA 94104
toll-free: 888-781-0283
fax: 415-520-5633
e-mail: Service@NewedgeGroup.com
category: Online discount broker
slogan: "The Preferred Way to Trade Options and Stocks!"
option tools = 7
usability = 7
site design = 8
overall = 7.33

- **general description:** Newedge USA caters to active option and stock traders. The web-based software offers an easy-to-use platform with fast execution speed for retail orders and large block orders for institutions. For options traders, the system allows the easy entry of single orders as well as some advanced options strategy orders from a single screen.

- **features:** Newedge USA's trading platform was designed by professional traders and provides a sophisticated and powerful trading platform to execute equities, options, and futures. The multiwindow application has many value-added features including user-friendly point-and-click trading as well as direct-access order routing. The firm currently offers online vertical spreads, calendar spreads, straddles, and strangles.

- **additional services:** Perhaps the most influential force in bringing portfolio margining to the investment community, Newedge USA is well positioned to provide experienced traders the opportunity to trade using risk-based margin. Customers also have access to online trading of stocks, futures, and spreads, as well as smart-routing to best stock or option markets or market of choice. Stop, contingent, and staging orders are available on stock and option orders. Customers can perform instant analysis by simulating changes in various factors, including stock prices, interest, dividend, and analysis date. The firm also offers real-time profit/loss of real or hypothetical option positions; real-time streaming option chain, or filtering options by expiration, class, or range of strikes; position greeks showing net position for all holdings; and real-time profit and loss calculation.

- **options:** $.95 per contract with a $9.95 minimum per order. (See Table 12.13.)

---

table 12.13   newedge USA

Trade [Apple Computer (AAPL) @ $172]	Margin	Commission
Long Stock 100 Shares	$8,600 (50 percent of stock)	$9.95
Long Call APL January 175 call @ $5.00	$500.00 (100 percent of options)	$9.95
Long Straddle Long 1 AAPL January 175 call @ $2.50 Long 1 AAPL January 175 put @ $5.00	$750.00 (100 percent of options)	$19.90
Short Straddle Short 1 AAPL January 175 call @ $5.00 Short 1 AAPL January 175 put @ $2.50	$4,190 (100 percent of options premiums plus 20 percent of the underlying stock)	$19.90
Bull Call Spread Long 1 AAPL January 175 call @ $5.00 Short 1 AAPL January 180 call @ $2.00	$300 (net debit or risk of spread)	$19.90
Butterfly Spread Long 1 AAPL January 170 call @ $8.50 Short 2 AAPL January 175 calls @ $5.00 Long 1 AAPL January 180 call @ $2.00	$50 (net debit)	$29.85
Portfolio Margin	**Available (yes/no)**	**Minimum Account**
	Yes	NA

- **stocks:** $.0095 per share with a $9.95 minimum per order; $9.95 flat fee for NASDAQ stocks.
- **account minimum:** $5,000.
- **quotes:** Real-time streaming quotes are available at no additional charge to clients if there is a minimum of three trades per month; otherwise the fee is $7.00 per month. Level II streaming quotes are available for $30 per month fee.

conclusion

This chapter deciphered the needs of an online trader by taking a close look at the advantages of using a live broker rather than an online brokerage firm. To become a securities broker, or stockbroker, candidates must pass a test called a Series 7 to receive a license, which gives them requirements to buy and sell on behalf of the brokerage firm clients. The Series 7 exam is designed to test a candidate's knowledge of the rules and regulations of stock trading, the formal definitions of various securities, the risks involved in trading, and some fairly basic macroeconomic variables that affect securities. What the test does not assess is a candidate's ability to make money in the markets. Many brokers are fairly young and get into the business with hopes of making lots of money in commissions, not necessarily making money in the markets.

We raise this issue because the most widely touted reason for having a live broker is to get his advice. However, the quality of the advice is directly proportional to your broker's ability to make money in the marketplace (commissions not included). There are many brokers who are very talented and could be a tremendous asset in your financial management. Then there are the others—the ones who may know less than you do about how to make money using stocks and options. That's why it is so important to interview prospective brokers carefully before you throw high commission dollars at them. All brokers are not created equal. Ask around. Talk to friends and relatives. Get referrals before trusting a complete stranger to handle your hard-earned money.

Brokers make money even if you don't. That's a very important thing to keep in mind. Have you ever gotten a call from a broker who just had to tell you about the latest hot stock that you just had to buy? If you decide to take that timely advice and buy the stock, and the stock price subsequently plummets, your broker still makes a commission getting you into and then out of that very same stock. Getting advice from a broker is a double-edged sword. With the advent of online financial commentaries, advisories, and chat rooms, much of the information that was previously limited to the broker's world is now readily available on the Internet. Once you learn how to interpret market signals for yourself, you probably won't need a broker to advise you at all.

On the flip side, let's look at the advantages that computers already bring to the table today. Most traders use the Internet to get charts, news, and analysis information. The research is out there and available at little to no cost. A good online broker will also provide additional information, research, and tools to trade options. And commissions, or the cost of buying and selling, have come down considerably and it's now more affordable than ever to trade. It really has become the era of do-it-yourself investing. Hopefully, this chapter will help you find the right online broker to work with you along the way.

chapter 13

order processing

placing an online order

Technology has made the execution of an order almost unnoticeable to the average trader. You just key in the trade and hit "Send." In many cases, the entire ordering process is completed in seconds or less. Simple buy and sell orders are so effortless that many traditional investors do not concern themselves with this end of the investment process at all.

But this does not hold true for complex option orders. Option traders have distinct needs that require special attention. If you are dealing with a brokerage firm that doesn't specialize in options, you may have a hard time getting a complex option order executed online. As an option trader, you need a brokerage that understands the tricks of the trade so that your order will be filled at the best possible price.

Trade execution depends on the type of trade you want to execute, the exchange, and the mood of the market. There are an assortment of order instructions (see Appendix A for a list of "Types of Orders") and a variety of exchanges to choose from. In addition, the advent of the Internet has changed the ordering process dramatically. Let's take a closer look at what happens when you place a stock order.

To make a trade, you begin by placing an order with your broker, who in turn passes it along to a floor broker. The floor broker takes it to the appropriate pit and uses the open outcry system to try to find another floor broker who wants to buy or sell your order. If your floor broker cannot fill your order, it is left with a specialist who keeps a list of all the unfilled orders, matching them up as prices fluctuate. In this way, specialists are brokers to the floor brokers and receive a commission for every transaction they carry out. Groups of specialists trading similar markets are located near one another in trading pits. Once your order has been filled, the floor trader contacts your broker, who in turn sends confirmation of the execution of your trade. The amazing part of this process is that a market order—one that is to be executed immediately—may take only seconds to complete.

Computerized trading handles a large percentage of orders today. But, no matter what, your broker gets paid a fee or commission for his efforts. Although some online brokerages have slashed commissions to less than $10 a trade, your chief concern as a trader should be to get the transaction executed as you desire and at the best possible price. That's why choosing the right broker is essential to your success. Brokers should be in the business of looking after your interests, not just generating commissions for their pockets.

designated order turnaround (DOT)
the computerized order entry system maintained by the New York Stock Exchange.

In addition to the specialists, there are also market makers who create liquidity by narrowing the spread. Market makers trade for themselves or for a firm. Once an order hits the floor, the market makers can participate with the other players on a competitive basis. However, if there is no action in the pit, they are obligated to "make a market" happen. Market makers are truly pros. They play the bid-ask spread like no one else on the planet, making their money on the spread—the difference between the bid and the ask price. This difference may be only a nickel or less. However, they process a very large number of trades and this tiny difference adds up quickly. Market makers are also experts at hedging their trades for protection.

> **market maker**
> an independent trader or trading firm that is prepared to buy and sell shares or contracts in a designated market in order to facilitate trading by making a two-sided market (bid and ask).

NASDAQ offers brokers the ability to trade directly from their offices using telephones and continuously revised computerized prices. In this way, brokers bypass floor traders and the need to pass along a commission to them. This means that they get to keep more of the commission for themselves. There are no specialists, either—but there are market makers.

Options exchanges, although much newer, are very similar to stock exchanges. They provide a safe place for buyers and sellers to trade options. The Chicago Board Options Exchange (CBOE) and the International Securities Exchange (ISE) handle the majority of the volume in stock options. However, the Philadelphia Stock Exchange (PHLX), the American Stock Exchange (AMEX), the Boston Options Exchange (BOX), the NASDAQ, and the New York Stock Exchange (NYSE) also house options trading operations.

The process for placing option orders is very similar to that of placing a stock order. In many cases, if you are trading both the stock and the options, your order will be guided to an exchange that can process both. However, since they are individual orders, you will be charged a commission on both orders. Commissions are charged to place an options trade and to exit one.

Behind each successful option spread trade stands a broker who understands the best method for executing a complex option order. Indeed, there are numerous decisions that contribute to an option spread order's success. The real trick of the trade comes into play when an option is listed on multiple exchanges. Each exchange has its own bid-ask spread, which may not be the same as other exchanges' bid-ask spreads. This can make things extremely confusing, especially since most quotes show the best inside market (best bid and best offer from an individual exchange). That's why choosing the right brokerage is essential to your trading success. Brokers with extensive options experience will know which exchange provides the better fill or whether the order should be split (one leg to be executed on one exchange and the other leg to be executed on a different exchange).

Once an order has been filled, executions are verbally given to the brokerage firm from the floor broker with individual strike price fills, which then need to be communicated to the customer. This execution should be confirmed with the customer or appear immediately within the customer's online order execution screen. Simple stock orders and buy/sell option orders can be processed electronically, but complex option spreads require manual labor. This leaves a wide margin for human error. Firms without the expertise to process specific strategies are just more likely to make mistakes and possibly cause forfeiture of profits or even major losses. This leads to client frustration as an enormous amount of time and energy goes into complaining and trying to find a solution. Look for a brokerage that employs brokers with experience on the floor of an options exchange. There is no substitute for options experience.

assignments and option exercising

The manner in which a trade is closed manifests the trade's profit or loss. There are three ways to exit a trade in which options are present. An option can be offset, exercised, or allowed to expire. Experience is the best teacher when it comes to choosing the best alternative. Since each alternative has an immediate result, learning how to profitably close out a trade is essential to becoming a successful trader.

If you want to exercise a long stock option, you simply notify your broker, who will then notify the Options Clearing Corporation (OCC). By the next day, you will own (call) or have sold (put) the corresponding underlying asset. You can exercise an option at any time, but generally you will do it—if you do it at all—just prior to expiration. If the market rises, you may choose to exercise a call option. Your trading account will then be debited for 100 shares of the underlying stock (per option) at the call's strike price. If the market declines, you may choose to exercise a put option. You will then short the stock and receive a credit to your account for 100 shares at the put's strike price.

An option seller cannot exercise an option. By selling an option, you are taking on the risk of having a buyer assigned who then exercises the option against you when market price movement makes it an ITM option. If you have an open position short call that is assigned and exercised, you are obligated to deliver 100 shares of the underlying stock to the option buyer at the strike price of your short call. If you have an open position short put that is assigned and exercised, you are obligated to buy 100 shares of the underlying stock from the option buyer at the strike price of your short put. The OCC randomly matches or *assigns* buyers and sellers to one another. If there is an excess of sellers by expiration, all open position ITM short options are automatically exercised by the OCC. In order to avoid being automatically exercised, short option holders can choose to offset their options instead.

Offsetting is a closing transaction that cancels an open position. It is accomplished by doing the opposite of the opening transaction. Obviously, the best time to offset an option is when it is in-the-money and therefore will realize a profit. Offsetting is also used to avoid incurring further losses. An option can be offset at any time—one second after it has been entered or one minute before expiration. In contrast, the best way to realize a profit from a short option is to let it expire and keep the credit received from the premium. That's why time is a short option's enemy. The longer a short option has till expiration, the more chances it has of being exercised.

Although most option holders and writers close out their option positions with an offsetting closing transaction, investors should be familiar with assignment and exercise. Understanding assignments and exercises can help an option holder determine whether exercise might be more advantageous than an offsetting sale of the option. Offsetting an option is the most popular technique of closing an option. In fact, 95 percent of all the options with value are offset. However, there are various reasons why a trader might choose instead to exercise an option. Of the 5 percent that are exercised, 95 percent are exercised at expiration.

In addition, option writers (short option sellers) need to understand exercise procedures because of the possibility of being assigned. Once a customer is assigned, he can no longer effect a closing transaction in that option, but must instead purchase (call) or deliver (put) the underlying stock for the exercise price (or, in the case of a cash-settled option, pay the cash settlement amount). Depending on the situation, it may be better for the customer to cover the assignment and deliver the underlying stock by hedging and selling a long option position or simply by exercising a long option position.

In the case of assignments, the OCC assigns exercises in standardized lots to clearing member accounts that reflect the writing of options identical to the exercised options. Once the exercises are assigned by the OCC to a clearing member firm, the clearing firm must then assign them to customers maintaining positions as writers of the exercised options series. These assignments are allocated either on a random selection basis or on a first in, first out basis.

To exercise an option, the holder must direct his brokerage firm to give exercise instructions to the OCC. In order to ensure that an option is exercised on a particular day, the holder must direct the brokerage firm to exercise before the firm's cutoff time for accepting instructions for that day—normally a half hour before the market closes. Once an exercise instruction has been given to a member clearing firm, it cannot ordinarily be revoked except to correct a bona fide error designated in a request filed by the clearing member prior to a deadline specified in the OCC's rules.

online order entry formats

Each online brokerage site has its own unique design format, but many of the available order screens are similar in scope. If you understand one, you can probably figure out the others. Let's take a walk through a few order screens using OptionsXpress as our prototype brokerage. OptionsXpress has created the following order entry screens for stock orders, spreads, and combination stock and option orders. These options order screens enable customers to revise a price or quantity prior to sending the order to the brokerage. Most brokerages also offer a symbol lookup feature that can be used to find the symbol for the stock or option you want to trade.

stock order screen   There are several different variables that clients enter to submit a stock order online (Figure 13.1). In addition to the ticker symbol, the investor must select an action: buy, sell, sell short, or buy to cover the stock of your choice. You also need to specify the quantity of shares, choose whether it's a market or limit order (and choose a price if you want a limit order), specify day or good till canceled (GTC), and add any advanced instructions you may have (stop order, stop limit, fill-or-kill, etc.). Additional fees may apply depending on your special instructions. Traders looking to trade outside of normal exchange hours can also trade after markets with the "Extended Hours" order entry tool.

figure 13.1   **stock order entry screen**

Stock Order Form

| Stock | Extended Hours | Trailing Stop | Contingent |

Stock Symbol   ORCL   Find Symbol

Action   Please Select ▾

Quantity   ⦿ Shares ◯ $ Amount   All or None ☐

Price
- ⦿ Market
- ◯ Limit $
- ◯ Stop $
- ◯ Stop Limit
- ◯ Market On Close

Duration   Day Order ▾

Routing   Default ▾

Advanced Orders   None ▾

Preview Order   Save

source: courtesy of OptionsXpress, reprinted by permission.

trailing stop
a stop loss order is an instruction to the broker to exit a position when a certain price level is breached. For example, an investor might set up a stop loss to exit a trade if Oracle (ORCL) falls below $20 a share. A trailing stop is a stop loss order that follows the prevailing price trend. For example, a stop loss might trail the price of ORCL by $2.00. If the stock moves from $22 to $25 a share, the trailing stock moves up from $20 to $23.

figure 13.2   option order entry screen

Options Order Form

| Option | Trailing Stop | Contingent |

Option Symbol	[ ] Find Chain
Action	Please Select ▾
Quantity	[ ] All or None ☐
Price	◉ Market
	○ Limit $ [ ] ↕
	○ Stop $ [ ] ↕
	○ Stop Limit
	○ Market On Close
Duration	Day Order ▾
Advanced Orders	None ▾

Preview Order   Save

source: courtesy of OptionsXpress, reprinted by permission.

option order screen   There are several different variables that the customer must enter to submit an option order (Figure 13.2): the option symbol (which also names the underlying asset, whether it is a call or put, the expiration month, and the strike price), open buy/open sell, close buy/close sell, quantity, limit price, day order or good till canceled, and any special instructions you may have. Once again, you may modify your order as to price and quantity or look up the option's symbol if needed.

> **contingent order**
> an order to be executed if another order is executed first. An example is to sell one specific security if another specific security has been bought. Many brokers don't accept contingent orders because of the extra work involved.

spread order screen There are two kinds of vertical spreads: credit and debit (Figure 13.3). Since a vertical spread consists of two options, the order screen has two rows of information that must be filled out to complete the order. Qualifiers such as day or GTC, limit price, and special instructions are entered only once.

straddle order entry A straddle consists of two option transactions—a put and a call with the same strike price and expiration date—executed at one price. The straddle order screen (Figure 13.4) consists of the same selections as a basic option screen, except the straddle order selection has two "Buy to Open" menus versus one buy and one sell menu.

butterfly order entry Butterfly orders are simply three option transactions at one price. A butterfly spread is often in a 1:2:1 ratio with regular strike increments. The screen shown in Figure 13.5 is used to trade butterflies in which the customer only needs to specify one price and whether it is for a credit or debit.

condor order entry Condor orders consist of four option transactions at a time. The screen shown in Figure 13.6 can be used to place a condor or an iron butterfly order. There are four rows of option information that must be completed and one row of qualifiers. For the most part, you should include a limit price for spreads, straddles, butterflies, and condors. In today's highly volatile market, placing limits on the amount of money you are willing to spend is the key to managing your risk.

system failures

On Tuesday, October 28, 1997, the New York Stock Exchange at 1.2 billion shares' worth and NASDAQ at 1.36 billion shares' worth broke

figure 13.3   vertical spread order entry screen

Xspreads® Option Spread Order

| Spread | Combo | Straddle | Butterfly | Condor | OCO |

Option Symbol

Action
Buy To Open ▾

Quantity

Find Chain

Option Symbol

Action
Sell To Open ▾

Quantity

Find Chain

Price

◉ Market

○ Limit/Credit* $

○ Limit/Debit* $

○ Even

Duration   Day Order ▾

Advanced Orders   None ▾

Preview Order   Save

source: courtesy of OptionsXpress, reprinted by permission.

the record for trading volume. Markets plummeted that day, and bargain-hunting traders clamored to take advantage of extremely low prices. A feeding frenzy ensued, but many small investors couldn't reach their brokerage firms to get their hands in the pie. Unfortunately, many online brokerages simply did not have the capacity to handle the increased flow of orders. Investors found it impossible to log on and even brokerage phone lines were busy. As losses accumulated and profits were missed, investor frustration soared sky high.

figure 13.4 **straddle order entry screen**

Xspreads® Straddle/Strangle Order

Ⓕ

Spread	Combo	**Straddle**	Butterfly	Condor	OCO

Option Symbol **Action** **Quantity**

Buy To Open ▾

Find Chain

Option Symbol **Action** **Quantity**

Buy To Open ▾

Find Chain

Price
- ◉ Market
- ○ Limit/Credit* $ [____] ⬍
- ○ Limit/Debit* $ [____] ⬍
- ○ Even

Duration Day Order ▾

Advanced Orders None ▾

[**Preview Order**] [Save]

source: courtesy of OptionsXpress, reprinted by permission.

After the exchanges closed, online financial chat rooms were filled with negative tirades from impassioned investors. Each brokerage cited a variety of excuses for system failures. Many big online brokerages had misjudged the intense volume a major move in the marketplace could create and did not have the capacity to handle it. In contrast, many of the smaller brokerages had an easier time processing the increased flow of orders because they service fewer clients to begin with.

This initial incident of system failure gave the online brokerage industry a new demon to deal with. But solving such difficulties is

figure 13.5 **butterfly spread order entry screen**

Xspreads® Butterfly Order

| Spread | Combo | Straddle | **Butterfly** | Condor | OCO |

Option Symbol   **Action**   **Quantity**
Buy To Open ▾

Find Chain

Option Symbol   **Action**   **Quantity**
Sell To Open ▾

Find Chain

Option Symbol   **Action**   **Quantity**
Buy To Open ▾

Find Chain

Price
⦿ Market
◯ Limit/Credit* $ ▲▼
◯ Limit/Debit* $ ▲▼
◯ Even

Duration   Day Order ▾

[**Preview Order**]   [Save]

source: courtesy of OptionsXpress, reprinted by permission.

not easy. System failures continue to plague electronic brokerages as online brokerages pursue various solutions to the high volume problem. Recent increases in stock trading volumes as well as wild price swings have produced a tidal wave of online brokerage failures. For example, E*Trade, the self-proclaimed leader of online brokerages, suffered critical outages on three consecutive days during the first week in February 1999. Thousands of E*Trade customers were unable to place orders. In addition, massive trading bottlenecks on a number of high-volume Internet stocks as well as periodic access

figure 13.6 condor order entry screen

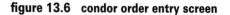

Xspreads® Condor Order

| Spread | Combo | Straddle | Butterfly | Condor | OCO |

Option Symbol

Action
Buy To Open ▼

Quantity

Find Chain

Option Symbol

Action
Sell To Open ▼

Quantity

Find Chain

Option Symbol

Action
Sell To Open ▼

Quantity

Find Chain

Option Symbol

Action
Buy To Open ▼

Quantity

Find Chain

Price
- ● Market
- ○ Limit/Credit* $
- ○ Limit/Debit* $
- ○ Even

Duration
Day Order ▼

Preview Order   Save

source: courtesy of OptionsXpress, reprinted by permission.

problems in quieter markets have triggered a variety of problems for traders across the board.

Unfortunately, everyone wants to place the blame somewhere other than their own backyard, and very few are bellying up to the bar with any concrete solutions. After the Securities and Exchange Commission (SEC) received 330 percent more investor complaints about online problems than the prior year, the SEC's chairman, Arthur Levitt, responded by warning investors to exercise caution when trading online. Not to be outdone, the NASD Regulation, the self-policing arm of the National Association of Securities Dealers, suggested that brokerage firms should warn investors of possible losses due to online capacity flaws.

Since that time, online trading has become a lot more reliable and there haven't been any major system outages due to capacity limits. There have been some problems with system outages at some of the futures exchanges, such as the Chicago Board Options Exchange and the New York Mercantile Exchange, but these have proved to be isolated and short-term events.

Nevertheless, if you do get burned by a system failure, you can attempt to find consolation by lodging a complaint in writing to the compliance officer at your brokerage firm and sending copies to the SEC, the NASD, and possibly your state regulator. Investors who want to take legal action do not have much of a case unless they can prove "a clear departure from established norms." Since antifraud provisions do not permit suits based on claims of lost profits, there is no recourse under federal antifraud provisions set up by national securities laws. If you still want to file a complaint, make sure to send a copy to the SEC at the Office of Investor Education and Assistance, Securities and Exchange Commission, Washington, DC 20549, or call your local NASD office (call 800-289-9999 to find it). You can also visit the NASD web site at www.nasd.com.

---

national association of securities dealers (NASD)
the self-regulatory organization of the securities industry responsible for the regulation of NASDAQ and the over-the-counter markets (www.nasd.com).

---

securities and exchange commission (SEC)
a commission created by Congress to regulate the securities markets and protect investors. It is composed of five commissioners appointed by the president of the United States and approved by the Senate (www.sec.gov).

conclusion

Order processing has come a long way since the late 1700s when traders met under a buttonwood tree on Wall Street. Today's floor traders can run up to 12 miles or more each trading day just to get the job done. At the same time, since we have crossed into the 21st century, the process has become more electronically synchronized.

For individual investors—like many of those who are reading this book—computers make the process of trading and tracking positions easier than ever before. Most brokerages provide detailed listings of any orders that you have open. You can also have closing prices on the stocks and options of your choice sent directly to your e-mail address, either from your brokerage or from a lengthy list of financial web site services. This is a far cry from checking prices in the *Wall Street Journal* every day.

Since the price execution of an option spread is critical to its success, I highly recommend working with online brokerage firms that specialize in options. In addition, easy ordering formats are very important to the avid option trader. Luckily, there has been a lot of advancement in this area over the past few years. It's time to take advantage of it!

chapter 14

ready, set, engage

trading to win

In March 2008, the Securities and Exchange Commission (SEC) filed suit against an investment firm in Salt Lake City, alleging that the group had duped investors by misrepresenting the risks associated with investing in one of their funds. According to the SEC, the group lost a substantial portion of the investors' funds through mistimed bets in the options market. According to a March 4, 2008, SEC filing:

> In an effort to recoup earlier losses by the hedge funds, the Commission alleges Thompson Consulting invested virtually all the hedge funds' assets in unhedged options on the VIX, the CBOE's volatility index, in July and August 2007. Virtually all of the hedge funds' assets were wiped out when the securities markets dropped sharply in mid-August. According to the Commission's complaint, from July 31 to Aug. 17, 2007, the net asset value of the hedge funds fell from approximately $54 million to approximately $200,000. (http://www.sec.gov/news/press/2008/2008-28.htm)

This case highlights two important things. First, so-called financial advisers are not necessarily better investors than you or me. In many cases, they are simply better at sales and marketing, but not necessarily astute at making money in the financial markets. Always deal with financial advisers whom you trust, which might involve getting referrals from friends and colleagues or looking at the long-term track record of the investment firm in question. Look closely at the portfolios and funds, including the holdings within those investment vehicles.

Second, the losses suffered by the Salt Lake City–based firm highlights one of the important risks that options traders sometimes fall victim to, namely that when losses are suffered, they try to make up for those losses with more and more aggressive trading. Conversely, aggressive trading is sometimes due to overconfidence after a few successful trades. However, it takes time and discipline to develop a sufficient trading knowledge base with which to make money in the markets—especially the options markets.

After all, the marketplace is the greatest equalizer of education. Whether you are a Harvard MBA, a rocket scientist, or a high school dropout, the markets prove on a daily basis who wins and who loses. One way or another, you will get your education in the markets, so be well prepared.

Trading options is a specialized business. Informed traders have the opportunity for high rewards while uninformed traders may end up experiencing just how devastating sporadic market movement can be. Just as an Internet stock can go up 10 times in value in a year, it can also lose popularity and sink like a stone. Beware of selling naked options unless they are hedged as part of a spread!

Regardless of technology's effects on the markets, the characteristics of basic trading instruments remain the same. An option by any other name is still an option. Never underestimate the importance of a comprehensive working knowledge of options and just how critical the nuts and bolts of options trading is to your success. There is absolutely no substitute for a healthy understanding of options' risks and rewards. Success should be measured in terms of long-term gain, not yesterday's gain.

If you want to become a successful online trader, take the time to gain market experience. Don't worry about missing out on a market's wild bull ride. Trending markets happen every day. Start by setting up online portfolios to monitor market movement to get a sense of how things work. Remember: For every Dell Computer success story, there are a million sad stories from traders who lost their whole account on a bad tip.

trading accounts

Determining how much money you need in order to start trading options can be very tricky. There are generally two types of transactions: cash and margin.

Cash trades require you to put up 100 percent of the money in cash. All costs of the trade have to be in the account before the trade is placed. For example, if you wanted to buy 100 shares of IBM at $100, you would have to pay $10,000 plus commissions up front. If IBM were to rise to $110, the account would show an open position profit of $1,000, or a 10 percent rise in the account.

In contrast, margin trades allow you to put up a percentage of the total cost of the trade amount in cash and the rest is *on account*. The brokerage company lends you an amount of money against the security of the investment you buy. The actual amount of money you are required to put on deposit with your clearing firm to secure the integrity of the trade is the margin amount. This amount changes depending on the market and size of the trade you are placing.

Most traders prefer margin accounts because these accounts allow them to leverage assets in order to produce higher returns. If the price of the stock goes against your position, you will be required to post additional money into your margin account to keep the position open. If you cannot provide the extra cash needed to fulfill the new margin requirements, you lose your position. This is one of the reasons that shorting the market is so dangerous.

Of course, brokers don't lend money for free. They charge a fixed rate of interest on the loan amount as well as the usual commission on the trade. The interest rate and commissions are paid regardless of what happens to the price of the stock. The rate is usually broker call rate plus the firm's add-on points. This rate is cheaper than most loans due to the fact that it is a secure loan.

Based on the SEC's rules, the margin on most stock purchases equals 50 percent of the amount of the trade. For example, 100 shares of IBM at $100 a share costs a total of $10,000. You would be required to have a minimum of $5,000 on deposit in your margin account.

If you choose to sell short, you are actually borrowing the stock shares from your broker at one price in anticipation of a drop in the market price. If the market price falls, you can buy back the shares at the lower price to repay the loan from your broker and pocket the difference. If the stock price rises, you eventually have to buy back the stock to cover your position at a higher price than you received for selling it. This can be a very expensive process, especially if a stock has been heavily shorted, because as the price starts to rise, a buying flurry among short sellers may drive the price sky-high. Margin on short selling is extremely expensive. You have to be able to cover the entire cost of the stock plus 50 percent more. This value will change as the market price fluctuates. At some brokerages, investors must have a minimum of $50,000 in their margin accounts plus the margin amount for the trade in order to short the market.

Long options do not require margin. They must be paid for up front, but at a fraction of the cost of buying the underlying stock. For example, since each premium point in stock options costs $100, a stock option at $3\frac{1}{2}$ will cost you $350 regardless of the underlying asset's current market price. However, if you choose to short sell the same option, you would have to have a certain amount of margin in your account. If you were short selling the option without a corresponding hedge, many brokers would require at least $50,000 in your account to place a short option trade. If you are hedging the short option, then the margin amount is subject to your broker's discretion.

Combining the buying and selling of options and stocks may create a more complex margin calculation. In some cases, investors can have reduced margin requirements due to a new set of rules known as *portfolio margining*. Portfolio margin accounts are different than traditional strategy-based accounts because the margin is based on risk. For example, the protective put is a combination of long stock and long puts. In a strategy-based margin account, the margin is 50 percent for the stock and 100 percent for the options. However, in a portfolio margin account the margin deposit is based on the true risk of the position, which is limited by the strike price of the short put, which is significantly less than the strategy-based margin. In general, since every trade is unique, margin will depend on the strategy you employ and your broker's requirements. If you're worried about the margin at the outset of the trade, you probably shouldn't place the trade. This rule can keep you from putting on positions that are larger than you can really handle. If you're interested in portfolio margin accounts you should ask your broker if they offer it. Many do, but only to accounts with equity in excess of $100,000.

trading levels

Getting started in options is sometimes a frustrating experience for new traders because options approval is required by all brokerage firms. The compliance department within the firm must ensure that clients have a certain level of experience in trading before allowing clients to open accounts and place more complex trades. Strategies such as uncovered sales, or naked options writing, are definitely not suited for inexperienced options investors.

---

compliance department
the group within the brokerage firm that approves new accounts and ensures that clients are not trading outside of what is suitable given their financial resources and experience.

For some traders, however, the requirements imposed by the brokerage firms serve as a catch 22: how can an investor become experienced in trading if brokers will not allow them to implement trading strategies to begin with? This process is sometimes frustrating at the onset, but there are ways to resolve the dilemma and begin trading. One of them is to gain experience trading equities first and then begin trading combination equity and options strategies, like covered calls or collars.

An individual's past options trading experience and financial resources will allow him to trade within certain strategy levels. For instance, level 1 strategies include relatively straightforward approaches like covered calls and protective puts. More complicated trades require a higher level of approval. Figure 14.1 shows a typical breakdown. Traders with a great deal of experience and significant financial resources can generally receive approval for level 5 trading, which would allow them to implement any type of trading strategy.

In order to avoid the frustration of opening an account with a firm that will not allow trading in more advanced levels, new traders will want to find out the brokerage firm's policy regarding options approval before funding an account. The best way to do this is to contact the firm's compliance department by phone or e-mail and share your concerns. If you have little or no experience, ask them what steps you need to take in order to trade the more complex options strategies (level 3). It sometimes helps to specify which trades (e.g., spreads, straddles, butterflies) you want to trade. Then ask if you will be approved for that type of activity. Don't fund the account until you get the okay.

figure 14.1 **options strategies and broker approval**

Strategy	Options Trading Level				
	Level 1	Level 2	Level 3	Level 4	Level 5
Covered call writing	a	a	a	a	a
Protective puts	a	a	a	a	a
Buying stock or index puts and calls		a	a	a	a
Covered put writing			a	a	a
Spreads			a	a	a
Uncovered put and call writing				a	a
Uncovered writing of straddles and strangles				a	a
Uncovered writing of index puts and calls					a

source: www.optionetics.com, reprinted by permission.

setting your goals

Competing in today's marketplace requires constant Net awareness. You have to pay attention to various sources of information to keep abreast of what's happening. To minimize the inherent frustration of searching the Net for useful information, a trader has to implement a master plan. Developing such a plan is a process of evolution; new sites are integrated into the daily routine as other sites are abandoned. The hardest part of this process lies in defining your starting point and destination.

After defining your goals—college for the kids, retirement by age 50, or a house in the country—it's time to assess where your starting point is. How much money can you afford to place in a trading account? What kind of returns will enable you to attain your goals? How much money can you afford to lose? To determine your financial capabilities, take a discerning look at how much cash you have readily available and the value of assets that could be converted into cash.

Once you come up with the total range of your capabilities, you should assess your real needs. Don't trade more than you can afford to lose. In other words, don't invest your rent payment, monthly food budget, or any funds critical to your family's future. Do not mortgage the house in order to start trading. Use funds that are readily available and can be traded without attachment. If you don't have enough to get started, start a nest egg, earmark it for your new trading career, and start to learn all you can about trading. When you finally have enough money to open an account, you'll be that much further ahead of the game.

Time is another important consideration. To determine the trading style that best fits your needs, you have to accurately assess your time constraints. In the beginning, you must allot the time you have available to learning about trading as well as monitoring your trades. To become a full-time trader, you have to monitor the markets more aggressively. If you have only 15 minutes in the morning and evening to track your positions, short-term trading is simply out of the question. You need to structure a trading program that will let you trade in your spare time until you have the resources to make trading a full-time profession.

You might want to think longer-term. LEAPS (Long-term Equity AnticiPation Securities), for example, are long-term options that are available on many more actively traded stocks. For traders with a traditional buy-and-hold orientation, these longer-term options, which expire in one or two years, often carry with them the stigma of being short-term trading tools with tax consequences. By the very nature of their long-term expiration dates, LEAPS help to overcome this stigma by giving traders significantly more time to be right about market movement.

LEAPS®
Long-term Equity AnticiPation Securities are long-term stock or index options with up to three years until expiration.

The next step is to determine the level of risk you can tolerate. Maybe it is naive to think that anyone should find any risk tolerable; however, the reality of investing is that risk exists no matter what you do. Yes, you can limit risk and you can manage risk; however, *risk is an inherent element of investing*. This includes both financial risk and opportunity risk.

To be a successful investor, you have to get the highest return for the amount of available capital you own. To reach this goal, always calculate the maximum risk a trade presents before placing it. If you are buying options, you risk the money paid to purchase the options. If you are selling options, your risk is unlimited depending on the price of the underlying stock. Unlimited risk is a dangerous endeavor. Hedging risk by using option spreads and delta neutral strategies is a viable way to create trades that leverage your resources and maximize profit potentials.

---

risk
the potential financial loss inherent in an investment.

Since a love affair with anything you do increases your chances of success, make your daily online routine fun. The excitement of surfing the Net drives your performance. To make your journey smooth, your entire computer system must be aligned to support your master plan. Everything from the software you use to the access provider that serves as your gateway to the Internet is an important part of the process. Choose carefully. The road you travel will be much less bumpy if you love the road you have chosen.

conclusion

When I first sat down to write this book, the immensity of the project was a bit overwhelming. Not only are the financial markets constantly changing and offering a wide array of new options strategies, but technology has changed the way we live our lives, do business, and trade. Without a doubt, online trading has emerged as the preferred way for options traders to buy and sell puts and calls. It is here to stay.

Yet, while trading options online is now an everyday reality, there are pitfalls and risks. For example, it is easy for investors who sit comfortably at home behind a computer to overtrade and develop a gambler's mentality. It's also possible to lose a lot of money on one bad trade. If anyone ever tells you they lost a ton of money with options, just ask them what they sold. Chances are they made a bad decision selling options short, as it is a high-risk trade. So, given the dangers, what can the active online option trader do right now to minimize losses?

In my humble opinion, there are 10 do's and don'ts that can help you through the world of online trading:

1. First and foremost, you have to assume that glitches and delays are rare but are part of the online trading process. It could be your broker, your ISP, your power, or the exchanges, but glitches happen. Don't panic.

2. Develop a backup plan for each trade beyond just calling your broker on the phone when your system is down.

3. Keep a hard copy of your trading account available for when your broker's server shuts down.

4. Place limited-risk trades; avoid naked positions.

5. Always calculate a trade's maximum risk before entering it and make sure you can afford to lose that amount. Ask yourself, what if I'm wrong?

6. Try using LEAPS options in the more volatile markets.

7. Don't expect instantaneous executions or confirmations, for sooner or later you will be disappointed.

8. If you believe the "fast" and "easy" claims advertised by online brokerages, get ready for disillusionment.

9. Always use limit orders. Market orders can be extremely dangerous, especially in heavily volatile markets.

10. There are specific risks associated with buying on margin. Be aware of what is expected of you before entering a trade.

When it comes to online trading, let caution be your guide until knowledge and experience coalesce to foster tangible trading intuition. To acquire experience, you need to be able to play the game long enough to get the big picture. Trading knowledge is acquired by learning which details to pay attention to. Before placing a trade, calculate the maximum risk and reward as well as the breakeven points to clearly establish a trade's profit range. A successful trader must know whether a trade is worth the risk. The practical application of limited-risk strategies can increase your chances of making consistent stock market profits and reducing trading-related stress.

The key to successful trading is the effective integration of the big picture coupled with a perceptive ability to prioritize small details. To become a confident trader, you need to be able to break down the complexities of trading strategies into simple, straightforward tasks that lead to moneymaking trades. Each time you study a new market, there are certain characteristics to be investigated. Likewise, every strategy has its own niche of applicability. By specializing in one or two markets at a time, you can learn which strategies work in which recognizable market conditions. As these conditions repeat themselves in other markets, the same strategy can be employed to reap rewards.

As we continue to experience the effects of technology on the investment community's evolution, it's up to you to find a balance—neither getting left behind nor moving too fast. I hope this book has helped give you a foundation for competing in the online trading revolution. Learning to trade options takes true-grit determination as well as passion, patience, and perseverance. Your pursuit of this journey affirms your personal decision to strive for increased financial success through managed-risk strategies. The Internet offers traders financial empowerment. With this in mind, you're ready to boldly go forth into cyberspace—mouse in hand—to seek out new web sites and explore trading opportunities, the likes of which have never before been seen by civilization.

appendix a

useful tables, data, and strategy reviews

option expiration month codes

	January	February	March	April	May	June
Calls	A	B	C	D	E	F
Puts	M	N	O	P	Q	R

	July	August	September	October	November	December
Calls	G	H	I	J	K	L
Puts	S	T	U	V	W	X

strike price codes

A	B	C	D	E	F	G	H	I
5	10	15	20	25	30	35	40	45
105	110	115	120	125	130	135	140	145
J	**K**	**L**	**M**	**N**	**O**	**P**	**Q**	**R**
50	55	60	65	70	75	80	85	90
150	155	160	165	170	175	180	185	190
S	**T**	**U**	**V**	**W**		**X**	**Y**	**Z**
95	100	7.50	12.50	17.50		22.50	27.50	32.50
195	200	37.50	42.50	47.50		52.50	57.50	62.50

variable option deltas   All options are provided a delta relative to the 100 deltas of the underlying security. If 100 shares of long stock are equal to +100 deltas, then the corresponding options must have delta values of −100. You can estimate an options delta as follows, depending on the movement of the underlying stock.

	Calls		Puts	
Option Deltas	**Long**	**Short**	**Long**	**Short**
ATM	+50	−50	−50	+50
	ITM			
1 Strike	+60 to +65	−60 to −65	−60 to −65	+60 to +65
2 Strikes	+70 to +75	−70 to −75	−70 to −75	+70 to +75
3 Strikes	+80 to +85	−80 to −85	−80 to −85	+80 to +85
	OTM			
1 Strike	+35 to +40	−35 to −40	−35 to −40	+35 to +40
2 Strikes	+25 to +30	−25 to −30	−25 to −30	+25 to +30
3 Strikes	+15 to +20	−15 to −20	−15 to −20	+15 to +20

option symbols   To understand quotes, you must be able to decipher option symbols. Option symbols vary depending on their source. However, all option symbols are composed of the following components:

- *Root symbol*—the symbol used to identify the underlying financial instrument on which an option is based.
- *Expiration month*—the month in which the option contract expires, represented by a letter of the alphabet that also designates the option as a call or a put. (An "Option Expiration Month Codes" chart can be found on the first page of this Appendix.)
- *Strike price*—the specific price at which the option gives the holder the right to buy or sell the underlying financial instrument. For stocks, strike prices are represented by a letter of the alphabet.
- *Option type*—in stock options, a letter designating the expiration of calls and puts.

stock example

INQ A A

Intel January 105 Call

INQ = Intel Stock

A = January call expiration

A = Strike price of 5, 105, 205, 305, 405, 505

option quote terms

Data	Definition
Last	The last price that the option traded for at the exchange. For delayed quotes, this price may not reflect the actual price of the option at the time you view the quote.
Open	The price of the first transaction of the current trading day.
Change	The amount the last sale differs from the previous trading day's closing price.
Percent change	The percentage the price has changed since the previous day's closing price.

(continued)

Data	Definition
High	The high price for the current trading day.
Low	The low price for the current trading day.
Bid	The highest price a prospective buyer (floor trader) is prepared to pay for a specified time for a trading unit of a specified security. If there is a high demand for the underlying asset, the prices are bid up to a higher level. Off-floor traders purchase at the ask price.
Ask	The lowest price acceptable to a prospective seller (floor trader) of a specified security. A low demand for a stock translates to the market being offered down to the lowest price at which a person is willing to sell. Off-floor traders sell at the bid price. Together, the bid and ask prices constitute a quotation or quote. and the difference between the two prices is the bid-ask spread. The bid and ask dynamic is common to all stocks and options.
52-week high	The highest price at which the stock traded in the past 52-week period.
52-week low	The lowest price at which the stock traded in the past 52-week period.
Earnings per share	The bottom line (net pretax profit) divided by the number of shares outstanding.
Volume	The total number of shares traded that day.
Shares outstanding	The total number of shares the company has issued
Market cap	Shares outstanding multiplied by the closing stock price.
P/E ratio	Stock price divided by the earnings per share (P = price; E = earnings per share).
Exchange	Where a company lists or registers its shares (e.g., the New York Stock Exchange).

intermarket relationships

Interest Rates	Bonds	Stocks	Dollar
Rising	Falling	Falling	Rising
Falling	Rising	Rising	Falling
Stable	Stable	Up/Stable	Stable

Note: If these relationships do not hold, then there is said to be a divergence. A good trader will look for reasons for a divergence and look for opportunities to make money under these circumstances.

market opportunities

Bullish Limited-Risk Strategies	Bullish Unlimited-Risk Strategies	Bearish Limited-Risk Strategies	Bearish Unlimited-Risk Strategies	Neutral Limited-Risk Strategies	Neutral Unlimited-Risk Strategies
Buy call	Buy underlying	Buy put	Sell underlying	Long straddle	Short straddle
Bull call spread	Sell put	Bear put spread	Sell call	Long strangle	Short strangle
Bull put spread	Covered call	Bear call spread	Covered put	Long synthetic straddle	Call ratio spread
Call ratio back-spread	Call ratio spread	Put ratio back-spread	Put ratio spread	Long butterfly	Put ratio spread
				Long condor	
				Long iron butterfly	

types of orders   As you get ready to trade, you will have to decide what kind of order you wish to place. A wide variety of orders exist that you will need to become acquainted with. Let's take a look at the most prevalent order types.

1. **At-even orders** should be placed without a debit or a credit to the account. That means that you may have to wait until the market gets to the right prices for your trade to be placed.
2. **At-the-opening orders** should be executed at the opening of the market or should be canceled.
3. **Day orders** remain good only for the duration of the trading day that they are entered. They are canceled at the end of the trading day, if not executed.
4. **Fill-or-kill orders** must be executed immediately as a whole order. If not, the order is canceled.

5. **Good till canceled orders** remain in effect until executed or explicitly canceled, or the contract expires.

6. **Immediate or cancel orders** must be executed immediately in whole or in part as soon as they are entered. Any part not executed is automatically canceled.

7. **Limit orders** specify a maximum buying price or a minimum selling price.

8. **Limit buy orders** must be executed below the current market price.

9. **Limit sell orders** must be executed above the current market price.

10. **Market orders** are the most common type of order. They are guaranteed execution at the best price prevailing in the market.

11. **Market-on-open orders** must be executed during the opening of trading.

12. **Market-on-close orders** must be executed during the closing of trading.

13. **Market-if-touched orders** combine market and limit orders, whereby an order becomes a market order when the options or stock reach a specified price.

14. **Market-if-touched buy orders** become market orders when the options or underlying asset fall below the current market price.

15. **Market-if-touched sell orders** become market orders when the options or underlying asset rise above the current market price.

16. **Stop orders** are used to limit risk. They become market orders when the options or stock reach a certain price. However, **buy stop orders** must be executed when the specified price is above the current market price; and **sell stop orders** must be executed when the specified price falls below the current market price.

17. **Stop limit orders** are an extension of stop orders where the activated order becomes a limit order instead of a market order.

risk profile basics   Use Figure A.1 to help you get the full benefits of the risk graphs scattered throughout this book. Risk graphs like this

figure a.1   put ratio backspread (short 1 July MO 40 put @ 5.50, long 2 July MO 35 puts @ 1.75 MO @ 3.38)

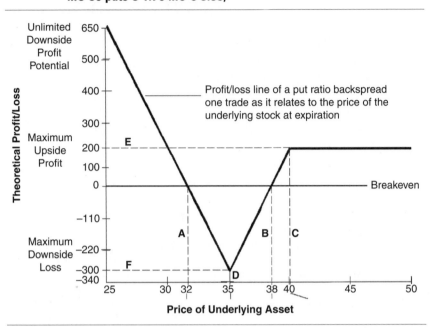

Profit/loss line of a put ratio backspread one trade as it relates to the price of the underlying stock at expiration

one enable traders to visually assess a trade's profitability in one glance. By analyzing the risk graph of a trade at expiration, you can assess a variety of important values:

- *The darker line* tracks the actual profit or loss of the trade depending on the price of the underlying asset. By looking at any price on the bottom axis, you can figure out the corresponding profit or loss the trade makes when the underlying asset expires at a certain price.
- *Line A* tracks the downside breakeven ($32) of the trade to the corresponding price of the underlying asset. If the price of the underlying asset falls below this point, the trade starts to make a profit that is unlimited in nature (the line continues to move upward and to the left as the price of the underlying asset falls).
- *Line B* tracks the upside breakeven ($38) of the trade to the corresponding price of the underlying asset. When the price

of the underlying asset rises above this point it starts to make a profit that is limited in nature.

- *Line C* tracks the point at which the trade hits a maximum limited profit ($40, the strike price of the short call). The underlying asset must move significantly in either direction for this trade to make a profit.
- *Line D* shows the price of the underlying asset at the point of maximum loss ($35, the strike price of the long option).
- *Line E* shows the maximum limited profit ($200).
- *Line F* shows the maximum loss amount (−$300).

popular indexes

Symbol	Index	Symbol	Index
$XAL	Airline Index	$TRIN	NYSE Short-Term Trade Index
$ISSA	AMEX Advance/Decline Issues	$XOI	Oil Index
$XAX	AMEX Composite Index	$DRG	Pharmaceutical Index
$XMI	AMEX Major Market Index	$BKX	PHLX Bank Sector Index
$XOI	AMEX Oil & Gas	$BMX	PHLX Computer Box Maker Sector
$AVOL	AMEX Volume	$FPP	PHLX Forest & Paper Sector Index
$BTK	Biotechnology Index	$XAU	PHLX Gold and Silver Index
$MNX	CBOE Mini-Ndx Index	$OSX	PHLX Oil Service Sector Index
$GAX	CBOE Gaming Index	$SOX	PHLX Semiconductor Sector Index
$DDX	Disk Drive Index	$DOT	PHLX TheStreet.Com Internet
$COMP	Dow Jones Composite Index	$PSE	PSE High Technology Index
$DJC	Dow Jones Composite Index	$RUI	Russell 1000
$INDU	Dow Jones Industrial Average	$RUT	Russell 2000

(*continued*)

Symbol	Index	Symbol	Index
$DJI	Dow Jones Industrial Index	$RUA	Russell 3000
$DJT	Dow Jones Transportation Index	$SOX	Semiconductor Index
$DJU	Dow Jones Utilities Index	$OEX	S&P 100 Index
$FCHI	France Cac-40 Index	$SPX	S&P 500 Index
$FTSE	FTSE-100 Index	$SGX	S&P Barra Growth Index
$GDAX	Germany Dax Index	$SVX	S&P Barra Value Index
$GLD	Gold Index	$CEX	S&P Chemical Index
$GNX	Goldman-Sachs Index	$IUX	S&P Insurance Index
$GSO	GSTI Software Index	$MID	S&P Mid-cap 400 Index
$JPN	Japan Index	$RLX	S&P Retail Index
$VIX	Market Volatility Index	$SRX	S&P Super Composite
$MEX	Mexico Index	$TRX	S&P Transport Index
$CMR	Morgan Stanley Consumer Index	$XBD	Securities Broker Dealer Index
$CYC	Morgan Stanley Cyclical Index	$ICX	TheStreet.Com E-Commerce Index
$MSH	Morgan Stanley High Tech Index	$TSE-TC	Toronto 35 Index
$ISSQ	NASDAQ Advance/Decline Issues	$TOP-TC	TSE 100 Index
$COMPQ	NASDAQ Composite	$UTY	Utility Sector Index
$QVOL	NASDAQ Volume	$XVG	Value Line Index (Geometric)
$NDX	NASDAQ-100 Index	$WSX	Wilshire Composite Index
$IXCO	NASDAQ High Tech Index	$TNX	10-Year T-Note Index
$ISSU	NYSE Advance/Decline Issues	$IRX	13-Week T-Bill Index
$NYA	NYSE Composite Index	$TYX	30-Year T-Bond Index
$XNG	Natural Gas Index	$FVX	5-Year T-Note Index

popular ETFs

Exchange-Traded Fund Type	Exchange-Traded Fund Description	Market Representation
DIAMONDs	Diamonds Trust Series	Dow Jones Industrial Average
FITRs	Fixed Income Exchange-Traded Securities	Various treasuries
HOLDRs	Holding Company Depositary Receipts	Very narrow industry sectors
iShares	Index Shares	Various countries and market sectors
QUBEs	NASDAQ 100 Tracking Stock (QQQ)	NASDAQ 100 Index
Spiders	Standard & Poor's Depositary Receipts (SPDRS)	Various Standard & Poor's indexes
StreetTracks	State Street Global Advisor ETFs	Various Dow Jones style indexes
VIPERs	Vanguard Index Participation Receipts	Several Vanguard Index funds

market acronyms

AAF—asset allocation fund
AAGR—average annual growth rate
AAR—average annual return
ABS—automated bond system
AD line—advance/decline line
ADR—American Depositary Receipt
ADX—average directional movement index
AGI—adjusted gross income
AMEX—American Stock Exchange
AMT—alternative minimum tax
AON—all or none
APR—annual percentage rate
APV—adjusted present value
APY—annual percentage yield
AR—accounts receivable
ARM—adjustable rate mortgage

ASX—Australian Stock Exchange
ATM—at-the-money
ATP—arbitrage trading program
ATR—average true range
BICs—bank investment contracts
BIS—Bank for International Settlements
BOP—balance of payments
BOT—balance of trade
BP—basis point
CAPEX—capital expenditure
CAPM—capital asset pricing model
CAPS—convertible adjustable preferred stock
CBOE—Chicago Board Options Exchange
CBOT—Chicago Board of Trade

(*continued*)

CCE—cash and cash equivalents
CCI—commodity channel index
CD—certificate of deposit
CEO—chief executive officer
CFA—chartered financial analyst
CFO—chief financial officer
CFP—certified financial planner
CFPS—cash flow per share
CFTC—Commodity Futures Trading Commission
COGS—cost of goods sold
COO—chief operating officer
CPA – certified public accountant
CPI—consumer price index
CPM—cost per thousand
CSI—commodity selection index
CUSIP—Committee on Uniform Securities Identification Procedures
DAT—direct access trading
DD—due diligence
DI—disposable income
DJIA—Dow Jones Industrial Average
DJTA—Dow Jones Transportation Average
DJUA—Dow Jones Utility Average
DMI—directional movement index
DPSP—deferred profit sharing plan
DRIP—dividend reinvestment plan
EAFE—European and Australasian, Far East Equity Index
EBIT—earnings before interest and taxes
EBITDA—earnings before interest, taxes, depreciation, and amortization
ECN—electronic communication network
EDGAR—Electronic Data Gathering Analysis and Retrieval
EMA—exponential moving average
EPS—earnings per share
ERISA—Employee Retirement Income Security Act
ESO—employee stock option

ETF—exchange-traded fund
FAD—funds available for distribution
FASB—Financial Accounting Standards Board
FDIC—Federal Deposit Insurance Corporation
FFO—funds from operations
FIFO—first in first out
FHLMC—Federal Home Loan Mortgage Corp
FNMA—Federal National Mortgage Association (Fannie Mae)
FOMC—Federal Open Market Committee
FRAs—forward-rate agreements
FRB—Federal Reserve Board
FRS—Federal Reserve Systems
GAAP—generally accepted accounting principles
GARP—growth at a reasonable price
GDP—gross domestic product
GIC—Guaranteed Investment Certificate
GNMA—Government National Mortgage Association (Ginnie Mae)
GO—general obligation bond
GSE—government-sponsored enterprise
GTC—good till canceled order
HOLDRs—Holding Company Depositary Receipts
HTML—HyperText Markup Language
IFCI—International Finance Corporation Investable Index
IPO—initial public offering
IRA—Individual Retirement Account
IRR—internal rate of return
ISO—International Organization for Standardization
ITM—in-the-money
IV—implied volatility
JSE—Johannesburg Stock Exchange

(*continued*)

KCBT—Kansas City Board of Trade
LBO—leveraged buy-out
LEAPS—Long-term Equity
   Anticipation Securities
LIFO—last in first out
LLC—limited liability company
LP—limited partnership
MA—moving average
MACD—moving average
   convergence/divergence
MEM—maximum entropy method
MER— management expense ratio
MIPS—monthly income preferred
   securities
MIT—market if touched
MPT—modern portfolio theory
MSCI—Morgan Stanley Capital
   International Index
NASD—National Association of
   Securities Dealers
NASDAQ—National Association of
   Securities Dealers Automated
   Quotations
NAV—net asset value
NMS—normal market size
NOI—net operating income
NPV—net present value
NSO—nonqualified stock options
NYSE—New York Stock Exchange
OBV—on balance volume
OI—open interest
OID—original issue discount
OPEC—Organization of Petroleum
   Exporting Countries
OTC—over the counter
OTM—out-of-the-money
PDF—portable document format
P/E—price to earnings ratio
PEG—price/earnings to growth
POP—public offering price
PPI—producer price index
QQQ—ticker symbol for
   NASDAQ-100 Trust
R&D—research and development
REIT—real estate investment trust

RIC—return on invested capital
ROA—return on assets
ROE—return on equity
ROI—return on investment
RPI—retail price index
RSI—relative strength index
SAI—statement of additional
   information
SAR—stop and reverse
SEC—Securities and Exchange
   Commission
SEP—simplified employee pension
SEMI—Semiconductor Equipment
   and Materials International
SIC—standard industrial
   classification
SIPC—Securities Investor Protection
   Corporation
SMA—simple moving average
SOES—small order execution
   system
SOX—Philadelphia Semiconductor
   Index
S&P—Standard and Poor's
SPDR—Standard & Poor's
   Depositary Receipts (ETF)
SSR—sum of squared rResiduals
SV—statistical volatility
SWIFT—Society for Worldwide
   Interbank Financial
   Telecommunication
TPO—time price opportunity
TRIN—trading index
TSE—Toronto Stock Exchange
UN—United Nations
VIX—CBOE Market Volatility Index
VXN—Nasdaq Volatility Index
VPT—volume price trend
WSE—Winnipeg Commodity
   Exchange
XD—Ex-Dividend
XR—Ex-Rights
XY—Ex-Warrants
YTD—Year-to-date
YTM—Yield to maturity

options strategies quick reference guide

Strategy	Trade	Market Outlook	Profit Potential	Risk Potential	Time Decay Effects
Long call	B1-C	Bullish	Unlimited	Limited	Detrimental
Short call	S1-C	Bearish	Limited	Unlimited	Helpful
Long put	B1-P	Bearish	Unlimited	Limited	Detrimental
Short put	S1-P	Bullish	Limited	Unlimited	Helpful
Covered call	B100-U S1-C	Slightly bullish to neutral	Limited	Unlimited	Helpful
Bull call spread	B1-LC S1-HC	Bullish	Limited	Limited	Mixed
Bull put spread	B1-LP SI-HP	Moderately bullish	Limited	Limited	Mixed
Bear call spread	S1-LC BI-HC	Moderately bearish	Limited	Limited	Mixed
Bear put spread	S1-LP B1-HP	Bearish	Limited	Limited	Mixed
Long straddle	B1-ATM-C B1-ATM-P	Volatile	Unlimited	Limited	Detrimental
Long strangle	B1-OTM-C B1-OTM-P	Volatile	Unlimited	Limited	Detrimental
Long synthetic straddle with puts	B100-U B2-ATM-P	Volatile	Unlimited	Limited	Detrimental
Long synthetic straddle with calls	S100-U B2-ATM-C	Volatile	Unlimited	Limited	Detrimental
Ratio call spread	B1-LC S2-HC	Bearish/ stable	Limited	Unlimited	Mixed
Ratio put spread	B1-HP S2-LP	Bullish/ stable	Limited	Unlimited	Mixed
Call ratio back-spread	S1-LC B2-HC	Very bullish	Unlimited	Limited	Mixed
put ratio back-spread	S1-HP B2-LP	Very bearish	Unlimited	Limited	Mixed

(*continued*)

Strategy	Trade	Market Outlook	Profit Potential	Risk Potential	Time Decay Effects
Long butterfly	B1-LC/P S2-HC/P B1-HP/P	Stable	Limited	Limited	Helpful
Long condor	B1-LC/P S1-HC/P S1-HC/P B1-HC/P	Stable	Limited	Limited	Helpful
Long iron butterfly	S1-ATM-C B1-OTM-C S1-ATM-P B1-OTM-P	Stable	Limited	Limited	Helpful
Calendar spread	B1-LT-C/P S1-ST-C/P (same strikes)	Stable	Unlimited	Limited	Helpful
Diagonal spread	B1-LT-C/P S1-ST-C/P (different strikes)	Stable	Unlimited	Limited	Helpful
Collar spread	B100-U B1-ATM-P S1-ATM-C	Volatile	Limited	Limited	Helpful

B = Buy/S = Sell
1 = 1 Contract
100 = 100 shares
U = Underlying stock
C = Call option
P = Put option
HC = Higher strike call
LC = Lower strike call

HP = Higher strike put
LP = Lower strike put
ATM = At-the-money
OTM = Out-of-the-money
ITM = In-the-money
LT = Long-term
ST = Short-term

options strategies review

long stock

> **Strategy** = Buy shares of stock
>
> **Market opportunity** = Look for a bullish market where a rise in the price of the stock is anticipated.
>
> **Maximum risk** = Limited to the price of the stock as it approaches zero.

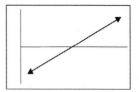

> **Maximum profit** = Unlimited as the stock price rises above the initial entry price.
>
> **Breakeven** = Price of the stock at initiation.
>
> **Margin** = Required. Usually 50 percent of the total cost of the shares.

short stock

> **Strategy** = Sell shares of stock.
>
> **Market opportunity** = Look for a bearish market where a fall in the price of the stock is anticipated.
>
> **Maximum risk** = Unlimited as the stock price rises.

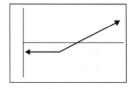

> **Maximum profit** = Limited to the full price of the stock shares as they fall to zero.
>
> **Breakeven** = Price of the stock at initiation.
>
> **Margin** = Required. Usually 150 percent of the total cost of the shares.

long call

> **Strategy** = Buy a call option.
>
> **Market opportunity** = Look for a bullish market where a rise above the breakeven is anticipated.
>
> **Maximum risk** = Limited to the amount paid for the call.

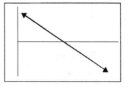

> **Maximum profit** = Unlimited as the price of the underlying instrument rises above the breakeven.
>
> **Breakeven** = Call strike + call premium.
>
> **Margin** = None.

short call

> **Strategy** = Sell a call option.
>
> **Market opportunity** = Look for a bear- 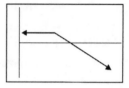 ish or stable market where you an- ticipate a fall in the price of the un- derlying below the breakeven.
>
> **Maximum risk** = Unlimited as the stock price rises above the breakeven.
>
> **Maximum profit** = Limited to the credit received from the call option premium.
>
> **Breakeven** = Call strike + call premium.
>
> **Margin** = Required. Amount subject to broker's discretion.

long put

> **Strategy** = Buy a put option.
>
> **Market opportunity** = Look for a bear- 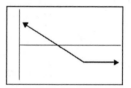 ish market where you anticipate a fall in the price of the underlying below the breakeven.
>
> **Maximum risk** = Limited to the price paid for the put premium.
>
> **Maximum profit** = Limited as the stock price falls below the breakeven to zero.
>
> **Breakeven** = Put strike − put premium.
>
> **Margin** = None.

short put

> **Strategy** = Sell a put option.
>
> **Market opportunity** = Look for a bullish 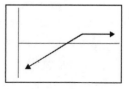 or stable market where a rise above the breakeven is anticipated.

Maximum risk = Limited as the stock price falls below the breakeven until reaching a price of zero.

Maximum profit = Limited. Credit received from the put premium.

Breakeven = Put strike − put premium.

Margin = Required. Amount subject to broker's discretion.

bull call spread

Strategy = Buy a lower strike call and sell a higher strike call with the same expiration dates.

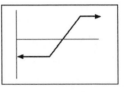

Market opportunity = Look for a bullish market where you anticipate a modest increase in the price of the underlying above the price of the short call option.

Maximum risk = Limited to the net debit paid for the spread.

Maximum profit = Limited. [(Difference in strikes × 100) − net debit]

Breakeven = Lower call strike price + net debit paid.

Margin = Required. Amount subject to broker's discretion.

bull put spread

Strategy = Buy a lower strike put and sell a higher strike put with the same expiration date.

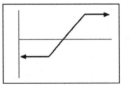

Market opportunity = Look for a bullish market where you anticipate an increase in the price of the underlying asset above the strike price of the short put option.

Maximum risk = Limited. [(Difference in strikes × 100) − net credit]

Maximum profit = Limited to the net credit received when the market closes above the short put option.

Breakeven = Higher strike − net credit.

Margin = Required. Amount subject to broker's discretion.

bear put spread

Strategy = Buy a higher strike put and sell a lower strike put with the same expiration date.

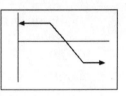

Market opportunity = Look for a bearish market where you anticipate a modest decrease in the price of the underlying asset below the strike price of the short put option.

Maximum risk = Limited to the net debit paid.

Maximum profit = Limited. [(Difference in strikes × 100) − net debit]

Breakeven = Higher strike − net debit.

Margin = Required. Amount subject to broker's discretion.

bear call spread

Strategy = Buy a higher strike call and sell a lower strike call with the same expiration date.

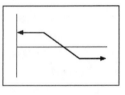

Market opportunity = Look for a bearish market where you anticipate a decrease in the price of the underlying asset below the strike price of the short call option.

Maximum risk = Limited. [(Difference in strikes × 100) − net credit]

Maximum profit = Limited to the net credit.

Breakeven = Lower strike price + net credit.

Margin = Required. Amount subject to broker's discretion.

long straddle

Strategy = Purchase an ATM call and an ATM put with the same strike price and the same expiration.

Market opportunity = Look for a market with low implied volatility options where a sharp volatility increase is anticipated.

Maximum risk = Limited to the net debit.

Maximum profit = Unlimited to the upside and downside (all the way to zero) beyond the breakevens. Profit requires sufficient market movement but does not depend on market direction.

Upside breakeven = ATM strike price + net debit.

Downside breakeven = ATM strike price − net debit.

short straddle

Strategy = Sell an ATM call and an ATM put with the same strike price and the same expiration date.

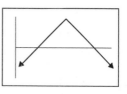

Market opportunity = Look for a wildly volatile market where you anticipate a period of low volatility.

Maximum risk = Unlimited to the upside and the downside beyond the breakevens.

Maximum profit = Limited to the net credit. Profit is possible if the market stays between the breakevens.

Upside breakeven = ATM strike price + net credit.

Downside breakeven = ATM strike price − net credit.

long strangle

Strategy = Buy an OTM call and an OTM put with the same expiration date.

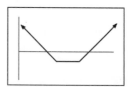

Market opportunity = Look for a stable market where you anticipate a large volatility spike.

Maximum risk = Limited to the net debit paid.

Maximum profit = Unlimited to the upside and limited to the downside (all the way to zero) beyond the breakevens.

Upside breakeven = Call strike + net debit.

Downside breakeven = Put strike − net debit.

short strangle

Strategy = Sell an OTM call and an OTM put with the same expiration date.

Market opportunity = Look for a wildly volatile market where you anticipate a drop-off into a very stable market with low volatility.

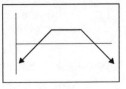

Maximum risk = Unlimited to the upside and downside beyond the breakevens.

Maximum profit = Limited to the net credit.

Upside breakeven = Call strike price + net credit.

Downside breakeven = Put strike price − net credit.

covered call

Strategy = Buy the underlying security and sell an OTM call option.

Market opportunity = Look for a bullish to neutral market where a slow rise in the price of the underlying is anticipated with little risk of decline.

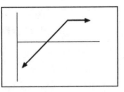

Maximum risk = Virtually unlimited to the downside below the breakeven all the way to zero.

Maximum profit = Limited. [Short call premium + (short call strike − price of long underlying asset) × 100]

Breakeven = Price of the underlying asset at initiation − short call premium.

covered put

Strategy = Sell the underlying security and sell an OTM put option.

Market opportunity = Look for a bearish or stable market where a decline in the price of the underlying is anticipated with little risk of the market rising.

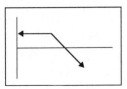

Maximum risk = Unlimited to the upside beyond the breakeven.

Maximum profit = Limited. [Short put premium + (price of underlying asset at initiation − put option strike) × 100]

Breakeven = Price of the underlying asset + short put premium.

long synthetic straddle

Market opportunity = Look for a market with low volatility where you anticipate a volatility increase resulting in stock price movement in either direction beyond the breakevens.

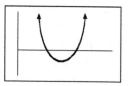

Long Stock and Long Puts

Strategy = Buy 100 shares of underlying stock and buy 2 long ATM puts.

Maximum risk = Net debit of options + [(price of underlying stock at initiation − option strike price) × # of shares]

Maximum profit = Unlimited above or below breakevens.

Upside breakeven = Price of underlying stock at initiation + net debit of options.

Downside breakeven = {[(2 × option strike) − price of underlying stock at initiation] − net debit of options}

Short Stock and Long Calls

Strategy = Sell 100 shares of underlying stock and buy 2 long ATM calls.

Maximum risk = {[Net debit of options + (option strike − price of underlying at initiation)] × # of shares

Maximum profit = Unlimited above upside breakeven and limited as the stock falls to zero below downside breakeven.

Upside breakeven = {[(2 × option strike) − price of underlying stock at initiation] + net debit of options}

Downside breakeven = Price of underlying stock at initiation − net debit of options.

ratio call spread

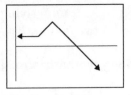

Strategy = Buy a lower strike call and sell a greater number of higher strike calls.

Market opportunity = Look for a volatile market where you expect a slight decline or a small rise not to exceed the strike price of the short options.

Maximum risk = Unlimited to the upside above the breakeven.

Maximum profit = Limited. [# of long contracts × (difference in strike prices × 100) + net credit or − net debit]

Upside breakeven = Lower strike + [(difference in strikes × # of short contracts) ÷ (# of short calls − # of long calls) + net credit or − net debit]

ratio put spread

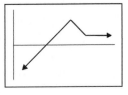

Strategy = Buy a higher strike put and sell a greater number of lower strike puts.

Market opportunity = Look for a market where you expect a rise or slight fall not to exceed the strike price of the short options.

Maximum risk = Unlimited to the downside below the breakeven.

Maximum profit = Limited. [(Difference in strike prices + net credit or − net debit) × 100]

Downside breakeven = Higher strike − [(difference in strike prices × # of short contracts) ÷ (# of short contracts − # of long contracts)] − net credit or + net debit

call ratio backspread

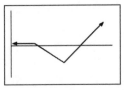

Strategy = Sell lower strike calls and buy a greater number of higher strike calls (the ratio must be less than 0.67).

Market opportunity = Look for a market where you anticipate a sharp rise with increasing volatility; place as a credit or at even.

Maximum risk = Limited. [(# of short calls × difference in strikes) × 100 − net credit or + net debit]

Maximum profit = Unlimited to the upside beyond the breakeven.

Upside breakeven = Higher strike + [(difference in strikes × # of short calls) ÷ (# of long calls − # of short calls)] − net credit or + net debit

Downside breakeven = Short strike + net credit or − net debit.

put ratio backspread

Strategy = Sell higher strike puts and buy a greater number of lower strike puts (the ratio must be less than 0.67).

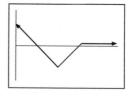

Market opportunity = Look for a market where you anticipate a sharp decline with increased volatility; place as a credit or at-even.

Maximum risk = Limited. [(# of short puts × difference in strikes × 100) − net credit or + net debit]

Maximum profit = Unlimited to the downside below the breakeven.

Upside breakeven = Higher strike − net credit or + net debit.

Downside breakeven = Lower strike − [(# of short puts × difference in strikes) ÷ (# of long puts − # of short puts)] + net credit or − net debit

long butterfly

Strategy = Buy lower strike option, sell two higher strike options, and buy a higher strike option (all calls or all puts).

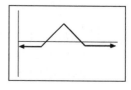

Market opportunity = Look for a range-bound market that is expected to stay between the breakeven points.

Maximum risk = Limited to the net debit paid.

Maximum profit = Limited. (Difference between strikes × 100) − net debit. Profit exists between breakevens.

Upside breakeven = Highest strike − net debit.

Downside breakeven = Lowest strike + net debit.

long condor

Strategy = Buy lower strike option, sell higher strike option, sell an even higher strike option, and buy an even higher strike option (all calls or all puts).

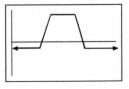

Market opportunity = Look for a range-bound market that is expected to stay between the breakeven points.

Maximum risk = Limited to the net debit.

Maximum profit = Limited. (Difference between strikes × 100) − net debit. Profit exists between breakevens.

Upside breakeven = Highest strike − net debit.

Downside breakeven = Lowest strike + net debit.

long iron butterfly

Strategy = Buy a higher strike call, sell a lower strike call, sell a higher strike put, and buy a lower strike put.

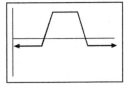

Market opportunity = Look for a range-bound market that you anticipate will stay between the breakeven points.

Maximum risk = Limited. [(Difference between long and short strikes × 100) − net credit]

Maximum profit = Limited to the net credit.

Upside breakeven = Strike price of upper short call + net credit.

Downside breakeven = Strike price of lower short put − net credit.

calendar spread

Strategy = Sell a short-term option and buy a long-term option using at-the-money options with as small a net debit as possible (use all calls or all puts). Calls can be used for a more bullish bias and puts can be used for a more bearish bias.

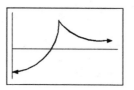

Market opportunity = Look for a rangebound market that is expected to stay between breakeven points for an extended time.

Maximum risk = Limited to the net debit paid.

Maximum profit = Limited. Use software for accurate calculation.

Upside breakeven = Use software for accurate calculation.

Downside breakeven = Use software for accurate calculation.

diagonal spread

Strategy = Sell a short-term option and buy a long-term option with different strikes and as small a net debit as possible (use all calls or all puts).

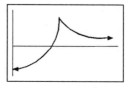

A *bullish diagonal* spread employs a long call with a distant expiration and a lower strike price, along with a short call with a closer expiration date and higher strike price.

A *bearish diagonal* spread combines a long put with a distant expiration date and a higher strike price along with a short put with a closer expiration date and lower strike price.

Market opportunity = Look for a rangebound market that is expected to stay between the breakeven points for an extended period of time.

Maximum risk = Limited to the net debit paid.

Maximum profit = Limited. Use software for accurate calculation.

Upside breakeven = Use software for accurate calculation.

Downside breakeven = Use software for accurate calculation.

collar spread

Strategy = Buy (or own) 100 shares of stock, buy an ATM put, and sell an OTM call. Try to offset the cost of the put with the premium from the short call.

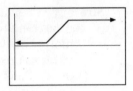

Market opportunity = Protect a stock holding from a sharp drop for a specific period of time and still participate in a modest increase in the stock price.

Maximum risk = Initial shares price − put strike + net debit or − net credit.

Maximum profit = Call strike − initial shares price − net debit or + net credit.

Breakeven = Initial share price + (put premium − call premium).

appendix b

market analysis terminology

fundamental analysis methodologies and indicators

accumulation/distribution This indicator reflects a stock's daily long shares compared to short stock shares. This is important in that it attempts to evaluate two of the most important indicators of strength or weakness in a stock—the percentage change of a stock's price and volume. The accumulation/distribution rating is calculated by multiplying a stock's daily price change percentage by its volume. This number is then added to or subtracted from the cumulative total for the stock depending on whether the price increased or decreased. *Investor's Business Daily* uses the following rating: A (strongest accumulation), C (neutral), and E (weakest—distribution). In general, a stock with an A rating means there is plenty of demand for the stock (high volume) and the price will probably continue to rise. An E rating means that the supply for a stock is greater than the demand and could trigger a drop in price. I like to focus on As only for buying and Es for a bearish perspective.

annual earnings change (percent) The historical earnings change between the most recently reported fiscal year earnings and the preceding.

beta coefficient A measure of the market/nondiversifiable risk associated with any given security in the market. A ratio of an individual stock's historical returns to the historical returns of the stock market.

closing price, net change These two points are important as they represent the dollar value by which a stock has changed. The net change value tells how much the price of the stock changed during yesterday's trading. If the fictitious stock XYZ is trading at $10 today and closed yesterday at $8, then the stock has risen $2. This 20 percent increase is significant. If XYZ is trading today at $10 and closed yesterday at $20, this $10 drop in value (50 percent) is very significant.

dividend yield Dividend yield is calculated by dividing a stock's dividend rate expected for the next 12 months by the current price of the stock. Unless you are buying stocks based on dividend yield (the return you receive on a dividend payout) and earnings, this is not a critical number. If you are building a long-term portfolio based on yields, then you will want to compare one stock versus another using this information. Many stocks—especially high-technology stocks—have a low dividend yield, yet still are good investments.

earnings growth This indicator is measured annually and quarterly. It divides a company's revenue by the outstanding shares. If a company starts to slump, you'll definitely see it on the quarterly earnings growth reports. If revenues decline, companies have to tighten their belts, and this can send out the bears.

earnings per share (EPS) EPS is a widely used measurement of a company's financial strength. It is calculated by dividing a company's net earnings for common stock by the number of outstanding common shares. The resulting number can then be compared to the EPS of the same quarter in the prior year to determine a company's earnings growth. The result of this comparison is used to forecast an increase or decrease in the future price of the stock. Also, pay attention to a stock's ability to consistently grow by researching the EPS at least five years back. If you find a consistent growth pattern, you can bet that investors are willing to pay more for that stock.

earnings per share rank This number is a measure of a company's growth over the past two quarters in comparison to the same quarters in the prior year. The past three- to five-year annual growth rate is factored in and the resulting number is compared to other companies and given a rank of 1 (lowest) to 99 (highest). The EPS rank basically tells a trader how profitable a stock is in comparison to the more than 10,000 stocks available to be traded. I like to focus on companies with stocks with the greatest strength when buying (an EPS ranking of 95 or better) and the weakest when selling (an EPS of 20 or less). It is a good idea to track the EPS rank of your stocks on at least a weekly basis. This will give you a chance to make changes to your portfolio if there is a dramatic change in the character of your investments.

52-week high and low This figure tells you the price change of a stock over the past year. The difference between the high and the low is called the range. If a stock has moved only $1 in the past year, it is likely to stay in this range again in the coming year. Also, if a stock is at its 52-week high, it may be ready to make new highs. This is one you want to look at as a potential buy. If a stock is at a 52-week low, it could break down and move lower, which may be a selling opportunity (going short). It is generally stated on Wall Street that strength leads to strength and weakness leads to weakness. Since many investors use this information to make investment decisions, it can have great influence on the directions of many stocks.

float (mil) The float represents the number of securities that are in the public's possession. You can deduct shares that are held by pensions, mutual funds, and other large investors to arrive at a float. This daily column indicates how many shares are available for trading. This number is important if you want to keep track of how supply and demand affect price. For example, if XYZ shares are in high demand, buyers will have to bid the price up to make it attractive to sellers to sell their shares to increase supply. When a company splits, it reduces demand by increasing supply. Therefore, a company with a smaller float will likely outperform one with a higher float.

greatest percent rise in volume This is often more perceptive than a most active list because it highlights stocks with exceptional activity—not just those with the highest volume of shares being traded. Noting this figure may enable you to discover those small- and mid-cap stocks with increasing volume above and beyond the norm.

high price yesterday/low price yesterday (hi/lo) Unless you are day trading (going in and out during one trading session), this information is not critical. Investors and traders look at this information to signal if stock traders will be running stops. This technique can also be used to look for orders from public traders. For example, if a trader sold a stock yesterday, he may place a buy stop (to cover losses) above yesterday's high. This is referred to as a resistance point. If the trader bought a stock, he may place a sell stop (to sell the stock they purchased) below yesterday's low. This is referred to as a support point. Stops are a technique used by many investors and traders for protection if the market moves against their original position; however, it is not recommended. I prefer to use options because I find them to be much more profitable and safer in the long run.

high-low index The high-low index (H/L index) is constructed by taking the net 52-week yearly highs and lows over a six-day period (for displays of one year or less) or a six-week period (for displays greater than one year). The number of new 52-week highs and lows is calculated as a percent of total issues traded, to compensate for the addition and subtraction of stocks to an industry group average.

management Changes in a company's management can mean big news, which often triggers public reaction to be bearish or bullish.

money flow A volume-weighted version of the relative strength index, but instead of using up-closes versus down-closes, money flow compares the current interval's average price to the previous interval's average price and then weighs the average price by volume to calculate money flow. The ratio of the summed positive and negative money flows is then normalized to be on a scale of 0 to 100.

most active issue The *Investor's Business Daily* and the *Wall Street Journal* list those stocks that are most active by volume— primarily blue-chip stocks with millions of shares available to be traded.

most percent down in price This listing is interesting to watch, but the information only describes what is happening, not what will happen.

most percent up in price These are stocks with the biggest increases in price. Although this information is interesting to scan, it can be dangerous to choose a stock based solely on the change in its price.

net change The daily change from time frame to time frame. An example would be the change from the close of yesterday to the close of today. It is the difference between the closing price of a security on the trading day reported and the previous day's closing price. In over-the-counter transactions, the term refers to the difference between the closing bids.

net earnings That part of a company's profits remaining after all expenses and taxes have been paid and out of which dividends may be paid.

odd lot An amount of a security that is less than the normal unit of trading for that security. Generally, an odd lot is fewer than 100 shares of stock or five bonds. An investor may pay a premium when trying to purchase odd lots. Historical theory says that the odd-lot investor is traditionally a small personal investor trading in less than 100 shares at a time. Odd-lot traders are usually guilty of bad timing, and profits may be made by acting contrary to odd-lot trading patterns. Those who believe this theory interpret heavy odd lot buying in a rising market as an indication of technical weakness and the signal of a market reversal. Heavy odd lot buying in a declining market is seen as an indication of technical strength and is thus a signal to buy. Analysis of odd-lot trading patterns over the years has failed to support this theory with any real consistency. Odd-lot investors tend to buy market leaders and have generally done well in the upward market of the past 50 years.

on balance volume On balance volume is an accumulation of volume where the current interval's volume is added to the total if the stock closes up, and today's volume is subtracted from the total if the stock closes down.

price-book ratio Compares a stock's market value to the value of total assets less total liabilities (book). It is determined by dividing current price by common stockholders' equity per share (book value), adjusted for stock splits. Also called market-to-book.

price-earnings ratio (P/E) The price-earnings ratio—otherwise known as the P/E—is very important because it compares a company's stock price to the amount of earnings per share. This comparison attempts to assign a rating to the difference between a company's profits per share and the actual price of each stock share. The P/E ratio tells you how many times the earnings a stock is trading at. To calculate the P/E of a stock, simply divide the current stock price by the latest 12-month earnings per share. Let's use our fictitious high-technology stock, XYZ as an example. If XYZ is trading at $20 per share and the earnings per share are $1, it has a P/E of 20. If the average for the high-tech industry is a P/E of 40, then this stock may be undervalued. If XYZ is trading at a P/E of 100 ($100 per share) with an industry average of 40, then the stock is overvalued; on any sign of weakness, the stock will likely come tumbling down.

How are industry averages established? Brokerage firm analysts establish guidelines for each industry. For example, a slow-growth industry, such as the steel industry, may have a P/E of only 10, while a high-growth industry, such as the Internet businesses, may have a P/E of 40 or higher. The P/E ratio is used to describe the current state of a stock's price. It is not generally used to forecast future prices; it simply lets traders know how well the stock is doing right now. A general rule of thumb states that faster growing companies have higher P/Es. Since faster growth is linked to higher future earnings, a company with a high P/E may have high future earnings. The trick is never to assume anything that isn't carved in stone. Valuing a company by its future earnings is a dangerous game since these earnings may range significantly.

"price percentage gainers and losers" This is one of my favorite *Wall Street Journal* columns. If there were only two pieces of information I could look at to make a smart investment, I would pick these two because they reveal the stocks with the greatest momentum (up or down). I have to admit that I believe that the best investments are based on momentum, at least in the short term. I like to watch these stocks like a hawk to see if they have momentum that is continuing (good or bad) or momentum that is slowing and reversing. I like to look for a chance to do the opposite on fast movers down (price percentage losers) by looking for buying opportunities. I also like to buy on a fast mover up (price percentage gainers). If I miss a move up, I look to sell as soon as I see the momentum slowing or reversing.

price to sales ratio (PSR) Tracking this indicator can help you to understand when a stock is overpriced or undervalued. To calculate a stock's PSR, divide the price of a stock by the company's sales per share.

quarter end fluctuations The end of each quarter is of special significance to portfolio managers. The SEC requires mutual funds to post performances and holdings for shareholder review. If there are some real clunkers in the portfolio, these are often jettisoned in favor of a stock or stocks that are the current favorite among the institutional crowd and traders in general. This is also called window dressing and creates some wild times on the last trading days of March, June, September, and December.

quarterly EPS percent change The historical earnings change between the earnings most recently reported and the quarter preceding.

quick ratio Indicator of a company's financial strength (or weakness). Calculated by taking current assets less inventories, divided by current liabilities.

relative strength (RS) The price strength of an individual stock relative to the strength of the market as a whole. A stock that is performing better than the market is said to have relative strength, which is a bullish sign for the stock in question. Relative strength compares a stock's price change over the past year to all the others. A relative strength of 99 puts that stock at the top of the list; a relative strength of 1, at the bottom. I prefer to buy call options on stocks with a relative strength weighting of 80 or better; I look for 40 or lower when buying put options. A relative strength line can also be found on *IBD*'s price charts. It is usually the unbroken line below the price bars and the stock's 50-day moving average. The relative strength value can be found at the end of the RS line. It charts the ratio created when a stock's closing price is divided by the closing price of the S&P 500 index. The relative strength line can be used to provide clues to the future price movement of a stock. If the relative strength line continues to move up, the price will most likely rise (and vice versa).

relative strength index (RSI) Technical analysts use RSI in a number of ways. For one, it can be used to determine whether a stock or index is overbought or oversold. The RSI is also used to gauge the strength of an advance or a decline—in other words, whether the trend is healthy and likely to continue, or whether it is becoming weaker and ready to change direction.

return on equity (ROE) This indicator rates a stock's profitability. It is derived by dividing the net income of the past 12 months by the common stockholders' equity (adjusted for stock splits). The result is shown as a percentage. If you can find a stock with an ROE higher than 20 over the past five years, then put it on your watch list.

short interest ratio A ratio that indicates the number of trading days required to repurchase all of the shares that have been sold short. A short interest ratio of 2.5 would tell us that based on the current volume of trading, it will take two and a half days' volume to cover all shorts.

standard deviation A measure of the fluctuation in a stock's monthly return over the preceding year.

"stocks in the news" A section of the *Wall Street Journal* that graphs 24 NYSE, 24 NASDAQ, and 4 AMEX stocks trading at their 52-week high. Each graph features a stock's price and volume activity over the past year, annual and quarterly earnings per share growth rates, shares outstanding, earnings per share and relative strength rankings, industry group strength, volume percent change, price-earnings ratio, percentage debt, management ownership of company stock, and relative strength line, as well as other pertinent indicators. These important charts give you the opportunity to scan for potential investment opportunities.

supply and demand The supply and demand for a company's shares is referred to as momentum. Companies typically issue earnings estimates and reports. In the meantime, Street expectation drives the price of the stocks prior to the release of a report. If investors feel the report will beat the Street expectation, then the price of the shares will be bid up, as there will be more buyers than sellers. If the majority of the investors feel that the company's earnings will disappoint the Street, then the prices will be offer down. In many ways, a stock exchange is like an auction. If there are more buyers than sellers, prices will rise. If there are more sellers than buyers, prices will fall.

volume (vol) The number of shares of stock traded per day is important when the volume is increasing significantly. For example, when a stock has had an average share volume of 100,000 shares and one day the stock trades five times that amount (500,000), this information is useful. If the stock has a high trading volume and is found on the price percentage gainers and losers list, then you have a confirmation signal that the stock is making a move. When volume is decreasing or stable, the stock will likely go nowhere, as interest in the stock is dwindling. It is important to watch the volume of the stocks you own or are trading to see whether there is a momentum increase or decrease.

volume percent change This interesting addition to *IBD*'s table of information shows how a stock's volume compares to the previous 50 trading days. *IBD* will highlight stocks with prices greater than $10 when their volume increases by 50 percent or more above the average volume over the past 50 trading days. Why is this so important? Volatility. Large increases in volume signal high volatility. Personally, I look for increases that at least double (200 percent) in average volume, because the larger the increase in volume, the more likely something important may be happening. This is a typical signal of momentum change that indicates strong impending moves either up or down in the price of a stock. Look for stocks that are greater than $10 in price that have volume percentage changes of 200 percent or greater, because this could signal the beginning of explosive growth in the price of a stock.

technical analysis methodologies and indicators

advance-decline line (A/D Line) A technical analysis tool representing the total differences between advances and declines of security prices. The advance-decline line is considered one of the best indicators of market movement as a whole. The A/D line is calculated by taking the percent of stocks advancing minus the percent of stocks declining (either daily or weekly) and adding this amount to a running total. This total is then plotted on top of the industry index so that when more stocks in the group are advancing than declining, the A/D line moves upward. A majority of stocks dropping in price causes the A/D line to move downward. Divergences are the most important feature of the A/D line. When a divergence occurs, the A/D line is believed to more accurately forecast the future because it reflects the action of the broad index rather than a small sample of the most highly market-capitalized issues. When a weighted industry index moves to new highs and the A/D line is in a decline, then an index top is indicated. The A/D line is usually much better at forecasting tops than bottoms. In general, it often turns at the same time or later than when an index bottoms.

alpha-beta trend channel The alpha-beta trend channel uses the standard deviation of price variation to establish two trend lines, one above and one below the moving average of a price field. This creates a channel (band) where the great majority of price field values will occur.

alpha coefficient This is a mathematical estimate of the amount of return expected from an investment's inherent values—such as the rate of growth in earnings per share—distinct from the amount of return caused by volatility, which is measured by the beta coefficient. An alpha coefficient of 1.3 indicates a stock is projected to rise 30 percent in price in a year when the return on the market and the stock's beta coefficient are both zero. When an investment price is low relative to its alpha, it is undervalued and considered a good selection.

andrews method A technique whereby a technician will pick an extreme low or high to use as a pivot point and draw a line (called the median line) from this point that bisects a line drawn through the next corrective phase that occurs after the pivot point. Lines parallel to the median line are drawn through the high and low points of the corrective phase. The parallel lines define the resistance and support levels for the price channel.

arms ease of movement This technique quantifies the shape aspects of equivolume charting tool plotted boxes to determine the degree of ease or difficulty with which a particular issue is able to move in one direction or another. The ease with which an issue moves is a product of a ratio between the height (trading range) and width (volume) of the plotted box. In general, a higher ratio results from a wider box and indicates difficulty of movement. A lower ratio results from a narrower box and indicates easier movement.

average directional index (ADX) The average directional index is a chart indicator designed to help traders identify trending markets. It does not give signals regarding direction, but tells traders whether the stock or index is in the midst of a healthy trend (either up or down). The idea is for directional traders to stay out of choppy or sideways markets, or when the stock or index is not trending, and only commit to the markets when the stock or index is moving within a clear trend.

beta (coefficient) A ratio of an individual stock's historical returns to the historical returns of the stock market. If a stock increased in value by 12 percent while the market increased by 10 percent, the stock's beta would be 1.2.

bollinger bands Bollinger bands can be used to determine overbought and oversold levels, locate reversal areas, project targets for market moves, and determine appropriate stop levels by plotting trading levels above and below a simple moving average. The standard deviation of closing prices for a period equal to the moving average employed is used to determine the bandwidth, with bands tightening in quiet markets and loosening in volatile markets. Bollinger bands are often used in conjunction with indicators such as RSI, MACD histogram, CCI, and rate of change. Divergences between Bollinger bands and other indicators show potential action points. As a general guideline, look for buying opportunities when prices are in the lower band, and for selling opportunities when the price activity is in the upper band.

box-jenkins linear least squares The additive structure of Box-Jenkins models with a polynomial structure. The Box-Jenkins method is from G. E. P. Box and G. M. Jenkins, who authored *Time Series Analysis: Forecasting and Control* (Prentice-Hall, 1994). The method refers to the use of autoregressive integrated moving averages (ARIMA), which fit seasonal models and nonseasonal models to a time series.

breadth-of-market theory A technical analysis theory that predicts the strength of the market according to the number of issues that advance or decline in a particular trading day.

breakdown A move below a major support area that paves the way for lower prices. A legitimate breakdown is accompanied by heavy volume as the stock or market falls through a support area and the decline gathers speed to the downside. Once it occurs, a longer-term period of weakness (lasting a few weeks or many months) normally ensues.

breakout In technical analysis, security movement above an area of resistance or below an area of support is referred to as a breakout. A breakout, accompanied by heavy volume, is generally indication that a stock or market is ready to make a significant move higher or lower. If the breakout is to the upside, and above a key resistance level, technicians will expect the rally to continue for a period of time. However, if the breakout is to the downside, and below key support, the stock or market is likely to experience a period of weakness.

candlestick charts A candlestick chart provides a visual representation of price movement during a specified period of fixed intervals. The price range between the open and close of each interval is symbolized as a rectangle. If the close is above the open, the rectangle is white, and if the close is below the open, the rectangle is black. In addition, vertical lines extend from the rectangles, indicating the high and low prices of that interval.

chi-square A statistical test to determine if the patterns exhibited by data could have been produced by chance.

cup and handle A price accumulation pattern that is often observed on bar charts. Patterns last from 7 to 65 weeks; the cup is U-shaped, and the handle, which is usually more than one or two weeks in duration, is a slight downward drift with low trading volume from the right-hand side of the formation.

directional movement index (DMI) The directional movement index is a technical indicator used to study trends. The indicator is generally not used for forecasting future direction or for market timing. Rather, it is used to gauge whether the stock or market is in a trending or nontrending pattern. A rising DMI indicates that the stock or index is trending.

elliott wave theory This method enables traders to determine where the market is currently in comparison to the overall market movement. There are three major aspects of wave analysis: pattern, time, and ratio. The basic Elliott wave pattern consists of a five-wave uptrend followed by a three-wave correction.

exponential moving average (EMA) A type of moving average that gives greater weight to the latest data. For example, to compute the 10-day exponential moving average, the analyst might multiply the closing price of the tenth day by 10, the ninth day by 9, the eighth day by 8, and so on, then add these products and divide their sum by the total number of days (in this case, 10). As a result, the EMA responds faster to new prices and less to old data. For that reason, some traders prefer exponential moving averages over simple moving averages because they offer better information regarding the most recent trends or prices.

fibonacci ratios and retracements Leonardo Fibonacci was an Italian mathematician who was born around the year 1170 A.D. According to some historians, Fibonacci developed what are now called Fibonacci numbers after studying the Great Pyramid of Giza in Egypt. Basically, the Italian mathematician discovered certain sequences of numbers in which each successive number is the sum of the previous two. For example, 1, 1, 2, 3, 5, 8, 13, 21, 34, 55, 89, 144, and so on. Similar types of ratios are believed to exist in financial markets. Originally used by Greek and Egyptian mathematicians as the golden mean and applied in music and architecture, a Fibonacci spiral is a logarithmic spiral that tracks natural growth patterns. In technical analysis, these can be applied to either price or time, although it is more common to use them on prices. The most common levels used in retracement analysis are 61.8 percent, 38 percent, and 50 percent. When a move starts to reverse, the three price levels are calculated (and drawn using horizontal lines) using movements low to high. These retracement levels are then interpreted as likely levels where countermoves will stop.

gann square Angles are at the core of Gann analysis. Mr. Gann initially divided a large square vertically and horizontally into 28 smaller squares. He then drew a 45-degree angle through the middle of it. He called this angle the "one-by-one," which means that for every one movement in price there is one movement in time. Hence, the Gann square is a mathematical system for finding support and resistance based on a market's extreme low or high price in a given period. Attainment of a particular price level in a square tells you the next probable price peak or decline of future movement.

head and shoulders A bearish price pattern that has three peaks resembling a head and two shoulders. The stock price moves up to its first peak (the left shoulder), drops back, then moves to a higher peak (the top of the head), drops again, but recovers to another, lower peak (the right shoulder). A head and shoulders top typically forms after a substantial rise and indicates a market reversal. A head and shoulders bottom (an inverted head and shoulders) indicates a market advance.

histograms A type of bar graph often used in statistics. The graph typically shows frequency distributions as evenly spaced vertical bars. Histograms are also used with computer-generated chart indicators and give trading signals when they move higher and lower.

kagi chart Originating in Japan, Kagi line charts display a series of connecting vertical lines where the thickness and direction are dependent on price action. If closing prices continue to move in the direction of the prior vertical Kagi line, then that line is extended. However, if the closing price reverses, a new Kagi line is drawn in the next column in the opposite direction. When closing prices penetrate the prior column's high or low, the thickness of the Kagi line changes.

lagging indicator A technical tool that turns after the market or investment has already changed direction. Lagging indicators are generally used to confirm existing trends rather than to predict future price movements.

leading indicator A technical tool that generally turns ahead of a market or investment. Leading indicators are used to try to predict movements in a stock or market before they take place.

linear regression Used to forecast future price action, a linear regression consists of a center line and a set of channel lines. The center line, the linear regression, is generated by a least squares calculation. The channel lines are placed on both sides of the center line at a percentage distance away. A positive line signals bullish opportunities and a negative line signals bearish ones.

linearly weighted moving average A type of moving average that gives greater weight to the latest data. For example, to compute the 10-day linearly weighted moving average, the analyst might take the closing price of the tenth day and multiply this number by 10, the ninth day by 9, the eighth day by 8, etc. These products are then divided by the sum of the multipliers. In the example of a 10-day MA, the sum of the multipliers is 55 $(10 + 9 + 8 + \ldots + 1)$. The linearly weighted and exponential moving averages are considered superior to simple moving averages because they assign more importance to new, rather than old data.

major resistance A resistance area is a price level at which a stock or market begins seeing increasing supply or selling pressure; it serves as a ceiling to higher prices. A *major* resistance area is one that has been tested on several occasions and over a sustained period of time. When a major resistance area is violated, and the stock or market finally begins to move higher, it generally foreshadows a more meaningful move to the upside. For that reason, major resistance levels are considered technically significant.

major support A support area is a price level at which a stock or market begins seeing increasing demand or buying interest; it serves as a floor to lower prices. A major support area is one that has been tested on several occasions and over a sustained period of time. When a major support area is broken and the stock or market begins to falter, it generally precedes a more meaningful move to the downside. For that reason, technicians consider major support areas to be significant.

major trendlines Lines drawn on stock charts along long-term uptrends or downtrends that span many months or even years. Technicians consider these long-term trendlines extremely significant, as they often serve as support or resistance to higher prices.

maximum entropy method (MEM) MEM can be used in two ways: as a tool for spectrum analysis and as a method of adaptive filtering and trend forecasting. As a tool for spectrum analysis, the MEM system provides high-resolution spectra for identifying the dominant data cycles within relatively short time series. As a forecasting tool, MEM can be used in conjunction with moving averages to forecast lower and upper trend channels in the data.

minor resistance A price level that serves as a ceiling to higher prices. A stock might retreat from this price level on a few occasions. However, it is not technically significant by virtue of the fact that it has not existed for a prolonged period of time and has not served as a resistance level numerous times.

minor support A price level that serves as a floor to prices. A stock might bounce off this price level on a few occasions. However, it is not technically significant by virtue of the fact that it has not served as a support level numerous times for a prolonged period of time.

minor trendlines Lines drawn along stock charts along short-term trends that last a few weeks or a couple of months. They are not considered extremely important when studying the markets using technical analysis.

momentum indicator This indicator alerts traders to overbought or oversold conditions for a stock or index. The momentum indicator is computed using a formula that considers closing prices over a number of days. Momentum will oscillate above and below zero. When it falls to low levels, it indicates that the stock or index is oversold and due to bounce higher. However, when it rises to the high end of its range, the stock is overbought and likely to move lower.

money flow indicator This indicator is designed to measure the volume associated with a stock's advance or decline. It compares today's average price to yesterday's average price and then weighs the average by volume. Generally, technical analysts use the money flow indicator to confirm an existing trend. For example, if a stock rises to new highs, money flow should also. If not, it is a sign that bulls are running out of buying power and the next move is likely to be to the downside.

moving average (MA) The moving average is probably the best known and most versatile indicator in the technical analyst's tool chest. It can be used with the price of your choice (highs, closes, or whatever) and can also be applied to other indicators, helping to smooth out volatility. It is a mathematical procedure to smooth or eliminate the fluctuations in data and to assist in determining when to buy and sell. A moving average emphasizes the direction of a trend, confirms trend reversals, and smoothes out price and volume fluctuations or noise that can confuse interpretation of the market. It is the sum of a value plus a selected number of previous values divided by the total number of values. As the name implies, the moving average is the average of a given amount of data. For example, a 14-day average of closing prices is calculated by adding the last 14 closes and dividing by 14. The result is noted on a chart. The next day the same calculations are performed with the new result being connected (using a solid or dotted line) to yesterday's, and so forth.

moving average convergence/divergence (MACD) The MACD is used to determine overbought or oversold conditions in the market. An MACD is composed of two lines—two exponentially smoothed moving averages—plotted above and below a zero line. The first line is the difference between the long-term moving average and the short-term moving average. The second line is a short-term moving average of the MACD line. Buy and sell signals come from any crossovers—movements across the zero line—and any divergences.

norton high/low indicator An indicator that uses results from the demand index and the stochastic study in order to pick tops and bottoms on long-term price charts. Two lines are generated: the NLP (low) line and the NHP (high) line. The system also uses level lines at -2 and -3. The NLP line crossing -3 to the downside is the signal that a new bottom will occur in four to six periods, using daily, weekly, or monthly data. Similarly, the NHP line crossing -3 to the downside indicates a new top in the same time frame. The indicator tends to be more reliable using longer-term data (weekly or monthly).

When either indicator drops below the −3 level, a reversal may be imminent. The reversal (or hook) is the signal to enter the market.

notis %V A way to measure volatility by measuring the daily price range. Volatility is high when the daily range is large and low when the daily range is small. The Notis %V study contains two separate indicators. It divides market volatility into upward and downward components (UVLT and DVLT). Both are plotted separately in the same window, and can be plotted as an oscillator. The upward component is also compared to the total volatility (UVLT + DVLT) and expressed as a percentage, thus the name %V.

oscillators Technical chart indicators that are used to identify overbought and oversold conditions in a stock or market. For example, the stochastics indicator is a commonly used oscillator. When it rises to high levels, the stock or market is considered overbought and due to correct. When it falls to low levels, the stock or market is oversold and set to move higher. Oscillators are generally used in sideways, rather than trending, markets.

on balance volume (OBV) On balance volume is tool for viewing trends with respect to volume. Developed by Joseph Granville and explained in the book *New Strategy of Daily Stock Market Timing* (Simon & Schuster, 1976), the indicator measures the buying and selling pressure by looking at daily volume during a stock or market's advance or decline. The math behind the indicator is straightforward: If a stock finishes the day higher, the volume is added to the running total, but if a stock finishes the day lower, the day's volume is subtracted. Traders want to see OBV moving in the same direction, or confirming the existing direction

point and figure charts (PF) There are several types of point and figure charting methods that analyze price variations in stocks and commodities using trend lines, resistance levels, and various other criteria. Point and figure charts are usually easy to read and interpret because they filter out the small, and often confusing, price movements, leaving only the most important price action movements.

price oscillator An indicator that displays the difference between a slow and fast time period, subtracting it from the current interval's price.

price patterns Formations that appear on stock price charts that have been shown to have a certain degree of predictive value, including double bottom (bullish), double top (bearish), head and shoulders (bearish), inverse head and shoulders (bullish), and triangles, flags, and pennants (can be bullish or bearish, depending on the prevailing trend).

rate of change (ROC) The rate of change is among the simplest and most popular charting tools. It is computed using the daily price changes of a stock or index over a period of time (5, 10, 20 days, etc.). There are no hard, fast rules for using the indicator, but it is generally used as a tool for identifying overbought and oversold conditions.

simple moving average (SMA) A series of successive averages that are defined by a set of variables. As each new variable is added, the oldest or last variable is removed. Moving averages are often computed for stock prices to view trends over time. Fifty- and 200-day moving averages are among the most common time frames.

stochastic indicator The stochastic indicator is a type of oscillator that is used to identify overbought or oversold markets. It is based on the momentum and price changes of a stock or index. Readings of 80 or more are generally viewed as an overbought signal, and 20 or less indicates oversold conditions. Above 80 is sometimes called the sell zone and 20 or less is the buy zone. Trading decisions are made with respect to divergence between % D (one of the two lines generated by the study) and the item's price, or when % K moves above % D (bullish) or below it (bearish).

swing chart A chart that has a straight line drawn from each price extreme to the next price extreme based on a set of criteria such as percentages or number of days.

trading bands A method of plotting lines in and around the price of a market to form an envelope. This information can be used to recognize when prices are high or low on a relative basis and predict when to buy or sell by using indicators that confirm price action.

true strength index A momentum indicator that double-smoothes the ratio of the market momentum to the absolute value of the market momentum.

variable-length moving average A moving average where the number of periods selected for smoothing is based on the standard deviation of price—the more volatile the price is, the shorter the number of periods used for smoothing.

weighted moving average Similar to a simple moving average, but it gives more weight to current data in the n-interval average calculation.

williams' %R An index that determines where the most recent closing price is in relation to the price range for an n-interval period. If Williams' %R rises above 80, it signals an overbought market. Conversely, if it falls below 20, it signals an oversold market.

sentiment analysis

confidence index A gauge of investor faith or optimism relative to the economy and the stock market. Technical analysts want to see an improvement in the confidence index in order to confirm a bullish move in the stock market. Conversely, deteriorating levels of confidence are considered a bearish omen for the market.

contrarian-style trading Taking the opposite view of the majority of investors, or the crowd. When investors are predominantly bullish or optimistic on the market, the contrarian will turn bearish. Similarly, excessive levels of bearishness or pessimism are reasons to be bullish.

put/call ratio A technical indicator that measures put volume divided by call volume. The ratio can be applied to stocks, indexes, or entire markets. Rising put/call ratios indicate that put activity is increasing and traders are becoming bearish. Low put/call ratios indicate that call activity is relatively heavy and traders are becoming predominantly bullish.

short interest indicator An indicator that measures relative levels of short selling to gauge bearish sentiment. Short sellers borrow stocks, sell them, and hope the price falls so they can buy the stock back. Therefore, when short interest is high, short sellers are active and bearish sentiment is considered high.

VIX The CBOE Volatility Index (VIX) measures the implied volatility of S&P 500 Index options. When it rises, traders are becoming more bearish and are worried about future market volatility. For that reason, VIX is sometimes called the *fear gauge*. Low VIX readings are a sign of bullishness or complacency among traders.

appendix c

financial software guide

available software programs

There are many different financial software programs currently available. I have used my fair share of trading programs and even designed a few of my own. Computers are well suited to financial planning and trading because of their inherent ability to crunch numbers and perform complex calculations at the push of a button. Now that real-time data is readily available directly over the Internet, option software programs are easier and cheaper to use than ever before.

Assessing a specific program is a difficult task because they are constantly being updated. That's why this section is not intended to be an in-depth review of these programs. Instead, this is a list of trading software and the web sites where they can be found. Most programs offer a 30-day free trial and many can be directly downloaded from the Net. Always demo a program before buying it!

Financial Engineering Associates	http://www.fea.com
Investment Enhancing Systems, Inc.	http://www.ies-invest.com
Option Edge	http://www.oedge.com
Option Master	http://www.options-inc.com
OptionPeer with OptionTutor	http://www.optionpeer.com
OptionStation, SuperCharts, and TradeStation	http://www.omegaresearch.com
Option Trader	http://www.optionsxpress.com/
Option Wizard	http://www.option-wizard.com
OptionVue Systems International, Inc.	http://www.optionvue.com
PMpublishing's Web POP	http://www.pmpublishing.com/webpop
Sunguard MicroHedge	http://www.sunguard.com/microhedge

recommended programs

optionetics Platinum   http://www.optionetics.com/platinum/

Award-winning Optionetics Platinum is a powerful web-based options analysis tool that helps you make money in virtually all market conditions. Traders of all levels rely on Platinum every day to scan the market for high-probability opportunities. The application features thousands of optionable stocks with complete chain and Greek data that puts you on the fast track to finding trade opportunities that meet your preferred trading style.

Optionetics Platinum combines the power of options analysis with the ease of a streamlined platform that's easy to navigate and visually appealing. The application offers three different subscription levels which allow new traders to start with a foundational tool that can be upgraded to include advanced functions suitable for more experienced traders. All subscription levels offer a user-friendly interface and provide detailed risk evaluation features.

A short list of features for each application includes:

- *Platinum Express*—Detailed option analysis capabilities including calculators and complete option chains with greeks, stock and option volatility data, strategy scans and backtest tools, trade management tools, and in-depth risk analysis capabilities.
- *Platinum*—Includes Platinum Express features plus additional strategy searches, advanced trade management tools (includes adjustments, alerts, and charting capabilities),

probability tools, and more detailed historical data. Data exports are also available.

- *Platinum Pro*—Platinum features plus futures data, advanced scan and back testing capabilities, weekly and quarterly option data, and advanced charting, graphics and overlay capabilities.

Use Platinum Express when just starting out to access option evaluation and risk management tools—it serves as a great resource for new option traders. When you're ready to move on to more sophisticated approaches, Platinum Express offers an easy upgrade to the Platinum Tool Suite. If you're not trading with Platinum, you're missing out on virtually *millions* of moneymaking opportunities.

ProfitSource www.optionetics.com/tools/software/profitsource/

ProfitSource is a sophisticated financial market analysis program designed to help you identify winning trades by harnessing the power of Elliott Wave as well as advanced scanning and searching functionalities. For seasoned traders with proprietary systems and ideas, ProfitSource enables system testing using five or more years of data, allowing users to test their systems automatically. ProfitSource provides basic indicators with user-defined settings, along with more sophisticated analysis tools and applications.

ProfitSource is designed to enhance your trading success by providing a full suite of technical analysis tools and powerful features, all developed with one thing in mind: to help you make a profit. ProfitSource also provides scanning tools that allow the trader to create a list of stocks with certain technical characteristics (e.g., all S&P 500 stocks with a 50-day moving average below the 200-day moving average and increasing toward it). More importantly, the software can back-test trading systems to determine how effective a moving average crossover approach would be on these stocks.

Using the latest software technology, ProfitSource combines many useful trading software features into one powerful package, including:

- Precomputed scans.
- System testing including manual walkthrough and automated back-testing.
- Elliott Wave Analysis via charting tools or preset scans. Charting options include time and price projections.

- Generation of custom scans using application tools and indicators.
- One-click exchange with Optionetics Platinum!

ValueGain www.optionetics.com/tools/software/valuegain/
Previously, analyzing the balance sheets and financial statements of companies has always been considered the territory of brokers and analysts because of the amount of work and information required. ValueGain is revolutionary software that helps you make light work of this task by compiling all of the information that you could possibly need into one easy-to-use interface!

ValueGain, a stand-alone software program, makes use of a data feed to provide the most current financial metrics available. In addition to financial statement data and basic scans, the software provides users with precomputed scans based upon the fundamental approach used by some of the leading names in analysis, including Benjamin Graham, Warren Buffett, Peter Lynch, and others. These scans are categorized by three investment styles: growth, value, and income.

ValueGain also provides users with easy access to an important comparison tool: the company's performance over time. This is accomplished by charting financial data for the firm so an analyst can readily see whether the reported value is improving or deteriorating. When an individual locates a company with a financial ratio that is healthier than its peers and can also quickly note that the value has been improving over the past five quarters, the information is that much more valuable to an investor seeking new opportunities.

Finally, ValueGain also includes calculators that provide the user with a theoretical value for a firm using current financial data and the selected valuation model (e.g., a Buffett value model). Results are provided in data and graphic formats, for ease of review. Similar to option pricing models, these calculators provide analysts with information about companies that may be overvalued or undervalued in the market.

ValueGain features include:

- Up-to-date company financial data.
- Precomputed and custom fundamental scans.
- Valuation calculators.
- User-friendly graphics and charting capabilities.

OptionGear   www.optionetics.com/tools/software/optiongear/

OptionGear is the latest in options trading software. Whether you're a novice starting out or a professional options trader, this sophisticated, real-time options analysis and trading program is simple to use, yet provides unrivaled power and capabilities.

OptionGear was designed with input from top option traders and analysts, so ease of use and efficiency were central to its innovative design.

OptionGear's features include:

- Real-time, end-of-day, or delayed option data with greeks and volatility.
- Option calculators.
- Scanning tools and back-test capabilities.
- Strategy analysis and risk graphs.
- Portfolio management to organize trades.
- Access to data for international markets.

appendix d

financial web site guide

internet resources

Appendix D contains reviews of financial investment web sites broken down into the following categories: supersites, news, research, education, technical analysis, options, webzines, high technology, exchanges, advisory sites, specialty sites, fun and games, and search engines, plus sites from George Fontanills. Since the Internet is an evolving medium, updates, additions, and changes to this list can be found at www.optionetics.com.

supersites

BMIquotes.com
http://www.bmiquotes.com
    BMI is a major dynamic quote service and supersite. They offer real-time, delayed, or end-of-day prices on stocks, futures, and options as well as up-to-the-minute news and market analysis for a fee. This information can be accessed in a variety of ways including

cable, FM, wireless networks, and directly from the Internet, and is compatible with various trading software. The main site provides free 20-minute delayed quotes, a link to CBS MarketWatch, and end-of-day global market information, including exchange rates and American Depositary Receipts (ADR) prices.

CyberInvest
http://www.cyberinvest.com

CyberInvest hosts a free web directory to a multitude of investing sites. It also focuses on investor education by providing portfolio tracking, market monitors, and tips for global investing. Lots of advertising, but it's still well worth visiting.

Daily Stocks.com
http://www.dailystocks.com

This mega-link site features a tremendous list of financial sites arranged by trading tool categories—from stock screening sites to market commentary sites. It also offers an excellent search tool that finds sites with the individual stocks of your choice. You can even opt to be notified of future postings by e-mail.

E*Trade Financial
https://us.etrade.com/e/t/home

This online brokerage from our top 12 list also provides the general public an immense number of financial trading tools. You have the market at your fingertips—get quotes, charts, earnings estimates, and company profiles. Set up a portfolio of your favorite stocks and they'll even e-mail you the latest breaking news and quotes.

EDGAR-Online
http://www.edgar-online.com

This first-rate site is a classic financial resource. It allows you to access the SEC's EDGAR filings using an electronic data gathering, analysis, and retrieval tool to locate the SEC filings that interest you. Check out the exclusive drill-down tools, the "IPO Express" feature, and insider trading updates, or program an alert to let you know when a company you are watching files a new document. Although this is a subscription-based site, it does offer a few free services including custom portfolios.

Investools
http://www.investools.com

This is a fully loaded, well-designed site dedicated to providing everything the savvy investor uses to make successful trading decisions. Investools' ultimate goal is to help you learn how to trust and rely on your own investing knowledge, instead of depending solely on someone else's advice. It offers education and training services, coaching services that help you apply what you learn, and trading tools to help you evaluate stocks, options and currencies—all within a community environment where you can meet other traders and investors like yourself. Try out the Investor Toolbox, which features state-of-the-art proprietary investment tools, award-winning technology, and analyst-quality data.

Investor Guide
http://investorguide.com

This excellent, comprehensive site focuses on investing, personal finance and education. In its "Stock Tracker" link, you can enter up to 10 of your stocks and view what's happening with any of that day's hot stocks. There is a great stock financial glossary, as well as a business glossary. That plus tons of up-to-the-minute news makes this site one of the best.

Investorlinks
http://www.investorlinks.com

Investorlinks is an extensive financial web directory with daily and weekly reports, as well as articles and commentary. It offers links to advisories, mutual funds, options services, quotes, charts, stocks, financial news, investor services, brokerages, stocks and bonds, research, and a free portfolio feature.

Kiplinger Online
http://www.kiplinger.com

Kiplinger is an excellent source for business forecasts, top business news, topical feature articles, and personal financial advice. Check out their portfolio tracker, calculator, forums, delayed quotes, and stock research capabilities.

Money.cnn.com
http://money.cnn.com/

Primarily a news site, CNNMoney.com features upbeat, edgy feature articles and columns, investing tools, and market summaries. Use the quote search and news search features, or set up custom charts and portfolios. Additional information can be found on real estate, insurance, autos, retirement, and taxes. This site offers free registration for access to their "My Portfolio" page.

Motley Fool

http://www.fool.com

One of the most popular sites on the Internet! The Motley Fool site seeks to educate, amuse, and continually enrich the investment process for the hundreds of thousands of eager investors that use its books and this site to maximize their trading profits. This extremely entertaining site has a vast amount of current and educational investment information including quotes, charts, financials, portfolios, news and ideas, and some of the most heavily trafficked bulletin boards on the Net.

In 2007, Motley Fool opened its second decade as "foolanthropists" and announced one of its great new focuses: financial literacy for youth, with the mission to ensure that "every young person in the world gets a basic financial education." If this second decade is anywhere near as interesting and gratifying as the first one, we say, bring it on! Truly a quintessential supersite!

MSN Money

http://moneycentral.msn.com/investor/home.asp

What don't they have at MSN's financial supersite? Here you can find quotes, charts, graphs, market reports, finders, screeners, research, online workshops, custom portfolios, feature news, blogs, and message boards. You'll also find excellent investment articles from the top news providers, including *Barron's, Forbes,* the *Wall Street Journal, Motley Fool,* and more, as well as impressive commentary from prime financial journalists. For a small fee, you can receive e-mailed market reports or link up using Microsoft Money Plus software.

OptionMonster

http://www.optionmonster.com

If you love trading options, this site is definitely worth looking into! Founded by ex-CBOE floor traders Jon and Pete Najarian, this site is excellent for both thrill-seeking, fast-paced options traders and longer-term strategists as well. Here you can find trading-related news stories, as well as a plethora of useful trading tools, resources, blogs, and webcasts. Check out their "Inside Options" blog!

Quicken.com

http://www.quicken.com

The Quicken site is geared for novice investors, would-be homeowners, and small business entrepreneurs. It offers an extensive array of quotes, advanced charting, custom portfolios, home and mortgage information (including a convenient calculator), news and analysis, company profiles, SEC filings, and reports. You can even find great information on health care!

Quote.com
http://new.quote.com/home.action

The Quote.com site offers a ton of useful information, including delayed and real-time quotes, charts, earnings estimates and reports, top business stories, NYSE most active gainers and losers, and a market guide with in-depth information on individual companies. You can also register for hourly updates, dynamic quote service, and timely news feeds.

Standard & Poor's Equity Investor Service
http://www2.standardandpoors.com

The S&P is not just a renowned index anymore, and its web site is one of the best in the business. The site features up-to-the-minute information on ratings, indexes, equity research, and risk solutions, as well as investment advisory and data services. You can create you own home page for a custom view of what you want to know immediately. Be sure to check out the stock reports and professional analysis.

Stock Smart
http://www.stocksmart.com

A well-designed, clean site that specializes in providing you with in-depth information on your chosen stocks and industry sectors. It offers excellent custom portfolios with automatic updates, earnings calendars, graphs, charts, research, and stock screening, plus a look at the global markets. "Smart E-lerts" can give you timely stock prices plus the latest news.

Yahoo! Finance
http://quote.yahoo.com

Yahoo Finance features a vast array of market information including quotes, financial news, calendars, the latest market news, bulletin boards, chat rooms, SEC filings, earnings estimates, and a custom portfolio feature to keep track of your favorite stocks. I just happen to enjoy Yahoo's format, and judging from Yahoo's popularity, so do millions of other Internet users.

news sites

ABC News.com
http://www.abcnews.com

ABC moves from TV to the Net! Scroll down long enough and you'll find plenty of up-to-date business news and a no-frills, global market overview. You can also check out small business information, company and industry sector news, quotes, and technical charts. ABC's site received a 1998 Webby for Best News Site.

BBC News/Business
http://news.bbc.co.uk/2/hi/business/default.stm

British news at its finest. Review international news, download articles from extensive archives, and check out the London stock market. Well written and thoroughly researched, this site offers a glimpse of how U.S. stocks are viewed form across the pond.

Bloomberg
http://www.bloomberg.com

Bloomberg's site has a staggering array of free and subscription services including up-to-the-minute headlines and daily news on stocks, bonds, treasuries, global indexes, IPOs, currencies, and commodities. You can access financial market updates by live video (Bloomberg Television) or audio (Bloomberg Radio). Bloomberg's subscription service integrates a variety of traders' tools including quotes, a chart builder, a portfolio tracker, the Dow 30, and its "Market Monitor," which can be used to hunt down the latest news on up to 10 companies. And just in case you're ready for a break, traders can monitor the latest sports news or check out some great interviews.

BusinessWeek
http://www.businessweek.com

This online version of a popular magazine offers a great selection of business news and commentary, quotes, portfolio, and an e-mail newsletter. Always a reliable favorite!

CNBC
http://www.cnbc.com

The CNBC television news channel is the leader in business news. Its web site seeks to continue this tradition. The CNBC site offers programming information for CNBC in the United States, Europe, and Asia. Biographies for the CNBC staff are also featured online. Extensive executive and job search web listings and phone numbers are available.

The Holt Stock Report
http://metro.turnpike.net/holt

The Holt Report is user-friendly and full of interesting investment ideas. Check out their hot stocks reports, stocks up 50 percent, and the most recent closings reports for stocks and options. There's a "Web Menu" listing of recommended investment web sites to explore as well as the Holt Report archives to research.

Insider Info
http://www.insiderinfo.com/LostandFound.php

This site is a search engine "For the people, by the people." You can search for just about anything on this site, but their top sponsored searches are all in the investment arena. If you're looking for a place to start learning about trading, this site is a good pick!

Internet.com
http://www.internetnews.com/stocks

This basic business news site specializes in current articles regarding Internet stocks, e-commerce, web development, and Internet technology. An easy way to keep on top of the latest highlights in the business world!

Investor's Business Daily
http://www.investors.com

IBD's online spin-off is a great place for novice investors to get their bearings and for active investors to keep abreast of market trends and company changes. Featuring topical daily news articles from daily newspaper sections such as "Inside Today," "Front Page," "Computers & Tech," "The Economy," "The Markets," and "Vital Signs," this site is also an excellent educational section with great tips from investment guru William O'Neil.

JagNotes
http://jagnotes.com

JagNotes is primarily a consolidated investment report on all the stocks that have had newly issued research, analyst opinions, upgrades, downgrades, and coverage changes. The information contained in the morning JagNotes is typically not released to the Street until after the start of trading. JagNotes also offers a fax transmission service with stock and options, daily news, and Wall Street insights. An interesting feature is Jag's "Rumor Room," which requires registration to peek into, but does offer a unique opportunity.

MarketWatch.com
http://www.marketwatch.com/avatar.asp?dist=

This is primarily a news site that offers its own links for information regarding market commentary, markets, mutual funds and ETFs, personal finance, technology, and more. It's a great source for catching up-to-the-minute news on just about every current market-related report out there. You can create your own account and take advantage of its "My Portfolio" feature, where you can view your transactions and sort your portfolios quickly and easily.

Money.com
http://money.cnn.com/

Primarily a news site, Money.com features upbeat, edgy feature articles and columns, investing tools, and market summaries. Use the quote search and news search features, or set up custom charts and portfolios. Additional information can be found on real estate, insurance, autos, retirement, and taxes. This site just completed a major design overhaul.

MSNBC
http://www.msnbc.com

Online spin-off of NBC television provides market updates and breaking news, feature articles, and commentary, plus a major exchanges chart and quote search tools. Lots of breaking news and video clips as well as links and advertisements. This site won a 1998 Webby award for Best News Site.

Reuters.com
http://www.reuters.com/

Reuter's is one of the primary international wire services, and its web site serves up a double dose of global news as well as top-notch investment commentary and market news. The site also provides links to news regarding politics, technology, entertainment, lifestyle, the environment, and more. You will also find some pretty great blogs here as well!

Silicon Investor
http://siliconinvestor.advfn.com/

Silicon Investor justifiably boasts being "A single source for worldwide financial data, news and discussion." In this site you can find just about everything you need for news regarding the markets. Its "Hot Subjects—Investments" page is a forum where companies are discussed, and that alone makes this site worth checking out.

TheStreet.com
http://www.thestreet.com
Hosted by controversial analyst Jim Cramer, this extremely popular site offers insightful articles on stocks, options, tech stocks, funds, taxes, and the international finance scene. Register for a free 30-day trial of their premium subscription service and you'll find yourself in the loop encountering the clever commentary of a cadre of bantering journalists three times a day, delivered right to your desktop. TheStreet.com's engaging articles and perceptive market analyses no doubt help to shape the mass psychology of the marketplace.

Thomson
http://www.thomsonreuters.com/
The Thomson Corporation serves professionals in the fields of law, tax, accounting, financial services, scientific research, and health care. The site contains software tools and applications that help its customers make better decisions, faster.

USA Today Money
http://www.usatoday.com/money/mfront.htm
One of America's premiere national newspapers creates a comprehensive and well-organized web site featuring a bounty of breaking news and feature articles. It also provides a lengthy list of trading tools including delayed quotes, most active lists, an IPO center, and industry research.

The Wall Street Journal Online
http://online.wsj.com/public/us
The *Wall Street Journal* online is a subscription-based site, but well worth it to the serious market watcher. The site offers 24-hour news updates, e-mail stock alerts, and has lots of information to help you track markets and investments. Within this site you may follow the technology sector, get a global perspective, and research your interests, with perspectives on over 10,000 companies and mailing lists. They also offer a 30-day free trial service, which you can access through http://interactive.wsj.com/.

research sites

Briefing.com
http://www.briefing.com

This site seems to have caught the ear of the market. The Briefing.com site offers three levels of subscription services. The Investor Index provides analysis, commentary, data, and broker ratings in an easy to navigate site. The Platinum Index provides live market commentary, stock analysis, quotes and charts, sector ratings, earnings reports, and an economic calendar. The Trader Index caters to the active trader with all kinds of money-making ideas, live information from, trading desks, and technical trading setups.

CNET News
http://investor.news.com/cnet

This is CNET's market news page within its bigger site. Here you'll find all kinds of up-to-the-minute news, featured articles, and commentary. Traders and investors can create their own portfolios within the site, and there is an interesting column called "CEO Wealthmeter," which offers brief but detailed profiles of the current movers and shakers.

Dow Jones
http://www.dowjones.com

The Dow Jones site offers global market updates, economic indicators, quotes, and news. Access to the Dow Jones Index pages and other business publications is also available.

Dun & Bradstreet
http://www.dnb.com

Dun and Bradstreet specializes in press releases and company profiles, focusing on news, views, and trends. Check out its renowned business database for report requests. With more than 125 million business records, D&B's global commercial database is enhanced by its proprietary DUNSRight Quality Process, which provides customers with quality business information.

FinanceWise
http://www.financewise.com

This no-frills site will enable you to search financial web sites by allowing you to query it using individual words. Searching by key terms or phrases, company names, or industrial sector locates special reports and news articles. You have to register and use a personalized post-registration bookmark to access the site again.

FinancialWeb
http://www.finweb.com

FinWeb is a comprehensive financial web site dedicated to providing the public with a vast amount of financial information and resources on topics including buying a home, rebuilding credit, or formulating an investment strategy. This site is designed to help people access the information they need to ask the right questions and maker good financial decisions.

Hoover's
http://www.hoovers.com

A premiere investment research web site, Hoover's makes it easy to research a company's financials while exploring historical market data. A small monthly subscription fee gives you access to proprietary profiles on 3,300 stocks. Get the jump on IPO filings, investigate industry overviews, quotes, and price forecasting each trading week. Access stock screeners, breaking news stories, research tools, and links, or download reports. This site has received numerous awards including the Dow Jones Business Directory's Select Site and Investor Link's Top Site.

InternetNews
http://www.internetnews.com/bus-news/

This site is designed primarily to deliver cutting edge news in the IT world. It's loaded with articles written by trade journalists who stay on top of what's happening with specific companies and their stocks that deal with technology, as well as broader news about the tech market as a whole. A great way to keep on top of this arena!

Stockhouse
http://stockhouse.com

Formerly Stock Group Information Systems, the Stockhouse web site offers feature articles, headlines, and interesting sector reports on tech stocks, petroleum, and diamond stocks. Quotes, custom portfolio managers, indexes, and an analyst corner are well-organized features.

Stocks.com
http://www.stocks.com

All stocks, all the time! If what you're looking for is a place to learn anything about the stock market, look no farther. There is also a link to an options page, where you can find great education services—including Optionetics!

StockSmart Pro
http://www.stocksmartpro.com

This site offers services that include tracking the market, following intraday trading, accessing company profiles and industry fluctuations, custom portfolios, automatic e-mail alerts, search engine tools, limited technical analysis tools, and stock screening.

Time
http://www.time.com/time/index.html

Time.com has partnered with CNN for this great new site. Here you can catch up on the most current news and global events—everything from the entertainment world to global finances. It features blogs, interviews with celebrities, and basically anything you would want in an interactive online newspaper. Not the strongest on stock quotes and news, but a good read nonetheless!

VectorVest
http://www.vectorvest.com

The VectorVest site provides services that integrate fundamental and technical analysis to sort, screen, rank, graph, and analyze over 6,500 stocks, industry groups, and industry sectors for price, value, safety, timing, and more. All stocks receive buy, sell, hold, and stop order recommendations as well as price and dividend risk assessments of low, high, or medium. If you're not ready for a subscription, you may want to take advantage of its free in-depth stock analysis service—just click on the "Free Stock Analysis" function.

World Wide Financial Network
http://www.wwfn.com

The World Wide Financial Network has an excellent variety of investor resources including company profiles, free real-time quotes and charts, upgrades and downgrades, real-time Globex, insider trading, news, extensive research, feature articles, and access to online brokers. Overall, a great site.

Zacks Investment Research
http://www.zacks.com

Zacks Investment Research is a very popular financial site that offers a variety of free and subscription services. It provides access to research produced by more than 3,000 analysts at the 240-plus brokerage firms as well as a vast array of brokerage and equity research, screening, and advisory tools.

ZDNet
http://www.zdnet.com

    ZDNet, "Where Technology Means Business," is an all-around site for searching the latest reviews in technological products and advancements. You'll find news, blogs, reviews, and white papers on the latest, greatest, and worst of what's available. So if you drool over all things techie, you can't go wrong by checking this site out—before and after you buy!

educational sites

American Association of Individual Investors
http://www.aaii.com

    This active investors' association boasts more than 70 local chapters across America. Dedicated to education, the friendly site offers free and member services. The home page features insightful articles and links to publications, message boards, articles and commentary, quote search tools, custom portfolios with portfolio management services, an extensive archival library, and a calendar of upcoming local events.

Dr. Ed Yardeni's Economics Network
http://www.yardeni.com/

    Dr. Yardeni's subscription-only site is an extensive research tool for weekly analysis, macroeconomics netbook, and a global and U.S. forecast table. There are online chat rooms, economic indicators, Dr. Yardeni's published articles, and polls. InvestorLinks rated this site on their Top Ten Financial Sites List and it also made *Smart-Money's* 10 Most Valuable Sites for Investors.

Financials.com
http://www.financials.com

    This site offers easy-to-follow, step-by-step guides that help you understand the basics of financial online investing and how to research companies that interest you. The site has links to investment news groups and investment clubs along with customized portfolios.

GreenJungle
http://www.greenjungle.com/
This site specializes in education for beginners with materials on everything from stocks to mutual funds to insurance. Make use of their articles, research resources, and valuable links on the web.

Investment FAQ
http://www.invest-faq.com
This site has free quotes, charts, graphs, and research reports. There is a basic tour with educational articles for beginners with info on mutual funds, stocks, bond basics, and P/E ratios, with a list of common errors to avoid. You can browse the site by categories or enter your own questions to find answers. This site also provides links to other sites in order to find additional answers to your investment questions.

Max's Investment World
http://www.maxinvest.com
This site seeks to help average traders get their investment bearings. Offering four main areas—Basics, Research, Ideas, and Investment Picks—Max IW fosters education on investing in a fun, light environment.

Stock-Trak
http://www.stocktrak.com
Stock Track provides portfolio simulations featuring stocks, options, futures, bonds, and more. More than 50,000 college students and 900 professors use this terrific educational site each semester in their finance and investment courses. Stock Track is now available to anyone, allowing you to manage a fake brokerage account in order to test strategies, place trades, and learn about the financial markets. It also provides links to trading guides on options and technical analysis as well as stock split information, upgrades and downgrades, historical prices, free annual reports, and lots more.

The Young Investor Website
http://www.younginvestor.com
This supersite for kids (and grown-ups, too) features several sections designed to entertain and educate. It's an outstanding way for kids to learn the fundamentals of money and investing in a comfortable, familiar, and interactive environment. For parents, this is a great place to learn how to help your kids develop good earnings,

savings, and investment habits. Makes you wish you would have had this site when you were a kid!

technical analysis sites

Ask Research
http://www.askresearch.com
    This well-organized site focuses on providing technical analysis tools using historical and real-time market data to create intraday and daily charts. You can also access option chains (delayed quotes) and take a look at the highest and lowest percentage option leaders. A good clean site with most of the amenities such as watch lists and customized portfolio tools.

Barchart.com
http://www.barchart.com
    Barchart.com is a comprehensive site that provides technical information on stocks, futures, and options. Customized charts and quotes are just the tip of the iceberg. Other advantages include options reports, a "trend spotter" feature, indexes, webmaster tools, and a learning center. This no-frills site is definitely worth checking out!

BigCharts
http://www.bigcharts.com
    BigCharts is sure to become one of your favorite free sites. It features easily customized intraday charts, historical quotes, and snapshot quotes and profiles on more than 34,000 stocks, mutual funds, and indexes. With an excellent design and very user-friendly, BigCharts.com also offers information on the big movers and losers in the main markets, momentum charts, and other goodies. You'll find links to this site from all over the Net!

ClearStation
http://www.clearstation.com
    This site focuses on technical information including customized charts, graphs, and company profiles. Enjoy custom portfolios, quotes, charts, message boards, and daily e-mail alerts plus recommendations that are actually worthwhile. Check out their "tag and bag" feature which lists stocks that are entering trends or experiencing events. These lists are updated throughout the day.

Daily Graphs Online
http://www.dailygraphs.com
Looking for new ideas? Here's a great collection of investment research tools. Its trademarked tools include Daily Graphs Online, Custom Screen Wizard, Industry Groups, Fund Center, and Options Guide. It also offers a stock selection discipline developed by William J. O'Neil, founder of *Investor's Business Daily*.

Equis.com
http://www.equis.com
This site offers the experience and expertise of its host corporation, Reuters International. Equis develops and markets the award-winning MetaStock range of products—the premier brand in the charting and technical analysis arena for the individual investor—and includes both real-time and end-of-day variants of the software, along with data subscriptions, plug-ins, and third-party products.

IQ Chart
http://www.iqc.com
This site provides stock charting software to individual investors and technical analysts. It maintains a variety of different news sources and an online "investors forum," as well as customized chart settings where you set up your own portfolio and can check on it instantly. There's a full-service educational center with a comprehensive technical analysis glossary of different terms and explanations of how to read the charts and graphs.

Market Edge
http://www.stkwtch.com
For traders and investors of all levels, this site combines fundamental analysis from Standard & Poor's with Second Opinion, the leading buy/sell stock timing service. Market Edge offers timely and actionable ideas in addition to daily and weekly market commentary, plus daily stock alerts that are designed to help keep you on the right side of the market.

Pristine
http://www.pristine.com
This educational site aims to educate individuals interested in self-directed trading while providing trading ideas for the seasoned pro. The Pristine Method includes a great explanation of the psychological challenges that day and swing traders face. Pristine.com also

answers the questions of not only what to trade, but when and why to trade. Day traders will appreciate their daily stock recommendations, market commentary, technical analysis charts, and unlimited real-time quotes.

StockMaster
http://www.stockmaster.com

StockMaster claims to have been the first financial site on the World Wide Web. It definitely has all the usual bells and whistles, including technical charts and graphs, customized portfolios, search engines, free software downloads, discussion groups, and a top 40 list of up-and-coming stocks to put on your watch lists. Check out its investor sentiment surveys and link to options trading.

StockTools
http://www.stocktools.com

The StockTools site has delayed quotes on all the major U.S. and Canadian exchanges. Nice features include a wide variety of industry groupings for selecting quotes. Customizable graphs and extensive historical quotes are also available.

Value Line
http://www.valueline.com

Best known for publishing the weekly *Value Line Investment Survey*, this subscription-based investment information center has it all: free quotes, graphs, and charts; featured articles; and research on mutual funds, stocks, and options. It also offers excellent interactive online investment tutorials. A first-rate site from a first-rate investment publishing and research company.

options sites

Committee on Options Proposals (COOP)
http://www.coop-options.com

COOP is comprised of respected options industry professionals and marketing personnel from 40 stock exchange member firms, the four options exchanges, and the Options Clearing Corporation (OCC). They work towards expanding the use of options in the marketplace through education, PR, and networking.

CoveredCall.com
http://www.coveredcall.com

This site offers options strategy advice and education including information on covered calls, credit spreads, LEAPS, and stock splits.

If you're unfamiliar with these terms, the site also offers an options covered calls primer with suggested readings and a tutorial. Take advantage of custom portfolios, a free newsletter, and features like the "War Room" message boards.

INO.com
http://www.ino.com

This privately held and independent company specializes in the futures and options markets. As a storefront for trading tools, charts, publications, educational courses, and other resources, INO serves traders worldwide with a continuous information service of quotes, charts, and news. They offer a Helpline link on every page within their site that is designed to allow you to quickly contact and get help from the right person.

Netpicks
http://www.netpicks.com

This is a site aggressive options traders, providing free stock quotes, graphs, and charts. Paid services include real-time paging on hot stocks, a daily updated morning and evening newsletter, investment links, and news headlines. There are quite a few different payment plans and a free two-week trial. Take advantage of their "AutoTrade" service, where they will execute your trades for you in your own account.

OptionInvestor.com
http://optioninvestor.com

This site offers a unique tour de force of options services, research, commentary, market analysis, trade recommendations, option quotes, live charts, S&P futures data, and a virtual options community of live chat rooms and message boards. This site is an excellent resource for both novice and seasoned options traders.

Options Industry Council
http://www.optionscentral.com

The basic mission of the Options Industry Council is to educate the public about the benefits and risks of exchange-traded equity options. Its excellent web site offers the latest educational tools, including audio and video podcasts, online classes, and webcasts. The FAQ section features intelligent questions and answers that are well written and easily understood. An excellent choice for the serious student!

Schaeffer's Research.com
http://www.options-iri.com

This comprehensive web site is the creation of option investment adviser and educator Bernie Schaeffer. Well organized and jam-packed with information, it provides stock and stock options quotes, lists of most active stocks and options, an options calendar and calculator, excellent options educational resources, as well as information concerning Schaeffer's *Option Advisor* newsletter and recommendation service, and access to his hardback book and options trading course.

The Option Strategist
http://www.optionstrategist.com

A web site that focuses on providing short-term stock and option trading resources developed by author and options educator Lawrence G. McMillan. This site features free options quotes, historical volatility data, volume alerts, a list of expensive options, chat rooms, and information regarding McMillan's seminars and other educational tools.

Stricknet.com
http://www.stricknet.com/index.htm

This site offers data on options and covered call picks, pure plays, and naked puts. There's daily commentary and screening of over 220,000 options a day, a calculator, plus market alerts. Check out the supplemental educational pages.

Strikeprice.com
http://www.strikeprice.com

This extensive site is one of my favorites for reviewing fundamental data and historical prices of options and stocks. In addition, it offers stock and option quotes and charts as well as a list of the most active options. Take advantage of its new custom portfolio manager system.

webzines

Barron's Online
http://www.barrons.com

This outstanding webzine offers breaking and scheduled financial news and commentary from the *Wall Street Journal* Interactive

Edition, plus exclusive, weekday coverage from industry giant and pioneer *Barron's*. In addition, subscribers are eligible to receive free annual reports, *Barron's* Roundtable, movers, and more.

The Economist
http://www.economist.com

The online edition of the *Economist,* a British business journal renowned for its excellent analysis of global politics and economic forces, offers thought-provoking articles, technical analysis, as well as access to archived editions.

Fortune Magazine
http://money.cnn.com/magazines/fortune/

With the splashy look of a top-notch magazine, this site presents an overview of what you'll receive as a print subscriber to *Fortune* and offers lists of top company performers and industry medians.

Inc. Online
http://www.inc.com/magazine/20080501/index.html

Hosted by Inc.com, this online magazine acts as an electronic consultant for small business owners and entrepreneurs. It provides hands-on advice, case studies, and big-picture overviews for growing companies. You can also find tutorials, glossaries, recommended readings, news and feature articles, and interactive networking opportunities. Check out the virtual consultant feature, chat rooms, and topical message boards.

Red Chip Review
http://www.redchip.com

This site focuses on undervalued and undiscovered small-cap companies. Over 200 companies in 28 industries are analyzed and evaluated including company specs, offerings, and timetables.

SmartMoney Interactive
http://www.smartmoney.com/mag/

SmartMoney Magazine calls itself "the *Wall Street Journal* magazine." This site specializes in addressing the needs and questions of professional and managerial Americans who may be overwhelmed by today's tough questions concerning the high-action world of finance. A very upscale site indeed!

Technical Analysis of Stocks and Commodities
http://www.traders.com

The online site of *Technical Analysis of Stocks and Commodities* magazine is designed to foster trader success by offering information on technical trading strategies, charting patterns, indicators, and computerized trading methods through well-researched feature articles and a wide variety of links and resources. Archived articles from the print magazine are also available.

Trader's Digest
http://www.tradersdigest.com

Trader's Digest offers information and resources for traders including feature articles, editorials and commentary, picks of the week, and free educational tutorials. This site also features a free e-mailed newsletter and invites readers to submit articles for the web site.

Wired Magazine
http://www.wired.com

This online version of *Wired* magazine is well-known for its cutting-edge style and lively commentary—perhaps a side-effect of being based in San Francisco. It has lots of interesting news, articles, commentary, and market analysis, especially regarding the world of high technology. There are custom portfolios, search tools for news or quotes, daily summaries and market indexes, and IPO reports with an inclination for the online dot-com companies. They also offer a worthwhile daily e-mailed newsletter.

Worth Online
http://www.worth.com

The online edition of *Worth* magazine offers a variety of investment articles, feature stories, and archived stories from previous editions. There is a link to the complete Peter Lynch archives, a section for investor resources, and investing 101 for beginners.

high-technology sites

Gartner Dataquest
http://www.dataquest.com

The Gartner Dataquest site is devoted to data, research, analysis, and advice with more than 140 annual strategic research programs, quarterly statistics programs and databases, and featured articles. Each subscriber receives a specified number of hours of strategic advice in areas including business plan development, user trends, technology developments, and overall industry directions.

Silicon Investor
http://siliconinvestor.advfn.com/

The Silicon Investor site claims to be the largest discussion community on the Web, with more than 3,500,000 messages in its database. This haven for tech stock investors specializes in computers, software, communication, semis, biotechnology and medical devices, and much more. Quotes and charts are supplied by North American Quotations, Inc., and are delayed 15 to 20 minutes.

exchanges

The American Stock Exchange
http://www.amex.com

The American Stock Exchange is comprised of companies that were too small to be listed on the New York Stock Exchange. Requirements include a pretax income of $750,000 in two of the past three years, stockholders equity of $4 million, and a minimum market capitalization of $3 million. The AMEX site is quite extensive and offers quotes, news, and exchange information as well as excellent educational materials.

The Chicago Board of Trade
http://www.cbot.com

The Chicago Board of Trade is primarily a futures and options exchange where the Dow Jones Industrial Averages (DJIA) futures trade. Its Webinars page helps you find information at all levels of industry knowledge, from beginner to advanced, in a variety of media that includes print, interactive tutorials, and videos.

The Chicago Board Options Exchange
http://www.cboe.com

The Chicago Board Options Exchange is the largest options exchange in the United States. Its web site offers news, new option listings, and exchange information on equities, options, and LEAPS. Specialization includes calls and puts on NYSE stocks, the S&P 500, U.S. Treasury bonds, and other indexes.

The International Securities Exchange
http://www.iseoptions.com/
The International Securities Exchange, a subsidiary of Eurex, is the largest global equity options trading venue. Its market's portfolio includes both an options exchange and a stock exchange. It offers options on equities, ETFs, indexes, and FX and its stock exchange trades approximately 6,000 products. It has a fully electronic equities platform with continuous price improvement.

NASDAQ
http://www.nasdaq.com
The National Association of Securities Dealers Automated Quotations (NASDAQ) system is also known as the over-the-counter market where, via online computer transactions, OTC and specific NYSE-listed securities can be bought and sold through licensed securities brokers and dealers. It features the internationally acclaimed NASDAQ overview and the world-wide NASDAQ network of NASDAQ performance data. There are quotes, charts, graphs, ticker search services, and features such as the 10 most active share volumes, polling volumes, and most active advanced performances. This is a good site to set up portfolio tracking and stock screening. An excellent site tour helps you get started.

NYSE Euronext
www.euronext.com
NYSE Euronext, the holding company created by the combination of NYSE Group, Inc., and Euronext N.V., offers a very diverse array of financial products and services. NYSE Euronext, which is a world leader for listings; trading in cash equities, equity and interest rate derivatives, and bonds; and for the distribution of market data, brings together six cash equities exchanges in five countries and six derivatives exchanges. This is definitely one of the most informative and user-friendly sites available.

Philadelphia Stock Exchange
http://www.phlx.com
The Philadelphia Stock Exchange (PHLX) was founded in 1790 as the first organized stock exchange in the United States. You'll find a daily market summary, exchange information, up-to-the-minute news, educational information, and a calendar of events. The site offers 15-minute delayed quotes for NASDAQ and 20-minute delayed

quotes for NYSE and AMEX. Volatility charts are available, along with news, research, and daily market analysis.

Securities and Exchange Commission
http://www.sec.gov/
 The Securities and Exchange Commission (SEC) has a lot of detailed securities-related information, such as SEC reports of listed companies, investor guides, and EDGAR. The database EDGAR performs automated collection of corporate information and reports required to be filed with the SEC.

advisory sites

Avid Trader
http://avidtrader.com
 Avid Trader calls itself the "Stock Trading Community for the Novice to Advanced Trader," and for good reason. Here you can find excellent publications, tools and resources, blogs, charts, news, and pattern types. *Online Investor* magazine believes this site's "Smart writing and design make this a comfy virtual hangout. . . . Includes chat rooms that attract a classier-than-average crowd."

Elliott Wave International
http://www.elliottwave.com
 This site is mostly about forecasting, with interactive billboards and discussion forums. Its host is master predictor Robert Prechter. There's expert international analysis with links to full-time analysis services. There are global market reports and a market watch as well as specialized forecasting services.

The Hedgehog
http://www.hedge-hog.com
 Created by a former naval officer with a talent for trading, this site offers his own evaluation of a long list of companies as well as IPO reports, featured articles, stock quotes, a portfolio tracker, and discussion forums.

StockPicks
http://www.stockpicks.com
 Are you looking to invest in the market while doing only a minimal amount of homework? If so, check out this site! StockPicks offers electronic data feeds that are both real-time and delayed.

Stockpicks.com offers real-time quote systems powered by Quote-Media. It also has a members' forum, which is an online discussion with open topics.

StockRumors
http://www.stockrumors.com
If you believe that rumors move equities, then StockRumors. com is the site for you. Instead of giving you yesterday's news, this site alerts its members in real time to where the volume and action is on the Street through Instant messaging and text messaging. StockRumors believes that "Knowing what is being said can earn you money!"

Strategic Organization Solutions
http://sosadvisors.com
This global consulting services firm offers a complete suite of management and human capital solutions. These services include business improvement solutions that enable organizations to meet strategic and tactical objectives and help to strengthen talent; consulting solutions that deliver improved operational performance and achievement of corporate goals; and much more.

TheStreet.com
http://www.smartportfolio.com
This is where you can find all things Jim Cramer, for starters! This site is quite complete, with tons of news articles, market research tools, options alerts, free newsletters, and even a "Beat the Street" game, a fantasy trading game where you could win some big money. Definitely worth checking out!

The Wolf
http://www.thewolf.cc/
The Wolf is basically an advisory-based analysis site with a daily service that uses option volume open interest to find options under accumulation. The Wolf filters out volume caused by other factors such as takeover rumors, hedges, and spreads.

specialty sites

Centrex
http://www.centrex.com
This group of international companies, which operates in the natural gas sector, focuses on the extraction and marketing of natural

gas reserves. Its autonomous, specialist subsidiaries operate in the gas industry along the entire value chain, from developing new reserves to transportation, trading, processing, and distribution. This site has a monthly subscription fee.

Direct Stock Market
http://www.dsm.com

Direct Stock Market provides investors and securities professionals with all there is to know about public and private offerings. In return, DSM also gives companies issuing stock in a public offering or completing a private placement with the ability to distribute their reports and company profiles to prospective investors. DSM is now accelerating its shift to a specialty life sciences and materials sciences company, promising to deliver faster growth, higher margins, and improved earnings quality.

DTN.IQ
http://www.dtniq.com/index.cfm

This is a real-time, streaming quote and news service that offers data direct from the exchanges. Since they own their own ticker plant and data centers, they guarantee fast, reliable quotes. Here you can watch the market move in real time and get state-of-the-art software program with a multitude of built-in investment tools.

Foreign Exchange Trading Education
http://www.fxte.com

This comprehensive site focuses on teaching investors and traders how to make money in the foreign exchange market (forex). FXTE offers a number of newsletters, articles, and resources, and provide excellent seminars on trading the forex, the world's largest and most liquid financial market, which trades more than $2 trillion per day.

FreeRealtime.com
http://www.freerealtime.com

FreeRealtime specializes in giving investors access to real-time quotes direct from the NYSE, NASDAQ, and AMEX. You can also access the latest breaking news, monitor your stocks and holdings, utilize research market indexes and stocks, and review featured articles. Links to charts, index updates, news, and commentary round out this one-dimensional site.

Good Money
http://www.goodmoney.com

This site is dedicated to helping people to invest in social and environmentally responsible companies. It provides a wealth of information including in-depth company profiles, online chats, social funds, and insightful articles, and studies—an excellent resource site for the conscious investor!

The Green Money Online Guide
http://www.greenmoneyjournal.com

The Green Money Online Guide specializes in socially and environmentally responsible business, investing, and consumer resources. Their motto is "Socially Responsible Investing—Greening the Global Economy." There is a web resource guide, a Green Money bookstore with recommended readings, and a calendar of upcoming events.

Investor Home
http://www.investorhome.com

The Investor Home page is a treasure trove of links, quotes, charts, research, profiles, and earnings estimates. The sites are coded to denote whether registration or payments are necessary, and each site is judged for market data, stock charts and charting tools, and fund-specific information gatherers.

Investor Words
http://www.investorwords.com

This is a consummate educational site with a full investment glossary containing more than 5,000 terms and 15,000 links between related terms. Need to know the difference between a *margin account* and a *margin agreement*, or between a *death benefit* and a *dead cat bounce*? This is the place. There are charts, quotes, investors' forums, and a comprehensive investors' guide—all laid out in an understandable, easy-to-use format.

MoneyMinded
http://www.moneyminded.com.au/

This site offers interactive polls, calculators, news, essays, articles, and advice columns for figuring out personal and investment finances, including college aid, bill consolidation loans, and even information on how to open a Swiss bank account.

Moody's Investment Services
http://www.moodys.com

Moody's Investor Services is the leading provider of credit ratings, research, and financial information to the capital markets, and it has set the standards for rating parameters since 1909. Different companies, from industries to medical research to banking, are investigated and rated to assess investment risks. You can also access continuous information gathering and updating of all the ratings.

Netquote
http://asx.www.netquote.com.au

This technical analysis site is geared to the Australian market, offering free quotes and portfolio management. For-pay services include Live ASX data, real-time AAP news and quotes, and e-mailed hot stock updates.

PC Quote
http://www.pcquote.com

PCQuote is an excellent quote service with a wide range of ticker symbol services, including stock analysis, profiles, and commodities delayed quotes, as well as access to real-time quotes.

Securities Industry and Financial Markets Association (SIFMA)
www.sifma.org

SIFMA's mission is to link "...investors and issuers locally and globally to create economic growth and financial security—around the corner, around the world." SIFMA represents more than 650 member firms of all sizes in all financial markets, not only in the United States but also around the world. They offer premiere educational resources for investors and for professional brokers. In this site you can find all the usual stock information, but what makes it stand out is their distinct global outlook.

Small Cap Investor
http://www.smallcapinvestor.com

This site specializes in small-cap stocks with a lot of potential that are considered to be undervalued and overlooked. There are the standard services including quotes, stock screeners, custom portfolios, news, humor, educational programs, and a newsletter.

Social Investment Forum (SIF)
http://www.socialinvest.org

The SIF is a nonprofit organization that promotes socially responsible investing. Members receive special reports on news, breaking issues, monthly reports, and a quarterly newsletter. There is stock screening, shareholder advocacy, and links to other socially responsible investment products and services.

Value Point Analysis Financial Forum
http://www.eduvest.com

Value Point Analysis Financial Forum is a community of investors who have been sharing their stock picks and analysis by using a common valuation model. By visiting the site, you can evaluate your stocks using a 13-field fundamental analysis model and then post the results, with additional message boards and chat rooms.

fun and games

Stock-Trak
http://www.stocktrak.com

This site is a huge educational exercise/game that is used by more than 900 professors and 50,000 students. You start with a portfolio simulation worth $100,000 and trade away. There's lots of information and explanations. The rules are very specific but this can be a great place for beginners in order to test strategies, place trades, and learn about the financial markets to get started before using real money.

Wall Street Sports
http://www.wallstreetsports.com

This is definitely a twist! Wall Street Sports looks a lot like a well-designed investment web site, but it's actually a sports stock market where you can buy and sell fantasy shares of your favorite athletes from all your favorite sports. It's free to play and you can win cash prizes. Create a custom portfolio to play along and get news analysis and commentary on your favorite stars, plus chat rooms and message boards.

search engines

Excite
http://money.excite.com/home.html

Excite's Money and Investing page has news articles, customized portfolios, quotes and charts, and links to some of the best investment sites on the Net. There is a lot of personal finance information as well as new tax assistant features.

Google
http://finance.google.com/finance

This well-laid-out and easy to access site offers several insightful sections including Market Summary, Top Stories, Sector Summary, Recent Quotes, and a Trends section. Google has, in fact, become the premier search engine—so much so that "google" is now a verb for searching the Internet.

Yahoo!
http://www.yahoo.com

The premier search engine hosts an excellent variety of news, articles, and investment tools. Expansive search engine and great graphics make this site a surefire bookmark.

sites from george fontanills

Optionetics
http://www.optionetics.com

The Optionetics site has comprehensive information available on all financial markets. Not only does it have a customized portfolio feature, but also quotes, most active gainers and losers, market analysis, index charts, research, bond quotes, and a large variety of market reports. You can also access updates on all major markets. This site also offers comprehensive options education, Optionetics Seminars, and a variety of educational materials.

Profit Strategies
http://www.profitstrategies.com

This active site, presented largely by Tom Gentile, offers message boards, traders' chat rooms, stock charts, quotes, news, a daily e-mailed newsletter, major index charts, resource links, investment ideas and technical analysis with global, domestic, and industrial views. It also presents a valuable mock trading portfolio analysis tutorial. Be sure to check out the weekly radio show! You'll find it here: http://www.profitstrategies.com/radio/?source=msb

appendix e

online brokerage directory

brokerage quick reference list

AB Watley Direct	www.abwatley.com	888-733-9000
Charles Schwab	www.schwab.com	888-245-6864
ChoiceTrade	www.choicetrade.com	877-731-9114
eOption	www.eoption.com	888-793-5333
E*Trade	www.etrade.com	800-ETRADE1
Fidelity Investments	www.fidelity.com	800-FIDELITY
Firstrade	www.firstrade.com	800-869-8800
Freedom Investments	www.freedominvestments.com	800-944-4033
Frontier	www.ffutures.com	800-777-2438
Interactive Brokers	www.interactivebrokers.com	877-442-2757
InternetTrading.com	www.internettrading.com	800-696-2811
InvesTrade	www.investrade.com	800-498-7120
MB Trading	www.mbtrading.com	866-628-3001
Newedge USA	www.preferredtrade.com	888-781-0283
NobleTrading	www.nobletrading.com	877-TRADE11
OptionsHouse	www.optionshouse.com	877-653-2500

OptionsXpress	www.optionsxpress.com	888-280-8020
RF Lafferty	www.laffertyny.com	800-221-8601
Scottrade	www.scottrade.com	800-619-SAVE
Sharebuilder	www.sharebuilder.com	866-747-2537
Siebert.net	www.siebertnet.com	800-872-0711
SpeedTrader.com	www.speedtrader.com	800-874-3039
TD Ameritrade	www.tdameritrade.com	800-454-9272
ThinkorSwim	www.thinkorswim.com	866-839-1100
TradeKing	www.tradeking.com	877-495-5464
Trading Direct	www.tradingdirect.com	800-925-8566
WallStreet*E	www.wallstreete.com	888-WALL-STE
Wyse Securities	www.wyse-sec.com	800-640-8668
Zecco	www.zecco.com	877-700-STOCK

brokerage descriptions

AB Watley

> **web site:** abwatley.com
>
> **address:** 50 Broad Street, Suite 1728, New York, NY 10004
>
> **toll-free:** 888-733-9000
>
> **fax:** 212-202-5204
>
> **e-mail:** accounts@abwatley.com
>
> **category:** Deep-discount brokerage
>
> **slogan:** "Wired to Wall Street"
>
> **site design:** 8
>
> **user-friendly:** 7
>
> **options usefulness:** 5
>
> **general comments:** Watley Trader (basic online service) and Ultimate Trader (premium software-based service) offer direct-access trading to the equity and options markets. AB Watley also offers foreign exchange, currency options, futures, physical commodities, mutual funds, and fixed-income products. Research, charts, and NADSAQ Level II quotes also available.
>
> **option commission:** $9.95 plus $1.50 per contract
>
> **stock commission:** Varies based on trading platform and trading activity. Check web site for accurate quotes.

Charles Schwab Online

web site: schwabat.com

address: 101 Montgomery Street, San Francisco, CA 94104

toll-free: 888-245-6864

e-mail: Located on the web site

category: Full-service discount brokerage

slogan: "Schwab gives Active Traders an edge in today's markets."

site design: 8

user-friendly: 7

options usefulness: 8

general comments: As the number one online brokerage, Charles Schwab has the lion's share of clients and boasts more than 450 offices nationwide. Schwab has it all: stock, stock options, mutual funds, bonds, Treasuries, stock screening, and portfolio management. It offers an extensive line of products and services that help options traders to compete in the marketplace. Commissions tend to run a little high but that hasn't stopped it from becoming one of the biggest brokers around.

option commission: $9.95 plus $.95 a contract (for 30 more trades per month)

stock commission: $9.95 (for 30 more trades per month)

ChoiceTrade

web site: choicetrade.com

address: 197 State Route 18, Suite 3000, East Brunswick, NJ 08816

toll-free: 877-731-9114

e-mail: Located on the web site

category: Online discount brokerage

slogan: "Trade Up"

site design: 8

user-friendly: 8

options usefulness: 8

general comments: ChoiceTrade is a good choice for frequent options traders looking for advanced tools and low commissions. Headquartered in New Jersey, the online brokerage firm offers stock and options trading using state-of-the-art trading platforms along with deeply discounted commissions. The firm offers several trading platforms designed for active traders. The commissions are low by industry standards. The tools have been upgraded and this firm is becoming one of the better choices for online options traders.

option commission: Online orders for 1 to 20 contracts are $0.99 per contract ($8.95 minimum—no trade fee). Online orders of 21 or more contracts are only $.75 per contract.

stock commission: $5.00 for online trades.

eOption

web site: eoption.com

address: 950 Milwaukee Avenue, Suite 101, Glenview, IL 60025

toll -free: 888-793-5333

e-mail: support@eOption.com

category: Full-service discount brokerage

slogan: "Exercise Your Option to Save"

site design: 7

user-friendly: 8

options usefulness: 7

general comments: Supported by over 30 years of options experience, eOption was established in 2007 as a division of Regal Securities, Inc., member FINRA/SIPC, a Chicago area broker/dealer since 1975. eOption offers execution capabilities on all major exchanges, simple order entry, and ultra low per contract prices. For options traders, eOption simplified the process of complex order entry with tools like strategy scanners and one-click closeout of multileg orders. A web-based platform allows traders to trade up to four legs from a single screen and displays a real-time quote on each leg of the order, as well as on the overall strategy. Direct-access trading and multiple platforms for active traders are also available.

option commission: $5.00 plus $.25 per contract.

stock commission: $5.00 unlimited shares

E*Trade

web site: etrade.com

address: 135 E. 57th Street, New York, NY 10022

phone: 678-624-6210

toll-free: 800-ETRADE-1

e-mail: tellmemore@etrade.com

category: Middle-cost discount brokerage

slogan: "E*Trade for Options"

site design: 8

user-friendly: 8

options usefulness: 8

general comments: E*Trade Financial is a powerhouse in the online financial services industry. E*Trade offers a variety of investment products along with a combination of low commissions and advanced trading tools for investors and traders. For options traders, E*Trade offers a comprehensive suite of tools and research including strategy chains that allow you to place simple and complex trades with one click. Real-time options analytics show implied volatilities, skew charts, theoretical values, and the greeks. For advanced options traders E*Trade offers free options Level II data, advanced options charting, direct order routing to exchanges, and integrated options trading in Excel Manager.

option commission: $6.99 to $12.99 or more per contract

stock commission: $6.99 to $12.99

Fidelity Investments

web site: fidelity.com

address: P.O. Box 770001, Cincinnati, OH 45277-0001

toll-free: 800-343-3548/800-FIDELITY

e-mail: sent via web site

category: High-cost discount brokerage

site design: 7

user-friendly: 5

options usefulness: 5

general comments: Fidelity Investments is an international provider of financial and investment services to individuals and institutions. Once known mostly for its family of mutual fund companies, Fidelity has evolved into a full-service brokerage firm with an online operation called Fidelity.com. In addition to more than 300 Fidelity mutual funds, Fidelity now offers discount brokerage, retirement planning, fixed-income trading, a tax center, money management, and life insurance. For options traders, offers OptionTrader ProSM, a Windows-based software application that provides streaming pricing, directed trading, Greeks, and some analytics. It is available for active traders (20 contracts per month).

option commission: Average is $10.95 plus $.75 a contract, but can be more or less depending on amount of trading activity.

stock commission: Average is $10.95, but can be more or less depending on amount of trading activity.

Firstrade

web site: firstrade.com

address: 133-25 37th Avenue, Flushing, NY 11354

phone: 718-961-6600

toll-free: 800-869-8800

e-mail: service@firstrade.net

category: Discount online brokerage

slogan: "Born to Invest."

site design: 6

user-friendly: 8

options usefulness: 6

general comments: FirstTrade offers cheap and easy to understand commissions. The firm charges just $6.95 for both stock and options trades. For options, add $.75 per contract, with no minimums. The firm has been around since 1985 and "continues to thrive on Low Costs, and High Standards," according to its web site. For options traders, the tools aren't all there yet. However, the firm does offer the ability to trade spreads and straddles online. It also received the "Best Deal among online discount brokerages" from *SmartMoney* in 2005. It also offers more than 10,000 different types of mutual funds and was *Kiplinger's* "Clear winner in mutual funds category" in 2006.

option commission: $6.95 plus $.75 a contract

stock commission: $6.95

Freedom Investments

web site: Freedominvestments.com

address: 375 Raritan Center Parkway, Edison, NJ 08837

toll-free: 800-944-4033

e-mail: support@freedominvestments.com

category: Middle-cost discount brokerage

site design: 4

user-friendly: 6

options usefulness: 4

general comments: Founded in 1994, this brokerage is small enough to be reliable and clients appear happy with executions and service. Option trading is not their main focus, but they do have a variety of services for active stock traders. The stock commissions are reasonable at $15 flat fee. However, the options commissions haven't changed since our first book and give the firm a serious competitive disadvantage.

option commission: $40 plus $2 per contract

stock commission: $15 flat fee.

Frontier

web site: ffutures.com

address: 4000 River Ridge Drive NE, Cedar Rapids, IA 52402

toll-free: 800-777-2438

e-mail: request@ffutures.com

category: Stocks/futures brokerage

site design: 3

user-friendly: 6

options usefulness: 3

general comments: Frontier is a no-nonsense broker, with an uninteresting web site, but a lot of experience in futures and options trading. This firm is probably not the ideal firm for most individual online options traders, but it might be worth a look if you need good execution and experience in handling larger volumes.

option commission: Based on number of round turns per month. Average is around $20 per contract. Check web site for details.

stock commission: NA

Interactive Brokers

web site: interactivebrokers.com

address: One Pickwick Plaza, Greenwich, CT 06830

toll-free: 877-442-2757

phone: 312-542-6901

e-mail: service@InteractiveBrokers.com

category: Direct access broker

slogan: "The Professional's Gateway to the World's Markets."

site design: 8

user-friendly: 8

options usefulness: 9

general comments: Interactive Brokers is one of the most widely used online firms by active stock and futures traders around the world. It has offices in Chicago, Switzerland, Montreal, Hong Kong, London, Sydney, and India. It is the best firm for traders who are looking for tools and capabilities to trade multiple financial markets in one location. It is also well suited for active do-it-yourself traders who want a one-stop shop for direct-access trading in multiple financial markets at deep-discounted commission rates. Futures traders give IB high scores. Active options traders also find value in the firm's advanced direct-access trading platform. The commissions are hard to beat.

option commission: $.50 to $.70 a contract (see web site for breakdown)

stock commission: $.005 or less per share

InternetTrading.Com

web site: internettrading.com

address: 100 Bush Street, 10th Floor, San Francisco, CA 94104

toll-free: 800-696-2811

fax: 415-362-0671

e-mail: info@internettrading.com

category: Middle-cost discount brokerage

site design: 4

user-friendly: 6

options usefulness: 5

general comments: InternetTrading.com is a brokerage firm with history going back to 1959. In addition to trading, the firm offers research, quotes, and news. Comments are very high from the few customers we spoke to, especially concerning reliability, execution, and customer service. Not a lot of perks for options traders. Commissions are high by industry standards. Web site needs an update as well.

option commission: $25 plus $2 per contract.

stock commission: $19.95 for up to 2,000 contracts; $.02 a share for over 5,000 contracts

Investrade

website: investrade.com

address: 950 Milwaukee Avenue, Suite 102, Glenview, IL 60025

phone: 847-375-6080

toll-free: 800-498-7120

e-mail: support@investrade.com

category: Deep-discount brokerage

site design: 7

user-friendly: 7

options usefulness: 7

general comments: Investrade Discount Securities is a division of Chicago area brokerage firm Regal Securities, which was founded in 1976. Investrade's division was established in 1997 and offers investors and traders online access to multiple markets, including stocks, options, and foreign exchange. The trading platform has come a long way since our first book and came just shy of being in the top 12. Investrade also offers direct-access trading, international stock trading, and options in IRA accounts.

option commission: $1.50 per contract ($14.95 minimum)

stock commission: $7.95 per trade (market orders)

MB Trading

web site: mbtrading.com

address: 1926 E. Maple Avenue, El Segundo, CA 90245

toll-free: 866-628-3001

e-mail: support@mbtrading.com

category: Direct-access broker

site design: 8

user-friendly: 6

options usefulness: 6

general comments: MB Trading is another firm that almost made it into our top 12 list. The firm offers direct access to a variety of different markets including equities, futures, and options. The commissions are very compelling and the web site is well designed. The trading platform is slick. However, for strategists, it doesn't provide all of the advanced options tools that many other firms now offer.

option commission: $1.00 per contract

stock commission: $4.95 per trade or $1.00 for 100 shares

Newedge USA

web site: www.preferredtrade.com

address: 220 Bush Street, Suite 650, San Francisco, CA 94104

phone: 415-781-0205

toll-free: 888-781-0283

fax: 415-520-5633

e-mail: Service@NewedgeGroup.com

category: Online discount brokerage

slogan: "The Preferred Way to Trade Options and Stocks!"

site design: 7

user-friendly: 7

options usefulness: 8

general comments: Newedge USA caters to active option and stock traders. The web-based software offers an easy-to-use platform with fast execution speed for retail orders and large block orders for institutions. For options traders, the system allows the easy entry of single orders as well as some advanced options strategy orders from a single screen.

option commission: $.95 per contract with a $9.95 minimum per order.

stock commission: $.0095 per share with a $9.95 minimum per order; $9.95 flat fee for NASDAQ stocks.

NobleTrading

web site: nobletrading.com

address: 50 Broad Street #408, 4th Floor, New York, NY 10004

toll-free: 877-TRADE-11

e-mail: info@nobletrading.com

category: Stock, futures, and options discount brokerage

site design: 8

user-friendly: 6

options usefulness: 5

general comments: Headquartered in New York, Noble Trading offers online trading of stocks, forex, options, commodities, and futures. It offers flexible commission plans and different platforms based on traders' needs. The web site was recently revamped and easy and straightforward to navigate. The platform is a good one for active futures and day traders. The commissions are also low by industry standards. For options strategists, however, the platforms don't provide the advanced order entry tools that several of the other firms now offer.

option commission: $7.95 plus $1.00 a contract

stock commission: $7.95 (Also offers per share plan and name-your-price plans. Details available on web site.)

OptionsHouse

web site: optionshouse.com

address: 303 E. Wacker Drive, Suite 700, Chicago IL 60601

toll-free: 877-653-2500

direct: 312-676-8801

e-mail: customerservice@optionshouse.com

category: Online discount brokerage

slogan: "Flat Fees. Sharp Tools"

site design: 9

user-friendly: 9

options usefulness: 9

general comments: OptionsHouse is one of the newer players on the options trading scene. Developed with institutional options market-making firm Peak6 Investments, LP, the OptionsHouse site was created using web technology so traders don't need to flip from page to page to execute a trade. It's all in one place.

option commission: $9.95

stock commission: $4.95

OptionsXpress

web site: optionsxpress.com

address: 311 W. Monroe Street, Suite 1000, Chicago, IL 60606

toll-free: 888-280-8020

direct: 312-629-5455

e-mail: info@optionsxpress.com

category: Low-cost online options brokerage

slogan: "Online Options, Stock & Futures Brokers."

site design: 10

user-friendly: 9

options usefulness: 10

general comments: For options traders, OptionsXpress stands out above the rest. As the firm's name implies, it is an options trading specialist and continues to develop new products and tools with the options community in mind. David Kalt, James Gray, and Ned Bennett came together to form optionsXpress in late 1999, pouring their 30 years of option industry experience into the firm. The firm is publicly traded and its shares trade under the symbol OXPS.

option commission: $1.50 per contract for 10 or more contracts, or $14.95 minimum per trade (examples: 5 contracts = $14.95, 10 = $15, 20 = $30)

stock commission: $14.95 up to 1,001 shares; $.015 per share @ 1,001 shares and above.

RF Lafferty

web site: laffertyny.com

address: 80 Broad Street, 26th Floor, New York, NY 10004

toll-free: 800-221-8601

e-mail: rob@laffertyny.com

category: Institutional brokerage

site design: 3

user-friendly: 4

options usefulness: 6

general comments: RF Lafferty is a brokerage firm with over 60 years experience and located in the heart of the financial district in Manhattan. The firm handles business for both institutional and individual investors. It also offers online trading access, including the ability to enter some complex options strategies online. However, that's not the firm's primary focus. Instead, the firm focuses on off-line execution services for professional traders and brokers. It is also involved in cash management, research, financial advising, and investment banking.

option commission: NA

stock commission: NA

Scottrade

web site: scottrade.com

address: 12855 Flushing Meadows Drive, St. Louis, MO 63131

toll-free: 800-619-SAVE

e-mail: support@scottrade.com

category: Deep-discount brokerage

site design: 6

user-friendly: 6

options usefulness: 2

general comments: Scottrade is a sizeable broker with a large client base. It is a deep-discount broker with very low commission rates on equity orders and average fees for options traders. ScotTrade offers three trading platforms based on the trader's level of trading activity. The ScotTrade Elite is most suitable for active stock traders. For active options trader, however, the firm doesn't offer much beyond relatively low commissions. It doesn't rank very well for that reason.

option commission: $7.00 plus $1.25 per contract

stock commission: $7.00

ShareBuilder

web site: sharebuilder.com

address: 1445 120th Avenue NE, Bellevue, WA 98005

toll-free: 866-747-2537

e-mail: Accessed through the web site

category: High-cost discount broker

site design: 8

user-friendly: 7

options usefulness: 5

general comments: ShareBuilder is a relatively new online broker that offers a variety of brokerage services with the smaller investor in mind, including automatic investing, real-time trading, options trading, and margin borrowing. The commissions are straightforward and within the industry average. The web site is well designed, but the trading and options tools for the strategist are still missing. Instead, the focus is on longer-term investing approaches like dollar cost averaging, stock ownership, and diversification.

option commission: $9.95 plus $1.00 per contract

stock commission: $9.95 per online trade

Siebert.net

web site: siebertnet.com

address: 111 Town Square Place, Suite 310, Jersey City, NJ 07310

toll-free: 800-872-0711

e-mail: Access available on web site

category: Middle-cost discount brokerage

site design: 7

user-friendly: 5

options usefulness: 2

general comments: This brokerage went online early in 1996 and has had more time than most to develop its infrastructure. Its online services have garnered more than a few kudos from *Barron's* and *Kiplinger's*. Although its live broker rates are a little pricey, it is rated as a middle-cost discount online brokerage. It has a reputation for excellent customer service and prompt executions. However, the commissions on options trades are steep and it has made very little effort to appeal to the active options trader.

option commission: $34 plus, depending on the number of contracts and the option's premium

stock commission: $14.95 per trade for up to 1,000 equity shares

SpeedTrader.com

web site: speedtrader.com

address: 1717 Route 6, Suite 101, Carmel, NY 10512

toll-free: 800-874-3039

e-mail: Access available on web site

category: Deep-discount brokerage

site design: 4

user-friendly: 5

options usefulness: 3

general comments: SpeedTrader.com is a division of Stock USA, a Carmel, New York–based institutional broker-dealer. The online broker offers trading in stocks, options, futures, and foreign exchange. Commissions are relatively cheap for very active traders, which is the group of investors the firm seems to target. Beyond that, Speedtrader.com doesn't offer options traders much to work with. Its platform is average and the firm has made very few efforts to appeal to the average online options trader.

option commission: $9.95 per ticket plus $1.25 per contract

stock commission: $2.95 per trade @ 1,500 or more trades per month

TD Ameritrade

web site: tdameritrade.com

address: P.O. Box 2760, Omaha NE 68103

toll-free: 800-454-9272

e-mail: starting@ameritrade.com

category: Full-service online brokerage

slogan: "Independence is the Spirit that drives America's most successful investors."

site design: 9

user-friendly: 8

options usefulness: 7

general comments: TD Ameritrade is one of the largest online brokerages offering a wide array of investment products, tools, and services, including a leading active-trader program, long-term investment solutions, and a national branch system, as well as relationships with one of the largest independent RIA networks. The firm offers both browser and software-based trading platforms and has been listed by *Forbes* as one of America's best big companies. The firm's options trading capabilities have been upgraded, but the commissions remain relatively high by industry standards. It is a great firm for an investor looking for a host of different financial products, including options. However, for butterfly and condor traders, the relatively high commission schedule makes TD Ameritrade an expensive online broker.

option commission: Online options trades are $9.99 plus $0.75 per contract.

stock commission: $9.99 for Internet trades with no share limits

ThinkorSwim

web site: thinkorswim.com

address: 3304 N. Lincoln Avenue, Chicago, IL 60657

toll-free: 866-839-1100

e-mail: support@thinkorswim.com

category: Discount options broker

slogan: "Join the Revolution."

site design: 8

user-friendly: 7

options usefulness: 9

general comments: ThinkorSwim's software-based platform stands out from the rest. For options traders, it offers a wide array of tools ranging from real-time quotes to the ability to create payoff charts with live data. The order entry tool is very slick and these guys really understand options. All around, this is a great firm and many of the traders we talk to agree. The company also offers stock and forex trading, relatively low commissions, and "Paper Money," a real-time trading platform for entering hypothetical trades.

option commission: The lesser of $2.95 per contract *or* $1.50 per contract plus $9.95

stock commission: $.015 per share with $5.00 minimum

TradeKing

web site: tradeking.com

address: P.O. Box 811690, Boca Raton, FL 33481-1690

toll-free: 877-495-5464

e-mail: service@tradeking.com

category: Online discount broker

slogan: "An Online Options and Stock Broker. Power to the Individual Investor."

site design: 9

user-friendly: 9

options usefulness: 9

general comments: TradeKing is a straightforward, no-nonsense online broker. The browser-based trading platform is easy to use and the firm offers a variety of tools and information to help make the decision-making process easier. The commissions on stocks and options orders are among the lowest in the business, and *SmartMoney* and *Barron's* have consistently given the firm top ratings for its tools and customer service. These are the main reasons many traders are turning to TradeKing.

option commission: $4.95 per trade plus $.65 a contract.

stock commission: $4.95

Trading Direct

web site: tradingdirect.com

address: 160 Broadway, New York, NY 10038

toll-free: 800-925-8566

e-mail: info@tradingdirect.com

category: Deep-discount broker

slogan: "Experience is the Difference."

site design: 8

user-friendly: 7

options usefulness: 3

general comments: Trading Direct has a slick web site and relatively low commissions. The firm executes orders on equities, options, mutual funds, and bonds. Outside of that and some free quotes and retirement planning services, Trading Direct doesn't offer much more for the active options trader.

option commission: $9.95 plus $1.00 a contract

stock commission: $9.95

WallStreet*E

web site: wallstreete.com

address: 5900 S.W. 41st Street, Miami, FL 33155

toll-free: 888-925-5783

e-mail: info@wallstreete.com

category: Online stock and options brokerage

slogan: "WallStreetE. . . where MONEY meets TECHNOLOGY"

site design: 8

user-friendly: 8

options usefulness: 7

general comments: WallStreet*E offers a wide array of services including traditional banking services, insurance, long-term investments, and trading of both stocks and options. The firm is best suited for those investors looking for a variety of solutions to longer-term financial planning needs and also tools and research necessary to trade various options strategies.

option commission: $25 plus $2.50 per contract

stock commission: NASDAQ OTC market orders are $14.95 per trade ($.02 per share above 1,000 shares). All other orders, NYSE listed, limit, stop, and GTC are $19.95 per trade plus $.02 per share plus frequent trader bonuses.

Wyse Securities

web site: wyse-sec.com

address: 20735 Stevens Creek Boulevard, Suite C, Cupertino, CA 95014

toll-free: 800-640-8668

e-mail: office@wyse-sec.com

category: Middle-cost discount brokerage

slogan: "A Professional Discount Broker You Can Trust"

site design: 8

user-friendly: 5

options usefulness: 4

general comments: We like the design of this site, but it lacks many of the amenities that options traders really need. Comments reflect reliability and good executions. In addition, the commissions are straightforward and midrange by industry standards. Wyse Securities also offers extended-hours trading, news and research, free IRA accounts, and cash management services.

option commission: $7.95 plus $.95 per contract (minimum $17.50)

stock commission: $9.95

Zecco

web site: zecco.com

address: P.O. Box 60126, Pasadena, CA 91116, USA

toll-free: 877-700-STOCK

e-mail: customerservice@zeccotrading.com

category: Middle-cost discount brokerage

slogan: "$0 Stock Trades"

site design: 9

user-friendly: 8

options usefulness: 5

general comments: Zecco is an innovative broker that came bursting to the scene with promises of unlimited free stock trades. The free trading has since been reduced to

10 free trades a month with accounts over $2,500 in equity. Nevertheless, the commissions remain cheap by industry standards. In addition, Zecco has developed a vibrant web community that includes participation from thousands of members. The firm also offers mutual funds, retirement planning services, tax planning, and performance tracking. Zecco offers a modest amount of options analytics, but not all of the tools most options strategists are looking for. Stay tuned, though, because the trading platform is still under development.

option commission: $4.50 plus $.50 a contract

stock commission: First 10 trades each month free, then $4.50 thereafter

index

ABC News.com, 404
AB Watley, 430
Accumulation/distribution (A/D) rating, 40, 375
Acronyms, market, 358–360
Adamsoptions.blogspot.com, 70
Adjustments, 103–104
Advance-decline line, 383
Advisory web sites, 70, 422–423
All American Brokers, 282
Alpha-beta trend channel, 383
Alpha coefficient, 383
American Association of Individual Investors, 59, 69, 411
American Stock Exchange (AMEX):
  exchange-traded funds traded on, 53–54
  Market Value Index, 51
  options trading on, 7, 15–17
  order execution through, 325
  structure and function of, 87–88
  web site of, 70, 266, 420
American-style options, 102–103
AMEX Market Value Index, 51
Analysis:
  of brokerage firms, 6, 9–10, 284–288, 320–321
  correlation, 276–277
  fundamental, 36–39, 68–69, 255, 257, 375–382
  of individual stocks, 34–50
  of investment information, 63–75
  of market, 32–34, 51–60

of options, 72–74, 267–268, 277
  sentiment, 392
  technical (*see* Technical analysis)
  of trading decisions, 3, 9–10
Andrews method, 383
Annual earnings change, 376
Appel, Gerald, 268
Apple Computer, 34–35, 38, 45–46, 184–186
Arbitrage players (arbitrageurs), 224–225
Archipelago, 15
Arms ease of movement, 384
Ask, 98–99, 121–122, 324–325
Ask Research, 413
Assets, underlying. *See* Underlying assets/underlying securities
Assignment, 125, 201–202, 327–328
Associated Press, 68
At-the-money options, 95–97, 137, 154–155
Auto-exercise, 100
Auto-trading, 65
Average directional index, 384
Avid Trader, 70, 422

Bank failures, 85–86
Barchart.com, 413
Bar charts, 42–43, 234–236, 238, 273, 275
Barron's, 19, 295, 417–418
BBC News/Business, 404
Bear call spreads, 148–151, 366
Bearish market:
  bear call spreads in, 148–151, 366
  bear put spreads in, 141–144, 366
  broad market analysis reflecting, 51–60

Bearish market (*Continued*)
    call options in, 92, 125, 127, 148–151,
        174–177, 366, 370
    definition of, 35
    put options in, 93, 128, 187–190, 371
    put ratio backspreads in, 187–190, 371
    ratio call spreads in, 174–177, 370
    short stocks in, 117, 120, 363
    strategies based on, 83, 250–252, 353,
        361–362
    vertical spreads in, 136
Bear put spreads, 141–144, 366
Bear Stearns, 85
Being Right or Making Money (Davis), 268
Bennett, Ned, 293
Bernanke, Ben, 57, 65
Beta coefficient, 376, 384
Beta version software, 76
Bias, 173–174
Bid, 98–99, 121–122, 324–325
Bid-ask spread, 99, 121–122, 324–325
BigCharts, 50, 69, 73, 235, 413
Blogs, 70
Bloomberg, 68, 262, 404
Blue-chip stocks, 84–85
BMIquotes.com, 399–400
Bollinger bands, 384
Bonds, 55–57, 352
Boston Options Exchange (BOX), 7, 15–17,
    325
Box, G. E. P., 384
Box-Jenkins linear least squares, 384
Breadth-of-market theory, 384
Breakdown, 385
Breakeven:
    of bear call spreads, 150–151, 366
    of bear put spreads, 143, 366
    of bull call spreads, 138–140, 365
    of bull put spreads, 146–147, 365
    of calendar spreads, 202, 373
    of call ratio backspreads, 185, 370–371
    of covered call strategy, 196, 368
    of diagonal spreads, 205, 373
    of long butterfly spreads, 208–209, 371–372
    of long call options, 122
    of long condor strategy, 211, 372
    of long iron butterfly strategy, 214–215,
        372
    of long put options, 129
    on long stock trades, 116
    of long straddle strategy, 160–161,
        366–367, 369
    of long strangle strategy, 166–167, 367
    of put ratio backspreads, 187–190, 371
    of ratio call spreads, 176, 370
    of ratio put spreads, 179–180, 370
    risk profiles graphing (*see* Risk profiles)
    of short call options, 126
    of short put options, 131
    on short stock trades, 120
    of short straddle strategy, 162–165, 367
    of short strangle strategy, 168–171, 368
Breaking news, 244–245
Breakout, 385
Briefing.com, 263, 408
Broad market analysis, 32–34, 51–60
Brokerage firms:
    analysis of (selection of), 6, 9–10, 284–288,
        320–321
    auto-exercising by, 100
    commission fees of, 8–9, 19, 281, 285–286,
        324, 341
    on covered call strategy, 194
    customer service of, 287
    deep-discount, 9
    direct access, 18
    discount, 9
    failing of, 86, 331–336
    full-service, 9, 282
    futures accounts with, 220
    information from, 9, 19, 26, 287
    live *versus* online brokers, 320–321
    loans from (margin impacted by), 285,
        341–342
    online (*see* Online brokerage firms)
    order execution by, 286, 323–326
    quote services from, 26, 287
    role in exercising options, 326, 328
    specializing in options trading, 282–285,
        325–326
    trading levels authorized by, 342–344
    trading software from, 247
    virtual trading by, 254
Buffett, Warren, 65
Bull call spreads, 137–141, 257, 258–261, 365
Bullish market:
    broad market analysis reflecting, 51–60
    bull call spreads in, 137–141, 257–261, 365
    bull put spreads in, 145–148, 257, 365
    call options in, 92, 124, 137–141, 183–187,
        257–261, 365, 370–371
    call ratio backspreads in, 183–187,
        370–371
    definition of, 35
    put options in, 93, 131–133, 145–148,
        178–181, 257, 365, 370
    ratio put spreads in, 178–181, 370
    strategies based on, 83, 250–252, 353,
        361–362
    vertical spreads in, 136
Bull put spreads, 145–148, 257, 365
Businesses. *See* Companies
BusinessWeek, 69, 404
Butterfly spread, 107, 206–210, 213–217,
    253–254, 331, 334–335, 371–372
Buy write. *See* Covered call strategy

Calendar spreads, 200–203, 373
Call options. *See also* Long call options;
    Short call options
  bear call spreads using, 148–151, 366
  in bearish market, 92, 125, 127, 148–151,
    174–177, 366, 370
  bull call spreads using, 137–141, 257–261,
    365
  calendar spreads using, 200–203, 373
  call ratio backspreads using, 183–187,
    370–371
  collar strategy using, 106, 198–200, 374
  covered call strategy using, 126–127,
    194–197, 343–344, 368
  definition of, 92
  diagonal spreads using, 203–206, 373
  exercising, 99–103, 125, 201–202, 326–328
  fundamentals of, 15, 91–93
  intrinsic value of, 96
  long butterfly spreads using, 206–210,
    371–372
  long condor strategy using, 210–213, 372
  long iron butterfly strategy using, 213–217,
    372
  long straddle strategy using, 159–162,
    366–367
  long strangle strategy using, 166–168, 367
  methods of using, 15
  moneyness and, 95–97
  offsetting, 99–100, 221, 327–328
  option premiums of, 92, 121–124
  put-call ratios using, 392
  ratio call spreads using, 174–177, 370
  risk profile of, 112–114
  settlement of, 101–103
  short straddle strategy using, 162–166,
    367
  short strangle strategy using, 168–171, 368
Call ratio backspreads, 183–187, 370–371
Candlestick charts, 42, 44, 46, 235–238, 385
Capital gains, 85, 118
Capital investment, 20, 83
Carrying costs, 219, 223–226
Cash flow, free, 255
Cash settlements, 101–103
Cash trades, 341
CBOE. *See* Chicago Board Options Exchange
    (CBOE)
CBOT (Chicago Board of Trade), 220, 420
Centrex, 423–424
CFTC (Commodity Futures Trading
    Commission), 220
Charles Schwab, 282, 289, 311–313, 431
Charts:
  bar, 42–43, 234–236, 238, 273, 275
  candlestick, 42, 44, 46, 235–238, 385
  Kagi, 387
  line, 42, 238, 269–272

  options analysis using, 267–268
  point and figure, 238, 390
  of risk-reward ratio (*see* Risk profiles)
  of sideways markets, 194
  swing, 391
  as technical indicator, 41–50, 194, 234–244,
    267–273, 275, 385, 387, 390–391
  tick, 238
Chat rooms, 79
Chicago Board of Trade (CBOT), 220, 420
Chicago Board Options Exchange (CBOE):
  option analysis by, 73
  options trading on, 7, 15–17
  order execution through, 325
  put-call ratios by, 59
  system outages at, 336
  Volatility Index of, 392
  web site of, 70, 420
Chicago Mercantile Exchange (CME), 220
Chips (computer), 22
Chi-squared, 385
ChoiceTrade, 289, 309–311, 431–432
Class of options, 90
Clearing margins, 222
Clearing member accounts, 328
ClearStation, 413
Closing price, net change, 376
CME (Chicago Mercantile Exchange), 220
CNBC, 263, 404–405
CNET News, 408
CNN Money, 245, 401, 406
Coca-Cola, 38
Codes (ticker symbol), 283, 349–350
Collar strategy, 106, 198–200, 374
Commission fees:
  of online brokerage firms, 8–9, 19, 281,
    285–286, 324, 341
  on options trades, 325
  on short stock trades, 120
Committee on Options Proposals (COOP),
    415
Commodities, 219–221, 223–230. *See also*
    Futures market
Commodity Futures Trading Commission
    (CFTC), 220
Common stock, 85–86
Companies:
  earnings of (*see* Earnings)
  exchange selection by, 88
  fundamental analysis of, 36–39, 68–69, 255,
    257, 375–382
  health of, impacting stock prices, 36–39, 84
  management changes in, 378
  quick ratio assessment of, 380
  size of, 84–85
  stocks of (*see* Stocks)
Competition, 36
Compliance departments, 343

Computers. *See also* Internet
  beta version software on, 76
  Internet browsers on, 25
  Internet service providers for, 4, 24–25
  purchasing appropriate, 21–24
  systems failures, 331–336
  trading software on, 75–78, 216–217,
    247–249, 257, 393–397
Confidence index, 392
Consumer price index (CPI), 58
Contingent orders, 331
Contrarian approach, 49–50, 58–59, 392
COOP (Committee on Options Proposals),
  415
Corporations. *See* Companies
Correlation analysis, 276–277
Costs. *See also* Prices
  carrying, 219, 223–226
  of computers, 22
  of data providers, 26
  of online trading (*see* Commission fees)
  of options (*see* Option premium)
CoveredCall.com, 415–416
Covered call strategy, 126–127, 194–197,
  343–344, 368
Covered put strategy, 368–369
Covering the short, 117
CPI (consumer price index), 58
Cramer, Jim, 407, 423
Credit spreads:
  bear call spreads as, 148–151, 366
  bull put spreads as, 145–148, 257, 365
  definition of, 136
  order entry format for, 331–332
Cup and handle, 385
Currency, 81–82, 191, 222, 352
Customer margins, 222
Customer service, 287
CyberInvest.com, 67, 400
Cyclical stocks, 86

Daily Graphs Online, 40, 69, 414
Daily Stocks.com, 400
Data providers, 25–28
Davis, Ned, 268
Day trader (definition), 235
Debit spreads:
  bear put spreads as, 141–144, 366
  bull call spreads as, 137–141, 257, 258–261,
    365
  definition of, 136
  order entry format for, 331–332
Deep-discount brokerage firms, 9
Delayed (delayed-time) quotes, 10, 25–28, 75,
  287
Delivery notice, 228
Dell Computer, 249
Delta, 154, 184, 350

Delta neutral trading:
  fundamentals of, 153–156
  long straddle as, 159–162, 331, 333,
    366–367, 369
  long strangle as, 166–168, 331, 333, 367
  short straddle as, 162–166, 331, 333, 367
  short strangle, 168–171, 331, 333, 368
Demand and supply. *See* Supply and demand
Designated order turnaround, 324
Desktop computers, 21–22. *See also*
  Computers
DIA (Dow Jones Industrial Average Index -
  "diamonds"), 54, 267
Diagonal spreads, 203–206, 373
Direct access brokerage firms, 18
Directional movement index, 385
Direct Stock Market, 424
Discount brokerage firms, 9
Discounting mechanism, 34
Discount rate, 55
Dividends, 86, 91, 118, 201–202, 376
Dividend yield, 376
DJIA (Dow Jones Industrial Average), 20,
  51–52, 54, 86
Dollar. *See* Currency
Dow, Charles, 51
Dow Jones Industrial Average (DJIA), 20,
  51–52, 54, 86
Dow Jones Industrial Average Index (DIA;
  "diamonds"), 54, 267
Dow Jones Industrial Index, 20, 267
Dow Jones (web site), 267, 408
Dr. Ed Yardeni's Economics Network, 411
DTN.IQ, 424
Dun & Bradstreet, 408

Earnings:
  annual earnings change, 376
  earnings per share rank, 376–377
  earnings per share value, 38, 376, 380
  exchange selection based on, 88
  growth of, 38–39, 255, 257, 376
  interest rate impact on, 56
  momentum, 255
  net, 379
  price-earnings (P/E) ratio, 38–39, 379–380
  prices-to-earnings growth rate formula
    (PEG), 39
  quarterly earnings per share percent
    change, 380
  reports on, 84, 245
Earningswhisper.com, 258
eBroker, 282
e-commerce, 13–14
Economist, The, 418
Economy, 51, 54–60, 85–86
EDGAR-Online, 400
Educational web sites, 69, 247, 411–413

Edwards, Robert D., 50
Elder, Alexander, 50
Elliot Wave International, 422
Elliot Wave theory, 257, 259, 385
e-mail newsletters, 71–72
Emotions. *See* Psychological market
   indicators
Employment report, 58
End-of-day quotes, 25, 27
Energy markets, 226
eOption, 289, 316–317, 432–433
Equis.com, 414
eSignal, 75
E*Trade Financial, 282, 289, 301–303, 334,
   400, 433
Eurex, 15
Euronext, 421
European-style options, 102–103
Exchanges:
   commodity, 220
   definition of, 87
   exchange-traded funds traded on, 53–54
   futures, 220, 222–223
   indexes tracking movement of, 51–53
   involvement in COOP, 415
   multiple, 18, 325–326
   options analysis by, 73
   options trading on, 7–8, 14–18, 59, 325,
     336, 415
   order execution through, 324–326
   put-call ratios by, 59
   structure and function of, 87–88
   system outages at, 336
   web sites of, 70, 263, 420–422
Exchange-traded funds (ETFs):
   fundamentals of, 53–54
   hedging strategies using, 266–267, 274,
     276–277
   popular, 358
   settlement of, 101–102
   short straddle strategy using, 163
Excite, 427–428
Exercise settlement amount, 102
Exercise settlement value, 102
Exercising options, 99–103, 125, 131,
   201–202, 326–328
Exit plans, 20, 137
Expiration date:
   in bear call spreads, 148–151
   in bear put spreads, 141–144
   in bull call spreads, 137–141
   in bull put spreads, 145–148
   of call options, 91–93, 122, 125–126
   in call ratio backspreads, 183–187
   cash settlement by, 101–103
   codes for, 349
   in covered call strategy, 196
   definition of, 122

exercising by, 99–100, 326–328
of futures contracts, 220–221, 223–226
intrinsic value impacted by, 97
in long butterfly spreads, 206–210
of long call options, 122
in long condor strategy, 210–213
in long iron butterfly strategy, 213–217
of long put options, 128–130
in long straddle strategy, 159–162
in long strangle strategy, 166–168
offsetting by, 99–100
of options contracts, 89–95, 122, 125–126,
   128–133
of put options, 93–95, 128–133
in ratio call spreads, 174–177
in ratio put spreads, 178–181
of short call options, 125–126
of short put options, 131–133
in short straddle strategy, 162–166
in short strangle strategy, 168–171
in vertical spreads, 135–137
Exponential moving averages, 270–275,
   385–386
Extrinsic value, 97

Fair value, 157
Fannie Mae, 85
Fear gauge, 392
Federal funds rate, 55
Federal Open Market Committee (FOMC),
   55
Federal Reserve System, 54–55, 57, 191
Fibonacci ratios and retracements
   (Fibonacci, Leonardo), 386
Fidelity Investments, 433–434
52-week high and low, 377
FinanceWise, 408–409
Financial futures, 220, 221–222
Financial market. *See* Market
Financials.com, 411
Financial Times, 68
FinancialWeb, 409
Financial web sites. *See* Web sites
FINRA/SIPC, 316
First notice date, 228
Firstrade, 434–435
Float, 377
Floor brokers, 324–325
Fooled by Randomness (Taleb), 265
Forbes, 69, 304
Forecasting:
   charts assisting with, 234
   fundamental analysis for, 36–39
   individual stock assessment for, 34–50
   market analysis for, 32–34, 51–60
   psychological factors impacting, 60
   technical analysis for, 40–50
   vertical spread dependence on, 136

Foreign exchange (forex; FX) trading, 81–82, 222
Foreign Exchange Trading Education, 424
Fortune magazine, 418
Forward volatility skew, 187–190, 192
Fox Business News, 68
Freddie Mac, 85
FRED economic database, 268
Freeburg, Nelson, 268
Free cash flow, 255
Freedom Investments, 435
FreeRealtime.com, 424
Frontier, 436
Full-service brokerage firms, 9, 282
Fun and games web sites, 71, 427
Fundamental analysis, 36–39, 68–69, 255, 257, 375–382
Futures market:
    definition of, 82
    fundamentals of, 219–223
    hedgers and speculators in, 226–230
    overnight trading in, 82
    spot market *versus*, 223–226
FX (foreign exchange) trading, 81–82, 222

Gann square, 386
Gartner Dataquest, 419–420
Gentile, Tom, 39, 64, 107, 428
Getting Started in Commodities (Fontanills), 230
Global financial market, 81–82, 220, 222
Goal setting, 344–346
Gold and Silver Mining Index (XAU), 101–102, 149–151
Goldman Sachs, 267
Gold market, 223–224
Good Money, 425
Google, 71, 245, 247, 266–267, 428
Google Finance, 67
Government, 54–55, 57–58, 86, 245
Granville, Joseph, 390
Graphs. *See* Charts
Gray, James, 293
GreenJungle, 412
GreenMoney Journal, 70, 425
Gross national product, 58
Growth stock, 86, 261–264

Hard drives, 23
Hass, John, 33
Hayes, Timothy, 268
Head and shoulders, 386–387
Hedge (definition), 5
Hedgehog, 422
Hedgers, 5, 226–227
Hedging strategies, 265–279
High-low index, 378
High price yesterday/low price yesterday (hi/lo), 377–378

High-technology web sites, 419–420
Histograms, 243, 387
Historical volatility, 157–158, 267–268
Holt Stock Report, 405
Hoover's, 68, 409
Housing starts report, 58
HUBB Financial Group, 265. *See also* ProfitSource
Humphrey-Hawkins testimony, 57

IBM, 47
IClub Central, 70–71
Implied volatility, 157–158, 183–187, 248–251, 267–268
Inc. Online, 418
Income stock, 86
Indexes:
    average directional, 384
    confidence, 392
    consumer price, 58
    directional movement, 385
    exchange-traded funds tracking, 53–54, 274, 276
    high-low, 378
    market, 222
    market activity assessed through, 51–53
    mini-indexes, 20, 52
    popular, 356–357
    relative strength, 241–242, 381
    sector, 52–53
    true strength, 391
    Volatility Index, 392
Index options, 101–103
Individual investors:
    cautions for, 17–20
    experience of, 342–343
    goal setting by, 344–346
    guidelines for online trading, 63–67, 72–74
    opportunities for, 20
    in options industry, 4–7
    strategies for, 246–254
    technological advances impacting, 2–3
    technology purchases by, 21–26
    trading methodologies of, 110–111, 115, 153, 190–192
Individual stocks, 34–50, 267. *See also* Stocks
Industry trends, 87
Inflation, 55, 58
Information:
    analysis of, 63–75
    from brokerage firms, 9, 19, 26, 287
    from data providers, 25–28
    from exchanges, 16–17
    Internet as source of, 2–3, 6, 14, 18–19, 31–32, 63–75, 262–263, 321, 344
    news providing, 244–247, 261–263, 381–382
    online trading impacted by, 244–247
    overload, 6, 32
    value of, 340

Initial margins, 222
Initial public offerings (IPO), 83
INO.com, 245, 416
Insider Info, 405
Intel, 249
Interactive Brokers, 220, 289, 299–301, 436–437
Interest rates, 55–58, 91, 222, 341, 352
Intermarket relationships, 352
Intermediate trends, 41
International market, 81–82, 220, 222
International Securities Exchange (ISE), 7, 15–17, 59, 70, 325, 421
Internet. *See also* online-related entries; Web sites
  browsers to access, 25
  chat rooms on, 79
  development of, 7
  financial web sites on (*see* Web sites)
  information available on, 2–3, 6, 14, 18–19, 31–32, 63–75, 262–263, 321, 344
  online trading impacted by, 2, 13–14, 31–32
  order execution via, 324
  research using, 3, 5–6, 9–10, 68–69
  search engines on, 71, 427–428
  service providers to access, 4, 24–25
  stock charts on, 50
Internet browsers, 25
InternetNews.com, 405, 409
Internet service providers (ISP), 4, 24–25
InternetTrading.com, 437
In-the-money options, 95–97, 137, 154–155, 257
Intrinsic value, 96–97, 137
Inverted markets, 225–226
Investment FAQ, 412
Investment information. *See* Information
Investools, 400–401
Investopedia.com, 244
Investor Guide, 401
Investor Home, 425
InvestorLinks.com, 67, 401
Investors, 262. *See also* Hedgers; Momentum investors; Speculators; individual investors
Investor's Business Daily:
  data provided in, 375, 378, 381–382
  financial news provided by, 67–68
  on growth stocks, 263
  influence of, 4
  online version of, 405
  on stock price fluctuations, 115
Investors Intelligence, 59, 69
Investor Words, 425
Investrade, 437–438
IPO (initial public offerings), 83
IQ Chart, 414
ISE (International Securities Exchange), 7, 15–17, 59, 70, 325, 421

ISP (Internet service providers), 4, 24–25
iVolatility.com, 69

JagNotes, 405–406
Japanese candlestick charts, 42, 44, 46, 235–238, 385
Jenkins, G. M., 384
JPMorgan, 85

Kagi chart, 387
Kalt, David, 293
Kiplinger's, 69, 401
Kirkreport.com, 70
Kiss principle (keep it simple, stupid), 244

Lafferty (RF Lafferty), 441–442
Lagging indicators, 45, 48–49, 387
Laptop computers, 21–22. *See also* Computers
Leading indicators, 387
LEAPS (Long-term Equity Anticipation Securities), 90–91, 267, 345
Lehman Brothers, 85, 187–190
Leverage, 89, 121, 227–228, 341
Levitt, Arthur, 336
Limit order/limit prices, 286, 329, 331
Linearly weighted moving average, 387
Linear regression, 387. *See also* Regression channel techniques
Line charts, 42, 238, 269–272
Liquidity, 73, 97–99, 227
Long butterfly spreads, 206–210, 331, 334, 371–372
Long call options:
  bear call spreads using, 148–151
  bull call spreads using, 138–141
  calendar spreads using, 200–203, 373
  call ratio backspreads using, 183–187
  diagonal spreads using, 203–206, 373
  fundamentals of, 91–92
  long condor strategy using, 210–213
  long iron butterfly strategy using, 213–217
  margin on, 342
  ratio call spreads using, 175–177
  strategies for using, 121–124, 362–363
  vertical spreads using, 135–137
Long condor strategy, 210–213, 331, 335, 372
Long iron butterfly strategy, 213–217, 331, 335, 372
Long options. *See* Long call options; Long put options
Long put options:
  bear put spreads on, 142–144
  bull put spreads using, 145–148
  calendar spreads using, 200–203, 373
  diagonal spreads using, 203–206, 373
  fundamentals of, 93–94
  long condor strategy using, 210–213
  long iron butterfly strategy using, 213–217

Long put options (*Continued*)
  margin on, 130, 178, 342
  put ratio backspreads using, 187–190
  ratio put spreads using, 178–181
  strategies for using, 128–130, 364
  vertical spreads using, 135–137
Long stock, 41, 114–117, 196, 363
Long straddle, 159–162, 331, 333, 366–367, 369
Long strangle, 166–168, 331, 333, 367
Long synthetic straddle, 369
Long-term Equity Anticipation Securities (LEAPS), 90–91, 267, 345
Lycos, 71

MACD (moving average convergence/divergence), 74, 242–244, 270–273, 275, 389
Macroeconomics, 54–58
Magee, John, 50
Maintenance margins, 222
Major resistance, 387–388
Major support, 388
Major trendlines/trends, 41, 388
Management, 378
Margin:
  in futures trading, 221–223, 227–228, 230
  loans from online brokerages impacting, 285, 341–342
  on long options, 130, 178, 342
  on ratio put spreads, 178
  on short options, 341–342
  on short stock, 117–118
  of short straddle strategy, 164
Margin trades, 341–342
Market:
  acronyms, 358–360
  analysis of, 32–34, 51–60
  bearish (*see* Bearish market)
  breadth-of-market theory, 384
  bullish (*see* Bullish market)
  energy, 226
  futures, 82, 219–230
  global, 81–82, 220, 222
  gold, 223–224
  interest rate impact on, 55–58
  intermarket relationships, 352
  inverted, 225–226
  liquidity of, 73, 97–99, 227
  neutral, 83–84, 250–252, 353, 361–362 (*see also* Sideways markets)
  premarket routines, 262–263
  psychological market indicators impacting, 33, 58–59, 392
  sideways, 193–194, 216–217 (*see also* Neutral market; Sideways strategies)
  spot, 223–226

stock prices reflecting, 115
volatility of, 1–2, 19, 59–60, 153, 156–158, 161–162, 331–336
Market capitalization, 85
Market Edge, 414
Market indexes, 222
Market makers, 324–325
Market orders, 324
Market price, 157–158
Market timing process, 268–269
Market Vane, 59
MarketWatch, 67, 72, 245, 263, 406
Maximum entropy method, 388
Maximum profits:
  of bear call spreads, 150–151, 366
  of bear put spreads, 142–143, 366
  of bull call spreads, 138–139, 365
  of bull put spreads, 145, 146–147, 365
  of calendar spreads, 202, 373
  of call ratio backspreads, 185, 370–371
  of collar strategy, 199, 374
  of covered call strategy, 196, 368
  of delta neutral trades, 156
  of diagonal spreads, 205, 373
  of long butterfly spreads, 208–209, 371–372
  of long call options, 122
  of long condor strategy, 211, 372
  of long iron butterfly strategy, 214–215, 372
  of long put options, 128
  of long stock trade, 116
  of long straddle strategy, 159–161, 366–367, 369
  of long strangle strategy, 167, 367
  of put ratio backspreads, 188–189, 371
  of ratio call spreads, 174–176, 370
  of ratio put spreads, 178–181, 370
  risk profiles graphing (*see* Risk profiles)
  of short call options, 126
  of short put options, 131
  of short stock trades, 119–120
  of short straddle strategy, 162–165, 367
  of short strangle strategy, 169–170, 368
  of vertical spreads, 136
Maximum risk:
  on bear call spreads, 150–151, 366
  of bear put spreads, 142–143, 366
  of bull call spreads, 138–139, 365
  of bull put spreads, 146–147, 365
  calculating tolerance for, 346
  of calendar spreads, 202, 373
  of call ratio backspreads, 185, 370–371
  of collar strategy, 199, 374
  of covered call strategy, 196, 368
  of delta neutral trades, 156
  of diagonal spreads, 205, 373
  of long butterfly spreads, 208–209, 371–372
  of long call options, 122

of long condor strategy, 210–211, 372
of long iron butterfly strategy, 214–215, 372
of long put options, 128
of long stock trade, 116
of long straddle strategy, 159–161, 366–367, 369
of long strangle strategy, 166–167, 367
of put ratio backspreads, 188–189, 371
of ratio call spreads, 176, 370
of ratio put spreads, 179–180, 370
risk profiles graphing (*see* Risk profiles)
of short call options, 126
of short put options, 131
of short stock trades, 119–120
of short straddle strategy, 162–165, 367
of short strangle strategy, 169–170, 368
of vertical spreads, 136
Max's Investment World, 412
MB Trading, 438
McMillan, Larry, 107
Media, 4, 67–69, 244–247, 261–263, 381–382, 404–407. *See also specific media by name*
Meg (megabyte), 22
Metaquotes.com, 244
Mid-cap stocks, 84
Mini-indexes, 20, 52
Mini-NASDAQ 100 Index, 52
Minor resistance, 388
Minor support, 388
Minor trendlines/trends, 41, 388
Modems, 23–24
Momentum indicators, 388
Momentum investors, 49–50
Monetary policy, 55
Money, 55–58. *See also* Costs; Currency; Prices
Money.cnn.com, 245, 401, 406
Money flow, 378, 389
Money flow indicators, 389
MoneyMinded, 425
Moneyness, 95–97
Monitors (computer), 23
Monsanto Company, 258–261
Monthly options expirations, 90
Moody's Investment Services, 426
Morningstar, 70
Mortgage crisis, 85
Most active issue, 378
Motley Fool, 69, 402
Moving average convergence/divergence (MACD), 74, 242–244, 270–273, 275, 389
Moving averages (MA):
    charting, 45, 47–49, 240–241
    definition of, 48, 241
    exponential, 270–275, 385–386
    linearly weighted, 387

simple, 240–241, 391
    as technical indicator, 257, 389
    variable-length, 391
    weighted, 387, 391
MSNBC, 406
MSN.com, 263
MSN Money, 67, 68, 402
Multiple exchanges, 18, 325–326
Multiple listed options, 18

Naked call, 93
Naked put, 95
NASDAQ 100 Index, 52, 53–54
NASDAQ Composite Index, 51
NASDAQ Level II, 75
NASDAQ Options Market, 8
NASDAQ Stock Exchange (National Association of Securities Dealers Automated Quotations System):
    exchange-traded funds traded on, 54
    options trading on, 7–8, 15–17
    order execution through, 325
    structure and function of, 87–88
    web site of, 70, 263, 421
NASD (National Association of Securities Dealers) Regulation, 336
Natenberg, Sheldon, 107
National Futures Association (NFA), 220
Net change, 376, 378
Net earnings, 379
Netpicks, 416
Netquote, 426
Neutral market, 83–84, 250–252, 353, 361–362. *See also* Sideways markets
Newedge USA, 289, 318–320, 439
News, 244–247, 261–263, 381–382
News services/news sites, 67–68, 404–407
New Strategy of Daily Stock Market Timing (Granville), 390
New York Composite Index, 51
New York Mercantile Exchange (NYMEX), 220, 336
New York Stock Exchange (NYSE), 87–88
New York Stock Exchange (NYSE) Arca, 7, 15–17, 70, 325
New York Stock Exchange (NYSE) Euronext, 421
New York Times, 67
NFA (National Futures Association), 220
NobleTrading, 439–440
Nondirectional spreads:
    fundamentals of, 173–174
    long straddle as, 159–162, 331, 333, 366–367, 369
    ratio backspreads as, 181–190, 370–371
    ratio call spreads, 174–177, 370
    ratio put spreads, 178–181, 370
Norton high/low indicator, 389–390

Notebook computers, 21–22. *See also* Computers
Notis %V, 390
NYMEX (New York Mercantile Exchange), 220, 336
NYSE (New York Stock Exchange), 87–88
NYSE (New York Stock Exchange) Arca, 7, 15–17, 70, 325
NYSE (New York Stock Exchange) Euronext, 421

Odd lot, 379
Offsetting, 99–100, 221, 327–328
On balance volume, 270–272, 379, 390
O'Neil, William J., 4
Online brokerage firms:
    advantages of, 8–9
    analysis of (selection of), 6, 9–10, 284–288, 320–321
    auto-exercising by, 100
    commission fees of, 8–9, 19, 281, 285–286, 324, 341
    comparison of, 290–291
    on covered call strategy, 194
    customer service of, 287
    directory of, 288–320, 429–449
    failing of, 86, 331–336
    futures accounts with, 220
    information from, 9, 19, 26, 287
    live brokers *versus*, 320–321
    loans from (margins impacted by), 285, 341–342
    order entry formats of, 328–335
    order execution by, 286, 323–326
    quick reference list of, 429–430
    quote services from, 26, 287
    reliability of, 286, 287, 331–336
    role in exercising options, 326, 328
    specialties of, 281–285, 325–326
    system failures of, 331–336
    top 12, 288–320
    trading levels authorized by, 342–344
    trading software from, 247
    user-friendliness of web design, 287–288
    virtual trading by, 254
Online routines, 63–66, 72–74, 110–111, 115, 153, 190–192
Online trading:
    charts as tool of (*see* Charts)
    costs of (*see* Commission fees)
    do's and don'ts of, 347–348
    fundamental/technical trading approach to, 255, 257–261
    goal setting for, 344–346
    growth stock trading routines, 261–264
    hedging strategies, 265–279
    history of, 7–8
    individual stock analysis for, 34–50

market analysis for, 32–34
news impacting, 244–247
order entry formats for, 328–335
order types for, 353–354
pros and cons of, 8–10, 17–20
purchasing appropriate technology for, 21–26
reliability of, 4, 25, 286, 287, 331–336
resources for, 63–79 (*see also* Information; Web sites)
risk in (*see* Risk)
sample trades, 258–261, 269–279
strategies for, 246–255, 257–279 (*see also* Strategies, trading)
systematic approach to, 6
system failures during, 331–336
technology impacting, 2–3, 13–14, 18, 31–32, 331–336
tools for, 2–3
tracking trades, 254–256
trade environment assessment for, 31–32
trading accounts for, 285–286, 341–342
trading levels in, 342–344
trading software used in, 75–78, 216–217, 247–249, 257, 393–397
Open high low close charts, 42–43, 234–236, 238
Option chains, 73, 283
Option class, 90
Optionetics:
    back-test trading strategies with, 254
    charting services by, 235, 244
    educational information by, 69, 247
    e-mail newsletters from, 71
    fundamental information by, 37
    option analysis by, 73–74
    trading software by (Platinum), 216, 247–249, 257, 394–395
    web site of, 428
OptionGear, 397
Option greeks, 154. *See also* Delta neutral trading
OptionInvestor.com, 416
OptionMonster, 402
Option premium:
    of call options, 92, 121–124
    definition of, 89
    delta relationship to, 184
    factors affecting, 91
    in long butterfly spreads, 209–210
    in long straddle strategy, 159–162
    price sensitivity of, 153–154
    of put options, 94–95, 128–133
    in short straddle strategy, 162–166
    in short strangle strategy, 169–170
    vertical spreads using (*see* Vertical spreads)
    volatility of, 157–158

Options. *See also* Call options; Put options
  adjustments impacting, 103–104
  American-style, 102–103
  analysis of, 72–74, 267–268, 277
  at-the-money, 95–97, 137, 154–155
  availability of, 73
  definition of, 6, 89
  deltas of, 154, 184, 350
  European-style, 102–103
  exercising, 99–103, 125, 131, 201–202,
    326–328
  fundamentals of, 88–95
  futures (*see* Futures market)
  index, 101–103
  in-the-money, 95–97, 137, 154–155, 257
  methods of using, 4–7, 15
  moneyness and, 95–97
  multiple listing of, 18
  offsetting, 99–100, 221, 327–328
  out-of-the-money, 95–97, 137, 155, 166–171
  prices of, 89–91, 96–97, 157–158
  risk of (*see* Risk)
  settlement of, 101–103
  stock, 101–103
  versatility of, 4–7
  volatility impacting, 156–158
  web sites focused on, 69, 415–417 (*see also*
    Optionetics; Profit Strategies)
Options analysis, 72–74, 267–268, 277
Options as a Strategic Investment (McMillan),
  107
Options calculator, 267–268
Options Clearing Corporation:
  auto-exercise implementation by, 100
  on contract adjustments, 103–104
  on growth of options industry, 2, 14
  involvement in COOP, 415
  put-to-call ratios by, 59
  role in exercising options, 326–328
Option series, 90
Options exchanges, 7–8, 14–18, 59, 325, 336,
  415
OptionsHouse, 282, 297–299, 440
Options industry, growth of, 2, 14
Options Industry Council, 416–417
Option spreads, 286
Options ticker symbols, 283, 351
Options trading:
  brokerages specializing in, 282–285,
    325–326
  education in, 340
  on exchanges, 7–8, 14–18, 59, 325, 336, 415
  fundamentals of, 88–95
  goal setting for, 344–346
  history of, 7–8
  pros and cons of, 17–20
  risk of (*see* Risk)
  tracking, 254–256

  trading accounts for, 285–286, 341–342
  trading levels in, 342–344
  web sites focused on, 69
Option Strategist, The, 417
OptionsXpress, 220, 282, 289, 292–294, 328,
  440–441
*Option Volatility & Pricing: Advanced Trading
  Strategies and Techniques* (Natenberg),
  107
Oracle, 249
Order execution:
  brokerage role in, 286, 323–326
  exercising options as, 99–103, 125, 131,
    201–202, 326–328
  offsetting as, 99–100, 221, 327–328
  order entry formats for, 328–335
  order types for, 353–354
  placing online orders, 323–326
  system failures during, 331–336
Orders:
  contingent, 331
  limit, 286, 329, 331
  market, 324
  stop loss, 329
  types of, 353–354
Oscillators:
  accumulation/distribution rating as, 40,
    375
  on balance volume as, 270–272, 379, 390
  definition of, 48, 242
  price, 390
  relative strength index as, 241–242, 381
  stochastics indicators as, 48–49, 270–273,
    275, 391
  as technical indicators, 390
  trends tracked by, 45, 48–49
Out-of-the-money options, 95–97, 137, 155,
  166–171
Overbought/oversold stock, 45, 48–49,
  241–242, 381, 388, 390–391
Overnight positions, 82, 264

Paper trading, 79, 171. See also Virtual
  trading
PC Quote, 75, 426
Peak6 Investments, 289, 297
PEG (price-to-earnings growth rate formula),
  39
Performance bond margins, 222
Philadelphia Stock Exchange (PHLX), 7,
  15–17, 70, 325, 421–422
Point and figure charts, 238, 390
Portfolio margin accounts, 342
Portfolio trackers, 3, 254–255
PowerShares NASDAQ 100 Index Trust
  (QQQQ), 53–54
Preferred stock, 86
Premarket routines, 262–263

Premium, option. *See* Option premium
Price-book ratio, 379
Price-earnings growth rate formula (PEG), 39
Price-earnings (P/E) ratio, 38–39, 379–380
Price oscillator, 390
Price patterns, 390
Prices. *See also* Costs; Quotes; Stock prices;
    Strike price
  bid and ask, 98–99, 121–122, 324–325
  of bonds, 55–57
  of commodities, 223–230
  consumer price index tracking, 58
  limit, 286, 329, 331
  market, 157–158
  of options, 89–91, 96–97, 157–158
  price-book ratio, 379
  price-earnings (P/E) ratio, 38–39, 379–380
  price oscillator, 390
  price patterns, 390
  price percentage gainers and losers, 380
  price-sales ratio, 38, 380
  prices-to-earnings growth rate formula
    (PEG), 39
Price-sales ratio, 38, 380
Pristine, 414–415
Profit reports, 84
Profits. *See also* Maximum profits
  of bear call spreads, 148–151
  of bear put spreads, 141–144
  of bull call spreads, 138–141
  of bull put spreads, 145–148
  of calendar spreads, 202–203
  of call options, 92–93, 121–127
  of call ratio backspreads, 184–186
  capital gains as, 85, 118
  of collar strategy, 199–200
  commissions impacting, 285
  of covered call strategy, 195–197
  of delta neutral trades, 156
  of diagonal spreads, 204–205
  of futures trading, 221–223, 227–230
  of long butterfly spreads, 206–210
  of long condor strategy, 211–213
  of long iron butterfly strategy, 214–217
  of long stock, 114–117
  of long straddle, 159–162
  of long strangle strategy, 166–168
  of put options, 94–95, 128–133
  of put ratio backspreads, 187–190
  of ratio backspreads, 181–183
  of ratio call spreads, 174–177
  of ratio put spreads, 178–181
  reinvestment of, 86
  risk profile graphing (*see* Risk profiles)
  of short stock, 117–120
  of short straddle strategy, 162–166
  of short strangle strategy, 168–171
  stock prices and, 15, 38

  from stock purchase/sale, 85
  tracking, 255
  of vertical spread strategies, 135–137
ProfitSource, 77–78, 234, 257, 264, 265,
  395–396
Profit Strategies, 69, 428
Protective puts, 198, 343–344
Psychological market indicators, 33, 58–60,
  392
Put-call ratio, 59, 392
Put options. *See also* Long put options; Short
    put options
  bear put spreads using, 141–144, 366
  bull put spreads using, 145–148, 257, 365
  calendar spreads using, 200–203, 373
  collar strategy using, 198–200, 374
  covered put strategy using, 368–369
  definition of, 94
  diagonal spreads using, 203–206, 373
  exercising, 99–103, 326–328
  fundamentals of, 93–95
  intrinsic value of, 96
  long butterfly spreads using, 206–210,
    371–372
  long condor strategy using, 210–213, 372
  long iron butterfly strategy using, 213–217,
    372
  long straddle strategy using, 159–162,
    366–367, 369
  long strangle strategy using, 166–168, 367
  margin on, 130, 178, 342
  methods of using, 15
  moneyness and, 95–97
  offsetting, 99–100
  option premiums of, 94–95, 128–133
  protective, 198, 343–344
  put-call ratios using, 59, 392
  put ratio backspreads using, 187–190, 371
  ratio put spreads using, 178–181, 370
  settlement of, 101–103
  short straddle strategy using, 162–166,
    367
  short strangle strategy using, 168–171,
    368
Put ratio backspreads, 187–190, 371

QQQQ (PowerShares NASDAQ 100 Index
  Trust), 53–54
Quadruple witch expiration, 90
Quarter end fluctuations, 380
Quarterly earnings per share percent
  change, 380
Quicken.com, 402–403
Quick ratio, 380
Quote.com, 403
Quotes:
  bid and ask, 98–99, 121–122, 324–325
  delayed, 10, 25–28, 75, 287

end-of-day, 25, 27
option, 73
pros and cons of, 25–28
real-time, 10, 25–26, 28, 75, 287
technology impacting obtainment of, 10
terminology of, 351–352
web sites offering, 75

Random access memory (RAM), 22
Rate of change, 391
Ratio backspreads, 181–190, 370–371
Ratio call spreads, 174–177, 370
Ratio put spreads, 178–181, 370
Ratio spreads, 174–181, 370
Real-time quotes, 10, 25–26, 28, 75, 287
Realtime Stockquote, 75
Red Chip Review, 418
Regal Securities, Inc., 316
Regression channel techniques, 269–272, 387
Relative strength, 381
Relative strength index (RSI), 241–242, 381
Reliability:
    of Internet service providers, 4, 25
    of online brokerages, 286, 287, 331–336
Reports, 57–58, 84, 245
Research. *See also* Information
    to assess trading environment, 32
    guidelines for, 63–67, 72–74
    on individual stocks, 34–50
    online, 3, 5–6, 9–10, 68–69
    on options, 73–74
    premarket, 262–263
    via news reports, 244–247
    web sites specializing in, 68–69, 408–411
Research Driven Investor, The (Hayes), 268
Resistance, 44, 193–194, 378, 387–388
Resources for online trading, 63–79. *See also*
    Information; Research; Web sites
Retail sales report, 58
Return on equity, 255, 381
Reuters, 68, 406
Reverse stock splits, 103
Reverse volatility skew, 178–181, 183–187,
    191–192
RF Lafferty, 441–442
Risk. *See also* Maximum risk; Risk profiles
    of bear call spreads, 148–151
    of bear put spreads, 141–144
    of bull call spreads, 138–141
    of bull put spreads, 145–148
    of calendar spreads, 201–203
    of call options, 92, 121–127
    of call ratio backspreads, 185–186
    of collar strategy, 198–200
    of covered call strategy, 196
    of diagonal spreads, 204–206
    of futures trading, 221–223, 227–230
    hedging, 5, 221–222, 225–227, 231, 346

of initial public offerings, 83
of long butterfly spreads, 207–209
of long condor strategy, 210–212
of long iron butterfly strategy, 214–217
of long stock, 114–117
of long straddle, 159–162
of long strangle strategy, 166–168
management of, 19–20, 59–60, 109–111,
    331, 346–348
margin reflecting, 285, 342
option greeks measurement of, 154
options-related, 4–5, 59–60, 92, 94–95,
    121–133, 339–340
of put options, 94–95, 128–133
of put ratio backspreads, 188–190
of ratio backspreads, 181–183
of ratio call spreads, 175–177
of ratio put spreads, 178–181
of short stock trades, 117–120
of short straddle strategy, 162–166
of short strangle strategy, 168–171
of stocks, 84–86, 114–120
tolerance for, 345–346
of vertical spread strategies, 135–137
Risk profiles:
    of bear call spreads, 150–151
    of bear put spreads, 143–144
    of bull call spreads, 140, 261
    of bull put spreads, 147
    of butterfly spreads, 207, 214–215, 254
    of calendar spreads, 203
    of call ratio backspreads, 186
    of collar strategy, 199–200
    of covered call strategy, 197
    of diagonal spreads, 205
    fundamentals of, 111–114, 354–356
    of long butterfly spreads, 207
    of long call options, 123
    of long condor strategy, 211–212
    of long iron butterfly strategy, 214–215
    of long put options, 129
    of long stock, 114–117
    of long straddle strategy, 160–161
    of long strangle strategy, 167–168
    of put ratio backspreads, 188–189
    of ratio call spreads, 176–177
    of ratio put spreads, 180
    of short call options, 126–127
    of short put options, 131–132
    of short stock, 117–120
    of short straddle strategy, 164
    of short strangle strategy, 170
Risk-to-reward ratio, 60, 111, 251, 253–254.
    See also Risk profiles
Rolling (rollover), 229–230
Routines, online, 63–66, 72–74, 110–111, 115,
    153, 190–192
Russell 2000 Index, 52

St. Louis Federal Reserve Bank, 268
Sales growth, 257
Sales-price ratio, 38, 380
Schaeffer's Research.com, 417
Scheduled news, 245–246
Schwab (Charles Schwab), 282, 289, 311–313, 431
Scottrade, 442
Screening, 9–10, 35, 68, 284
Search engines, 71, 427–428
Sector indexes, 52–53
Securities. *See* Bonds; LEAPS; Options; Stocks
Securities, underlying. *See* Underlying assets/underlying securities
Securities and Exchange Commission (SEC), 8, 335–336, 339, 341, 422
Securities Industry and Financial Markets Association (SIFMA), 426
Sentiment analysis, 392
SentimenTrader, 59
Series 7 exam, 320
Settlement of options, 101–103
ShareBuilder, 442–443
Shares. *See* Stocks
Short call options:
　bear call spreads using, 148–151, 366
　bull call spreads using, 138–141, 365
　calendar spreads using, 200–203, 373
　call ratio backspreads using, 183–187, 370–371
　diagonal spreads using, 203–206, 373
　fundamentals of, 92
　long condor strategy using, 210–213
　long iron butterfly strategy using, 213–217, 372
　margins on, 341–342
　ratio call spreads using, 175–177, 370
　strategies for using, 125–127, 364
　vertical spreads using, 135–137
Short interest indicator, 392
Short interest ratio, 381
Short options. *See* Short call options; Short put options
Short put options:
　bear put spreads on, 142–144, 366
　bull put spreads using, 145–148, 365
　calendar spreads using, 200–203, 373
　diagonal spreads using, 203–206, 373
　fundamentals of, 94–95
　long condor strategy using, 210–213
　long iron butterfly strategy using, 213–217, 372
　margins on, 341–342
　put ratio backspreads using, 187–190, 371
　ratio put spreads using, 178–181, 370
　strategies for using, 130–133, 364–365
　vertical spreads using, 135–137

Short stock, 41, 117–120, 363
Short straddle, 162–166, 331, 333, 367
Short strangle, 168–171, 331, 333, 368
Sideways markets, 193–194, 216–217. *See also* Neutral market; Sideways strategies
Sideways strategies:
　calendar spreads as, 200–203, 373
　collar strategy as, 106, 198–200, 374
　covered call strategy as, 126–127, 194–197, 343–344, 368
　diagonal spreads as, 203–206, 373
　long butterfly spreads as, 206–210, 331, 334, 371–372
　long condor strategy as, 210–213, 331, 335, 372
　long iron butterfly strategy as, 213–217, 331, 335, 372
Siebert.net, 443
SIFMA (Securities Industry and Financial Markets Association), 426
Silicon Investor, 406–407, 420
Simple moving averages, 240–241, 391
SmallCapInvestor.com, 70, 426
Small-cap stocks, 84
SmartMoney, 295, 418
Social Investment Forum, 426–427
Social networking, 70–71
Software, trading, 75–78, 216–217, 247–249, 257, 393–397
S&P 100 Index, 51–52
S&P 500 Depositary Receipts (SPY; "spiders"), 54, 269–279
S&P 500 Index, 52, 54, 276
Specialists, 324–325
Specialty web sites, 70, 423–427
Speculators, 5, 227–230
SpeedTrader.com, 444
S&P MidCap 400 Index, 52
Spot market, 223–226
Spread orders, 6, 331
Standard deviation, 381
Standard & Poor's, 267. *See also S&P-related entries*
Standard & Poor's Equity Investor Service, 403
Statistical volatility, 157–158, 267–268
Stochastics indicators, 48–49, 270–273, 275, 391
StockCharts.com, 42, 50, 69, 235–238
Stock exchanges. *See* Exchanges
Stockhouse, 409
Stock market. *See* Market
Stock Market Course, The (Fontanills and Gentile), 39
StockMaster, 415
Stock options, 101–103
StockPicks, 422–423

Stock prices. *See also* Strike price
  advance-decline line of, 383
  in calendar spreads, 202–203
  call options impacted by, 121–124
  charting (*see* Charts)
  closing price, net change in, 376
  in collar strategy, 106, 199–200, 374
  in covered call strategy, 126–127, 195–197,
    368
  in diagonal spreads, 204–206
  factors impacting, 36–39, 83–87
  52-week high and low, 377
  forecasting (*see* Forecasting)
  high-low index of, 378
  high price yesterday/low price yesterday,
    377–378
  indexes tracking, 51–53
  interest rate impact on, 56–58
  in long butterfly spreads, 206–210
  in long iron butterfly strategy, 214–215
  in long put options, 128–130, 364
  in long stock trades, 115–117, 363
  most percent up/down in price, 378
  net change in, 376, 378
  news impacting, 244–247
  price-book ratio, 379
  price-earnings (P/E) ratio, 38–39, 379–380
  price oscillator, 390
  price patterns, 390
  price percentage gainers and losers, 380
  price-sales ratio, 38, 380
  prices-to-earnings growth rate formula
    (PEG), 39
  profits from change in, 15, 38
  quotes of (*see* Quotes)
  rate of change in, 391
  risk profile graphing (*see* Risk profiles)
  in short call options, 125–127, 364
  in short stock trades, 117–120, 363
  in sideways markets, 193–194
  stock split based on, 103–104
  supply and demand impacting, 36, 40, 45,
    48–49, 83, 382
  volatility of (*see* Volatility)
StockRumors, 423
Stocks. *See also* Stock prices; Strike price;
    Underlying assets/underlying securities
  assessment of individual, 34–50
  blue-chip, 84–85
  collar strategy using, 106, 198–200, 374
  common, 85–86
  covered call strategy using, 126–127,
    194–197, 368
  cyclical, 86
  definition of, 33
  deltas of, 154
  fundamentals of, 83–87, 255, 257
  growth, 86, 261–264

  in hedging strategies, 267
  income, 86
  individual, 34–50, 267
  intermarket relationships with, 352
  long, 41, 114–117, 196, 363
  mid-cap, 84
  most active issue, 378
  in the news, 381–382
  order entry format for, 328–329
  overbought/oversold, 45, 48–49, 241–242,
    381, 388, 390–391
  preferred, 86
  relative strength of, 241–242, 381
  risk of, 84–86, 114–120
  short, 41, 117–120, 363
  small-cap, 84
  splitting, 103–104
  supply and demand of, 36, 40, 45, 48–49,
    83, 382
  technical analysis of (*see* Technical
    analysis)
Stocks.com, 409–410
StockSmart Pro, 68, 403, 410
Stock splits, 103–104
StockTA.com, 258
StockTools, 415
Stock Trak, 71, 412, 427
Stop loss orders, 329. *See also* Limit
    order/limit prices
Straddle. *See* Long straddle; Short straddle
Strangle. *See* Long strangle; Short strangle
Strategic Organization Solutions, 423
Strategies, trading:
  based on trader's experience, 343–344
  delta neutral, 153–156, 159–171, 331, 333,
    366–368, 369
  determining appropriate, 246–254
  fundamental/technical, 255, 257–261
  growth stock trading routines, 261–264
  hedging, 265–279
  quick reference guide to, 361–362
  sideways, 106, 126–127, 194–217, 331,
    334–335, 343–344, 368, 371–374
  for specific markets, 83, 250–252, 353,
    361–362
  summary of, 363–374
Strategists (definition), 5
Stricknet.com, 417
Strike price:
  in bear call spreads, 148–151, 366
  in bear put spreads, 141–144, 366
  in bull call spreads, 137–141, 365
  in bull put spreads, 145–148, 365
  buying/selling at, 89–90
  in calendar spreads, 202–203, 373
  of call options, 91–93, 121–127, 364
  in call ratio backspreads, 183–187, 370–371
  codes indicating, 283, 350

Strike price (*Continued*)
   in collar strategy, 198–200, 374
   in covered call strategy, 195–197, 368
   definition of, 122
   in diagonal spreads, 203–206, 373
   in long butterfly spreads, 206–210, 371–372
   in long call options, 121–124, 362–363
   in long condor strategy, 210–213, 372
   in long iron butterfly strategy, 214–215, 372
   in long put options, 128–130, 364
   in long straddle, 159–162, 366–367, 369
   in long strangle strategy, 167–168, 367
   option premium impacted by, 91
   of put options, 93–95, 128–133, 364–365
   in put ratio backspreads, 187–190, 371
   in ratio call spreads, 174–177, 370
   in ratio put spreads, 178–181, 370
   of short call options, 125–127, 364
   of short put options, 130–133, 364–365
   in short straddle strategy, 162–166, 367
   in short strangle strategy, 169–170, 368
   underlying asset price *versus*, 95–97
   in vertical spreads, 135–137
Strikeprice.com, 417
Supersites, 66–67, 399–403
Supply and demand:
   of commodities, 225–226
   stock prices impacted by, 36, 40, 45, 48–49,
      83, 382
Support, 44, 193–194, 378, 388
Swing chart, 391
System failures, 331–336

Taleb, Nassim, 265
TD Ameritrade, 282, 289, 304–306, 444–445
Technical analysis:
   charting as, 41–50, 194, 234–244, 267–273,
      275, 385, 387, 390–391
   definition of, 42
   fundamentals of, 40–50, 383–392
   strategies based on, 257, 265–278
   trading software providing, 75–78
   web sites offering, 69, 413–415
*Technical Analysis: Power Tools for Active
   Investors* (Appel), 268
Technical Analysis of Stocks and Commodities
   magazine, 419
Technical Analysis of Stock Trends (Edwards
   and Magee), 50
Technology. *See also* Internet
   online trading impacted by, 2–3, 13–14, 18,
      31–32, 331–336
   purchasing appropriate, 21–26
   stock assessment using, 35
   systems failures of, 331–336
   trading software as, 75–78, 216–217,
      247–249, 257, 393–397
TeleChart, 265

TheStreet.com, 70, 74, 407, 423
ThinkorSwim, 282, 289, 307–309, 445–446
Thompson Consulting, 339
Thomson, 407
Tick charts, 238
Ticker symbol, 38, 283, 351
Time.com, 410
Time decay, 123, 145, 196, 201, 253
Time periods. *See also* Expiration date; Time
      decay
   of call options, 91–93, 121–126
   charting stock prices over (*see* Charts)
   to devote to trading, 345
   of futures contracts, 220–221, 223–226
   intrinsic value impacted by, 97
   of long call options, 121–124
   of long put options, 128–130
   in long stock trades, 115
   moving average based on, 45, 47–48
   in moving average
      convergence/divergence, 243
   of options contracts, 89, 90–91
   of put options, 93–95, 128–133
   for settlement, 101–103
   of short call options, 125–126
   of short put options, 131–133
   volatility measured within, 157
Time Series Analysis: Forecasting and Control
      (Box and Jenkins), 384
Time value, 96–97, 137, 193–194, 209–213
*Timing Models and Proven Indicators for
      Today's Markets* (Freeburg), 268
Tracking trades, 254–256
TradeKing, 70, 289, 295–297, 446
Traders (definition), 262. *See also* Investors
Trader's Digest, 419
Tradethenews.com, 258
Trading:
   accounts, 285–286, 341–342
   auto-trading, 65
   bands, 391
   environment, 31–32
   levels, 342–344
   online (*see* Online trading)
   options (*see* Options trading)
   paper, 79, 171 (*see also* Virtual trading)
   sheets, 277–279
   software, 75–78, 216–217, 247–249, 257,
      393–397
   strategies (*see* Strategies, trading)
   virtual, 254 (*see also* Paper trading)
Trading Direct, 446–447
Trading for a Living (Elder), 50
Trailing stops, 329
Trend-following indicators, 242–244
Trends:
   alpha-beta trend channel, 383
   average directional index of, 384

charts tracking, 41–50, 234
definition of, 42
directional movement index of, 385
in indexes, 53, 384–385
industry, 87
intermediate, 41
major/minor, 41, 388
moving averages tracking, 45, 47–49,
    240–244
profits driven by, 87
technical analysis of, 265–266
types of, 41
vertical spread dependence on, 136
True strength index, 391

Underlying assets/underlying securities.
    See also Stock prices
call options on, 92–93, 121–127
charting, 234–244
definition of, 15
delta reflecting price change of, 153–156
exercising options and, 326–328
in futures market, 228
in long butterfly spreads, 206–210
in long iron butterfly strategy, 213–217
long put options on, 128
in long strangle strategy, 166–168
options on, 89–91
price of, 111–114
put options on, 94, 128, 130–133
in ratio call spreads, 176
in ratio put spreads, 181
settling for, 101–103
short call options on, 125–127
of short put options, 130–133
in short straddle strategy, 162–166
strike price *versus* price of, 95–97
volatility of, 157–158
Unemployment rate, 58
U.S. Department of Commerce, 58
U.S. Department of Defense, 7
USA Today Money, 407
User-friendliness, 287–288

Vacation trades, 182
Value. *See also* Costs; Prices
earnings per share value, 38, 376, 380
exercise settlement, 102
extrinsic, 97
fair, 157
of information, 340
intrinsic, 96–97, 137
time, 96–97, 137, 193–194, 209–213
ValueGain, 77–78, 257, 264, 396
Value Line, 415
Valueline.com, 258
Value Point Analysis Financial Forum, 427
Variable-length moving average, 391

VectorVest, 68–69, 410
Vertical spreads:
bear call spreads as, 148–151, 366
bear put spreads as, 141–144, 366
bull call spreads as, 137–141, 257, 258–261,
    365
bull put spreads as, 145–148, 257, 365
fundamentals of, 135–137
order entry format for, 331–332
Virtual trading, 254. *See also* Paper trading
VIX (Volatility Index), 392
Volatility:
of economy, 59–60
historical (statistical), 157–158, 267–268
implied, 157–158, 183–187, 248–251,
    267–268
long straddle impacted by, 159–162
long strangle impacted by, 166–168
of market, 1–2, 19, 59–60, 153, 156–158,
    161–162, 331–336
of option premiums, 157–158
options strategies responding to, 91
ratio backspread impacted by, 181–190
ratio spread impacted by, 174–181
short straddle impacted by, 162–166
short strangle strategy impacted by,
    168–171
skews, 178–181, 183–192
stock prices impacted by, 38–39, 84
stock splits triggering, 103
system failures impacted by, 331–336
of underlying assets, 157–158
volume as indicator of, 382
Volatility Course, The (Fontanills and
    Gentile), 107
Volatility Index (VIX), 392
Volume (of money), 55
Volume (of stock trades):
analysis of, 382
on balance, 270–272, 379, 390
charting, 45–46
greatest percent rise in, 377
investment sentiment gauged by, 59
liquidity impacted by, 73, 98
most active by, 378
percent change in, 377, 382
system failures due to, 331–336
as technical indicator, 40, 240
Volume spike, 240

Wall-Street*E, 289, 313–315, 447
Wall Street Journal, 4, 67, 378, 380–382, 407
WallStreetSports, 71, 427
Washington Mutual, 86
Weblogs, 70
Web sites:
advisory sites, 70, 422–423
blogs on, 70

Web sites (*Continued*)
  educational sites, 69, 247, 411–413
  exchange sites, 70, 263, 420–422
  fun and games sites, 71, 427
  fundamental analysis sites, 68–69
  guide to, 258, 399–428
  high-technology sites, 419–420
  news sites, 67–68, 404–407
  options sites, 69, 415–417 (*see also*
    Optionetics; Profit Strategies)
  quotes offered on, 75
  research sites, 68–69, 408–411
  specialty sites, 70, 423–427
  supersites as, 66–67, 399–403
  technical analysis sites, 69, 413–415
  user-friendliness of, 287–288
Webzines, 69, 417–419
Weighted moving average, 387, 391
WhatsTrading.com, 245
Wilder, Welles, 241
Williams %R, 391
Winning on Wall Street (Zweig), 268

Wired magazine, 419
Wolf, The, 423
Worden Brothers, Inc., 265
World Wide Financial Network, 410
World Wide Web, 7. *See also* Internet
Worth Online, 419
Wyse Securities, 447–448

XAU (Gold and Silver Mining Index), 101–102,
  149–151

Yahoo!, 428
Yahoo! Finance, 58, 67, 71, 74, 245–246, 258,
  263, 268–269, 403
Yardeni's Economics Network, Dr. Ed's, 411
Young Investor Website, The, 412–413

Zacks Investment Research, 72, 74, 410–411
ZDNet, 411
Zecco, 448–449
Zero position delta. *See* Delta neutral trading
Zweig, Martin, 268

free trading kit

From George Fontanills
(a $100 value)

Request your FREE Trading Kit and learn more about high-profit, low-risk, low-stress trading strategies *that really work!*

My Trading Kit is full of practical tips and useful information to guide you down the path toward successful trading. The trading fundamentals presented are based on the same proven techniques taught by the expert traders at Optionetics (www.optionetics.com), which I created in 1993 to show individual investors how to profit in all market conditions. Since that time, Optionetics has become a leading provider of investment education services, portfolio management techniques, market analysis, and online trading tools to more than 250,000 people from more than 50 countries worldwide.

To receive your FREE Trading Kit, simply complete and mail (or fax) the form below to:

Optionetics
255 Shoreline Drive, Suite 100
Redwood City, CA 94065
Fax: 650-802-0900

You may also call 888-366-8264 (or 650-802-0700 outside of the United States), or e-mail customerservice@optionetics.com.

Free Trading Kit

☑ **Yes!** I would like to learn more about managed-risk trading strategies. Please send me my FREE Trading Package today.

Name: _____

Address: _____

City, State: _____ Zip Code: _____

Telephone: _____

Fax: _____ E-mail: _____

I purchased this book from: _____
